Putting CLIL into Practice

Published in this series
Oxford Handbooks for Language Teachers

Putting CLIL into Practice

Phil Ball, Keith Kelly, and John Clegg

OXFORD
UNIVERSITY PRESS

UNIVERSITY PRESS

Great Clarendon Street, Oxford, OX2 6DP, United Kingdom

Oxford University Press is a department of the University of Oxford.
It furthers the University's objective of excellence in research, scholarship,
and education by publishing worldwide. Oxford is a registered trade
mark of Oxford University Press in the UK and in certain other countries

ISBN: 978 0 19 442105 8

Printed in China

This book is printed on paper from certified and well-managed sources

ACKNOWLEDGEMENTS

*The authors and publisher are grateful to those who have given permission to reproduce
the following extracts and adaptations of copyright material*: p.13 Figure adapted
from *Bilingualism and Special Education* by Jim Cummins (Multilingual Matters,
1984). Reproduced by permission of Multilingual Matters. p.22 Extract from
"Language across the curriculum. The British example: The National Literacy
Strategy" by John Clegg (2002). Reproduced by permission of Ikastolen
Elkartea. p.31 Graph from "Promoting the Minority Language Through
Integrated Plurilingual Language Planning: The Case of the Ikastolas" by
Itziar Elorza and Inmaculada Muñoa, *Language, Culture and Curriculum* (http://
www.informaworld.com), Volume 21 (1), 2008. Reproduced by permission of
Taylor & Francis Ltd. pp.36, 39, 141, 143, 187, 283 Extracts from *Subject Projects
1: The World of Inventions* by Phil Ball et al. (2005). Reproduced by permission
of Ikastolen Elkartea. p.43 Extract from *SSLIC English: Workbook 1* by Inma
Muñoa et al. (2008). Reproduced by permission of Ikastolen Elkartea. pp.46,
56, 170, 185, 189, 195,196, 197, 204, 205 Extracts from *Geog 3* by Phil Ball et
al. (2009). Reproduced by permission of Ikastolen Elkartea. pp.51, 171, 178,
188 Extracts from *Subject Projects 1* by Phil Ball et al (2005). Reproduced by
permission of Ikastolen Elkartea. p.59 Figure from *Language, Power and Pedagogy:
Bilingual Children in the Crossfire* by Jim Cummins (Multilingual Matters, 2000).
Reproduced by permission of Multilingual Matters. p.60 Figure from *Scaffolding
Language, Scaffolding Learning: Teaching English Language Learners in the Mainstream
Classroom, 2nd Edition* by Pauline Gibbons. © 2015 by Pauline Gibbons; Published
by Heinemann, Portsmouth, NH; figure adapted from "Teacher support and
teacher challenge in promoting learner autonomy" by Luciano Mariani from
Perspectives, a Journal of TESOL Italy, Volume XXIII (2), Fall 1997. Reprinted by
permission of the Heinemann and TESOL Italy. p.62 Figure from *The roles of
language in CLIL* by Ana Llinares, Tom Morton and Rachel Whittaker (Cambridge
University Press, 2012). Reproduced by permission of Cambridge University
Press. p.62 Extract from *Discourse in Content and Language Integrated Learning (CLIL)
Classrooms* by Christiane Dalton-Puffer (John Benjamins Publishing Company,
2007). Reproduced by permission of John Benjamins Publishing Company.
p.73 Extracts from *Language and Literacy in Science Education* by Jerry Wellington and
Jonathan Osborne (Open University Press, 2001). Reproduced by permission

of Open University Press. p.80 Extract from *Handbook for Teachers of English as
an Additional Language* by Diana Bousfield Wells (Hounslow Language Service).
Reproduced by permission of Hounslow Language Service. p.82 Extracts
from *Integrated Curriculum For Secondary Schools*: Science Year 6 by Ministry of
Education Malaysia, 2006. Copyright © 2007 Curriculum Development Centre,
Ministry of Education Malaysia. Reproduced by permission. p.89/p.152 Extract
from *What did you eat?* and Figure 2 from "How Acid Rain is Formed" from
Acid Rain, www.scienceacross.org, © ASE/Bp.1999. Reproduced by permission
of Association for Science Education. pp.94, 110, 115, 119, 133, 145, 162, 167,
169 Extracts from *New Coordinated Science: Biology for Higher Tier* by Brian Beckett
and RoseMarie Gallagher (3e, Oxford University Press, 2001), copyright © Brian
Beckett and RoseMarie Gallagher, 2001, reproduced by permission of Oxford
University Press. p.111 Figure from *New Coordinated Science: Biology* by Brian
Beckett and RoseMarie Gallagher (2e, Oxford University Press, 1996), copyright
© Brian Beckett and RoseMarie Gallagher, 1996, reproduced by permission of
Oxford University Press. p.111 Definitions from the *Oxford Advanced Learner's
Dictionary*, www.oxfordlearnersdictionaries.com. Reproduced by permission
of Oxford University Press. pp.112, 117, 120 Extracts from *Access to History:
Medieval Britain* by Walter Robson (Oxford University Press, 1991), copyright
© Walter Robson, 1991, reproduced by permission of Oxford University
Press. p.113 Extract from *Geog.1 EAL Workbook* by John Clegg and Keith Kelly
(Oxford University Press, 2009), copyright © John Clegg and Keith Kelly,
2009, reproduced by permission of Oxford University Press. p.114 Extracts
from *Geog.2 Students Book* by RoseMarie Gallagher and Richard Parish (Oxford
University Press, 2005), copyright © RoseMarie Gallagher and Richard Parish,
2005, reproduced by permission of Oxford University Press. pp.118, 149 Extract
from *New Coordinated Science: Physics* by Stephen Pople and Peter Whitehead
(2e, Oxford University Press, 1996), copyright © Stephen Pople and Peter
Whitehead, 1996, reproduced by permission of Oxford University Press. pp.122,
150 Extracts from *New Coordinated Science: Physics for Higher Tier* by Stephen
Pople (3e, Oxford University Press, 2001), copyright © Stephen Pople, 2001,
reproduced by permission of Oxford University Press. p.123 Extract from *Geog.1:
Students Book* by RoseMarie Gallagher, Richard Parish and Janet Williamson (2e,
Oxford University Press, 2008), copyright © RoseMarie Gallagher, Richard Parish
and Janet Williamson, 2008, reproduced by permission of Oxford University
Press. pp.125, 144, 154, 157, 168 Extracts from *New Coordinated Science: Chemistry
for Higher Tier* by RoseMarie Gallagher and Paul Ingram (3e, Oxford University
Press, 2001), copyright © RoseMarie Gallagher and Paul Ingram, 2001,
reproduced by permission of Oxford University Press. pp.126, 128, 129, 130
Extracts from *Oxford Content and Language Support: Science* by Saema Kauser and
Sarah O'Donoghue (Oxford University Press, 2010), copyright © Saema Kauser
and Sarah O'Donoghue, 2010, reproduced by permission of Oxford University
Press. pp.140, 167 Figure from *New Coordinated Science: Chemistry* by RoseMarie
Gallagher, Paul Ingram and Peter Whitehead (2e, Oxford University Press, 1996),
copyright © RoseMarie Gallagher, Paul Ingram and Peter Whitehead, 1996,
reproduced by permission of Oxford University Press. pp.177, 180 Extracts from
Subject Projects 2: Healthy U by Phil Ball et al. (2006). Reproduced by permission
of Ikastolen Elkartea. p.177 Extract from "Present Perfect or Past Simple
Worksheet", Pre-Intermediate, www.esl-lounge.com. © 2001–2015 esl-lounge.
com. Reproduced by permission. pp.182, 200 Extracts from *Subject Projects 2,
Europe: United in Diversity* by Phil Ball et al. (2006). Reproduced by permission of
Ikastolen Elkartea. pp.191, 192, 194, 202, 218 Extracts from *History 4* by Harri
Beobide and Phil Ball (2010). Reproduced by permission of Ikastolen Elkartea.
pp.198, 224, 225, 227, 229, 230 Extracts from *Subject Projects 1: We've Got Talent!*
by Phil Ball et al. (2005). Reproduced by permission of Ikastolen Elkartea. p.201
Page from *Science in Action Book 3* by Patricia Harrison and Christine Moorcroft,
Folens, 1996. Reproduced by permission of HarperCollins Publishers Ltd.
© 1996 Patricia Harrison and Christine Moorcroft. p.217 Graph from "Mounting
a Good Offense against Measles" by Walter Orenstein, M.D., and Katherine Seib,
M.S.p.H. *The New England Journal of Medicine*, Volume 371 (18), pp.1661–1663.
Copyright © 2014 Massachusetts Medical Society. Reprinted with permission
from Massachusetts Medical Society. p.291 Extract from 20th Century History
for Cambridge IGCSE by John Cantrell, Neil Smith, Peter Smith and Ray Ennion
(Oxford University Press, 2013), © John Cantrell, Neil Smith, Peter Smith and
Ray Ennion, 2013, reproduced by permission of Oxford University Press. p.293
Extract from *New Star Science: Year 4: Habitats Pupils' Book* by Rosemary Feasey,
Anne Goldsworthy, John Stringer and Roy Phipps (Ginn, 2000). Reproduced by
permission of Pearson Education Limited.

Sources: p.81 "Ethical English: Teaching language through content, and content
through language" by Keith Kelly and Stefka Kitanova (Science Across The
World, 2002). p.206 "Theory of relativity", https://en.wikipedia.org, accessed
February 2015. Design including redrawn illustrations by Oxford Designers and
Illustrators.

For Diana, Vino, Dara, and Sam.

CONTENTS

ACKNOWLEDGEMENTS

We would like to say thank you to the teachers in the Ikastola network in the Basque Country, and to colleagues in Ikastolen Elkartea (The Federation of Basque Schools) for their optimism, hard work and willingness to innovate. We'd also like to thank the Austrian Technical College teachers who have gone through CLIL training at the University of Education in Vienna, for trying out and giving feedback on three-dimensional CLIL. We are also grateful to the teachers in the FACTWorld (www.factworld.info) network of over 3,500 colleagues, for their continued enthusiasm for integrating content and language.

INTRODUCTION

CLIL stands for '**content and language integrated learning**' and is a way of teaching and learning subjects in a second language (**L2**). Within this broad category, it is a relatively recent set of practices which had its origin in Europe in the 1990s and has since then gradually spread throughout the continent and further afield. It is used within primary and secondary schools; and as English-medium teaching in tertiary education expands across Europe, the term is increasingly applied at this level.

CLIL is related to all forms of education in which subjects are learned through L2 or through two languages simultaneously. In Chapter 1, we outline some of these forms. They are distinct from CLIL in a variety of respects. Some are designed for learners from language minorities. Some are found in developing countries. Some, such as bilingual education or **immersion education**, encompass the whole, or a large part of, the curriculum. And some, such as English-medium maths and science programmes, cover only a part of the curriculum, but may be compulsory for all schools. CLIL is different from all of these. It tends to be offered mainly to students who speak the majority language (though clearly minority learners will form part of many cohorts). It was originally—and is still largely—a European phenomenon, though again CLIL programmes are also offered elsewhere, for example in South America. It is normally restricted to one or two subjects in any school curriculum, and it is self-selecting: schools opt to offer it.

CLIL is often also wrongly used to refer to forms of practice which do not conform to its requirements. Some English language teachers, for example, give the name 'CLIL' to content-based language teaching. This, as its name suggests, is a form of language teaching into which subject contents are imported, but which is taught by language teachers, assessed as language teaching, and makes no formal contribution to the subject curriculum. CLIL is also wrongly used to refer to local forms of **L2-medium subject teaching** in other parts of the world, such as South Asia, South East Asia, and Africa. Here, there are both long-established forms of L2-medium education and more recent introductions—for example, English-medium science and maths—which are adapted to the local context. As we show in Chapter 1, these are very different from CLIL in terms of aims, curriculum coverage, and learners.

However, even within Europe, CLIL is a broad term which embraces a variety of different school practices. We will emphasize the fact that it comes in many forms. The key versions we will draw attention to are 'hard' and 'soft'. '**Hard**' **CLIL** programmes are taught by subject teachers with a strong emphasis on the acquisition of subject knowledge, occupying all the available hours for the subject for a year or more and sometimes culminating in a public examination. '**Soft**' **CLIL**, on the other hand, is normally a shorter programme, taking up only part of the curriculum time allocated to the subject, valued for its language benefits and often involving language teachers. This book is addressed to teachers of both types of programme.

CLIL is also a diverse phenomenon in other ways. It has, notably, developed from the bottom up. Individual teachers have often initiated it; individual institutions have developed practice within their own walls, without reference to wider schools of practice; individual regions and countries have made it work to suit their own needs. It has taken time for practices to be codified, researched, and taught to teachers in training, and for resources to be developed. Indeed, in many contexts, training and resources are still not available. CLIL is therefore by no means a uniform set of practices; neither does it necessarily provide principles which apply in every circumstance: what works in one place may not work in another. In this book, we have tried to take some account of this variety.

The book is divided into ten chapters, some tending towards the more theoretical, others to the more practical. The first chapter describes some relations of CLIL: a range of types of education in L2 in varying socio-economic and geographical contexts in different parts of the world. Some of these are more successful than others, and we attempt to indicate why this is. The chapter then looks carefully at the key factors which seem to make education in L2 work and discusses the extent to which they determine effectiveness in CLIL programmes in particular.

In Chapter 2, we attempt to say what CLIL is by discussing its methodology. We discuss the two focuses—on concepts and language—which CLIL is said to have and the variants of CLIL which emphasize one or other of these focuses. The chapter also proposes ten features which distinguish CLIL as a particular way of teaching. These are concerned with: the role of subject concepts and their relationship to language; the role of the **task** and how CLIL highlights language within it, alongside concepts and thinking skills; the relation of task to text and other media; and finally the importance of speaking, writing, and thinking in the process of coming to know something through the medium of a second language.

In Chapter 3, we explore the crucial relationship in CLIL between language and content. We propose that in CLIL lessons, teachers negotiate three dimensions of classroom discourse: concepts, language, and procedures—or thinking skills. They can see any of these as objectives, turning each dimension up or down as the lesson proceeds. The chapter also discusses the idea of academic language proficiency and how this relates to cognitive complexity in classroom tasks. We show how academic language becomes more important as learners progress through school.

Chapter 4 describes what we mean by 'language' in CLIL. Here again, we are concerned with the academic variety of language and give examples of how it appears in subject teaching. We also explore the subject teacher's relationship with language in CLIL and offer seven principles which determine this relationship. They show how teachers need to be able to think about the language demands of both lessons and whole subjects, plan how they can highlight language in their teaching, and focus in particular on the use of speaking and writing in helping learners to grasp new subject concepts.

Chapters 5 and 6 belong together in that they deal with two sides of the same coin: the concept of **language support**. This is the key element of CLIL methodology which distinguishes it from conventional forms of teaching through the first language (**L1**). The principle is simple: learning through an L2, if the learner is still developing fluency in it, tends to restrict learning. In order to counteract this tendency, language support amplifies the messages of reading and listening and reinforces the ability to speak and write. To do this, it uses a range of task types and visuals not normally used in conventional L1-medium teaching. Chapter 5 exemplifies these task types in relation to the processing skills; and Chapter 6 does the same for **productive skills**.

The design of CLIL materials is the subject of Chapter 7. We list key principles which should shape CLIL materials design, concerning the idea of the learning task, how it can be the basis for focusing on the three dimensions of CLIL (concepts, procedures, language), and how it provides support for reading and listening on the one hand and for speaking and writing on the other. Other principles have to do with highlighting language, varying task difficulty, and planning task sequences.

In Chapter 8, we discuss assessment in CLIL. We deal with issues which regularly draw attention in relation to CLIL assessment, such as the roles of **formative** and **summative assessment**; the focus of assessment on language, content, or both; the risk of learners failing to demonstrate knowledge because of inadequate language ability; and the role which CLIL can play in the assessment of **competence-based education**.

Chapter 9 looks at CLIL from a school management viewpoint. Many aspects of CLIL programmes need to be managed at a whole-school level; and in this chapter, we outline the main ones, such as the selection of students, the training of teachers, teacher collaboration, communication with parents, and programme design and monitoring. We also propose how these matters can be governed through the design and application of practical whole-school CLIL policy.

Teacher education in CLIL is the subject of the last chapter. Here, we attempt to describe what makes a good CLIL teacher, and what might constitute good practice in CLIL, in order to propose what teacher education should concentrate on. We discuss what CLIL teachers need to know about, what they need to be able to do, methodologically speaking, and how they should see themselves as professionals. The chapter briefly discusses current teacher education capacity in CLIL and recommends how it might be improved.

The final section of the book contains practical tasks relating to Chapters 2 to 10 and suggested answers to these where possible. There is also a comprehensive Glossary of the key terms, acronyms, and abbreviations used in the book.

CLIL is a way of teaching which is growing in scope and proving ever more interesting to education authorities in Europe and beyond. Many schools and education authorities have long-established experience in CLIL, while others are interested in starting a programme—we intend the book to be of use to both. We have also tried to address the different interests of both subject teachers and language teachers.

What makes CLIL interesting is its distinct pedagogy. Its purpose is to amplify the conceptual content of the lesson in a way which allows learners without full command of the medium of instruction to understand and express new subject concepts. By reducing the language demands of classroom tasks, CLIL pedagogy makes subject knowledge accessible to students whose incomplete language ability would normally limit their ability to learn. It does this without reducing the cognitive challenge of subject learning. It generates what Gibbons (2009) calls a high-challenge, high-support classroom. This is an enriched pedagogy which makes use of a range of tasks not normally taught to teachers in training—and not normally available in subject textbooks. It enables teachers to use a more transparent form of talk with learners, and to get extended responses from them in a way which conventional teaching would not prepare them for. Above all, it makes the academic variety of the language, which is crucial to school learning, evident and available in the lesson for learners to use. Of all the contributions CLIL makes to education, this pedagogy is its major achievement. To many teachers who are used to the more restricted code of conventional teaching, this has value beyond CLIL and is something which they can take back to their work in the learners' first language, and which adds value to teaching across the curriculum.

1

WHAT IS CLIL?

Overview

In this chapter, we will relate CLIL to other forms of education in a second language throughout the world. The focus will be specifically on immersion education, **minority education**, bilingual education, **English-medium education** (**EME**) in developing countries, and recent English-medium maths and science developments. In each case, we will look at a series of key learner features, such as ability in L2, literacy and cognitive skills, exposure to the L2, and social background. We will also examine teacher language ability and appropriate pedagogy, and institutional issues such as programme structure and resourcing. In the second half of the chapter, we will isolate these features and discuss them in more detail, in an attempt to establish what it is that enables learning in an L2 to be successful, and in particular what distinguishes schools which make a success of CLIL.

What is meant by 'CLIL'?

CLIL is a term that encompasses a wide range of differing school practices. When you talk to someone about CLIL, it is advisable to establish what you both mean by the term in order to avoid talking at cross-purposes. In this book, we will focus on two main versions. The first, known as 'hard' CLIL, is a form of subject teaching in L2 which highlights academic achievement within the subject and treats language development as important, but as a bonus. A school which runs this kind of CLIL programme offers one or two subjects in L2—but rarely more—for one, two, or more years full-time; in other words, the programme occupies all the hours allocated to the subject. In this type of school, language teaching can sometimes have little or no involvement in the CLIL programme.

The other main type of CLIL, known as 'soft' CLIL, may be offered for a short period—perhaps half a year—and it will only occupy a portion of the hours available to the subject; perhaps one in three. A school offering this kind of CLIL programme will certainly look for high achievement in the subject, but it will also place emphasis on language development. With this in mind, it may involve language teachers in several possible roles within the CLIL programme and highlight collaboration between subject and language staff. We will return to the matter of collaboration in Chapter 9, and deal in more detail with both these 'hard' and 'soft' variants of CLIL in Chapter 2.

In this book, we use the term 'L1' to refer to a language used in the home or community, in which learners are most fluent when they enter school. We use the term 'L2' to refer to any languages which students learn in addition to this L1, most often in a formal school setting. In CLIL programmes, L2 is the **medium of instruction** (**MoI**). We use 'bilingual education' to mean any form of school learning through the medium of two languages. We use EME to refer to the teaching of subjects through the medium of English; in the relevant literature, this is sometimes referred to as 'English-medium instruction' (EMI).

Education in a second language: diversity of contexts

Education through the medium of L2 happens in varying contexts all over the world. CLIL is thus a relation in this family of similar practices. However, these practices differ considerably, and it is important to establish, where we can, what the distinguishing features of their contexts are and, in particular, what makes them succeed or fail.

Indeed, one crucial thing to bear in mind is that L2-medium education sometimes works well and sometimes does not. CLIL has, by and large, a good track record: it tends to work—in the sense, for example, that learners can acquire good levels of subject knowledge (Zydatiss, 2009; Sierra, 2008). But we need to know why it works, how to make it better, and when it sometimes does not work, why that might be. Here, we will look at some of the features which influence the success of L2-medium education in general in its various guises in different parts of the world. In some contexts, such as minority and immersion education in the USA generally, we are helped by the fact that L2-medium schooling is well researched. In other contexts, little is known about why some learners thrive while others do not. However, some potential determining factors are available for consideration:

- the educational background of learners
- the level of learners' L2 ability
- the degree to which learners are literate in L1 and have acquired strong cognitive academic language proficiency (CALP) in L1
- the degree to which teachers are trained to teach subjects in L2
- the degree to which teachers are sufficiently fluent in L2
- whether the whole curriculum or just a part of it is taught in L2
- learners' exposure to L2 in the community
- the degree to which authorities are informed about L2-medium education and provide appropriate support.

In this chapter, we will briefly outline some of the better defined of these L2-medium contexts, with a view to establishing what CLIL has in common with them. In doing so, we will focus on the role played by some of the determining factors listed above.

Immersion education

Immersion education as a form of state schooling originated in Canada, but it has since expanded to various parts of the world, including the USA and Europe. Immersion programmes start at various points in a child's school career: 'early' (for example, kindergarten), 'mid' (for example, nine to ten years old), and 'late' (for example, secondary). Immersion programmes also vary in terms of the amount of curriculum time delivered in immersion: they may be either '**total immersion**' (100%) or '**partial immersion**' (say, 50%), and L2-medium curriculum time often decreases throughout an immersion programme (Baker, 2001). Learners often start with low ability in L2 and are not normally exposed to the language to any considerable extent in the community.

The MoI in an immersion programme is normally a high-status language, such as French in Canada. Similarly, learners in these programmes tend to speak high-status majority languages at home, such as English in North America. Notably, they are often literate in these high-status home languages, and schools running the programme support development in this first language and aim for **additive bilingualism** (Baker, 2001)—i.e. a second language is added to the first, as opposed to replacing it.

Teachers in immersion programmes are normally bilingual. Teacher-education programmes are necessary, but vary in their availability from context to context. Immersion programmes tend to be populated by learners from backgrounds with higher **socio-economic status** (**SES**) (Cummins, 2000); the programmes are also often driven by parental motivation and are thus self-selective in nature, i.e. they are provided for sections of the community which demand them.

There has been a great deal of research on immersion programmes, concerning levels of subject and language ability, as well as classroom processes. Learners are considered to achieve good levels of both subject knowledge and L2 ability, though there is a concern that learners are sometimes said to have insufficient accuracy in productive skills (Johnson & Swain, 1997).

Minority education

Minority education provides for the schooling of language minorities. Debate about minority education mainly concerns migrant and immigrant communities in industrialized countries, for example the USA, the UK, and various other countries in Europe and Australasia. However, there is also a growing interest, especially in South and South East Asia, in the early years education of indigenous communities speaking **minority languages** (Benson & Kosonen, 2013). Minority children in industrialized countries learn the whole curriculum in L2 at all ages and levels of language ability. When they enter the host school system, their L2 entry level is often low. They are educated mainly in mainstream classrooms, with or without specialist support, and they may in addition learn L2 in withdrawal classes. Exposure to the MoI in the community tends to be high. In contrast to immersion programmes, learners often come from low-SES families, speaking languages which often have low status in the community—for example Urdu speakers in the UK. Minority education in these contexts is often associated with relatively low school achievement: learners may struggle to get a good education. However, this is not always the case: some language minority communities have high SES and achieve well in schools, for example some Chinese speakers in the UK (Hollingworth & Mansaray, 2012).

Forms of practice in minority education vary hugely. Creese (2005) outlines some of these as they apply to the UK. Often learners are placed, unsupported, in mainstream subject classrooms. They may or may not benefit in some of these lessons from support from a specialist teacher trained in L2-medium education or from a bilingual support teacher, or indeed from a mainstream subject teacher with some minority education expertise. They may also be withdrawn from mainstream lessons for weekly sessions in L2 development. In some cases, the school may have developed a whole-school policy for the support of minority L2-medium learners which enables mainstream subject teachers to provide a degree of support within their lessons. In some contexts, particularly in the USA, various forms of bilingual education for minority language users are also available (Thomas & Collier, 2002). Teacher-education facilities also vary, from sophisticated university-based **in-service education and teacher training** (**INSETT**) and **initial teacher education** (**ITE**) courses to the absence of any teacher development opportunities at all.

In the USA, research into minority education is widespread and influential. It has focused in particular on the differential forms which the education of minority learners may take. These vary, for example, in the degree of attention they pay to the learners' L1. In many countries, the minority learners' L1 is not valued, additive bilingualism is not pursued, and the L1 may have no place in the curriculum. The work of Thomas and Collier (1997), however, has established that in the USA, bilingual education—**two-way developmental bilingual education** in particular—is more beneficial to learners than unsupported 'immersion' in mainstream classrooms. The work of Cummins (2000 inter alia) has focused attention on the role of **CALP** in the schooling of minority learners, leading to widespread acceptance that it is crucial for minority learners to acquire academic language ability in L2. Learners may become conversationally fluent in L2 relatively quickly, but it may take many years of formal intervention for them to develop the level of CALP necessary to learn effectively in L2.

Bilingual education

Bilingual education is practised in various parts of the world; extensive research exists in both the USA and Europe. Several distinct models are used. '**Maintenance bilingual education**' in the USA educates minority language learners in two languages (Baker, 2001). Half or more of curriculum time is taught in the minority students' home language. This form of bilingual education aims to maintain a language which might easily be lost in a community in which the majority language predominates. Maintenance models of bilingual education enable children both to maintain their home language and to achieve academically in core curriculum subjects on a par with conventional education (Baker, 2001). Most schools using this model of bilingual education are primary schools.

In **dual-language bilingual programmes** (for example, in the USA), roughly equal numbers of **language-minority students** and **language-majority students** are taught in the same classroom. Many schools aim for a 50:50 division between languages as media of instruction. Languages are separated as MoIs; for example, they may be used on alternate days or in alternate subject lessons. **Code-switching**, while it occurs, may be thought officially to be unhelpful (Baker, 2001). Dual-language programmes aim to produce bilingual and multicultural learners; they also aim for—and in the case of American schools, can achieve (Lindholm-Leary, 2001)—higher-than-average levels of subject knowledge. Dual-language bilingual schools cater for all grades.

English-medium education in developing countries

In some parts of the world, the vast majority of learners learn through an L2. This is the case, for example, in **sub-Saharan Africa** (**SSA**), where for more than a hundred years students have learned through the media of European languages. Similarly, in many parts of the world, students do not learn through the medium of their home language but instead through a language of wider participation, as in Tanzania, for example, where they learn through Kiswahili and not through the many African community languages. In South Asia also, students may often learn through a language which is not their home language. The same goes for the education of communities through the medium of a national language, such as Spanish in South America. In these contexts, L2-medium education may start from day one of schooling or—as in most of SSA—after three years of education in a local language. L2 ability at the start of L2-medium education is normally low (MacDonald, 1993). Education in L2 is system-wide, and students learn most subjects in the L2. Because many of these contexts are developing countries, the majority of learners may come from low-SES, often impoverished, and **print-illiterate** backgrounds. Societal exposure to the MoI may be low, especially in rural communities.

Strong research evidence (see Heugh, 2006) shows that English-medium education in Africa is often ineffective, as many learners have neither a strong enough CALP base in their L1 to allow them to benefit from early-exit L1-medium schooling, nor strong enough L2 ability to enable them to make an early switch to L2-medium education. Many teachers also feel insufficiently confident in the L2 to teach subjects in it effectively (Brock-Utne, 2010). Infrastructure to support the development of education in L2 is often non-existent: ITE, for example, tends to be unfamiliar with bilingual education (Probyn, 2006) and trains learners as if they were L2-fluent. Education in L2 in Africa, therefore, often has a depressive effect on national and individual school achievement. One African language-in-education research tradition calls for the strengthening and extension of education in L1 (Brock-Utne & Skattum, 2009).

Recent English-medium science and maths programmes

In some parts of the world, there has recently been a new interest in education through L2, mainly in English. In a few contexts, new English-medium education initiatives have been system-wide, i.e. they involve all children, often from day one of schooling, as has been the case in Malaysia and Qatar, and at low levels of L2 ability, at least in the early years. In other countries, such as other Gulf States, South Asia, or China, English-medium education has been introduced selectively, and often in response to parental demand. Some programmes do not involve the whole curriculum, but sections of it, such as science, maths, and ICT in Malaysia and Qatar. Where programmes are self-selecting, schools tend to cater for children from educated, higher-SES backgrounds. In system-wide programmes, exposure to L2 in society may be low, especially in rural areas, whereas in self-selecting programmes, exposure to L2 in both the home and the community can be high.

The success of recent introductions in L2-medium education is varied. One thing that can be learned from them is that self-selecting programmes in educated communities can often thrive without extensive support. On the other hand, we also realize that to cater for all schools, age-ranges, and social backgrounds requires major, long-term, and expensive infrastructural provision. Without these, national educational standards can be at risk. In these system-wide programmes, large numbers of learners and teachers can struggle with English as MoI in school. In these cases, good ITE and INSETT are needed, as are published materials tailored specifically to meet the needs of learners and teachers working in L2, and school-based management practices to raise whole-school achievement in L2. Provision of this kind is rare, as it takes many years to develop. Without it, system-wide programmes can struggle to achieve sufficiently high national subject standards across the board. Low school achievement in maths and science was a key reason why the Malaysian English-medium science and maths programme, started in 2003, was terminated in 2012. On the other hand, English-medium programmes which are self-selecting and driven by motivated parents from high-SES backgrounds tend to deliver good results in both subjects and language.

How is CLIL different?

CLIL is obviously related in one way or another to all the very varied school practices mentioned above in which learners learn partly or wholly through an L2. However, one way in which it differs from many of the programme types described above is that it tends to be taught in a particular school in one or a limited number of subjects; it rarely involves large proportions of the curriculum. Like immersion education and bilingual education, it tends to be self-selecting in that it is a programme which schools offer as an option as opposed to one which is imposed on all schools by an education authority. Unlike all the system-wide forms of L2-medium education described above, CLIL learners have a basic minimum level of L2 ability when they enter a programme, which is considered adequate for them to flourish in it. Like all the forms of schooling to which we have already referred, CLIL is dependent on good levels of CALP on the part of learners. CLIL is normally offered in secondary schools, though many primary schools do offer effective CLIL courses; and secondary school learners will have had time to develop CALP in their L1 in primary school.

CLIL programmes differ somewhat from some forms of bilingual education in that they tend not to pursue overtly 'political' aims in terms, for example, of equity, equal language status, or multiculturalism; but they are often sold to parents in terms of their value in a multilingual world of work and sometimes in terms of a wider cultural view. The experience of CLIL is radically different from that of learners learning in L2 in many developing countries where levels of poverty, L2 exposure and ability, and resourcing lend weight to the value of education in the child's home language. In European CLIL, by contrast, learning a subject in an L2 can have high social value for parents and can achieve high levels of language and subject knowledge.

In the next section of this chapter, we will look more closely at the criteria which, when taken together, can help a school to design a successful CLIL programme.

Criteria for success in CLIL

Several potential determining factors emerge from the forms of L2-medium education described above, which make it easier or more difficult for learners to learn through a second language.

Learner L2 ability

Subject teachers can teach their subject to learners with good levels of ability in the MoI. With skilled CLIL strategies, it is also possible for these teachers to teach their subject to learners with an ability level of intermediate or below in the MoI and still maintain acceptable levels of subject knowledge. However, there must clearly be a level of learner ability in the MoI below which teaching and learning subjects in an L2 becomes ineffective. In this case, learners have to learn both new language and new subject concepts; when too much of both is unfamiliar, the cognitive load is simply too heavy. This 'bottom line' language ability is usually described in terms of academic rather than social language. What this level is, however, is difficult to define because it is dependent on so many variables.

Pedagogical skill makes a big difference when dealing with learners of different L2 ability: a skilled CLIL teacher working with learners whose ability approaches this 'bottom line' can maintain levels of subject knowledge, whereas a good subject teacher without CLIL strategies may not. In addition, some subjects are less linguistically demanding, and students can learn them more easily in L2. High-context subjects, for instance those with high visual content such as art or physical education (PE), could fall into this category. Learner subject knowledge is also important: learners who know a subject well can cope with lower levels of L2 ability; and learners who are well motivated can sometimes do the same. Moreover, it is possible to run a good CLIL programme starting with learners with low or even zero L2 ability. Early years bilingual education is a case in point: programmes of this kind take into account a strongly bilingual classroom; initial L2 ability may be minimal, and effective L2-medium learning is often delayed until learners are more skilled in L2.

Nevertheless, when deciding whether to offer a CLIL programme, a school will often think carefully about whether the learners know enough L2. Some may offer **language-booster courses** both before and during the CLIL course. Others may specify a level on an internationally recognized scale: to enter CLIL programmes in the Netherlands, for example, learners may have to demonstrate a level equivalent to **Cambridge ESOL Advanced** (2013). In other contexts, such as in Bulgaria, a whole transitional year—which includes high-intensity language development— serves as a preparatory step to CLIL programmes. For some schools, highly skilled CLIL teachers may make up partly for lower learner L2 ability. However, in some parts of the world, such as SSA, low learner ability in the MoI can seriously depress school achievement (Alidou & Brock-Utne, 2006).

Exposure to L2

CLIL learners can benefit from living in a society in which exposure to the L2 is fairly high. The L2 may be widely used in the society itself, as is obviously the case for minority learners of a majority language, such as migrant communities in European countries or in the USA. Indeed, these learners pick up the majority language from their environment—in the street, for instance, and especially in the playground—and often become fluent in the social variety of it without much intervention from teachers. This helps them to then develop the cognitive academic variety of the language in school. In some countries, the L2 may be widely available through the media, as is the case with English in northern Europe. Here, this kind of exposure can help learners achieve fairly high levels of L2 ability. High exposure may also be achieved within school by learning large proportions of the curriculum through L2, for example in timetabled CLIL lessons. Learners learning more than half of the curriculum through L2—especially when they start early, such as in the Spanish Ministry of Education and Culture (**MEC**)/British Council bilingual programme (2010)—will get a lot of exposure to the language over time. By contrast, low levels of social exposure to the language may be a barrier to succeeding in L2-medium education. For example, low and often close to zero exposure to English in rural areas of English-medium education in Africa can make it very hard for rural learners to succeed in school. Similar claims were made about rural schools in the English-medium science and maths programme in Malaysia mentioned on page 10. Crucially, however, it must be remembered that social exposure and social fluency alone is not enough: learners need focused teaching of CALP in L2 (Cummins, 2000), and we will return to this in Chapters 4–7.

Literacy and cognitive skills

CLIL programmes are taught through L2, but as has been emphasized in this chapter, and will be emphasized again in Chapter 4 and in the book as a whole, this is crucially through the academic variety of the L2. Teachers and learners use this variety when they handle school subjects. It is therefore important that key stakeholders in CLIL programmes are aware of its features. We will look more closely at this in Chapter 4.

It is widely accepted and well supported by research (Cummins, 2000) that learners with good L1 literacy skills and academic language proficiency are better equipped to learn in L2. Cummins makes the point that a set of underlying academic language skills—what he calls a 'common underlying proficiency' consisting of CALP skills—once learned in one language, can transfer to a second. In other words, once children have learned these skills in their first language, they don't have to learn them again in their second. Cummins's (1984) diagram of a 'dual iceberg'—slightly adapted in Figure 1.1 below—has become familiar in bilingual education as a way of making this very point.

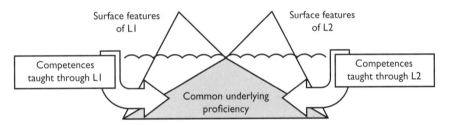

Figure 1.1 Cummins's 'dual iceberg' representation of bilingual proficiency (adapted from Cummins, 1984.)

There is also some discussion of the length of time needed for learners to have acquired these skills in their L1 so that they are established well enough to be usable in the L2. Students in many SSA countries, for example, learn for three or four years in their L1 before switching medium to L2, and some commentators do not consider this 'early-exit' form of L1 proficiency to be long enough for transfer to L2 to take place (Heugh, 2006). They would prefer six to eight years' learning in L1. Cummins (2000) also suggests that while a minority language learner in the USA might become socially fluent in L2 within two years, it may take them seven years to develop good CALP skills. CLIL programmes in Europe normally take place in secondary education, by which time good foundations in L1 literacy and cognitive skills have been established.

Socio-economic status

All learners can benefit from learning in L2. It is not the case that learners with lower socio-economic status and without the advantages of an educated family background are not good candidates for CLIL programmes. They are, but they do need more support. Just as learners from more educated backgrounds take to school education more easily in general, they may also have advantages when it comes to learning in L2. Those features of an educated family background which are widely known to give a child an educational advantage in the L1—for example, the presence of books, the high status of reading, and the use of a 'literate' form of family talk between parents and children (Wells & Chang-Wells, 1992)—may also make it easier for students to learn in L2 at school (Brice Heath, 1982). In particular, L1 literacy and an acquaintance with the beginnings of L1 CALP can make it easier to learn in school through L2 (see 'Literacy and cognitive skills' above). Immersion education, for example, is easier for educated families, especially those with L1 literacy (Cummins, 2000). In minority education, learners from migrant families will often learn better through L2 in mainstream classrooms if they have educated family backgrounds, or have experience of good L1-medium schooling with good foundations in L1 CALP. Students learning through the medium of English as an L2 in Africa can also manage much better if their families are educated (Fleisch, 2008). We see similar indications in South East Asian English-medium education, for example in Hong Kong or Malaysia where schools with middle-class intakes do better in English. Also, L2-medium education tends to thrive in selective education systems—and indeed in private schools—where middle-class schools and parents approve of it and often demand it. By contrast, in system-wide contexts, where learners from every social background are required to learn through L2, the L2 can become one more barrier to education, on top of conventional class barriers, and socially disadvantaged children and schools may struggle.

There are obvious dangers in this. Learners from all socio-educational backgrounds can succeed in CLIL programmes; and learners in both mixed-ability schools and mainly low-SES **catchment areas** can learn effectively through CLIL. Indeed, the growing popularity of CLIL attests to the view that its methods can, with good teacher support, work well in mixed-ability classrooms. However, it can happen that middle-class parents push for CLIL programmes, that schools with high-SES learners offer them effectively, and that learners from educated backgrounds progress more easily within them. By contrast, learners with lower SES and less experience of CALP may succeed only with more support. Schools must therefore pay particular attention to these learners, and the support they give should take the form of additional explicit focus on CALP. Appropriate support of this kind should ensure that in L2—and also in L1 where possible—learners get explicit instruction in those basic features of academic discourse that they may not control well enough, such as aspects of cohesion, academic **language functions**, academic vocabulary, and the fundamentals of reading, writing, and speaking in learning contexts.

Finally, it should be noted that, as shown in Figure 1.1, transfer of academic language skills can occur in either direction—from L1 to L2 or vice versa (Cummins, 2000). In other words, learners do not necessarily have to learn them first in L1. In the Basque Country, for example, learners learn three languages— Basque, Spanish, and English—with Basque being the first and principal language of schooling. Here, a learner might speak Spanish at home, but acquire CALP in Basque, an L2, and later transfer those academic language skills to Spanish, the L1.

Teacher L2 ability

Teacher ability in the L2 is also crucial. Teachers must feel confident enough in it—and especially in the cognitive academic variety and subject-specific requirements of it—both to control the language of the subject and to give expression to a good range of pedagogical strategies in order to teach it. Teacher language ability, like learner language ability, can affect the success of CLIL programmes. Without confidence and adequate fluency in the L2, CLIL teachers cannot teach their subject effectively enough, and this can contribute to a fall in subject standards. Teacher language ability in education through European languages in Africa is often insufficient for them to teach their subject to an acceptable national standard (Brock-Utne, 2010).

Teacher language ability varies: in some parts of Europe, for instance, CLIL teachers speak the L2 well. In others they do not; and in these cases, authorities may feel that this insufficient level of teacher language ability limits the extent to which they can introduce 'hard' CLIL programmes. Teacher language ability can be upgraded, but that takes both time and a language programme which is preferably geared towards the requirements of teaching a subject in L2. Courses like this are few and far between. In recent introductions of English-medium education—for example in Malaysia and Qatar—authorities quite properly felt it important to institute teacher language-upgrading courses. However, it is difficult to make such courses work: offered to all teachers on a system-wide basis, they are often too short to raise teacher language ability to a level which makes a marked difference to learner subject achievement. It is often easier simply to procure a subject teacher who can teach in the language well enough.

Teacher pedagogical skill

Teacher language ability is not as crucial as some authorities seem to think it is. Fluent speakers of the MoI would, for example, be of little use in the CLIL classroom if they could not get learners of low L2 ability to understand them. For this reason, appropriate teacher pedagogy is also vital. Indeed, teachers who are well-trained in CLIL pedagogy can counterbalance a certain lack of fluency in the MoI. For instance, if their front-of-class talk in L2 is not perfect, but they are good at adopting a comprehensible CLIL talking style and supporting their presentation of concepts with visuals, they will do a better job than a fluent talker who cannot help learners to understand. CLIL teachers, therefore, need to be trained to use CLIL pedagogy, especially if they are working with learners whose L2 abilities are still developing. We will return in detail to the teacher strategies which constitute such a CLIL pedagogy in Chapters 5, 6, and 10.

Resourcing

CLIL programmes need resources. The most valuable resource is learning materials. Learners need to be able to read about their CLIL subject in the L2. Where learners have a high level of L2 ability, a book intended for L2-fluent or native-speakers of the language may be appropriate. Where learner L2 levels are lower, however, a book intended for native-speakers may be linguistically too difficult and therefore slow learning down. Some CLIL teachers may be tempted to choose a book which is linguistically easier because it is intended for native-speaker learners in a lower age range, but this reduces the cognitive demands on learners—a step which CLIL programmes are keen to avoid. Because publishers see only small markets in CLIL books, few are published. Expertise in designing books which offer language support of the kind which CLIL programmes depend on (see Chapters 4 and 5) is not common anywhere in the world. CLIL teachers therefore spend a great deal of time sourcing improvised materials from textbooks meant for native speakers and from the internet, then building in their own language support. Preparation devoted to this time-consuming exercise takes up much more of a CLIL teacher's time than lesson preparation for a conventional teacher and can prove daunting. We will return in detail to the matter of resources in Chapter 7.

Self-selecting or system-wide programmes

As already mentioned, some CLIL programmes are adopted only in certain schools, whereas in other contexts the aim is to teach CLIL subjects in all schools, and perhaps even to all age groups. Self-selecting CLIL programmes work more easily than system-wide programmes. They select the learners who are best fitted for the programme, by virtue of their L2 ability, but also taking into account other factors such as their subject ability, motivation, general learning ability, etc. The school may select the learners by reference to measured L2 ability. Or the learners may self-select, with teacher advice and often with parental support, on the basis of their L2 ability as well as their interests and motivations. Schools which offer CLIL programmes normally offer the opportunity to learn a subject either in L1 or L2. They may also, in electing to offer CLIL, be influenced by parental demand. Some schools may be more able than others to find the resourcing which a CLIL programme requires. In this way, self-selecting CLIL programmes are often linked unintentionally to higher SES.

Most European CLIL programmes are self-selecting: that is, only some schools offer programmes, and they offer them only in some subjects to some learners. System-wide education programmes, such as African L2-medium education, face a grossly different task. The same might be said of system-wide English-medium science and maths programmes, even in rich countries, such as Qatar. System-wide programmes involve the delivery of either the majority of the curriculum (as in Africa) or part of it (as in Qatar) through L2 from day one of schooling, or maybe from Year 4. Thus all learners, including the poorest, least academically able, and sometimes also the youngest (with close to zero L2 ability), learn subjects in L2 in schools which include the least well resourced and those in the most impoverished catchment areas. To achieve high levels of education in L1 in these schools requires high-quality teaching, but to achieve it in L2 is often even more difficult. The lesson here, as pointed out under *Socio-economic status* above, is that if you want to do CLIL with all learners in all schools, some will need more help; and the kind of help they need is an explicit reinforcement of CALP skills.

Time allocation

At the beginning of this chapter, we outlined a range of different forms of education which can go by the name of CLIL. One thing which can distinguish them is the amount of the subject syllabus which is taught through L2. If a school asks a learner to study the whole of the science curriculum for three years in L2, this is very different from offering one out of the three timetabled hours of science per week in L2 for a module of 25 weeks. In the latter form of CLIL, the focus is often on the language more than, or as much as, the subject; and the extra degree of L2 fluency which learners are claimed to acquire is often the main reason for offering the programme. It is a low-risk enterprise: if learners fail to understand subject concepts in the L2 in one lesson, they can probably retrieve them in L1 in the next. It may also not matter so much if teachers are not L2-fluent. However, learners who study all their science for a number of years in L2 need effective L2-medium subject teaching and sufficiently fluent teachers to ensure that their science achievement in L2 is as good as in L1, if not better. That is a much higher-risk undertaking. In this way, full-time, long-term CLIL requires a greater commitment from a school than short-term, part-time CLIL, and schools need to be sure that they have the means to make it work.

The language syllabus

Language teachers, if they collaborate with CLIL subject teachers, should also know something about CALP and spend some time helping learners in CLIL programmes to use it. CLIL can be more effective if L2 language teaching is orientated to its requirements. We will return to this issue in Chapters 3 and 4. Language-teaching syllabuses and materials—and the training of language teachers—are not normally orientated to learning subjects. They are geared to the learning of social language skills to be used in the street, in shops and social transactions, and in the family and wider society. Learners who are using a second or foreign language to learn subjects need a kind of teaching which is at least partly focused on the language of these subjects and of academic learning. This is often the case in minority education; but in schools which offer CLIL programmes, this orientation is often lacking in the language syllabus. A language teacher who can steer the teaching of L2 partly towards the **cross-curricular language skills** of L2-medium learning, and perhaps even to the basics of some subject-specific language, can have a positive impact on the capacity of learners to use the language in learning subjects in CLIL programmes. This is especially the case if the school encourages collaborative practices between language and subject teachers—another question to which we will return in Chapter 9.

Planning

CLIL programmes work better if they are planned. Planning may happen at the level of the education authority, of the school management, and of the subject teacher. We will look at this issue in more depth in Chapter 9. An education authority may plan a regional CLIL programme, for example, by setting standards of staffing and resourcing, adjusting assessment and examination procedures, or providing teacher support. A school may plan at the level of senior management by setting school entry requirements for CLIL programmes, monitoring levels of teacher language ability, funding resources, or encouraging collaboration. Planning at this school level is familiar in minority education: for instance, the UK has well-established whole-school management procedures for **EAL (English as an additional language)**, known as 'partnership teaching' (Bourne & McPake, 1991). The subject teacher may plan by developing an L2-medium subject syllabus, designing teaching materials, or collaborating with colleagues. It is crucial for planning that decision-makers be informed about the theory and practice of successful CLIL—about, for example, materials, appropriate pedagogy, fair assessment, etc. Some CLIL programmes may suffer from poor planning: authorities may establish programmes without knowing quite what they are good for and how they best work. Training and support are sometimes scarce. By contrast, well-planned and informed programmes can lead to high-quality education and high L2-medium subject standards.

Summary

Several criteria for success in CLIL have emerged from this chapter.

- Learners need to be able to speak the L2 well enough. If their level is on the low side, good CLIL pedagogy on the part of the teacher is especially important. Social or media exposure to the L2 can help raise this level of language.
- Strong literacy and cognitive skills are crucial.
- Learners from all social backgrounds can succeed in CLIL, but the socially disadvantaged may need extra support.
- Teachers need to be able to speak the L2 well enough, and they should also have specialist teaching skills which highlight language in learning, especially if they teach learners with lower levels of L2 ability. They will be helped in this by resources tailored to their needs, but may find that such resources are scarce.
- Schools which opt to offer CLIL will find it easier than those which are required to do so as part of a system-wide programme. Those which offer long-term, full-time programmes will need to pay more attention to subject standards than those in short-term 'softer' programmes. Language courses can help learners studying subjects in L2.
- School development planning can raise achievement in CLIL programmes.

What distinguishes CLIL is a certain concern with language in the subject classroom and a distinct subject pedagogy which allows the subject teacher to deploy a range of **language-supportive strategies** which are unfamiliar in conventional teaching. In the next chapter, we will look more closely at how teachers do this in the different forms of CLIL in which they work.

Further reading

Baker, C. (2001). *Foundations of bilingual education and bilingualism*. Clevedon, UK: Multilingual Matters.
Chapters 9–11 are an excellent source of readable, informed, well-summarized information on all aspects of bilingual education, mainly in industrialized countries.

Benson, C., & **Kosonen, T.** (Eds.). (2013). *Language issues in comparative education*. Rotterdam: Sense Publishers.
A selection of authoritative articles on aspects of EME in different parts of the developing world.

Coyle, D., Hood, P., & **Marsh, D.** (2010). *CLIL: Content and language integrated learning*. Cambridge: Cambridge University Press.
A good overview of CLIL as it occurs mainly in Europe. Chapters 1 and 2 define the term and the aspects of education it refers to.

García, O. (2009). *Bilingual education in the 21st century: A global perspective*. Chichester: Wiley-Blackwell.
Classic account of bilingual education in its various forms across the world by one of the leading experts in the field. See Chapters 6–7.

2 DEFINING PARAMETERS

Overview

In this chapter, we will attempt to narrow the parameters of CLIL through a more methodological framework, suggesting ten principal features that are explored in further detail in subsequent chapters. We will examine the shift from teacher talk to student intervention, the bridges between language teaching and subject teaching, and the beneficial effect that successful CLIL practice can also have on whole-school policy and on L1 teaching in schools.

Teacher talk to student intervention

Sometimes the simplest of stories have the most impact, especially for teachers just setting out on their particular CLIL journeys. Consider the following anecdote about a CLIL trainer on a substantial, long-term CLIL programme in the north of Spain:

> Every June, local teachers whose schools were about to join the project attended a short briefing course with the trainer in question. During the very first of these sessions, a secondary school history teacher explained that he was nervous about teaching CLIL in September because of his language level. He had been teaching history in Spanish for 25 years, and he felt confident in his delivery of the content. However, doing the same in English was a frightening prospect. The trainer tried to reassure the teacher by praising his English, but the teacher was unconvinced. 'What can I do between now and September?' he asked. 'How can I improve my English so that I feel more confident?' Various teachers had suggestions, ranging from 'Go and do a crash-course in the UK this summer' to 'Just read lots of history books in English over the summer'; but most of the solutions proposed were based on improving the teacher's oral fluency—and therefore his confidence in delivering the material. The teacher turned to the trainer and asked him which of the proposals he thought was the best. The trainer shrugged and replied, 'None of them'. Shocked by this rejection of the proffered advice, the teacher asked the trainer, 'OK, so what do you propose?' The reply that the trainer gave was to become the leitmotif for all his subsequent CLIL training sessions: 'When you get to September, and you're standing in front of the class, just don't talk so much.'

The simplicity of this observation unlocks a treasure trove of truths regarding CLIL. It is also powerful advice because it would have been counter-intuitive to language teachers, particularly those brought up on a diet of 'model teacher talk'. It would have been similarly alien to those subject teachers whose mantra it is to transmit knowledge by way of explanation. Particularly in Spain, from where this anecdote originated, the traditional (and often current) view of 'good teachers' is that they are the ones who can demonstrate their knowledge of the subject. Teachers teach; students listen and learn. Whether this is true or not—and there are good reasons to suspect that it is not—then the first consequence of a 'just don't talk so much' approach in a CLIL classroom where the lesson is planned and under control, will be that the students do more. The teacher volume is, as it were, turned down, and the student volume (in the positive sense of their intervention) is turned up.

Why is this a good idea? Why is talking good for learners, and why is it just as beneficial when learning through another language as it is when learning in the L1? According to Clegg:

> Talking about something which one is learning is important, because it is when we express a new concept linguistically that we gradually develop it. The concept may be partly developed in our minds, but until we start to communicate it linguistically, we don't know how clearly—or unclearly—it is formed. (Clegg, 2002a)

Teacher support

Of course, we must be careful here. Appropriate teacher talk is no less significant in CLIL contexts than it is in any other context where the **language of instruction (LoI)** is not the learners' L1; and teacher talk is particularly important in CLIL where learners may have low L2 ability. When presenting new concepts to the whole class, the characteristics of comprehensible teacher talk become especially important, as do the variety of teacher techniques used to prompt learner responses in the L2 in the same context (Mercer, 2000). But learner talk is important too. In fact, it is surely more important, because the function of teacher talk is ultimately to give way to student talk, whether in pairs, groups, or in **plenary**. (Or perhaps we should say student <u>production</u>, so as to include writing as well.) Learners were never intended to remain passive recipients of teacher-delivered wisdom. Crucially, therefore, in CLIL the teacher's craft is moving towards a greater consideration of how to offer support to learners. As we shall see in Chapters 5 and 6, CLIL (and perhaps competence-based education in general) is focused on guiding input and supporting output. It is a clear-enough mantra.

There seems to have been a shift in thinking since the publication of the EU's *Key competences for lifelong learning* (2006), a shift that favours competence-based performance. This has been good news for CLIL, because right from the outset, the instincts of successful CLIL practitioners have been in line with this. In good CLIL classes, the students are intervening and the teacher is facilitating. The students are doing things, are engaged with the lesson and its materials, and are more likely to be producing some of the **vehicular language**. The inevitable three-way dynamic, between the teacher, the students, and the materials (since all three elements always exist), is the dominant force, not the teacher's ability to transmit knowledge. The history teacher in the anecdote above was to be applauded in his desire to improve his level of English and to consequently increase his sense of self-confidence, but CLIL was never intended as a methodology to encourage teachers' oral demonstration of their knowledge. So what does CLIL seek to engender, apart from 'turning down the teacher volume'? What are the features that best define its aims and its essence?

CLIL as a methodology

As we noted in Chapter 1, CLIL (as a paradigm) shares an interface with a number of other approaches whose broad aim has been to facilitate the learning of subject content in circumstances where the learners are **non-native speakers** (**NNS**) of the vehicular language. Some of these approaches have been more successful than others, usually, we suspect, in circumstances where the authorities implementing the approach realized that language support was necessary. Exactly what this language support constitutes is the main focus of this book, for it can be provided in many forms. What is clear, however, is that this support can only be understood and then practised by teachers if they view CLIL as a methodology, with a set of tried-and-tested practices that can be applied across the board. We need to be able to identify these parameters in order to state what CLIL is, and what it is not. We need to be able to say, 'Try doing it like this' and 'Try to avoid doing it like that'.

Where CLIL has been unsuccessful (see Chapter 1), there seems to have been a prevailing assumption that there is no distinction between teaching through L1 to native speakers and teaching through an L2 to non-native speakers. Bluntly speaking, in such cases, there has probably been no real integration of language and content. As Kees de Bot insisted:

> It is obvious that teaching a subject in a foreign language is not the same as an integration of language and content … language teachers and subject teachers need to work together … [to] formulate the new didactics needed for a real integration of form and function in language teaching.
> (Marsh, 2002)

But first, teachers need to know what they are going to do once they decide to 'work together', as Kees de Bot suggests. In this chapter, we will try to identify the fundamental classroom-based features of CLIL practice. This is important, because we cannot simply say that a project failed because it was not CLIL, or that CLIL equals good practice and that therefore any defective models cannot be awarded the label. On the other hand, if we say, for example, that CLIL methodology consists of X, Y, and Z, we can begin to identify and then increase its presence. And once the features have been identified and are in place, we can begin to improve the quality of our classroom practice.

CLIL *sans frontières?*

Other variables can contribute to CLIL's downfall, of course, but we should be especially wary of portraying it as an educational life-force suited to some cultures, but out of bounds for others. If it comes with too many ideological demands attached, it will never really work *sans frontières*, i.e. in many different national contexts. However, as a set of methods, CLIL can potentially be applied to any scholastic context, regardless of the prevailing philosophy of the host system. Baetens Beardsmore (1993) did CLIL a potential disservice by suggesting that 'no model, however successful, is for export', by which he (broadly) meant that what works for Belgium does not necessarily work for Brazil, and vice versa. This was an important warning, due to the obvious problems of transfer from one socio-political context to another, but surely the transfer of methodological parameters is more feasible? Methodology comes with nothing attached save the twin needs for training and implementation. These might indeed be conditioned by national circumstances, but a clear methodological model works whatever the context. It can be considered, copied, and adapted if necessary. Indeed, the sharing of good practice across national boundaries has always been a strong feature of ELT, and there appears to be no reason to assume that CLIL cannot prosper in the same way. Coyle seems to think the same:

> Since effective CLIL depends on a range of situational and contextual variables, the need for a shared understanding about CLIL pedagogies became a priority. Identification of underlying fundamental principles and effective classroom practice must contribute to creating a framework for assuring quality in diverse contexts ...
> (Coyle, 2008)

An 'umbrella term'

For many teachers, CLIL remains a rather elusive concept (Ioannou-Georgiou, 2012). It is not entirely clear why this is the case, given that the acronym first appeared over 20 years ago, but it may have something to do with the problematic notion that CLIL is an 'umbrella term, covering a dozen or more educational approaches' (Mehisto, Marsh, & Frigols, 2008). According to Mehisto et al., these approaches included immersion, bilingual education, multilingual education, language showers, enriched language programmes, etc. They went on to add: 'What is new about CLIL is that it synthesises and provides a flexible way of applying the knowledge learnt from these various approaches.'

Whilst no one would seek to deny the eclectic nature of CLIL and its historical links to other areas of education, it is also worth noting that the 'dozen or more' alleged ingredients which help to constitute the potpourri that is CLIL are themselves multifaceted and difficult to pin down. The exact nature of their benefits and the good practices that have derived from them are by no means readily available to either the general public or to the teaching profession as a whole. Teachers starting out with CLIL need to be able to identify something with clearer parameters—something more workable from this rather inchoate notion of CLIL as an eclectic mixture, from which we can allegedly extract whatever we see fit, according to our own particular contexts.

Dual or single focus?

A similar problem occurs with the generalized notion that CLIL is a 'dual-focused' approach. It would certainly seem to be, because it appears to involve two things, namely content and language. As Coyle, Hood, and Marsh (2010) claim, 'CLIL is an educational approach in which various language-supportive methodologies are used which lead to a dual-focused form of instruction where attention is given to both the language and the content.'

There are two problems with this idea. Firstly, since the start of institutionalized education, content has always involved language, and language has always involved content. The two are philosophically and practically inseparable. Secondly, the notion that 'attention is given to both the language and the content' sounds feasible and laudable, but no further reason for this practice has ever been offered. Why would we want to give attention to 'content' (itself a contentious and multi-faceted term), and why would we want to give attention to 'language'? It is an interesting question, and one that lies at the heart of the CLIL paradigm. The dual focus does indeed exist in good CLIL practice, but what is the sum of its benefits? What is the aim behind this alleged fusion, this synthesis of two elements which are both in actual fact examples of content? Language is content, if it is viewed in a certain way—for example, as the basis of a language syllabus. If it is viewed in a different way, for example as the discourse of a subject syllabus, it is more the vehicle of the learning, not the learning itself.

Similarly, subject content, by which we usually mean conceptual or declarative content, can also be viewed in different ways. The factual basis of a syllabus—its quantitative content—can be seen as the product to be learned. But another view of conceptual content, as with the language example, might be to see it as the vehicle for another type of learning, namely subject competences. It is our view that both language and content are actually vehicles for the development of subject competences (geography, history, science, mathematics, etc.) and that language and content are never, as it were, aims in themselves. Maybe CLIL has a single focus after all, namely the more efficient development of subject competences.

CLIL and competences

In Chapter 3, we will profile this notion in more detail, within the framework of CLIL's three dimensions of knowledge (concepts, language, and procedures), where the third of these—procedural knowledge—is the key to understanding what CLIL does best, and why it can make an important contribution to a competence-based future. For now, suffice to say that CLIL may not be a dual-focused approach at all, but rather a single-focused methodology which enables subject-based competences to take shape more clearly, using language as the primary contributor to the cause. One of CLIL's most innovative and thought-provoking slogans—'using languages to learn and learning to use languages' (Marsh et al., 2000)—says very much the same thing. Language is a means to an end, and in CLIL, this idea finds its maximum expression and achieves its maximum exposure. What we want students to do is to perform in the vehicular language and to develop their discourse, as far as possible, in the direction of the text types and subject genres that predominate in their school lives. In the biology class, there is a certain kind of discourse used in the classroom, and when students move to the history class an hour later, the discourse changes again. This is as true of the L1 experience as it is of the L2 experience; but in the latter context, teachers and students soon realize that the particular language that frames the subject is either a support or an obstacle to learning. If CLIL has taught us this, then it has done us a great favour.

As Graddol (2006) remarked, English has ceased in many ways to be a language and has become a 'core skill' instead, without which people are 'disabled' in terms of their job prospects. Although CLIL is not by default English-centric, Graddol's message is a central component of the CLIL package and a crucial observation, since it lies at the heart of the educational and social change that has taken place since the development of the internet and the parallel growth in globalization. As English has become an essential add-on to any curricular programme around the world, it has evolved to become a subject that pupils learn 'in order to do something else' (ibid.). CLIL's 'dual-focused' exterior, underpinned by its single, competence-based aims, fits this post-millennial, utilitarian view of the English language perfectly. Liberal educationalists may not agree with it, but for the time being it is here to stay. More importantly, perhaps, we should simply view language (and not exclusively English) as the central component of learning, without which students are 'disabled', to use Graddol's word. It is not so much about learning languages per se, but about the impact that language has on learning. Bullock (1975) made very much the same point in his desire to include language considerations across the entire L1 curriculum.

Is it still not possible to consider language teaching an activity that has value in itself? The answer is of course 'yes', but CLIL represents the extreme end of the instrumental spectrum: you learn a language in order to do something else with it. The implication is that a lesson entitled 'The differences between the present perfect and the past simple' will be given short shrift by a CLIL teacher or learner. What CLIL learners need to know is how those differences help them to carry out the series of tasks that they are being asked to do.

'Soft' and 'hard' CLIL

An added difficulty when attempting to define CLIL is the question of for whom the paradigm is most intended: language teachers or subject teachers? As mentioned in Chapter 1, this dilemma has caused CLIL practitioners to invent the twin terms 'soft' and 'hard' (sometimes 'strong' and 'weak') to describe language-led and content-led approaches respectively. 'Soft' CLIL is used to describe the broad linguistic aims that a language teacher brings to the classroom, whereas 'hard' refers exclusively to subject-based aims and objectives, where subjects from the conventional curriculum are taught in an additional or foreign language.

In its origins, CLIL was intended as a set of methods that could help subject teachers support the language needs of their students, where the gap between the students' language levels and the complexity of the syllabus was causing potential problems in both understanding the material and producing the target language in the required discourse. As Kelly (2010) puts it, 'hard' CLIL is basically about guiding input and supporting output. As a framework for building a set of language-supportive methods and techniques, the axiom conveys a simple and practical notion that subject teachers—who are not trained to deal with the language implications of their subject content—can understand and put into practice.

Language teachers, on the other hand, were more on the margins of the movement in its earlier days, but 'soft' CLIL has made gradual inroads into the general scene and has become a branch of CLIL in its own right. This is partly because publishers had experienced difficulties in providing satisfactorily for the numerous niche areas that constitute the school curriculum, and also because a textbook for geography (for example) for a specific age level, in a foreign language, for a limited number of schools in a specific country is almost always unfeasible from a financial point of view. This still remains a problem, albeit to a lesser degree. On the other hand, incorporating features of CLIL practice into, say, an English-language textbook, could cater for a much wider market, just as long as the approach made sense to the teachers and learners.

Objectives and assessment

One key problem that has emerged in the wake of the growth of 'soft' CLIL is the fact that this version has linguistic objectives (the teacher is paid to teach a language), whereas the 'hard' version has content objectives (the teacher is paid to teach biology, for example). This raises the question of what to assess, particularly with regard to the language teacher. If the topical content of a language textbook is increased to the extent that it begins to resemble 'hard' CLIL, then how does the teacher assess the students? If conceptual content is to be incorporated meaningfully, it must be assessed. If not, the students sense very quickly that the topics themselves are mere slaves to the linguistic objectives, and motivation and interest levels drop accordingly.

On the other hand, imagine a biology teacher spending a fortnight on photosynthesis, to eventually test the students only on the associated language. The absurdity of this is undeniable, but for language teachers, who are paid a salary to improve their students' target-language levels, the assessment of 'content' is a tricky terrain to negotiate. We will return to this issue specifically in Chapter 8, but as we shall see during the course of the book, the demarcation lines between the nature of language teaching and 'content' teaching are beginning to blur (if we take Graddol's 'core skill' proposition seriously), with CLIL as the driving force.

Language teachers can be trained to assess conceptual content and **procedural content**, and indeed to consider these to be the *raisons d'être* of their courses.

Subject teachers, on the other hand, can be trained to first identify key language areas and issues within their specialism, and to then make these issues more salient to students. There is no need for them to suddenly become language teachers to achieve these aims. But the notion of salience is a crucial one, and it will also run throughout this book.

Building bridges between content and language

Another suggestion of this book is that the future health of CLIL depends on building bridges between content and language. This process requires subject teachers to understand the impact of language on cognition (and on their students' ability to understand the material), and language teachers to understand more fully the nature of subject-based texts and discourse. It is an enduring myth in CLIL circles that language teachers automatically grasp the linguistic issues involved in the understanding and production of subject-based content, and that they therefore represent an immediate and convenient source of support and advice for their subject teacher colleagues. This is no criticism, of course. Language teachers have not, up to now, been trained to cater for the often different demands that CLIL makes—something that this book aims to remedy.

Feeding L1 teaching

Before we consider the actual features that comprise a working model of CLIL, it is worth pointing out the impact the practice can have on L1 teaching and school life in general (Muñoa, 2011). This is a crucial and often overlooked benefit of CLIL, and in many ways it is becoming the main argument for its further application in a world that is increasingly multilingual and competence-based. In short, if a school adopts some form of CLIL practice into its curriculum, it seems strange to isolate it as a mere feature—as just another component of the timetable. If CLIL is successful within the school, then the rest of the staff should be made aware of why it has been successful. Besides, they may already be asking: 'Can we have some of that?'

Several writers have observed that CLIL is 'just good practice', although 'good practice' itself is a notion that is difficult to define precisely. The list of virtues attributed to the 'Core features of CLIL methodology' (Mehisto et al., 2008) allegedly include:

- multiple focus
- safe and rich learning environment
- authenticity
- active learning
- scaffolding
- co-operation.

However, these are only applicable where the practice is well established, well supported, and fed back into the general teaching in the school—and where it is not simply limited to CLIL-based practice, with its small band of smiling practitioners and its happy, motivated students. CLIL cannot be viewed as being 'over there', as if it were some mysterious alchemic practice with which the rest of the school had no concern.

Supporting awareness

However, it can be intimidating for those not practising CLIL to hear that all these wonderful things are going on, as if by default. A good way to combat scepticism (and thus spread the good word) is to emphasize that the core features of CLIL are basically these:

- supporting language learning in content classes
- supporting content learning in language classes.

If these things happen, the development of subject competences can follow. And it may even be worth changing the two features to read:

- supporting language awareness in content classes
- supporting content awareness in language classes.

We will look at this in more detail in Chapters 7 and 9, but for now, consider the way in which students come to understand the impact that language has on the content they study within the framework of their subject classes, and on cognition in general. Equally, in their language classes, students come to appreciate more keenly the role of content in helping them to understand a range of topics in order to then express themselves intelligently in a foreign language. And since the students may still be young and in the process of developing their ideas, identities, and perspectives, the things they can achieve through a foreign language become inextricably intertwined with what they can achieve in L1. Teachers, too, working solely through L1, might similarly be persuaded to consider adding some CLIL techniques to their repertoire, if only in the sense that they begin to see the cross-curricular power of language. LEST (Language Enhanced Subject Teaching) is an alternative acronym suggested by Ball and Lindsay (2010) for those teachers who begin to take an interest in what is going on in the 'CLIL corner'.

The Basque experiment

A long-term curricular project in the Basque Country, known as *Eleanitz* ('multilingual' in Basque), has a story to tell which serves as an example of CLIL influencing the standard mother-tongue curriculum. The Basque Country, in the north of Spain, is an officially bilingual region (Basque, Spanish); but in 1991, a section of the Basque-medium schools called *Ikastolas* decided to introduce English at the age of four. This was a radical move at the time, given that across Spain in general, English was introduced at either eight or ten years of age. The introduction of a third language was also seen as risky with regard to the recuperation of the Basque language, Euskara, which had been prohibited for 40 years under Franco and was at that time at a delicate stage of maintenance and redevelopment.

However, the planners of *Eleanitz* did an interesting thing at the beginning. They not only mapped out an entire materials-writing and training programme to accompany a ten-year external evaluation of the initiative carried out by the University of the Basque Country; they also stated that when the first cohort of students reached Grade 9 of secondary school (14 to 15 years of age), they would study the entire official social science syllabus (i.e. history and geography) in English for the next two years. They would do history in Grade 9 and geography in Grade 10. At the time, this seemed an enormously ambitious plan, given the general absence of English in Spanish society, the absence of any CLIL-like awareness, and the relatively low level of English of 15-year-olds in Spain at that time.

To cut a long and interesting story short, the research team from the university tested the 'experimental' cohorts in 2002 after they had completed the first year of social science, taught entirely through the medium of English. The materials were designed and written by a team of CLIL specialists from inside the project, but the content of the syllabus itself conformed exactly to the official one. By then, almost 80 schools were participating in the project, which had been renamed **Social Science and Language Integrated Curriculum (SSLIC)** for these age levels, and the sample selected for testing was a substantial one—as was the control group. Since the control group had studied history in Basque, the test was also conducted in Basque, as different test languages would have introduced an invalid variable. This put the experimental group at a further disadvantage because, although they were Basque speakers, and although language transfer is perfectly possible at this cognitive level, their whole conceptual, procedural, and linguistic experience of the subject had been through English.

The results, shown in Figure 2.1, were very interesting. The *Eleanitz* group scored higher in the English language tests, which was only to be expected because they had received substantially more contact hours of English from the age of four. The interesting result was in the history exam.

The test team wrote two broadly different types of question and distributed them evenly throughout the exam paper. The students were unaware of the typology. One type (Type A) was known as *Gizabasi*—meaning 'social science basic'. The questions tended towards **declarative knowledge**, with simple comprehension questions involving facts and figures, dates, events, etc. The other type (Type B) was known as *Gizasupe* and involved much more cognitive demand, and crucially, more written production. It asked the students to interpret, to infer, and to express opinions, often through more 'open' question types. In short, Type B questions required them to demonstrate what we might refer to as 'social science competences', often based around the crucial skill of critical analysis.

The results in Figure 2.1 are very clear. In the basic, memory-based Type A questions, the experimental CLIL group scored slightly higher, but not significantly so. However, in the Type B questions, the CLIL group massively outscored the control group, despite the disadvantage of taking the exam in Basque.

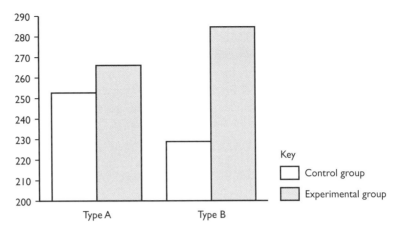

Figure 2.1 Results of history exam: CLIL students versus control group (Elorza, 2008.)

The CLIL effect—what are we doing wrong?

There were various conclusions to be drawn from the test described above, but it seemed obvious that the 'CLIL effect' had been strongest in the areas of academic thinking skills and written production. When published, the results initially caused some controversy, particularly among the teachers of the region who taught social science in Basque. But little by little, a period of reflection set in, and the Basque teachers began to ask the difficult question: 'So what are we doing wrong?'

This book will try to make suggestions with regard to the above question, but perhaps it was not so much a case of what the Basque teachers were doing 'wrong' but rather what the CLIL teachers were doing 'right', which could then be applied back into the L1 curriculum. It was clear that the teachers who had taught the same content through English had been doing it differently—obliged by the language issues to rethink their methodology, and also influenced by the CLIL materials available to them, which had also guided their new framework of practice. Now the standard curriculum was interested in this practice, and this brought about what Muñoa (2011) has called 'CLIL as a catalyst for change', which proved to be an unexpected but crucial consequence of the original project.

A further point to make is that other research (Jaeppinen, 2005; Dobson, Perez Murillo, & Johnstone, 2010; Grandinetti, Langellotti, & Teresa Ting, 2013) also suggests that CLIL/immersion students do not do worse in terms of content than their monolingual counterparts. In terms of language gain, Lasagabaster (2008) notes in relation to the Basque CLIL students: 'CLIL groups significantly outstripped their non-CLIL counterparts in speaking (pronunciation, vocabulary, grammar, fluency, and content) and writing (content, organization, vocabulary, and use of language).'

It is important to emphasize these facts. In this light, schools should be encouraged to carry out their own investigations into student achievement during CLIL courses and publish their findings.

What features most obviously characterize CLIL?

If teachers are interested in what CLIL can do for them, they need to be aware of its basic features. There is no magical way of determining how many there are, but we must be prepared to say what we expect to see in a CLIL-based landscape. What are the features that mark out the territory?

1 Conceptual sequencing

All the traditional school subjects—mathematics, science, history, geography, etc.—are fairly linear in the way they accumulate knowledge. One thing tends to lead on to another in terms of complexity, chronology, or simple logic. Subject-based textbooks, or coursebooks, tend to contain enough content for an academic year, and the progression of the content tends to be linear, with digestible chunks following a pattern of gradually increasing complexity. Whether or not the concepts should really respond to this linear progression is debatable, and the digital revolution is changing our view of the 'left-to-right journey' textbook; but perhaps this 'sequencing' of concepts is actually helpful for learning. We know more or less where we are going, and we know where we have been.

Language teaching, on the other hand, has none of this **conceptual sequencing**. In terms of linguistic content, teachers might prefer to present the first conditional before the second, but there is scant evidence to show that real usage prioritizes these structures in this order. In terms of conceptual content, a snapshot of some of the contents of a conventional language textbook may often look like this:

Unit 1: Saving the rainforests

Unit 2: Pop stars and their problems

Unit 3: My ideal school

There is no thematic connection, and each unit may last around three lessons. There is no logical reason for the sequence above, other than the support it will (hopefully) offer to the underlying language objectives. CLIL, on the other hand, always has conceptual sequencing, largely because in its 'hard' guise it is teaching the official content, and because in its 'soft' guise it must also deal with a sudden importation of real thematic content. So if language teachers want to incorporate more conceptual content into their classes and make that content the priority (thereby moving the language back into a more vehicular role), they must first consider the implications, because they are considerable! If language teachers now regard the thematic (conceptual) content as the priority, the classroom landscape will inevitably change quite radically.

To begin with, themes are studied for much longer in CLIL, and in clearly mapped-out sequences. In a CLIL textbook or syllabus, the themes are often divided into more substantial units, with real tasks to complete and real outcomes to pursue. Subject teachers working in CLIL have no particular problems with this, but they must understand the way in which the inherent language of each unit progresses, repeats, recycles, and grows in complexity. Language teachers working in CLIL, on the other hand, must embrace the prospect of dealing with real content, understanding how it develops and the way in which the accompanying language supports the whole framework of learning.

What is a 'sequence', and why is it important in CLIL?

A sequence is a succession of related activities and tasks, usually culminating in some form of assessment. The sequence can be as short as a single class, or as long as a school semester. So why is conceptual sequencing important in CLIL-based theory?

The simplest answer to this question is to assert that a didactic **activity**—namely one that takes place for the purpose of learning—never exists in isolation. There is always a 'before' and an 'after'. So, for instance, if the topic 'The discovery of the Americas by Columbus' is introduced, the students may well already know what a 'discovery' is (in broad terms) and what 'the Americas' represent, even if they know nothing of the specific events which led to their discovery. If you imagine yourself to be the teacher, or the materials designer (see Chapter 7), the shape of the first activity of the first lesson will be conditioned for you by these parameters. You know, more or less, what the students know, and so the initial phase of your sequence will reflect this. And then the subsequent activities in your sequence, which may last for two lessons or for two months, will also be conditioned by this initial phase. The 'domino effect' of conceptual sequencing is absolute.

This may seem a rather mundane observation—that one thing follows on from another and that we always have some sort of pre-knowledge, however basic—but it is crucially important in terms of the type of language that will be used at any point in the sequence. This is neither obvious to a subject teacher, nor a standard consideration for a language teacher. But when we plan and teach CLIL, we have to take the impact of sequencing on board. These sequential concerns, as we shall see in subsequent chapters, are also closely linked to other distinct CLIL-based considerations. Some are mentioned in Figure 2.2, but there will be more to consider.

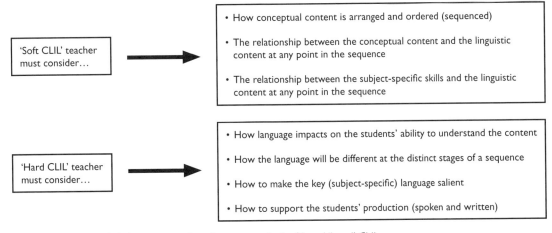

Figure 2.2 Sequence-related concerns for 'soft' and 'hard' CLIL

The stages of a sequence

We should be able to identify five stages of a sequence:

0   Establishing pre-knowledge/stimulating interest
1   Introductory
2   Main conceptual content
3   Concluding the main conceptual content (pre-assessment)
4   Synthesis and/or assessment activity(ies).

If the black line is <u>the total time</u> of the sequence, the five stages might be temporally distributed by most teachers in this way.

———————————————————————————————
0 1 2   3   4

Identify the likely stages by placing the teacher/textbook language on this 'sequence line'. The topic is 'Microorganisms'.

a) Everyone gets ill sometimes.

b) Other white blood cells digest any cells that the antibodies adhere to.

c) $C_6H_{12}O_6 \rightarrow 2C_3H_6O_3 + 2ATP$

Glucose $\rightarrow$ lactic acid + (energy)

As opposed to aerobic, anaerobic respiration refers to the oxidation of molecules in the absence of oxygen, to produce energy.

Figure 2.3 *Different language at different stages of a sequence*

Different stages, different discourse

Further illustrating the importance of sequencing is the example shown in Figure 2.3, which is from a training course for non-native CLIL subject teachers, designed to raise their awareness of this issue of sequencing. The example is a shortened version, but note how the task requires the teachers to consider two fundamental things: firstly, what the stages of a sequence are, and secondly, what the language used to teach about microorganisms looks like at any of those given stages. The language is exclusively teacher talk, but in order for it to be effective, it has to be understood by the 15-year-old students, and some of it then reproduced and used at the assessment stage. It is therefore, in effect, the target discourse that the students will eventually need to use.

It is obvious that utterance (a) in Figure 2.3 belongs to what we might broadly term the 'orientation' stage of a sequence. In classroom terms, this probably occurred in the 'zero' stage, which is a point during the very first lesson when the teacher needs to keep the conceptual volume as low as possible. This decision results in a clear absence of academic language. 'Everyone gets ill sometimes' could be the very first utterance of the two-month sequence. It is comprehensible and could easily lead on to a functional question such as 'When was the last time you were ill? Ask your partner. One minute.' And so the sequence has begun.

The answers from the students in plenary, in a CLIL context, will involve the vocabulary of illnesses, some of which will be unknown territory to students in the L2. This means the sequence is moving to stage 1, which is simply a slightly more technical version of stage 0, in that it may involve some of the language related to the topic in question—in this case, the vocabulary of illness and disease.

Sentence (b), however, could not possibly belong to this orientation stage, unless the lesson is at university (it is not) and the knowledge level of the students is much higher. The language is much more technical, with specific lexis from the field (e.g. 'white blood cells', 'digest', 'antibodies') and grammatical structures (e.g. 'adhere to') which are low frequency in terms of normal everyday speech. Sentence (c), therefore, hardly needs any introduction: if, like sentence (b), it belongs to stage 2, we would have to conclude that (c) belongs to the far right of that continuum, and that the relative lack of technical weight in (b) situates it to the left of the stage 2 continuum. If we were teaching this content in the L1, then we would still need to be highly aware of this discourse slope, which steepens as we climb further to the right. In L2, it becomes crucial to our very planning. The distance between sentences (a) and (c) is enormous, and yet they belong to the same sequence, the same two-month topic of microorganisms. We will see in later chapters that there are ways and means to cope with the challenges posed by these linguistic slopes, however steep or gradual they may be. For now, it is enough to simply be aware that they exist and that they clearly have an impact on learning.

'Soft' CLIL sequencing

If the above is interesting information for the 'hard' CLIL teacher, then Materials extract 2.A (overleaf) is a snapshot example of what an English teacher in a 'soft' CLIL programme can face, once the language syllabus takes on more conceptual content. It shows the cover page of a unit for 12-year-olds studying English in pilot schools in Italy, the Netherlands, and Spain, through units of work derived from particular subject areas (in this case, technology). The unit shown, about inventions, can take up to two months (i.e. 35 hours of class time).

Materials extract 2.A maps out four central 'sequences' (Introduction, Inventions through time, etc.) with an accompanying 'content box' summarizing the main conceptual focus of each sequence. Then, below each content box, there is a 'retrieval task' which assesses (retrieves) the box's content through a production-based communicative task.

Interestingly, both the conceptual and the procedural content are indicated, but there is no explicit mention of the language. This is because the sequencing and organization of the content are the priorities here, but the likely linguistic weight (both the structures and the lexis) are highly predictable, given the fact that the students are 12-year-olds.

In Materials extract 2.A, the lack of any explicit mention of language does not mean that 'soft' CLIL has no interest in the linguistic content of this unit. The language is also mapped out for the teachers in the Teacher's Guide, and is made salient throughout the unit. But crucially, it does not determine the order

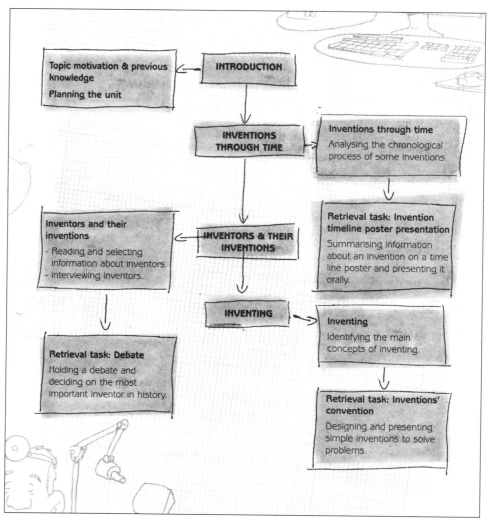

Materials extract 2.A Example of a unit outline ('soft' CLIL) (Ball et al., Subject projects 1: The world of inventions, Ikaselkar, p.47.)

of the sequence. It is not the objective, as such; it is the vehicle delivering the topic ('Inventions'), and the language should occur naturally through discourse determined by the content.

2 Conceptual fronting

It seems clear enough that the priority of CLIL is the content. We will see in Chapter 3 how the word 'content' can be broken down into three dimensions (concepts, language, and procedure), but for now, let us just say that CLIL is primarily concerned with 'things' (concepts), with 'communicating things' (language), and with 'doing things' (procedure). The criteria for assessing the understanding of these 'things' are based primarily on conceptual and/or procedural (skills-based) content. The language is crucial for the process, but it is not the priority. It is there to help.

If in CLIL we assess the content (see Chapter 8), it follows that we 'front', or prioritize, the conceptual and procedural content, as in the 'Inventions' example above. Such **'conceptual fronting'** is not normally practised in language teaching. CLIL is clearly different in this respect, and in this book we will attempt to argue that 'soft' CLIL can also move towards this content-based orientation. In turn, this can quite radically change the appearance of the language syllabus and bring it more in line with the competence-based outlook that is becoming ever more influential in the European educational sphere. Language cannot remain 'over there', forever the orphan of the curriculum, confined to its own world and to its own considerations. To bring language learning more clearly into the realm of education seems to be a role that CLIL can play.

3 Task as priority, language as vehicle

Language is not assessed as a separate entity, but as the vehicle for the accomplishment of production-based objectives (observable as tasks). As we will see in Chapter 3, language occurs naturally in the discourse framework associated with the conceptual content, and as a result of the communicative exchanges required by task-based methodology. In other words, if students are asked to research the progress of an invention over time (see the right-hand column in Materials extract 2.A, for example), and then communicate their findings, they will be obliged to use a whole array of temporal **discourse markers** ('first', 'then', 'ten years later', 'in the 19th century', 'in the early 20th century', 'in 1961', 'finally', etc.). And those are simply the basic tools for the production task. The language could get much more difficult if students are asked to describe what an invention actually does. But the point is that the language occurs naturally through the concepts (inventions and time) and the procedures (the explanation and/or narration of the inventions' progress). The language depends on the conceptual and procedural choices, and not vice versa. By 'procedural', we mean both the nature of the tasks that the teacher chooses to use in order to make the conceptual content comprehensible, and the cognitive skills that they might involve (see Chapter 3).

4 Making key language salient

Didactic material in L2 is subject to particular patterns of task design, in which the content undergoes a greater procedural 'breakdown' than one might associate with standard L1 materials. Language support is either scaffolded (explicitly provided) or embedded into the text, where it is picked up by usage in a succession of recycled contexts. These two notions (**scaffolding** and **embedding**) will be discussed in greater detail in Chapters 5, 6, and 7. Both of these techniques help to make key language more salient for the students, a theme that is also explored in the aforementioned chapters.

5 CLIL in three dimensions

The outcome objective (that one can assess) of a CLIL activity can be expressed in terms of three dimensions, beginning with the conceptual aim, carried out by means of a procedural decision, supported by the language that occurs as a result of its particular discourse. This idea, which is one of the leitmotifs of this book, could merit a chapter of its own, and it is offered (see Chapter 3) as a way of breaking down the problem of the word 'content'. It seems obvious, given that the 'C' in CLIL stands for 'content', that any book on this topic would discuss the notion at some point. Interestingly, however, few books on CLIL have actually done so.

By considering content in a three-dimensional framework—consisting of concept, procedure, and language—teachers can make daily decisions in their classrooms about which dimension they wish to prioritize at any given point. If they have already seen, for example, that the task they are to work on that day is language-heavy, and that their students may encounter problems, they will think of ways to confront this linguistic dimension, either by means of 'embedded' language support (having the key language recur in the text, be supported by graphics, etc.) or by explicit scaffolding, whereby teachers make the language issues salient or, in certain cases, actually work on the vocabulary and structures. If the designer of the materials was already aware of this before the teachers ever opened the textbook, so much the better (see Chapter 7).

There will also be days when teachers will not need to be so concerned with language, although by default it is always present. It is merely a question of volume. The next day, the conceptual 'volume' may be louder, and teachers will have to find ways of dealing with this. Teachers become like sound engineers in a music studio, adjusting the relative volume of items on the mixing desk (see Chapter 3). The constant interplay between these three dimensions, and the accompanying readjustments that teachers have to make, are in a sense the very essence of CLIL practice. This is discussed in more detail in Chapter 3.

6 *The text–task relationship*

The relationship between a text and the task that precedes or follows it is an enormously significant consideration for CLIL practitioners, which will be explored in more detail in Chapter 7. For now, as an introduction to the idea, it is worth pointing out that what the CLIL learner most appreciates is knowing what to do. There is plenty of evidence from L1-based research to suggest that student failure or misunderstanding is often more related to procedural comprehension issues than to any that are conceptual (Marcus et al., 1996). This often means students simply misunderstood the (usually) written instruction in a textbook or in an exam. Oral instructions can be challenging too, because of the number of steps they may constitute. Primary school teachers, for example, soon learn that it is much more effective to model a game and its rules than to explain those rules beforehand.

In CLIL-based situations, where both teachers and learners are non-native speakers of the target language, the potential for problems can increase; and as even native-speaker teachers who have been asked to write exams will confirm, one of the most difficult aspects of materials design is the writing of clear, unambiguous instructions. In L2, the difficulty is further accentuated.

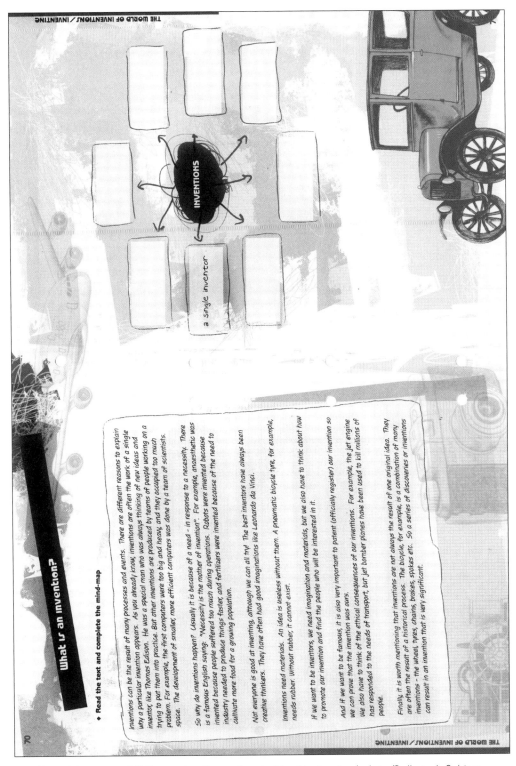

Materials extract 2.B Example of wrongly prioritized instruction/rubric (Ball et al., Subject projects 1: The world of inventions, Ikaselkar, pp. 70–71.)

In general, the best way to avoid unnecessary misunderstandings (and possible failure on the students' part) is to 'front' the task or activity, so that students know exactly what is required from the start. This will be explored in more detail in Chapter 7, but for now the following serves as a simple example.

The social sciences (e.g. geography and history) are typically quite 'text-heavy'. For some, this is a good reason to use these subjects for CLIL, because of the rich variety of language they provide, whereas for others it is a reason to avoid them, because of the sheer amount of language involved and the difficulty in breaking this down into digestible chunks.

Even in subjects perceived to be less 'text-heavy' (e.g. technology), the principle still holds. The activity shown in Materials extract 2.B is aimed at 12- to 13-year-old CLIL students studying technology in Spain through the medium of English. The short and clear instruction underneath the title asks the students to 'Read the text and complete the mind map'. The activity is fine—clear and well constructed—but the instruction fails to explicitly link the reading of the text with the completion of the diagram: the steps are 'Read the text, then complete the mind map', presented as two potentially separate processes. This may seem an unnecessary objection to make, but consider the alternative instruction 'Complete the mind map by reading the text'. The improvement is immediately obvious, because now there is an explicit reason for reading the text, and the task is given priority.

The instruction could be longer so that the task is prioritized, with the text as vehicle: 'Now, to help you fill in the "Inventions" mind map, read the text and find the main idea in each paragraph.' This way, the text is now neither a burden nor an obstacle, but rather the support mechanism for the completion of the task.

This prioritization of the task also has implications for the concept of 'difficulty' in scholastic material in general, and in CLIL-based pedagogy in particular. Again, this will be illustrated in Chapter 7, but it is surely obvious from even the brief example above that the 'difficulty' of a text is always conditioned by its related activity or task. In fact, as we shall argue, there is no such thing as a 'difficult' or an 'easy' text in CLIL. It depends entirely on how the author chooses to plan and manipulate the task. The power we have to do this means that CLIL can function in even the most hostile and resource-deprived circumstances.

7 *Enhancing peer communication*

Classroom research, both in standard teaching and in CLIL, has found that the most common form of interaction remains the teacher–student pattern, whereby the former initiates and the latter responds. Other research has demonstrated that although there may be opportunities for students to talk in class using a variety of interactional patterns, if it is mainly limited to whole-class teacher–student interactions, then student interventions tend to be brief (Dalton-Puffer, 2007) and fairly clipped, aimed at satisfying the teacher's demand as swiftly and as painlessly as possible. In a non-native language, this is even more likely to be the case. Also, the **initiation–response–feedback** pattern of questioning by the teacher-initiator (often abbreviated to **IRF**) is by far the most common pattern of dialogue, with CLIL classrooms no exception. Although this is not necessarily a problem, an over-emphasis on the sort of pattern exemplified by the following may limit both language development and cognitive progress:

Teacher What is the capital of France? (*initiation*)
Student Paris. (*response*)
Teacher Very good. (*feedback*)

Peer communication, or student–student interaction, can often break the IRF trap, and if the appropriate classroom-management techniques are employed, the classroom atmosphere can change radically, and the quality of the learning too. In CLIL, peer work feels safer, because it reduces the harsh public glare of plenary response. It is also interesting from a linguistic perspective, because although students may use a less formal register than demanded by the topic, they are often more adept at helping each other to understand. They instinctively know at which level their peers think. As we will see in Chapters 3 and 4, just as the academic language required for written and spoken accuracy can be insisted on at later stages of a sequence, so can accuracy in the time span of a single class. In peer-work dialogue, which involves students 'discussing' matters which they are later expected to offer in plenary, the peer work serves as rehearsal, under safer conditions. The old ELT myth that peer talk in a foreign language provides a 'bad' model, has largely disappeared. Besides, if materials such as **scripted** information-gaps are being used (see Chapter 6), with most of the language provided, there is no reason for the students to revert to the L1. As ever, it will depend on the objective—and in CLIL, the objectives are rarely linguistic ones.

Perhaps the best way to support the idea of peer communication is to ask a CLIL teacher the following question: 'When you congratulate yourself on a fantastic class that you taught, what reason do you identify for the lesson's success?' The teacher is surely unlikely to reply, 'I delivered an excellent lecture to my 13-year-old students for almost an hour, and they seemed rapt with attention.' More probably, the teacher was happy because the tasks that had been proposed and then facilitated had worked, the students had intervened and been involved, and the teacher talk remained at a minimum. As Illich (1971) remarked, 'Most learning is not the result of instruction. It is rather the result of unhampered participation in a meaningful setting.'

In Chapters 6 and 7, we will see a range of examples of CLIL tasks and activities based on the principles and uses of peer communication, at the same time trying to illustrate the difficult notion of what constitutes 'meaningful'.

8 *Guiding multimedia input*

In Chapters 5 and 7, we will look in detail at the idea of 'guiding input', by which we mean reading and listening/watching. In the purely analogue world, the second of the two classic processing skills (originally referred to as 'passive' skills) was always referred to as 'listening'. However, with the possibilities that digital media now offer to education, it seems odd to simply limit the processing skill to listening, especially since the majority of contemporary media is experienced through a more natural combination of aural and visual stimuli. A young student learning English in the digital age has a vast array of sources to choose from. In CLIL, the same principle applies, and teachers of any subject can find plenty of good material on the Web to support their syllabus. However, instead of devoting pages to the digital possibilities of CLIL—always a problem, since a book is static, whereas digital media progresses and changes almost daily—it seems more appropriate here to briefly mention certain related issues, most of which practising CLIL teachers will already be aware. Nevertheless, they are now an integral part of the CLIL landscape, especially considering the difficulties (see Chapter 7) for many CLIL teachers when it comes to finding off-the-shelf subject-based materials.

The internet is a fantastic source of information, but in an educational setting, it can have its pros and cons. One danger to avoid in CLIL is the following type of instruction: 'Research on the internet everything you can find out about micro-organisms.' Students, in a desperate attempt to narrow this instruction down, will naturally revert to 'copy and paste', rendering the task pointless. It is much better, of course, to narrow down the scope of the task from the beginning and make the research useful in terms of the ICT skills, the language, and the science involved, as shown in Materials extract 2.C.

Researching on the internet

You have to find out several facts about a specific microorganism. But there is too much information on the Web, and most of it is very technical. What can you do?

Try the following steps, using a search engine such as Google.

1 Find its technical name, using the following phrases.
Tetanus

Caused by the _____ microorganism.

The microorganism that causes tetanus is called _____.

2 Find its size.
Clostridium tetani

What is the size of _____?

Other phrases?

3 Find its structure.

The structure of _____ is _____.

What is the structure of _____?

The _____ is made of / consists of _____.

Other phrases?

4 Diseases they cause.

What diseases _____?

What diseases are associated with _____?

Other phrases?

Materials extract 2.C Narrowing the scope of CLIL-based internet research

Check the list and tick those you think could be useful if researching the Roanoke mystery. Try to find **four definite** ones, although there could be more! Be ready to justify your choices.

☐ **THE LOST COLONY: Roanoke Island, NC ~ Packet by Eric Hause ...**
The lie of the land of modern **Roanoke Island** appears much as it did at the time of the ... Amadas and Barlowe wrote glowing reports of **Roanoke Island**, ...
www.coastalguide.com/packet/lostcolony01.htm - 15k - 3 Jul 2005 –

☐ **Manteo / Roanoke Island, NC: HISTORY -**
A visit to Roanoke Island vividly illustrates the community's commitment to ... The Roanoke Island Festival Park interprets the area's early history with a ...
www.outerbanks.com/manteo/history/ - 9k - 4 Jul 2005 -

☐ **First English Settlement -**
The explorers described Roanoke Island as "a most pleasant and fertile ground,...The next spring, Raleigh sent a colony of 108 persons to Roanoke Island. ...
statelibrary.dcr.state.nc.us/nc/ncsites/english1.htm - 18k -

☐ **The Roanoke Island Freedmens Colony -**
Welcome to the site dedicated to the Roanoke Island Freedmen's Colony During the Civil War, Union-occupied Roanoke Island, which lies between the North ...
www.roanokefreedmenscolony.com/ - 17k -

☐ **Visit Roanoke Island North Carolina -**
Visit Roanoke Island, North Carolina, the Crown Jewel of the Outer Banks.
www.roanoke-island.com/ - 15k -

☐ **Roanoke Island Festival Park -**
Located on the Outer Banks on Roanoke Island at the Manteo waterfront - rain or shine there's always something to do. Explore the island's unique role in ...
www.roanokeisland.com/ - 4k - 3 Jul 2005 -

☐ **Roanoke Island -**
Amadas and Barlowe endorsed Roanoke Island, a three-mile strip of land off the coast of ... Many theories exist about the settlers' fate on Roanoke Island, ...
www.u-s-history.com/pages/h602.html - 10k -

Materials extract 2.D Helping students to use search engines (Muñoa et al., SSLIC English workbook 1, Ikastolen Elkartea, p. 41.)

There are actually seven steps, but the four examples in Materials extract 2.C are sufficient to make the point. Even better would be to provide a table listing the target characteristics of the microorganism (e.g. name, size, structure, etc.), as this would help students to avoid the dreaded 'copy and paste' problem so prevalent in poorer examples of CLIL practice.

We can also teach students explicit ICT skills within the context of the subject content. In Materials extract 2.D, taken from a 'soft' CLIL English unit entitled 'Unsolved mysteries', the activity helps the students (who are searching for information regarding the Roanoke Island mystery) to use search engines more efficiently, by focusing them on the text type used to summarize the content of websites. Clearly, the penultimate site, entitled 'Roanoke Island Festival Park', would waste the time of a young non-native reader anxious to find the relevant information for this particular objective (which is to research the historical mystery, not the island's contemporary tourist attractions). These skills are now crucial in both the L1 and the L2.

Perhaps the other important thing to bear in mind when considering this type of input is that the attractiveness of the authentic materials which can be found on the Web, and the often polished production techniques that accompany them, cannot substitute teacher mediation. This is also true of L1 teaching, but it is particularly important in CLIL practice. Basically, we must always give the student something to do 'while listening'. Previously, good language practice established the notions of 'pre-listening', 'while listening', and 'post-listening'. We can still apply these supportive techniques—even a simple instruction like 'Note down two things that the historian says about the building' can help to focus the listener. Students are not automatically engaged by visual media in class. They have enough access to it in their lives outside school. What they need, particularly in CLIL, is to have their learning facilitated and guided.

It should also be stressed that the process of educational technology has almost relegated the linear text—as the sole source of information—to the margins. Boxed sets of resources are now offered in tandem with textbooks, where teachers are offered a CD collection of all the visuals, animations, videos, and digital slideshows used in the course. This actually means teachers can present the content in the way they prefer, and not just as text on the textbook page. Online video tutorials (for example the Khan Academy) offer non-linear, highly visual input. Tablet-led lessons are another example. Written text itself can never be ignored, nor can the importance of providing students with strategies to cope with it, but there is now a much greater range of input tools on offer.

We will look at other ways of guiding input in Chapters 4 and 7.

9 Supporting student output

If we can guide student input, we can also support student output. The two verbs 'guide' and 'support' seem to contribute usefully to creating a working principle for CLIL. By 'output' we mean the two traditional productive skills derived from language study, namely speaking and writing. We will go into more detail on this in Chapters 5 and 7, but here we simply need to establish the basics of production in a CLIL context.

As we have seen with the notion of peer communication, students need to express themselves in order to convince both themselves and their teachers that they are learning. This is as true of primary and secondary school children as it is of university students. It sounds absurdly simple, until we actually take a hard look at the reality of many teacher-centred educational cultures, or even at those that claim to be learner-centred, where we find that teacher talk still dominates in the classroom. Chaudron's original research (1988) found teacher talk occupying up to 85% of bilingual classroom time (with a median of around 70%), and this has not significantly reduced in subsequent investigations. If CLIL claims to adopt the ideas contained in Swain's useful '**output hypothesis**' (1985), then CLIL practitioners must encourage and maximize student output across the curriculum. They must also support these acts, of course, and recognize the inherent differences in the various speaking acts that take place on the educational stage. For example, expressing an opinion is very different from describing data, and expressing an opinion to a peer in pair-work is very different from expressing an opinion through a PowerPoint presentation to the whole class.

When we come to look at writing, we also need to consider the array of text types, genres, and discourse that permeate the curriculum. These are often areas which are not within the remit of the language teacher, but if they remain neglected in subject-based classrooms, then students fail. The write-up of an experiment in science is a vastly different act from the writing of an opinion essay on Marxism. Not only are they hugely different acts of writing, but they also serve as culminations of different sequences of activities and tasks, most of which should have served as support mechanisms for these crucial acts of production. As we will see in Chapter 4, firstly the provision and then the support of academic language are the twin responsibilities of all teachers. CLIL simply brings this issue into greater focus.

10 Supporting thinking skills

Whilst it would be foolish to suggest that higher-order thinking skills are in some way the exclusive preserve of CLIL, there is a growing body of evidence to suggest that multilingual people think in different ways, and that those ways might be better suited to the sorts of competences that people are going to need in the future. Knowledge is no longer so static, and the pace of change brought on by the exponential growth of technology is challenging our entire concept of education. To prepare students for a role in this complex future, we will need to equip them with problem-solving skills, to engage them interculturally, to develop their sense of initiative, and to ground them in an awareness of the ethical consequences of their actions—if indeed we as educators are deemed capable of doing this (see Chapter 10 for further discussion).

The good news is that multilingual students already seem to possess a decent grounding in these sorts of competences. As Baetens Beardsmore noted:

> Bilingual children have a greater faculty for creative thinking at their disposal. They perform significantly better in tasks which require not the finding of the single correct answer to a question, but where they are asked to imagine a number of possible correct answers.
> (Beatens Beardsmore, 2008)

Looking at the various kinds of student that can populate the multilingual continuum, we can say that they have at least one thing in common: they have all learned in different ways from their monolingual counterparts. Bulgarian students who are studying the official programme of history in English know that they are working harder (cognitively speaking) than the students in the school down the road who are learning history in Bulgarian. CLIL students should embrace such value-added practice if they want to reap the rewards and prosper further. They cannot depend on memorizing everything, because the teacher no longer asks them to. They have to try to develop both their spoken and written English, because the discourse of social science requires them to. It is not easy; they have to understand basic history, and then demonstrate critical awareness, in their second language. They have to research the relevant topic on the internet, and synthesize the information they find (often expressed in formal, authentic English), and then maybe present this information to their peers, employing the discourse of the social sciences. Are they working harder than the students studying in Bulgarian?

3   *Read these eight statements by holiday-makers. Try to match four of them to the four sentences (issues) below them (a–d). The first one is done for you.*

"We really enjoyed England. We stayed in London for two weeks."

1

"The Costa del Sol is great! There are loads of English people to meet and the pubs all serve English beer."

2

"We're not going to that country again. The food was so strange and all their customs and traditions were so difficult to understand."

3

"The trouble with travelling abroad is that there are SO many tourists!"

4

"I'm not going there again. We had to cover our arms and wear long skirts."

5

"I quite enjoyed some regions of the country, but there were a lot of beggars. We didn't know what to do."

6

"The trek to Nepal was great. We climbed part of Mt Everest, and even at 4,000 metres there was a café for climbers."

7

"The holiday was amazing. We stayed in native huts, watching the natives carrying out their traditional customs. They even took us hunting for alligators. It was really authentic and traditional."

8

Issues

a) Many people from the developed world want to travel to developing countries to see exotic cultures, but then they cannot understand why the poorer indigenous people ask them for money, and they are shocked at the poverty.

b) Many people travel to a country and just visit the most famous places. Then they think that they have experienced the whole country.

c) Some tourists want 'home comforts' wherever they go. They go to wild, remote places, but then expect to find the same infrastructures. This can also affect the natural beauty of the countries they visit.

d) Some people think that everybody else is causing the problems.

Statements	6			
Issues	a	b	c	d

4   *Now take the other four statements that you have not put into the table, and write similar sentences about the issues that they are talking about.*

5   *Finally, try to guess the top 5 countries from where tourists come. So, who are the top travellers? Your teacher has the answer, but see if you can guess, in pairs. Winners get a prize!*

Materials extract 2.E Guided task (adapted from Beobide & Ball, Geography 3, Ikastolen Elkartea, p.72.)

Yes, of course. But if they succeed, the benefits are considerable—as we saw on page 29 of this chapter, with reference to the Basque Country.

However, CLIL teachers must not assume that thinking skills will develop by default through the L2. They will not. Of equal importance is the avoidance of the notion that, because the learner is 'language defective' (in comparison to a native speaker), the cognitive levels of study must somehow be reduced or sheltered. What CLIL seems to foster is the development of a wider range of tasks and activities to engage the higher cognitive skills. This is because, as we said, both teachers and learners acknowledge the greater challenge. In L2, we must continue to make students think and to offer them more opportunities for employing a range of operations. And of course, the greater the range of thinking that takes place, the richer the range of language that accompanies it.

Perhaps the real strength of CLIL lies in its role as a pathway to competences (see Chapters 8 and 10). 'Language through content for competences' sounds like an attractive new slogan.

As a final example, we can consider the task in Materials extract 2.E. It is taken from a CLIL geography unit on the service sector and requires students to think carefully (the matching and discrimination component is by no means simple) to produce their own language based on the models provided (Step 4), and then to carry out a little guesswork (Step 5). The mini-sequence challenges, engages, and attempts to motivate, whilst simultaneously guiding the conceptual input and supporting the linguistic output.

Summary

In this chapter, we have suggested that CLIL encompasses a certain set of practices, and that the methods constituting this set of practices best characterize its parameters. These methods are themselves redolent of certain beliefs as to how students can best learn subject matter in another language. We have also suggested that these methods might improve the practice of language teaching by extending the quantity and quality of the content available, and focusing the objectives more towards the conceptual and procedural content. We also introduced the concept of the three dimensions of content, which will be taken up in more detail in the next chapter.

Task

If you would like to look at a practical task to explore your own practice related to the content of this chapter, see Appendix 1 (page 289).

Further reading

Bentley, K. (2010). *The TKT course CLIL module*. Cambridge: Cambridge University Press.
A clear and useful introduction to CLIL, with most of the basic features covered. Each chapter has a series of useful short exercises and activities to help the reader revise and assimilate the basic concepts of CLIL.

Dellar, S., & **Price, C.** (2007). *Teaching other subjects through English*. Oxford: Oxford University Press.
A very practical book, based almost entirely on examples, ideas, and procedures for subject teachers unused to coping with language demands in their lessons.

Mehisto, P., Frigols, M. J., & **Marsh, D.** (2008). *Uncovering CLIL*. London: Macmillan Education.
A bold and innovative book, and the first attempt to truly explain the phenomenon of CLIL. Each chapter features anecdotes from practising teachers and advice on the issues surrounding both the practice and the implementation of CLIL programmes.

Ruiz de Zarobe, Y., Sierra, J. M., & **Gallardo del Puerto, F.** (2011). *Content and foreign language integrated learning: Contributions to multilingualism in European contexts*. Bern: Peter Lang.
An excellent and highly readable collection of research-based articles, featuring contributions from a range of European contexts.

3 THE CONTENT–LANGUAGE RELATIONSHIP

Overview

In Chapter 2, we suggested that CLIL is more easily defined and described as a methodology, with a set of classroom techniques and practices that we can identify. These methods help us to establish the parameters of CLIL by clarifying what it is, and what it is not.

In this chapter, we will look more closely at the elements of the CLIL acronym itself, in order to analyse the nature of the relationship between content and language. We will examine the notion of 'content', and offer a three-dimensional model of its components, to be used as a practical tool for CLIL teachers. We will then look at academic language as content, analyse the notion of cognitive academic language proficiency (CALP), and examine the perspectives on learning and language that derive from this analysis. Note that English is assumed to be the L2 MoI throughout this chapter, due to the nature of the examples used. Although it is the most common L2 used in CLIL, it is, of course, not the only one.

What is 'content'?

We also said in Chapter 2 that the acronym 'CLIL' has always been in danger of saying nothing special, since content has always involved language, and language has always involved content. Since the relationship is so obviously a symbiotic one, why is there so much interest in CLIL? The answer resides in our interpretation of the word 'integration' and in our understanding of the complex word 'content'. Content and language have always worked side by side, but as we saw in the previous chapter, it is the job of the teacher to make this relationship more salient. The problem, however, is that the acronym 'CLIL' separates the word 'content' from its language partner, as if language were something other than 'content'. Furthermore, if we talk about 'language skills', then we are still talking about content, albeit of a different kind. In short, it is impossible to understand CLIL and its potential to change our way of working unless we are prepared to confront the word 'content' and the notions that it might entail.

Objectives

All teachers have objectives, even if it sometimes seems unnecessary to make them explicit. However, it is surely impossible to divorce the 'content' of a lesson from its objective. The proposition would make no sense. This being the case, the objective of a lesson, or of a sequence of activities, will always contain certain elements that make up the content. Consider, for example, part of a science objective for 12-year-old CLIL students:

> To differentiate between the planets in the solar system.

This is a valid objective because it describes an outcome which can be assessed. For example, at some point in the process, we can, if we wish, test the ability of the student to tell us the differences between Earth and Jupiter, perhaps on the basis of their size, distance from the Sun, and some of their inherent characteristics. Those three concepts (size, distance, characteristics) would be appropriate for a 12-year-old learner, either studying in the L1 or through an L2.

The problem is that the description of this objective is merely conceptual. The student learns that the planets are different, and learns about some of the features that constitute those differences. But how is this achieved? For instance, the teacher could spend the entire lesson dictating the differences for the students to copy or note down. Or the teacher could hand out a fairly lengthy piece of text, ask the students to read it in silence, and then instruct them to answer the questions that follow. These two examples of classroom practice are particularly mundane, of course, but as procedures, they support the conceptual aspect of the objective. However, consider the following addition to the objective:

> To differentiate between the planets in the solar system, by interpreting, transcribing, and producing descriptions.

The addition of the three verbs extends the remit of the original 'To differentiate'. They describe the process imported from language teaching, known as a 'running dictation'. Colour pictures of the planets (with their relative sizes roughly indicated to scale) are handed to students grouped in threes, with the planets' names provided. In turn, the students in each group find on the classroom wall a series of short texts describing each planet. Materials extract 3.A, for example, describes the planet Jupiter. They must memorize each text, 'run' (within reason!) back to their group and then dictate the text to their partners, one of whom writes it down verbatim. They continue in this way until all the texts have been written down. Only then do they attempt to match the texts with the pictures and label each text with the corresponding planet's name.

It is a more chaotic lesson than many science teachers are accustomed to managing, but in a CLIL context, it is easy to see why the procedure might help students to engage with the concepts, and to view the process as significant (Fink, 2003). The three verbs ('interpreting', 'transcribing', 'producing') support the conceptual content by introducing procedural content, or the cognitive skills involved in the process. The runners must <u>produce</u> a description of the texts by memorizing chunks, then dictating them to the best of their oral ability. The writers must <u>interpret</u> the spoken text of the runners in order to write it down comprehensibly. The group will later interpret the texts more deeply in relation to the pictures. The writers also <u>transcribe</u> the spoken text to written text.

The fifth planet from the Sun, it is 11 times bigger than the Earth. One year on this planet is almost the same as 12 years on Earth, and the day is shorter than on Earth, about ten hours. The brightly coloured stripes on the surface are actually clouds. It emits more power than it absorbs from the Sun. It is named after the Roman king of the gods.

Materials extract 3.A Running dictation on the planets (adapted from Ball et al., Subject projects 1. Ikastolen Elkartea, p. 8.)

But in terms of content, there is still a missing element. Consider this third (underlined) addition to the objective:

> To differentiate between the planets in the solar system, by interpreting, transcribing, and producing descriptions using derived adjectives, comparative and superlative forms, and language to express relative distances.

This specifies the linguistic content which is inherent to the conceptual and procedural choices that the teacher has made. It is impossible to differentiate between the planets without, at some point, using comparative and superlative structures. The language frames are inescapable: 'Jupiter is bigger than the Earth'; 'Jupiter is the largest planet in our solar system'. The linguistic content is a natural product of the discourse context. In other words, it occurs naturally as a result of the need to differentiate.

The three dimensions of CLIL

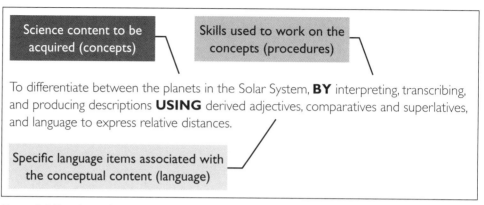

Figure 3.1 The three dimensions of CLIL

Figure 3.1 shows how the entire objective of the task described above could be represented. The description is a powerful summary of what CLIL is attempting to do. The activity teaches <u>conceptual</u> content, by means of <u>procedural</u> choices (cognitive skills), using specific <u>language</u> derived from the discourse context. All the words underlined here can be described as 'content', but it is the interplay between them that lies at the heart of CLIL practice. The concepts are ultimately understood <u>by</u> doing something, <u>using</u> a certain type of discourse.

We could consider these three types of content as learning 'dimensions', and go on to suggest that teachers in CLIL-based contexts might use these three dimensions as both planning tools and priorities, according to how they see the demands of any particular objective. In this sense, we can talk about two types of objective: outcome objectives (discussed above) and 'priority' objectives.

When using priority objectives, CLIL teachers decide which of the three dimensions they wish to emphasize at any given point in a sequence of activities or tasks. This contradicts the original idea of CLIL as a 'dual-focused approach', where Marsh's (2002) oft-quoted definition can seem insufficient when considering CLIL from a three-dimensional perspective: 'It is dual-focused because whereas attention may be predominantly on either subject-specific content or language, both are always accommodated.'

The word 'content' remains ambiguous in Marsh's definition, and also overlooks the fact that language, as we have said, is also 'content'.

The 'mixing desk' metaphor

One way of looking at CLIL in three dimensions is to see it in terms of an analogue mixing desk in a music studio. Teachers have three 'volume' controls which they can adjust, depending on the particular demands of the activity, task, or class. For example, in the lesson about the solar system, we could argue that the most important thing the students should gain is the body of conceptual knowledge about the different features of the different planets. In this case, we would 'turn up' the conceptual volume of the mixer, and reduce the other two accordingly (see Figure 3.2). The dimension with the highest volume is the dimension that the teacher makes the most salient, by whatever means.

Of course, the corollary of this decision is not that the other two dimensions are ignored. It is merely a question of emphasis. The three dimensions co-exist by default. Just as concepts cannot exist without language and vice versa, procedural content is always present. What concerns us as teachers is the quality of that procedural content, and whether or not it really is the most important dimension in the objective. As we noted in the 'Objectives' section above, the teacher could choose to teach 'The solar system' in a variety of ways, as long as the students could identify and differentiate between the planets by the end. Indeed, though we might object to the methodology, the teacher is of course at liberty to project a text onto a screen and ask the students to copy it and learn it for homework.

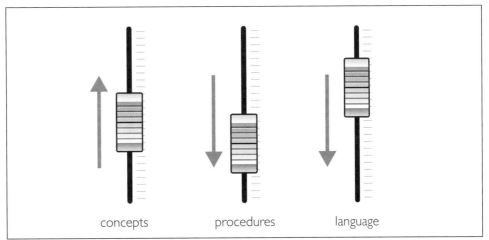

Figure 3.2 The CLIL 'mixing desk'

But why would we feel that this methodological choice was a defective one? Surely we would think this because of the poverty of the procedural content. After all, the concepts are still the same, as is the language. But the limitation of the procedural range imposed by the decision to 'copy from the board and learn for homework' means that neither the conceptual nor the linguistic content are made sufficiently salient. The students go away and learn the concepts, but the learning is not significant. They will probably have forgotten the content in a week's time. But turn up the procedural volume (for example, by deciding on a running dictation, managing it well, insisting on certain steps being fulfilled, and drawing the students' attention to the language of differentiation) and the students will pick up much more. They speak, listen, interpret, and transcribe, and will then need to negotiate (another skill) in order to reach a consensus regarding the matching of the texts to the pictures. Thus a reconsidered dimensional balance (with the volume levels readjusted) for the running dictation might be as shown in Figure 3.3 (overleaf).

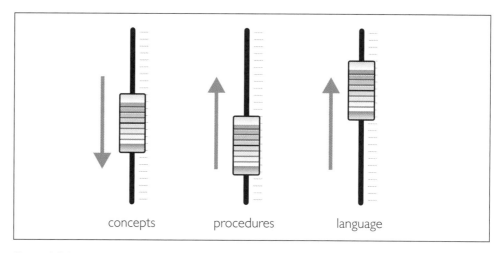

Figure 3.3 Readjusting the 'volume levels' for the running dictation

So, given the three-dimensional aspect of content that we have identified, it might be useful to think in terms of extended, or priority, objectives, in which we can emphasize any of the three dimensions of content at any given moment in a didactic sequence. We can decide on the relative priority or weight of a single dimension, according to the amount of support we deem necessary. By using the 'mixing desk' as a planning tool, the teacher is constantly aware of the demand–support relationship.

Language and concepts as vehicles

In CLIL, as we have already mentioned in Chapter 2, language is rarely an objective in itself. In 'hard' CLIL, the teacher's job is to emphasize and assess the 'content', which we can now recognize as 'dual' in a different way (conceptual and procedural). However, this also entails helping the learner to see how important language is in the process of learning. This is the special nature of CLIL, from which it derives its paradigmatic strength. By reconsidering language as an equal part of the three-dimensional paradigm, it becomes easier to see it as an essential part of a subject teacher's methodological repertoire. Language is clearly a vehicle for the understanding of concepts; but concepts themselves can also be vehicles for competences. In Figure 3.3, we are merely saying that the relative lack of conceptual volume means that, in this particular instance, the content serves as the 'vehicle'. Both the conceptual content and the linguistic content can be considered 'vehicles' for the cognitive skills contained within the procedural content. In many ways, the process can sometimes be more important than the product.

This sounds similar to Biggs's notion of 'constructive alignment' (2003), which entails drawing an important distinction between two types of knowledge. For Biggs, there is 'declarative knowledge' (second-hand knowledge, which can be retold or 'declared' to someone) and 'functioning knowledge' (putting knowledge to work, making it function), and good education is effectively a journey from one to the other. To illustrate this, the knowledge that Columbus sailed to the Americas in 1492 is important because it situates the event historically. But if we were to begin analysing the consequences of Columbus's discovery of the Americas, and perhaps proffer an opinion about it, then we would be dealing with functioning knowledge.

The distinction between **higher-order thinking skills (HOTS)** and **lower-order thinking skills (LOTS)**, derived from Bloom's original work (1956), is similar to this idea. CLIL does not have a monopoly on HOTS, but experienced CLIL teachers who talk of the benefits of the methodology seem to agree that students make more cognitive effort to fulfil the academic demands of the syllabus, probably because they are more aware of the gap between their cognitive level and the language required to nail down their learning. It therefore follows that teachers, aware of the (relatively) language-defective nature of their students, will make more methodological effort to get their content across. This 'effort' will almost inevitably manifest itself in procedural form.

We will return to this in subsequent chapters, but for now we are more concerned with seeing the advantages that the interplay between the three dimensions of content can provide us. We are also concerned with the relationship between cognition and language, and how we can support CLIL students who will be grappling with the same content syllabus as their native-language counterparts. We will look in detail at this support structure in Chapters 5 and 6, but for now, how can we best understand the balance between task difficulty and language support? What is 'difficulty' for a CLIL student, and how can we not only support but also enhance their learning?

Three-dimensional activities and sequences

As we argued earlier in this chapter, teachers can regard their objectives not only in terms of measurable, observable outcomes, but also in terms of the weight, or priority, they choose to give to their content-based dimensions. The word 'objective' is often used synonymously with 'aim' and 'goal', but for the purposes of this book, we will say that a 'goal' is the outcome of a series of successfully completed objectives, and that an 'aim' expresses a longer-term purpose.

The distinction is useful because we might wish to apply the 'mixing desk' metaphor not simply to an activity with a single objective but also to a sequence of activities, possibly culminating in a final production-based task. We might even apply the notion of **three-dimensional CLIL** to help us plan the stages involved in the attainment of an entire long-term aim. In fact, subject teachers rarely think in terms of single isolated activities, but rather in terms of didactic sequences. These sequences are often (but not always) linear, and they tend to increase in complexity as they progress. Language teachers rarely operate within this sort of framework, probably due to the non-linear nature of language acquisition. But non-linear planning is unusual in the educational world.

We will look at sequencing again in Chapter 7, but for now, let us consider how a subject teacher might offer support for a series of activities, probably lasting for a whole class, from the enhanced perspective of the three dimensions.

The activities shown in Materials extract 3.B are from a CLIL geography textbook for 14- to 15-year-old students in the Basque Country. The theme is 'Industry', and the particular lesson is focused on energy sources. The students' task, which the various stages/activities lead to, is to decide which of the sources of energy are valid candidates for future use. The lesson is clearly divided into three stages, indicated by the numbers 1 to 3 on the page. However, the interesting thing to note is how the three stages correspond to the three dimensions of CLIL described in this chapter.

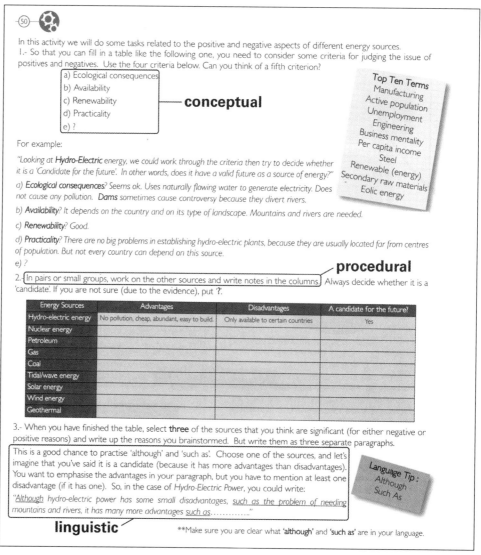

Materials extract 3.B The 'three dimensions' of the energy-sources task (Beobide & Ball, Geography 3, Ikastolen Elkartea, p. 72.)

Stage 1 is clearly dealing with the conceptual dimension. We would expect this anyway, given that the teacher is dealing partially with new information. This is the 'orientation' period of the lesson or sequence, but note that the activity number is 50 (see top left of the page), which means that the lesson is not dealing with entirely new information. The students have almost certainly encountered the energy sources themselves already, but not the criteria listed a–d at the top of the page. These criteria are intended to help the students to judge whether or not the energy sources are viable for the future.

The author provides four of the criteria, asks the students to think of a fifth (e.g. 'economic viability'), then gives examples of how they might make notes (in pairs) about the various energy sources. The language is quite varied, switching from the informal ('Seems OK') to the more academic in tone ('Uses naturally flowing water to generate …'). But the weight of this stage is clearly conceptual (i.e. the conceptual 'volume' is turned up quite high). This is because the students need examples of how to judge the energy sources, and the examples require a certain amount of pre-knowledge. The stage depends on the students knowing something themselves or speculating intelligently. But they have to bring their own conceptual content to the activity here.

Stage 2 is clearly procedural. The students work in pairs and systematically note down the advantages and disadvantages of the sources in the table provided. The conceptual content (both the sources and the judgement criteria) has been provided, so now the students are required to do several things. They must analyse the relationship between the sources and the criteria, and then arrive at a value judgement (yes or no) regarding each individual source. These are skills for which the conceptual content provides the necessary fuel, and the focus on these skills tends to coincide with the most valuable and busiest period of a lesson as far as active learning involvement is concerned.

Stage 3 focuses on the linguistic dimension. The language required to both carry out the activities and reflect the conceptual range of the overall task is made salient. In fact, it is made explicit in the Language Tip at the bottom of the page, where the terms 'although' and 'such as' are justified as necessary for both the procedural and the conceptual content. The activity is also an accuracy exercise, using what are known as 'scaffolds' (explicit language models) which contrast with the more embedded language and rougher input of the previous two stages. It reverses the elements of the old template of early communicative practice in ELT, the notion of 'presentation, practice, and production' (PPP), whose driving philosophy was the idea that students could not be allowed to simply 'jump in at the deep end' and speak if they struggled to cope. PPP provided students with some support, but effective CLIL actually reverses this process and expects them to 'jump in' and communicate as best they can. There are other forms of support within the CLIL framework to help them, but the important point is that production begins at the initial stages of the sequence.

In the 'resolution' stages of the sequence here, the teacher can fine-tune and make the language more salient. But the students have been required to use it first. Nevertheless, from the perspective of the three dimensions of CLIL, it is only in the final stage that the volume of the language dimension is turned up high. The 'Top Ten Terms', on the top right-hand side of the page, refer to the key language from the previous sequence and are intended as communicative revision items. They are not integral to the energy task, and further examples of this language-salience technique can be found in Chapter 7.

It is useful to see any didactic sequence in terms of <u>orientation</u>, <u>complication</u>, and <u>resolution</u>. The three dimensions are present at each stage of the sequence in the paragraphs above. But to refer back to the beginning of this chapter, we said that an objective could be seen as both an outcome and a priority. Here, teachers can prioritize the three elements at different stages of the sequence. But when making one dimension salient, they will always be backed up by the presence of the other two dimensions.

Perspectives on learning and language: visualizing the three dimensions

Any teaching and learning context has, at its core, a body of content that needs to be delivered to the learner. Teachers should ideally act as facilitators in this process. Their depth of involvement in this facilitation process can depend on many conditioning factors that lie outside the scope of this book: their own learning experiences as a pupil, pedagogical training experiences, personal variables, time constraints, etc. However, despite these factors, CLIL enables teachers to fulfil two simple methodological aims. One of these is to determine the mode of delivery of the content, and the other is to decide on the degree of facilitation provided by the teacher in the learning process. Effective CLIL achieves these aims firstly by identifying learners' language needs for the purposes of learning the content in question, and secondly by making strategic decisions about classroom activities based on information regarding those needs, such as to what extent learners are able to give presentations in the foreign language, or how experienced they are in writing a lab report. See Chapters 5 and 6 for more examples of such strategic decisions.

This information gathering is important because learners in a CLIL classroom have a wide range of language needs. A key factor in a CLIL environment, as we are beginning to see, is that the language needs are driven exclusively by the conceptual and the procedural content. If we look at learning needs in this way, in terms of concepts, procedures, and language, we should be able to provide effective learner-driven experiences for the students in our classrooms.

Cummins's matrix (see Figure 3.4) offers a useful framework for teachers to make strategic decisions about learning and support for their classrooms.

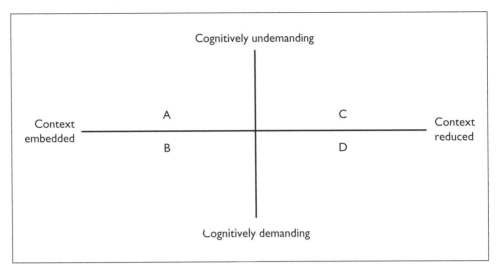

Figure 3.4 Cummins's matrix (Cummins, 2000.)

The quadrants on the left of the matrix (A and B) represent situations or materials which offer learners plenty of context in order to support understanding, whereas the opposite is true of the quadrants to the right (C and D). 'Context' can mean a range of things to learners. It can be previous experience of the content; it can be visual materials to enable learners to make connections between new content and something tangible; or it can be the language of the content itself, which adds to the degree of context for the learner. More concrete language provides a context (for example, 'this table here'), whereas more abstract language reduces it (for example, 'the term "dialectics" is not synonymous with the term "debate"').

More generally, a simple example of embedded or reduced context can be seen in the difference between offering an academic description of the water cycle (context reduced), as opposed to a narrated educational animation (context embedded) of the same.

Also, the quadrants at the top of the matrix (A and C) demand less cognitive effort than the quadrants at the bottom. With difficult thinking tasks to perform and very little context, quadrant D can be a very challenging learning space for an NNS learner. With NNS learners, a teacher's decision regarding the necessary support to provide for 'D' activities will determine the success or failure of the class. To hold a group discussion about how the students can modify their personal behaviour in order to minimize the collective carbon footprint of the class is considerably more challenging than asking students to describe factors which affect climate change, visible in a picture on a screen.

It is important to note that Cummins (2000) emphasizes cognition and context within 'language learning tasks and activities', suggesting that the issue of language is implicit within the matrix. The matrix can simply be applied to learning in general—for example, for measuring the cognitive weight of the learning experience in a biology class. But the crucial advantage of three-dimensional CLIL is that we can actually <u>see</u> the language dimension. It offers teachers not just concepts and procedures, but also a gauge for making decisions about language. In short, what is implicit in Cummins's matrix is made explicit in three-dimensional CLIL. This is important for the obvious reason that CLIL teachers need to see the language dimension in a planning matrix (see Chapter 4 for further examples).

Gibbons (in Mariani, 1997) develops Cummins's matrix further (see Figure 3.5), offering the notion of 'learning zones' in parallel with axes of challenge and support. This matrix is a useful gauge for teachers to reflect on how they generate thinking in the classroom, while at the same time helping them to decide on the amount of support they need to provide for their learners.

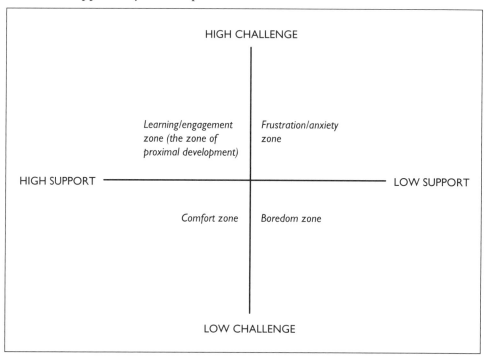

Figure 3.5 Gibbons's learning zones (Gibbons, 2009, adapted from Mariani, 1997.)

Let us consider Figures 3.4 and 3.5 in relation to a typical CLIL classroom. Gibbons, taking her cue from Vygotsky, believes that the best learning takes place when learners are most challenged and receiving the most support. We have already seen that the language 'volume' is difficult both to gauge and alter within Cummins's matrix because the language dimension is not visible. In Gibbons's matrix, however, it is possible to see the three dimensions of CLIL—concepts, procedures, and language—in relation to each other. For instance, we might place language along the horizontal support axis, because it plays a crucial role where HOTS are involved. The other two dimensions (conceptual and procedural) might fit along the vertical 'challenge' axis.

It can be useful for teachers to visualize the language variable alongside concepts and procedures in a diagram which incorporates all three dimensions (as with the 'mixing desk'—see Figures 3.2 and 3.3 on pages 53 and 54). This not only makes the language more visible, but also supports the idea that a central aspect of the

CLIL teacher's role is to make certain language issues salient, depending on their students' particular needs. This involves including an explicit linguistic focus at the planning and preparation stages.

How learning works in CLIL

Haslam et al. (2005) describe the 'Seems OK' trap, whereby learners of EAL sail along happily in seemingly favourable classroom conditions. But when the inevitable storms arrive—for example, in the form of complex concepts or abstract language—learners often lose confidence and underachieve due to a lack of sensitive tuition in the complexities of the key language within the curriculum. In response to this phenomenon, Smyth argues for a language-explicit approach to curriculum design—one which informs teachers about the language of the learning they are delivering in their subjects. In her book *Helping bilingual pupils to access the curriculum* (2003), Smyth stresses the need for teachers to use functions of language as a planning tool for supporting bilingual learners. She also suggests that curriculum materials should highlight cognitive academic language skills and exemplify them using structures which teachers should model and which students should practise during classes.

In this book, we offer 'three-dimensional CLIL' and 'mixing desk' as analogies to support teachers in their decision-making when considering the language needs of their students in CLIL-based contexts. But, of course, we will need to look in more detail at what we mean by 'language'. We may have established its status as an equal and valued member of three-dimensional CLIL, but we have not looked in any detail at the types of language learners encounter in the CLIL classroom.

As we have already seen, language does not exist in a vacuum but rather acts as the vehicle for both understanding and expressing conceptual and procedural content. But as Cummins noted, this content may be either complex or relatively simple. It is also true that, as children grow older, they experience a quantitatively expanding range of conceptual abstraction. Llinares et al. (2012), citing Bernstein (1999), refer to this as 'horizontal' and 'vertical' knowledge—as shown in Figure 3.6 (overleaf), which illustrates how younger children new to the schooling environment are exposed to learning experiences which relate to the 'here and now' and their everyday world (horizontal). As children get older, their learning experiences become more abstract (vertical).

This is true for all children, of course, but the obvious point to make here is that the vertical journey is both conceptual <u>and</u> linguistic. Children in an L1 scholastic environment experience an increase in academic discourse—a language type far removed from those of the home and the playground. As we saw in Chapter 1, Cummins (1979) coined the term 'cognitive academic language proficiency' (CALP) to identify this particular variety of language. CALP is crucial to learning, and children's gradual development of it largely determines their success or failure at school.

Importantly, Cummins also contrasted CALP with '**basic interpersonal communicative skills**' (**BICS**)—an informal, more oral, interpersonal variety of language. We will look in much more detail at CALP and its counterpart BICS in Chapter 4, with regard to their crucial influence in CLIL-based contexts. But for now, let us consider Figure 3.6, which shows that BICS, which encompasses the everyday language experience, is widely used and developed in the early years curriculum, but that the focus moves inexorably towards CALP as the child progresses through school.

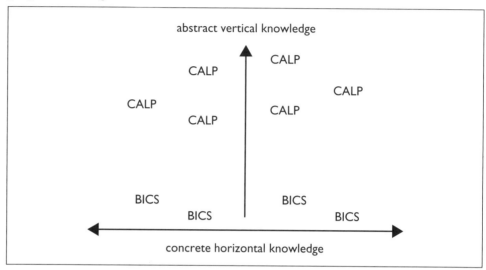

Figure 3.6 Bernstein's model of horizontal and vertical knowledge (Llinares et al., 2012.)

The problem this can create for students learning the curriculum through an L2 is that they have fewer opportunities to develop and use their well-honed 'horizontal' language skills the further they move up the vertical learning continuum. CLIL is CALP-rich, as we shall go on to see. It is rich by default in what we have called 'hard' CLIL, but it is also prominent in parallel language-syllabus CLIL programmes, which we have termed 'soft' CLIL—certainly more prominent than in conventional language lessons. Effective CLIL harnesses CALP, makes it salient, then practises and balances it through the calming influence of BICS.

The management of the relationship between CALP and BICS is crucial to the effective practice of CLIL, particularly if, as would seem to be the case, students learn more effectively when they are required to produce language. An example of the relative absence of this practice can be found in the work of Dalton-Puffer describing a range of CLIL classrooms in Austria:

> If one generalizes about students and teachers, it is evident and quite striking that neither group asks for explanations, reasons, and opinions with any frequency. The bread and butter of Austrian CLIL classrooms is obviously facts, facts, facts. This may also be an additional factor in the observation that signals of non-comprehension do not occur very often. Maybe the participants rarely signal to each other that communication has failed because facts just are, and there is nothing to comprehend, really.
> (Dalton-Puffer, 2007)

While Dalton-Puffer's research represents a limited number of learning samples through the medium of English, the argument presented is nevertheless a strong one. It reflects the concerns expressed by Bernstein (1999) and Llinares et al. (2012), namely that content classrooms without communicative opportunities are poor environments for foreign-language development. More importantly, perhaps, they are also poor environments for cognitive development in general—if we are to take Swain's 'output thesis' seriously (Swain, 1985). Swain has always argued that learners can only develop linguistically (and therefore cognitively) by actually producing language. Given the likely truth of this assertion, we cannot therefore allow the alleged scarcity of output in Austria or anywhere else to blind us to the fact that we as teachers must try to establish the conditions that will enable NNS students to generate both spoken and written language. And it follows, of course, that we must also help them to understand input.

Chapters 5 and 6 will deal with these dual axes of CLIL: supporting output and guiding input. But first, we will look in more detail in Chapter 4 at the types of language that an L2 learner must both understand and produce, as well as the variety of teacher discourse that occurs in CLIL contexts, with particular reference to how we provide support for learners in CLIL classes.

Summary

In this chapter, we have suggested that there is an intimate relationship between content and language, as befits the acronym CLIL, but that the word 'content' requires careful definition. Not only is content both conceptual and procedural, it is also linguistic. Language is in itself a form of content, and it therefore requires close attention when it comes to the planning of CLIL programmes. It is not simply a vehicle or an add-on.

We also considered the notion of educational objectives, and how they were normally expressed in terms of observable outcomes. We suggested that it might be useful to think in terms of priority objectives, through which we can emphasize any of the three dimensions of content at any given moment in a didactic sequence and adjust the levels of support as we deem necessary. We described this process using the analogy of an audio mixing desk, whereby the volume of any one content dimension can be adjusted in relation to the other two.

We further developed this by suggesting that if language is an equal member of three-dimensional CLIL (and not merely a vehicle), then it is necessary to examine its impact on cognition and learning. We looked at a series of models which dealt with the issues of conceptual complexity and its accompanying linguistic demands, and emphasized the fact that it is not merely the comprehension of language but rather its production that determines whether students learn in a significant way. This is true of normal L1 learning contexts, but its importance is magnified when we consider it with regard to CLIL-based contexts. This led us to the notion of teacher support, and finally to a brief consideration of the importance of academic language in the cognitive development of all learners.

Task

If you would like to look at a practical task to explore your own practice related to the content of this chapter, see Appendix 1 (page 290).

Further reading

Brinton, D., Snow, M., & **Wesche, M.** (1989). *Content-based second language instruction.* New York: Newbury House.
An influential book and a precursor to the CLIL phenomenon. It is principally concerned with case-study examples from tertiary education, but its emphasis on the importance of literacy and academic language established the bases for the wider reach of CLIL practice today.

Dalton-Puffer, C. (2007). *Discourse in content and language integrated learning (CLIL) classrooms.* Amsterdam: John Benjamins Publishing Company.
This book was the first in-depth analysis of the kind of communicative events typical of CLIL classrooms. It examines teacher and student talk at secondary school level from different interactional perspectives, with examples of classroom discourse from a variety of school subjects.

Gibbons, P. (1991). *Learning to learn in a second language.* Portsmouth, NH: Heinemann.
Although the book pre-dates the CLIL acronym, it provides a wealth of sample assessment tools, checklists, and helpful planning tools that can be implemented in any current CLIL-based classroom.

Mohan, B. (1986). *Language and content.* Reading, MA: Addison-Wesley.
Another influential book in the field, and an early affirmation of the importance and effectiveness of content-based language teaching. It also provides an organizing framework for developing content-based language curricula.

4 PRINCIPLES AND PRACTICE OF LANGUAGE IN CLIL

Overview

> For many pupils, learning to use language to express mathematical ideas will be similar to learning to speak a foreign language.
> (Lee, 2006)

As the above quotation suggests, learning a technical or abstract subject is akin to learning a foreign language. CLIL can help identify the linguistic features of this phenomenon and incorporate the information into a methodology for teaching the subject content through an additional language (L2). This chapter sets about identifying this language information in order to then present a series of principles for 'language in practice' in the CLIL classroom.

We will also look in detail at language in the CLIL classroom, by investigating further this 'foreign language' of learning, and suggest some ways in which teachers can support learners who are faced with studying a school subject in another language. The chapter concludes with seven principles of language in CLIL and examples for related practice in the classroom.

The subject–language relationship

As we examined in Chapter 2, CLIL is fundamentally about developing subject competences through language. In practice, this means learners must be taught in a way that helps them use language in order to acquire subject knowledge. However, when we teach subjects through a majority language, we tend to forget about this fact. If learners are orally fluent in the MoI, teachers may get the impression—often wrongly—that they do not need any help with the language of learning. This is reflected, for example, in subject syllabuses, as we will explore in this chapter. Subject language demands are rarely afforded explicit mention in subject curricula. Teachers often assume that learners have the necessary subject-specific language skills; or they assume that learners will 'pick them up', and that the skills therefore do not need to be taught. Teaching is, in this sense, 'assumptive' (Marland, 1977): it assumes learners already possess certain abilities which we need not teach. In addition, many subject teachers do not want to be particularly concerned with language. They feel that this is the job of language teachers. They also sometimes feel that they are not qualified to talk to learners about language.

In CLIL, subject teachers do not have the luxury of disregarding language. Unlike learners working in their L1, CLIL learners cannot be assumed to be fluent listeners, speakers, readers, and writers in the L2. They have to learn to develop these skills so that they can use them for learning subjects, and they have to do that, to a degree, at the same time as they learn the new subject content. In addition, they will not learn the language of the subject well enough without having it explicitly taught to them. Language teachers can do this to an extent, but they are not normally equipped with the necessary tools. CLIL subject teachers thus need to widen their view of their job to include some teaching of language. They do not have to be language experts and they do not have to devote a lot of time to it, but they do need to pay more attention to language than they would if they were teaching in L1. To what extent they should do this, and in what ways, will be examined in this chapter.

We also need to be clear about what we mean by 'language' in CLIL programmes. In the school context, we expect learners to use the academic variety of language referred to as CALP (Cummins, 2000). CALP comprises the ways in which we listen, read, speak, and write academically. It includes the vocabulary of subjects and of academic learning in general. It also includes some of the rather formal grammar we use when we write about school subjects, as well as the signals of organization we use to show structure and cohesion in formal writing. And it includes the crucial thinking skills which academic learning requires learners to engage in, and how those are expressed in language terms. These academic language skills are clearly different from the ways in which we use language in informal social interaction. But it is important to note that we do also use informal language skills for learning, alongside CALP. Indeed, education discourse places emphasis on how the two varieties interact in good classroom practice, and so it naturally follows that CLIL programmes should also pay close attention to the interaction between basic L2 communication and academic language skills.

What does 'language in CLIL' refer to?

Any discussion regarding the language required for teaching the curriculum needs to specify the type of language we are talking about. In the case of non-native speakers of English studying geography, for example, it can be useful to identify categories for describing the language involved. Taking the topic of global warming as an example, we could look at the following categories:

- grammar
- vocabulary
- discourse markers
- thinking skills/language functions
- language skills.

Grammar

The very notion of 'grammar' can be a concern for CLIL teachers coming from a subject-orientated background. However, being aware of grammar and having an understanding of subject-specific grammatical features can help a teacher provide better for the CLIL learner. It is not a question of 'teaching' grammar, but rather building an awareness of the types of sentence that occur frequently in a given subject and making decisions about how to present them to learners, helping them to see and hear this language, and supporting them when they are required to produce it themselves.

Returning to geography, a common perspective on global warming is how life on Earth is affected by the phenomenon. Aspects of life which are affected include, among others: health, water, land, weather, global population, and vegetation. The geography teacher might ask learners to make predictions about the impact global warming will have on these. In order to do this exercise, learners will need to have available a number of appropriate grammatical structures which will enable them to speak or write about the impact they predict global warming will have. And their sentences will also need to include the relative probability and certainty they attach to each of these effects.

Fortunately, we can find instances of the relevant grammatical structures in the standard text types of the subjects themselves. For example, a range of geography texts provides us with a representative sample of standard cause-and-effect structures being used to make statements about the consequences of changes to the aspects of life on Earth (see Figure 4.1).

Squeezing caused by colliding plates **causes** faulting.

The rising water **causes** landslides, triggering tsunamis.

Pressure **causes** rock to fracture and there is an upward movement of the land between the parallel faults.

Joints are enlarged through chemical weathering and this **causes** the edges of the blocks to become rounded.

As well as adding weight to the material, water also **causes** some soil particles to swell.

This swelling **causes** nearby particles to be moved and it lubricates the soil, making it move downslope.

Figure 4.1 Examples of statements using 'cause'

Immediately, we can see that all of the sentences in Figure 4.1 have the simple verb 'causes' at their heart. A closer look (see Table 4.1 overleaf) reveals several related structures. And another similar sample range of geography texts demonstrates the use of other aspects of grammar, such as cause-and-effect adverbs and conjunctions (see Table 4.2 overleaf).

X causes	*y* to be _____ -ed
	y to + infinitive
	a (noun phrase) (of *y*)

Table 4.1 Related cause-and-effect structures

As If	*x* happens *x* is _____	, *y* happens , then *y* happens	
X happens X is _____		because of *y* owing to *y* due to *y*	
		because *y* happens since *y* happens	
		and	therefore *y* happens is therefore *y* thereby *y* happens *x* is thus *y* thus has *y*

Table 4.2 Cause-and-effect adverbs and conjunctions

Vocabulary

Vocabulary can be subject-specific, general academic, cross-curricular, or not related to learning at all (which we refer to as 'peripheral' in this book). **General academic vocabulary** (e.g. 'thus' and 'whereas') can cause particular difficulties because it occurs frequently and is crucial to this type of discourse, but is not specific to any one subject. It is also less visible on the page than **subject-specific vocabulary** (for example 'photosynthesis'). We will explore these three layers of language later in the chapter.

The list in Figure 4.2 is an example of the range of verb-phrase vocabulary in a single topic area. It also reveals grammatical patterns which are useful to highlight for the purposes of written production (see Table 4.3). In addition, vocabulary can come in the form of noun phrases and involve a range of grammatical structures (see Table 4.4).

Discourse markers

Discourse markers are phrases used for organizing ideas in both written texts and in conversations. A simple example of discourse marking would include sequencing phrases which help describe the stages of a process: 'first', 'then', 'after that', 'next', 'as a result', 'the next thing', 'and then', 'finally'.

> **cause:** Compression of rock *causes* shock waves to spread out from the focus of an earthquake.
>
> **result in:** This *results in* heavy leaching, which deprives tree roots devastated by acid of the nutrients they need.
>
> **lead to:** Describe how plate movements *lead to* the formation of earthquakes.
>
> **be responsible for:** Tourism has *been largely responsible for* the development of a new airport and a ski run.
>
> **give rise to:** Good rainfall and summer heat *give rise to* prosperous agriculture.
>
> **trigger (off):** Building or quarrying can sometimes *trigger off* a landslide.
>
> **create:** Cloudless skies *create* high daytime temperatures and high pressure.
>
> **generate:** Running water turns wheels called 'turbines', which *generate* electricity.

Figure 4.2 Verb phrases synonymous with 'cause'

X	causes	*y* to be _____ -ed *y* to + infinitive verb a (noun phrase) of *y* a (noun phrase)
	results in	a (noun phrase) a / the (verb + *-ing*) of *y* *y* being / getting _____ -ed
	leads to triggers (off) creates generates	(change in) *y* (noun phrase)

Table 4.3 Structure in cause-and-effect verb phrases

A reason for				
A / An	consequence result cause source effect	of	*x* *x* happening	is *y*
A reason why			*x* / this happens	

Table 4.4 Structure in cause-and-effect noun phrases

Thinking skills/Language functions

Another key type of language resides in the thinking skills being engaged in any given lesson. For example, in addition to the causal language presented above, the topic of global warming might also include 'giving examples', or 'comparing', and perhaps 'prioritizing'. A good place to look for thinking skills and language functions in any subject is in the curriculum guidelines. As we will see, curriculum objectives which refer to these skills are very important for plotting and preparing for language practice in CLIL.

Language skills

Last but not least, a teacher working on the topic of global warming may have students working extensively on all four language skills, with listening/watching and reading input, and speaking activities which culminate in written production. The processing skills of listening/watching and reading and the productive skills of speaking and writing are dealt with in Chapters 5 and 6 respectively, but it is important here to emphasize that each skill makes different language demands on the learners.

Language in CLIL is clearly no simple matter, as our brief examination of 'cause and effect' and 'global warming' in geography demonstrates. What CLIL teachers need is a set of clear principles for dealing with language skills in class. To start with, teachers need to experience language in their classrooms from the perspective of their learners. This means teachers need to be aware of what language they use (and what language typifies their subject), what the component parts of this language are, and the challenges it causes for learners. Teachers then need a wide range of techniques and strategies to help learners manage these challenges.

We believe that language development and subject acquisition are interdependent and happen together, in both the L1 and CLIL-based classroom. Language in CLIL is by default an integral part of the support of any learning moment (Gibbons, 2002), and it serves as a bridge that helps learners move from their current position to further learning (Vygotsky, 1986). Just as engineers build with suitable materials using their knowledge of strengthening techniques and physical structures, teachers need to be able to construct the scaffolding of their lessons effectively by including language support based on an understanding of their learners' current level of subject knowledge and language ability. In order to build effective instructional scaffolds, teachers need to be familiar with the tools and materials they have at their disposal. In short, teachers need to understand the various aspects of language in the CLIL classroom and build up a repertoire of techniques to support learners in their learning experiences.

Principles for language practice in CLIL

Our aim is to equip teachers with a foundation for understanding language, as well as a basis for effective language practice in the CLIL classroom, and we will do this by offering the following set of principles. Firstly, we will describe language in the subject classroom. This description will cover different layers of language for learning and give teachers the terminology they need to be able to discuss the language of the subject and how it works in the classroom. Secondly, we will develop a framework for making decisions about classroom activity based on an understanding of language in a given subject. Chapters 5 and 6 will look directly at specific activity types in terms of '**input content**' and '**output content**' and offer a comprehensive range of strategies to use in the classroom.

These are the seven principles for language practice in CLIL:

1 'Mediate' language between the learner and new knowledge

2 Develop subject language awareness

3 Plan with language in mind

4 Carry out a curriculum language audit

5 Make general academic language explicit

6 Create initial talk time

7 Sequence activities from 'private' through to 'public'.

1 *'Mediate' language between the learner and new subject knowledge*

A general principle for language considerations in the CLIL classroom is that teachers need to work as language mediators in order to 'build bridges' between the learners and the new subject knowledge.

This principle suggests that CLIL teachers have an extra 'eye' which is constantly scouring input content for examples of language which might be above the reach of the learners. In terms of output, teachers monitor the learners' production and feed their observations into further planning.

The terms 'input content language' and 'output content language' are helpful to use in this discussion. CLIL teachers who are successfully mediating between the learners and the subject content will recognize potential language problems which are likely to occur at the point of content input and then plan to deal with them accordingly (see Chapter 5). The same CLIL teachers working to intercede between the learners and output content language will provide the scaffolding necessary for robust learner language production (see Chapter 6).

The description above applies equally to L1 learning contexts, with the difference residing in degree, extent, and application. Materials extract 4.A (overleaf) illustrates the issue in more detail.

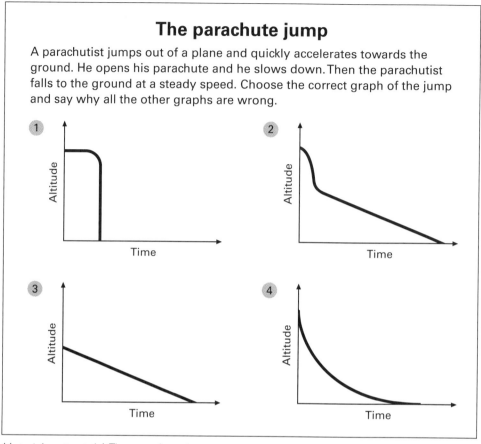

Materials extract 4.A The parachute jump

The problem shown in Materials extract 4.A is part of an upper-secondary mathematics CLIL course and exemplifies the curriculum objective 'Generate and solve problems with functions and graphs'. The question is in two parts. The first part asks learners to decide which graph represents the parachute jump. This part of the problem, in terms of language, demands that the learners understand the question and make a choice from the four graphs. The second part of the problem asks learners to then explain why the other three graphs are wrong.

The second part of the problem increases the language demand considerably. In order to explain why the other three graphs are wrong, learners need to carry out a number of operations: 1) to <u>describe</u> shape in line graphs, 2) to <u>draw conclusions</u> about shape in line graphs, and 3) to <u>give reasons</u> for the suitability (of a graph) using comparison.

CLIL teachers will need to think about how to mediate between the learner and the content in question. They will need to exploit contexts for presenting 'the language of shape in graphs', possibly with an example graph on the board or a screen using 'shape terms' embedded around the example graph for learners to see and hear, and perhaps note down, as they provide an explanation. In this sense, CLIL seems to involve a culture of mediation unlikely to exist to the same degree in L1 contexts.

The language of mathematics is challenging for native speakers. Lee (2006) identifies three distinct types of mathematical vocabulary, each carrying potential difficulties for learners:

1 Words that have the same meaning in everyday language as they do in mathematical discourse, which are used to set mathematics in context (for example, 'size', 'shape', 'area', 'distance').

2 Words that have a meaning which is specific to mathematical discourse (for example, 'hypotenuse', 'isosceles', 'coefficient', 'graph').

3 Words that have different meanings in mathematical discourse and everyday language (for example, 'difference', 'odd', 'mean', 'volume', 'value', 'integrate').

A maths teacher who makes these issues salient will be more effective. This clearly applies to other subjects too. For instance, Wellington and Osborne (2001) identified three categories of vocabulary in the discourse of science—scientific, semi-technical, and non-technical. They also ranked words according to their degree of abstraction. In order to help teachers go about organizing words in science classes, they created a taxonomy of scientific words which includes naming words, process words, concept words, and mathematical words and symbols, with the level of abstraction and potential difficulty for learners increasing respectively from level 1 to level 4 (see Figure 4.3).

Level 1: Naming words

1.1 Familiar objects, new names (synonyms)

1.2 New objects, new names

1.3 Names of chemical elements

1.4 Other nomenclature

Level 2: Process words

2.1 Capable of ostensive definition, i.e. being shown

2.2 Not capable of ostensive definition

Level 3: Concept words

3.1 Derived from experience (sensory concepts)

3.2 With dual meanings, i.e. everyday and scientific: for example 'work'

3.3 Theoretical constructs (total abstractions, idealizations, and postulated entities)

Level 4: Mathematical words and symbols

Figure 4.3 A taxonomy of the words of science (Wellington & Osborne, 2001.)

We can see that within subject-specific terminology, some words are more abstract and more difficult to learn and express than others. As such, the role of the teacher in facilitating the learning of subject-specific terminology is vital (Hayes-Jacobs, 2006; Lee, 2006; Wellington & Osborne, 2001; Roth, 2005; Zwiers, 2008).

But while it is clear that the specific language of the content curriculum can present a barrier to learners, research has shown that non-technical words (often taken for granted) can be at least as problematic as technical, specialist terms, if not more so (see Wellington & Osborne, 2001). This can be seen if you open a textbook at random to see if the subject-specific words are visible on the page. They may well be highlighted or made to stand out in some other way. According to Wellington and Osborne (2001), it is the rest of the 'invisible' language which poses the greatest challenge. For example, they stress that it is the many non-technical everyday words used in science with dual meanings which cause difficulties for learners: '… the logical connectives used to link sentences and ideas can present a barrier to the reading and understanding of science.'

Table 4.5 shows examples of logical connectives which cause especial difficulty in English.

The lower-case words shown are classed as 'difficult'; those in CAPITALS are 'very difficult'; italicized CAPITALS are 'extremely difficult'.		
AS TO	hence	on the basis of
consequently	i.e.	RESPECTIVELY
CONVERSELY	IN PRACTICE	similarly
ESSENTIALLY	*MOREOVER*	thus
FURTHER	nevertheless	whereby

Table 4.5 Some logical connectives in English which cause difficulty (Wellington & Osborne, 2001.)

So as Wellington and Osborne put it, 'Meaning has to be taught not caught.' The L1 teaching community has also realized that subject language in all its aspects needs to be made more salient to learners. And where CLIL is concerned, language must be plotted alongside the content in the curriculum.

A particular worry of some NNS teachers is that they are expected to 'teach' this language. They are concerned about their ability to teach grammar, to explain structure, and to generally deal with language problems they may not be sure about themselves. But CLIL is really more about language mediation. Language-sensitive teachers are more aware of the problems presented by subject language. This means they can offer a standard model of content subject language themselves. They also create opportunity and time for practising the language of the subject. They listen, note problems and errors, and consider moments for focusing on models from themselves and from the learners in order to facilitate the development of the 'standard' language of the subject. Whilst we are not suggesting that CLIL teachers should all be grammarians, the ability to confer language awareness on learners does require the teacher to have a certain level of language sensitivity and a familiarity with language-friendly pedagogy.

2 Develop subject language awareness

CLIL teachers, therefore, need to have a solid understanding of the language of their subject. They need to know what types of language occur in their subject and create an awareness of these types in their learners.

Subject teachers might use the following procedure:

- Recap the previous lesson
- Introduce a new topic and activate prior knowledge
- Deliver a short monologue on the new topic
- Set up an individual reading activity related to the new topic
- Go through questions and answers in plenary feedback after the reading
- Organize students into small groups to carry out an investigation as a follow-up to the reading
- Coordinate the groups to report back their findings to the whole class
- Summarize what has been learned before bringing the lesson to an end.

In such a lesson, the teacher language is not simply a uniform stream of words. There are three layers of language in classroom discourse (see Figure 4.4). One is related specifically to the subject area (for example, 'epithelial'). Another is cross-curricular, referred to as general academic language (for example, 'It's a type of cell which ...'), and finally, there is language which forms the 'conversation' of the classroom, the **interactional language** of communication between the people in the lesson, often referred to as '**peripheral language**'.

Figure 4.4 Types of classroom language

Layer 1: Subject-specific language

Subject-specific language, like **content-obligatory language** (Snow et al., 1989; Met, 1994), is language you cannot do without. An example is the word 'epithelial' in biology. Biology teachers consider it necessary for learning about the topic of 'cells and tissues'. In the same way, a geography teacher may highlight 'oxbow lake' as essential for learning about the stages of a river's development. Without this 'obligatory' vocabulary, learner language would stray too far from the non-standard. Any consideration of subject-specific language has to look at standard subject usage in this way. Similarly, teachers will need to develop an awareness of word frequency in the subject being taught. While frequency of subject-specific language is very different from frequency of general language, teachers still need to develop strategies for making decisions about which language they should draw attention to in any given lesson, clearly depending on the topic being taught and the activity.

Subject-specific vocabulary tends to be much less frequent than general-purpose language, and highly dependent on context within subjects. While it can sometimes be made visible on the page through highlighting or with explanatory notes in the margin, this varies from textbook to textbook. In any case, teachers will need to have techniques for helping learners to identify key terminology. Where key terms are not highlighted, teachers will need to be able to organize these key terms and offer learners help in memorizing them for future use. Mind maps and **concept maps** are examples of such techniques. Buzan's (1996) mind maps offer learners the opportunity to personalize maps according to learning preferences and styles. Concept maps (for example, CMaps) give teachers and learners the opportunity to embed all language within maps. Along the branches of maps, it is possible to embed verb phrases, prepositional phrases, and the 'rest' of the language. Maps like these can be used as a reference tool containing all the basic language in a given curriculum item or textbook unit. Materials extract 4.B shows an example concept map of the human organism.

It is important to differentiate between generic concept maps and those maps generated by learners themselves. Naturally, helping learners develop the skill of creating personal concept maps for learning is to be encouraged; but the challenge is for materials designers and publishers to produce generic key-concept and language-reference maps which will facilitate the learning process. In CLIL, there are two clear advantages to mapping out language in this way. The first of these is that the map presents a generic structure of the key concepts—generic because it is determined by the subject itself. The second advantage is that learners have all the basic terms in one place for ease of reference.

As mentioned above, there is a strong argument for the students themselves creating their own concept maps for learning. This should involve learners incorporating all manner of personal mnemonic devices (involving sound, colour, images, organization, etc.) to make memorization more effective. Clearly, personal maps like these would be very effective techniques for learners to use on their learning journey. The suggestion here, however, is that there is a need for concept maps to be available at the initial stage of a lesson, offering generic input structures for reference and organization of key language. We are thus focusing here on input content. When learning a content subject like biology through English as the L2 MoI, generic concept and language maps like these give learners a checkpoint or base to refer back to. Ideally, CLIL textbooks would all provide one content and language map in each unit. And the generic nature of these maps would allow for learners to edit the original at a later stage in order to create a personalized version for their own learning purposes in the way Buzan proposes. Getting learners to use mind-mapping software is an important part of the process of learning and the production of output content.

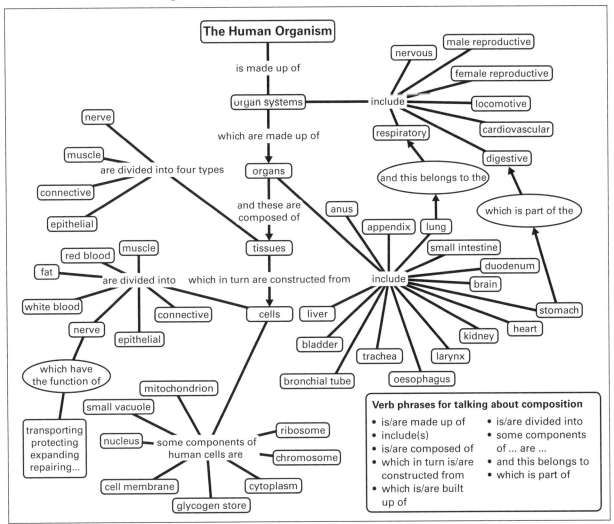

Materials extract 4.B Concept map of the human organism

Generic maps of noun-phrase vocabulary (and maps including other parts of sentences, such as verb, adjective, and adverb phrases) like the one shown in Materials extract 4.C (overleaf) can be used in any number of ways in the classroom. They can be broken up into sections and exploited for organizing vocabulary, as and when learners meet them in a given unit. One simple method is to offer a gapped map which learners fill in as they work through a unit. In this way, they reconstruct the overall structure of the unit content.

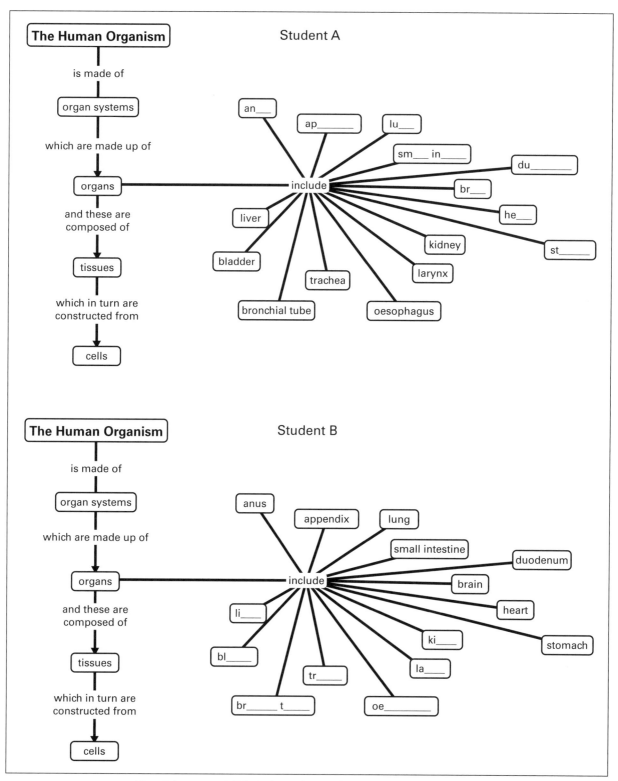

Materials extract 4.C Paired speaking with a gapped concept map

Concept maps can also be used to guide learners when listening to the teacher talking about a specific area. Here, learners are provided with sections of gapped maps to fill in while listening and watching. The maps can also be copied and used for paired speaking work to get learners actively listening to new vocabulary. The example shown in Materials extract 4.C exploits the concept map of the human organism for this purpose.

Learners familiarize themselves with the 'shape' of content in a given unit by using concept maps in this way. By building structures of key vocabulary and other parts of sentences, learners are constantly building the overall language and structure of a unit of work that will enable them to personalize content more effectively at a later stage. We will look further at speaking activities in Chapter 6.

Layer 2: General academic language

Subject-specific vocabulary is just the first layer of language in the classroom. Let us take a look at another layer of language which can cause a lot of difficulty for learners.

If we re-examine the concept map of the human organism (Materials extract 4.B on page 77), we can see that the language distributed along the branches of the map is made up of general academic language, with its wealth of verb phrasing, as opposed to the noun phrasing which is predominant in subject-specific vocabulary. General academic language is cross-curricular in nature, which means that the language is not specific to any one subject. Moreover, unlike subject-specific language, it is also largely invisible on the page and needs to be made visible for learners to be able to organize and assimilate it for future use.

General academic language relates closely to thinking skills within subject areas, and teachers may be able to identify the functions of language involved in these thinking areas by consulting their curriculum documents. Let us take a look at thinking skills and language in the curriculum.

Thinking and language in history

History is by definition a subject which moves learners away from the 'here and now', and this default focus on the past clearly influences discourse relating to the teaching and learning of the subject.

Figure 4.5 (overleaf) shows a summary of the language demands of history. A key aspect of this, which serves as an example of the challenges involved in the language of learning and thinking skills, is 'hypothesis'. Bousfield Wells highlights 'hypothetical questions', an aspect of empathy questions (vii(f)—an example is given below), both as a common aspect of history teacher talk and also as a challenge for non-native learners of English.

> 'If William had not won the Battle of Hastings, what would England be like today?'

The language of history

i) Vocabulary
 a) Historical terms
 b) Vocabulary and culture
 c) Abstract nouns
 d) Concepts
 e) Common core words
 f) Foreign words
 g) Register at word level

ii) Word formation
 a) Word families
 b) Nations and nationalities
 c) Word-formation specific to history
 d) Prefixes

iii) Pronunciation

iv) Adjectives used as collective nouns

v) Capital letters
 a) Proper nouns
 b) Titles
 c) Common nouns given a proper usage

vi) Roman numerals

vii) Tenses
 a) The simple past tense
 b) Habitual past tenses
 c) Tenses for source work
 d) The language of inference and uncertainty
 e) Speculative statements
 f) Empathy questions
 g) The passive

viii) The language for notes, summaries and maps

ix) The language for historical skills
 a) Development, change and continuity
 b) Comparing and contrasting
 c) The dependent clause preceding the main clause

x) Historical metaphors

Figure 4.5 A summary of history language demands (Bousfield Wells, n.d.)

Thinking and language in science

It is quite common to find thinking skills described in curriculum documents. For example, learners in science may be expected to be able to 'group and classify' different phenomena and 'compare' them. However, what are rarely described in L1 curriculum documents, and which are invaluable to the CLIL teacher, are examples of structures and phrases or whole example sentences which exemplify the function of the language in question. For example, learners would need to make use of phrases such as 'belongs to', 'is part of', and 'is characteristic of' among others, in order to talk or write about groups and classifications of scientific phenomena.

Clegg (2002b) describes 14 functions of language corresponding to cross-curricular thinking skills (such as 'classification', 'hypothesis', 'cause and effect') and presents language in terms of 'teacher questions' and 'learner statements'. The aim of the description is to make general academic language explicit to the CLIL teacher.

The learner statements are presented in an 'easy-to-use' **substitution table** (see Table 4.6). In this example, there are two substitution tables for learners to create statements for classifying phenomena (the second represents more formal versions of the first). Identifying general academic language and presenting it in this form is valuable for CLIL teachers. With language presented in this way, teachers can take the next step and embed the language in classroom activity (see Chapters 5 to 7 for examples).

Teacher questions	**Learner statements**			
How would you classify ...?	There are	three	kinds types forms classes categories	of	_____

Teacher questions	**Learner statements**					
How many kinds of ... are there? Who can classify ...?	_____	fall can be	divided classified	into	three	kinds types classes
	We/you/one can classify ... according to ... criteria This class has ... characteristics/features					

Table 4.6 The language of thinking: classifying (Kelly & Kitanova, 2002)

Like the generic concept map in Materials extract 4.B (on page 77), the language of thinking needs to be presented in reference form in textbooks for teachers themselves, and/or in CLIL curriculum documents offered as language samples to accompany CLIL curriculum objectives. Both L2 and L1 learners of subjects may find this general academic language problematic. Wellington and Osborne (2001) suggest that this is the case for L1 learners of science. As we have mentioned, learners do not readily notice general academic language. Learners in CLIL programmes need this language to be made clearly visible to them.

Language of thinking

It is unfortunate that not all curriculum documents are explicit about the thinking skills needed in a given subject, as CLIL curriculum writers need to begin from the idea that all thinking skills must be visible on a curriculum document page, due to its symbiotic relationship with language. Ideally, all curriculum documents available to teachers working in CLIL will be designed in a way that makes thinking skills visible, and with these skills linked explicitly to the language demands involved. When this does not happen, teachers may risk simply not knowing how to express thinking skills in L2 when planning teaching and learning.

Table 4.7 shows the curriculum specifications for Science Year 6 from the Ministry of Education, Malaysia.

Scientific skills	Thinking skills
Science process skills Observing Classifying Measuring and using numbers Inferring Predicting Communicating Using space–time relationships Interpreting data Defining operationally Controlling variables Hypothesizing Experimenting *Manipulative skills*	*Critical thinking skills* Attributing Comparing and contrasting Grouping and classifying Sequencing Prioritizing Analysing Detecting bias Evaluating Making conclusions *Creative thinking skills* Generating ideas Relating Making inferences Predicting Making generalizations Visualizing Synthesizing Making hypotheses Making analogies Inventing

Table 4.7 Curriculum specifications for Science Year 6 (Ministry of Education, 2006.)

This table of skills is a very valuable summary of the kinds of thinking to be expected of learners of science. The scientific skills that we can see in this list include both process skills and manipulative skills.

Two examples of process skills, as indicated in the table, are:

Observing

- Using the senses of hearing, touch, smell, taste, and sight to compile information about an object or a phenomenon.

Classifying

- Using observations to group together objects or events according to similarities or differences.

Manipulative skills are the kinds of skill used during practical work that enable students to use and handle science apparatus and laboratory substances correctly. The Malaysian curriculum also shows how thinking strategies are seen to include steps in planning which involve both critical and creative thinking skills. But the language demands of these skills are not shown in the curriculum document; and to arrive at what these language demands are, we need to specify them further. The more exactly we do this, the closer we see how the thinking skills relates to language, as in these two examples:

Grouping and classifying

- Separating and grouping objects or phenomena into categories based on certain criteria, such as common characteristics or features.

Making generalizations

- Making a general conclusion about a group based on observations made on, or some information from, samples of the group.

As shown in Table 4.8, science-related process skills are linked at another point in the curriculum document to thinking skills.

Science process skills	Thinking skills
Observing	Attributing Comparing and contrasting Relating
Classifying	Attributing Comparing and contrasting Grouping and classifying

Table 4.8 Thinking skills related to science process skills: observing and classifying

At this point, we are able to identify what the language demands actually are. Let us look at comparing and contrasting. A study of 'standard' science textbooks reveals the language of comparison shown in Table 4.9 (overleaf).

Comparative phrases	
smaller	The atom can be broken into **smaller** fragments.
x is smaller than *y*	The electron has a negative charge and **is** at least a thousand times **smaller** and lighter **than** any atom.
more	The steam engine was a far **more** efficient machine.
more than	Mercury is **more than** 13 times denser than water.
less than	Sliver is **less** dense **than** gold.
The more …, the harder …	**The more** accurately a particle's position was pinned down, **the harder** its momentum was to measure.
as … as	Pores in the unglazed porcelain capture particles **as** small **as** bacteria.
Superlative phrases	
smallest	The cell is the **smallest** unit of an organism that can survive on its own.
greatest	Archimedes was the **greatest** mathematician in the ancient world.
most	To the naked eye, **most** stars appear to be white.
the most	**The most** common isotope of carbon is carbon-12.
the least	**The least** electronegative element of the well-known elements is cesium.
Verb phrases	
compare	Grouping living things allows scientists to **compare** millions of organisms.
differ	The numbers of similar elements **differ** by seven or multiples of seven.
vary	Offspring **vary** from each other in many ways.
is / are similar to	Birds **are** essentially **similar to** reptiles.
is / are unlike	The fossilized bones discovered **were unlike** those of any living animal.
reduce	A ramp lined with a smooth material was used to **reduce** friction.
Noun phrases	
difference	The **difference** in upthrust between the two is small.
Prefix / Suffix terms	
over-	**Over**fishing of the lake led to a dramatic fall in the fish population.
under-	An **under**active thyroid means your thyroid gland does not produce enough chemicals called hormones.
-like	Not only did light have particle-**like** properties, but particles had wave-like properties too.
-shaped	Chromosomes are the rod-**shaped** structures that carry genes.
Discourse markers	
… on the other hand …	Hydrogen gas, **on the other hand**, is extremely combustible.
… while …	Half were given the medicine, **while** the other half got placebo.
… whereas …	Earth has most of its carbon underground, **whereas** on Venus it's in the atmosphere.
… however …	Birds had differently shaped beaks, **however**, adapted to different diets.

Table 4.9 Comparison in science textbooks

What we see from this is that CLIL teachers need a further dimension—a language dimension—added to curriculum documents. Some curriculum documents do sometimes make quite explicit the concepts and the procedures of learning to be carried out. But in very few cases is reference made to the language demands involved. Let us take the curriculum excerpt in Table 4.8 (on page 83) and the need it identifies for learners to compare things. Table 4.10 shows how we can add a column labelled 'Useful language' which lists sample phrases to exemplify the thinking skills of comparing and contrasting.

Science process skills	Useful language
Observing	**Comparative phrases** more than *Mercury is **more than** 13 times denser than water.* as … as *Pores in the unglazed porcelain capture particles **as** small **as** bacteria.*
Thinking skills	**Superlative phrases** the most ***The most** common isotope of carbon is carbon-12.* the least ***The least** electronegative element of the well-known elements is cesium.*
Attributing Comparing and contrasting Relating	**Verb phrases** differ *The numbers of similar elements **differ** by seven or multiples of seven.* is / are similar to *Birds **are** essentially **similar to** reptiles.* **Noun phrases** difference *The **difference** in upthrust between the two is small.* **Discourse markers** … whereas … *Earth has most of its carbon underground, **whereas** on Venus it's in the atmosphere.*

Table 4.10 Example of sample language for specific curriculum skills

It does not make sense for curriculum documents to be so full of language suggestions as to make them difficult for the science teacher to use. In an ideal context, a practising teacher will be able to edit the curriculum document based on their knowledge of learner needs in terms of the three dimensions of content, namely language, concepts, and procedures (see Chapter 3). This would mean that teachers would be able to take prompts from the curriculum, specify the language required, and aim it at the level of their learners, recycling essential structures and pre-empting those complex structures which will later be necessary with regard to student production.

A major challenge for CLIL teachers is where to find and make this language available to learners in their subject classrooms. Useful lists of academic language do exist. For example, a far-reaching audit of the most common academic words from a range of content areas, including law, medicine, business, and many others, has been carried out at university level. Coxhead's (2000) academic word list is widely used to give students practice using the most common non-specific, general academic terminology across academic subjects. In addition, the language is available in textbook reading material, as we have seen, and also in 'texts', or chunks of subject knowledge, that come from the teachers themselves. CLIL teachers need to find this language and make it available for teaching and learning purposes.

Layer 3: Peripheral language

Subject-specific language and general academic language make up the CALP of the curriculum. The third layer of language in the classroom is what we refer to as 'peripheral language' (similar to BICS referred to in Chapter 3). Peripheral language corresponds largely to the organizational language of the classroom. This is the language that teachers use to delegate roles, to give instructions, and generally to co-ordinate the activity taking place. Organizational language can sometimes also overlap with general academic language, for instance when teachers refer to content when setting up activities. Peripheral language also refers to the 'conversation' of the classroom, the interactional language between learners and between the teacher and the learners. On one level, it is quite simple to audit this language in a similar way to that of the two layers described above. We just need to reflect on the language and examine its structure and usage in order to make it visible and available to teachers and learners.

On another level, teacher talk itself can be said to be part of this peripheral classroom language. This can be clearly understood by examining the language used by teachers in their classrooms. We might look at how native-speaker teachers communicate with their learners and look at this alongside NNS teachers working with their classes through the medium of an L2. By and large, native-speaker teachers talk much more quickly, take more language for granted, and exhibit characteristics of language you would find in 'real-world' native-speaker interactions. On the other hand, NNS teachers tend to speak more slowly with their NNS learners, they tend to repeat things, focus on language, and use simpler 'caretaker' language in a way that you are less likely to find in a classroom run by a native-speaker teacher. In CLIL classrooms, whether they are led by native-speaker or NNS teachers, it is vital that the level of the peripheral language is adjusted to the level of the learners.

Whether it is in CLIL classrooms where both teachers and learners are developing their L2, or in CLIL classrooms led by native-speaker teachers, it can be useful to 'script' the peripheral language. This may be simply a question of plotting interactional language opportunities, making decisions about the kind of phrases that are going to be used, then sticking to this 'script' without varying too much from the plan. Table 4.11 shows an example of scripted teacher classroom language.

Teacher Language	
Getting students' attention	**Asking students to answer**
OK, listen, please.	Who can answer?
Attention, please.	Who'd like to answer?
Pay attention, please.	Who can give me an answer?
Let me have your attention, please.	Who thinks they know (the answer)?
Can I have your attention, please?	Put up your hand/hands.
Can you listen to me, please?	Hands up if you know/can answer.
Look this way, please.	Do you know the answer?
Look at me, please.	Do you know what to do?
I want you to listen, please.	Any volunteers?

Table 4.11 Scripted teacher language

3 Plan with language in mind

CLIL teachers need to have language at the forefront of their minds while planning lesson activity. The planning stage gives teachers time to predict language challenges in a given unit of work. This should not detract from teachers taking on a 'trouble-shooting' role during the lesson itself—it is impossible to predict all language demands. But at least for a given unit of work, teachers should be able to look at what language will be given in the form of content input, and what language is to be expected as content output.

Figure 4.6 (overleaf) shows a generic lesson plan with relevant questions about language in a CLIL lesson. The purpose of an instrument such as this is to encourage CLIL teachers to plan with language in mind. The planning frame helps them to pinpoint possible difficulties for learners in terms of language. These difficulties may come from any one of three directions: concepts, procedures, or language. As our 'mixing desk' analogy from Chapter 3 illustrates, teachers may decide to turn up the support volume in any of these areas within a lesson, depending on where the learners are in terms of both content and language.

There are language questions which teachers can predict and prepare for when planning a lesson. Effective planning will produce materials and activities which reflect language considerations and have terms and phrases embedded within them, according to the challenges predicted. There are other language questions which arise during lessons, and the better teachers are equipped, the more successfully they will be able to deal with these issues during the course of the lesson. For example, during a plenary session, teachers can expect learner responses to questions addressed to the whole class. If teachers hear several examples of the same language problem from these responses, they may decide to interrupt the course of the content sequence in order to focus the whole class on an appropriate 'standard' phrase by simply writing it up on the board, after which the plenary presentation continues with the class's attention maintained on the standard phrase.

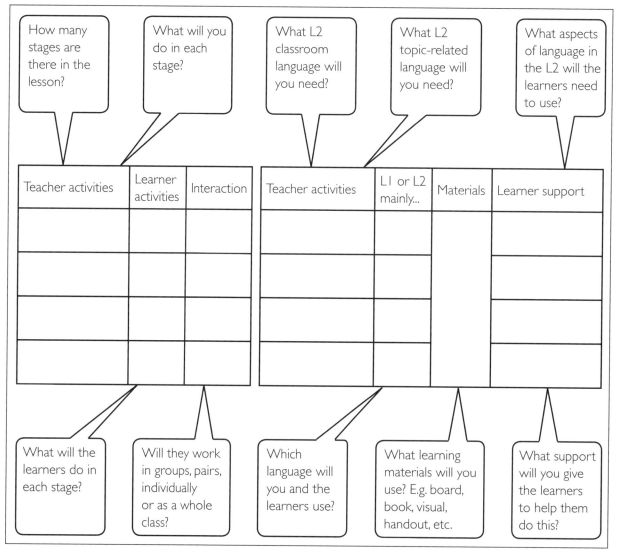

Figure 4.6 CLIL lesson questions

Let us take a look at a sequence of lesson activities in terms of materials and planning, to show language planning occurring for a CLIL lesson. Materials extract 4.D consists of linear text with headings in bold italic type.

The text names and describes a number of health problems that are related to diet. Each section of the text describes some of the causes of health problems and the consequences of eating too much of certain food groups. There are also suggestions as to how some of these effects can be avoided. The context for the reading of the text is a school exchange project on eating and drinking habits. The text is given as background information for learners investigating their own eating habits and those of their families and their country as a whole. It is presented alongside data for a number of diet-related illnesses in a variety of countries.

Diet and disease

Certain diseases, such as coronary heart disease, breast cancer and bowel cancer are more common in some countries than in others. It is thought that some of these diseases may be linked to diet. Below is some information about them.

Obesity

People who weigh 20% more than the ideal are overweight. They have a shorter life expectancy and are more likely to suffer from diseases that include heart disease, diabetes, gallstones, high blood pressure, arthritis and varicose veins.

Some people put on weight easily. The reasons are not understood. They do not necessarily eat more than other people, but they eat more than they need and lay down the excess as fat.

Tooth decay

Tooth decay (dental caries) has been linked to diets high in sugars. Your mouth contains bacteria that break down sugars to make acids. Acids attack tooth enamel, making it more porous. Tooth decay begins as the enamel wears away.

Heart disease

Death rates from coronary heart disease are often higher in countries where people eat diets high in 'saturated' fats such as butter, red meat, milk and cheese. A high-fat diet can raise the level of cholesterol, a fat-like substance in the blood. Your body needs cholesterol, but when it collects on the inside of blood vessels you have a greater risk of heart attacks.

High blood pressure

High blood pressure is a condition that may lead to ill health. Doctors may advise patients to eat food without added salt, and avoid processed foods and ready meals which tend to be high in salt.

Cancer

People in different countries tend to suffer from different types of cancer. Scientists think that diet could be a major factor. It is difficult to be sure, because countries collect their statistics in different ways, so that the figures given here may not represent exactly the same thing. New studies should soon give more reliable statistics.

Breast cancer is increasing in many countries. Its cause is not known.

Some scientists suspect that many people could avoid getting stomach cancer if they ate fruit and vegetables every day. Cancer of the bowel may also be linked to a diet high in fat. Eating enough dietary fibre may help to reduce the risk of bowel cancer.

Alcoholic drinks may be linked to cancers of the mouth and gullet (oesophagus) as well as to cirrhosis of the liver and high blood pressure.

Materials extract 4.D 'Diet and disease' (The Association for Science Education, 2004.)

Table 4.12 gives a curriculum descriptor for this area of the L1 secondary curriculum. What is missing from this descriptor, and what is crucial for CLIL teaching, is information about procedure and language. In other words, the CLIL curriculum document would make explicit to the teacher what language is needed, and how to activate this language during the lesson.

Year	Subject	Topic	Concepts	Skills
Year 9	biology	diet and disease	food groups, diet-related illnesses	naming, describing origin, cause and consequence, suggesting solutions
Learners will: • be aware of their own diet with respect to information on diet and disease • name common food groups and food items which belong to these groups • name diseases related to diet • explain the causes of different diet-related diseases • suggest ways these diseases may be avoided.				

Table 4.12 Sample curriculum objectives for 'Diet and disease' text

Of course, there are many ways of working with a linear text like the one in Materials extract 4.D, as we will also see in Chapter 7. A procedural decision might be to create a read-and-sort activity to get learners discussing the content of the text in small groups. This small-group discussion would enable learners to share their own ideas and understanding of the topic in initial 'private talk'. In order to create this opportunity, teachers would need to identify a generic structure in the text to produce a diagram of the content, which the learners could use to process the input content. An example of such a structure is a blank version of the table shown in Figure 4.7, which shows the completed diagram with the embedded language. The purpose of this instrument is to support learners in producing the output content, by showing the diagram on the board or a screen and asking learners to feed back on what they have learned about diet and disease. Two examples of what we might expect learners to say or write are:

> Obesity is caused by eating more than we need and too many of the wrong things. It can result in heart disease and diabetes among others, and could be avoided by eating a balanced diet and taking plenty of exercise.

> High blood pressure is caused by eating too many processed foods and ready meals high in salt content. It can lead to very ill health. High blood pressure could be remedied by avoiding too much salt in the diet.

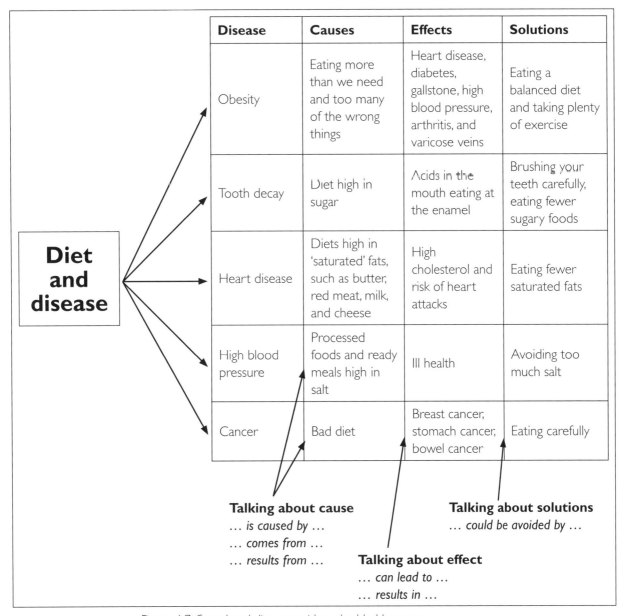

Disease	Causes	Effects	Solutions
Obesity	Eating more than we need and too many of the wrong things	Heart disease, diabetes, gallstone, high blood pressure, arthritis, and varicose veins	Eating a balanced diet and taking plenty of exercise
Tooth decay	Diet high in sugar	Acids in the mouth eating at the enamel	Brushing your teeth carefully, eating fewer sugary foods
Heart disease	Diets high in 'saturated' fats, such as butter, red meat, milk, and cheese	High cholesterol and risk of heart attacks	Eating fewer saturated fats
High blood pressure	Processed foods and ready meals high in salt	Ill health	Avoiding too much salt
Cancer	Bad diet	Breast cancer, stomach cancer, bowel cancer	Eating carefully

Talking about cause
... is caused by ...
... comes from ...
... results from ...

Talking about solutions
... could be avoided by ...

Talking about effect
... can lead to ...
... results in ...

Figure 4.7 Completed diagram with embedded language

The teacher who created the example shown in Figure 4.7 has predicted what language will be needed in the final 'public' expression of the content output. This is the language used to describe origin, cause, and consequence, and also how to avoid bad eating habits that can lead to diseases. The teacher has also made a procedural decision (not shown in the diagram) to create small-group discussion work and follow this up with a public plenary feedback session. This kind of procedural planning, prediction of language demands, and provision of language support is an important principle for CLIL classrooms.

4 Carry out a curriculum language audit

Curriculum documents offer teachers all over the world detailed instructions for the content of their lessons. The extent of explicit instruction differs from country to country. In some countries, curriculum documents are light, and the ministry of education creates a list of approved books for schools to choose from and purchase. These books are approved on the basis that they are seen to be following the instructions provided in the curriculum documents. In other countries, curriculum documents are more detailed and carry explicit information for teachers to follow.

Where CLIL is concerned, we need to look at redesigning key aspects of curriculum documentation. This is because a CLIL curriculum document will need to carry information about the three dimensions of CLIL as described in this book: concepts, procedures, and language.

We saw in Table 4.12 (on page 90) an L1 curriculum item describing biology objectives for the 'Diet and disease' lesson discussed above. We can see in this item that the objectives focus on the subject content without any indication of the language goals. Table 4.13, however, presents the same biology objectives for the 'Diet and disease' lesson with the addition of references to language and procedures.

Original curriculum descriptor					CLIL curriculum features	
Year	Subject	Topic	Concepts	Skills	Example phrases	Procedures
Year 9	biology	diet and disease	food groups, diet-related illnesses	naming, describing origin, cause and effect, suggesting solutions	An example of … is is caused by can lead to could be avoided by	Read text and sort disease, cause, consequence, solution

Table 4.13 A CLIL curriculum descriptor for the 'Diet and disease' lesson

Smyth (2003) writes extensively about the need for 'language' information to be included in curriculum documentation in the UK to support teachers who work with EAL learners. In the context that Smyth describes, L1 teachers are working with L2 learners. Her recommendation is that the curriculum be redesigned to offer teachers both a) information about language in a given unit of content work, and b) language targets for a given learner working on this unit. Working in this way will help teachers to prepare for their teaching, but will also facilitate ongoing formative assessment of learners to better feed into their future learning programme.

The idea of carrying out a language audit for the whole curriculum will sound daunting to most teachers who are already busy with day-to-day teaching. The challenge is thus for curriculum designers to include this information in CLIL curriculum documents, to make planning more efficient for teachers. Publishers too need to include unit language maps in CLIL textbooks, along with a range of ideas on how to use this language in the CLIL classroom. Teachers can, of course, carry out their own audit, but it would be useful to do so collaboratively. This is because if teachers are left to their own devices to identify what language to focus on in their lessons, there is a risk that language will be used randomly in a non-standard fashion in the classroom. It therefore makes sense for teachers interested in producing a curriculum language audit to track language usage on a unit-by-unit basis over the course of a school year and work together with colleagues to allow the audit to develop over time. Needless to say, networking with like-minded teachers in other schools, whether locally, nationally, or internationally, can also help avoid creating extra work.

Hayes-Jacobs (2006) advocates auditing and mapping out the language dimension of an entire curriculum. A curriculum language audit would inform all teachers in the same school about who is doing what language, when, and in which context. This information would enable teachers to build on the work that had just been done in a colleague's class, and present language in the curriculum in a meaningful sequence for learners. This is often referred to as an 'integrated curriculum' (Muñoa, 2008). The time is right for technology to support a move to cross-curricular sharing of literacy information for learners in schools in this way. Teachers can use technology to share language demands and needs across subjects in a given year, across all grades. Any system which shares information between teachers about learner language development is clearly most beneficial for learners, and especially for CLIL learners. Indeed, the difference between L1 and CLIL contexts is that this information sharing is an essential ingredient for success in CLIL contexts. Until schools adopt a whole-school approach to dealing with language in the curriculum, this aspect of CLIL will remain hard work.

5 Make general academic language explicit

We have suggested that, in an ideal situation, CLIL teachers would benefit from an investigation of the language used across the school curriculum so that this language could inform teaching and learning in the L2. This 'audit' would include the three layers of language described in this chapter: subject-specific language, general academic language, and peripheral language. Kelly (2009a, 2009b) has audited general academic language for geography and science subjects to produce reference lists of phrases in context for CLIL teachers and learners. This audit includes a range of language and thinking skills, such as hypothesizing, from these subjects. The language is contextualized with lessons including the audited language. As we have mentioned, it is unrealistic to expect individual teachers to undertake this work themselves, but teachers could investigate language on a lesson-by-lesson basis over a school term or year, and this would eventually accumulate to become a do-it-yourself language audit.

Here, we offer a five-step approach to activating general academic language:

1 Find a content 'text'

2 Highlight key 'concepts'

3 Identify general academic language

4 Decide what the 'procedure' of the lesson will be

5 Embed general academic language into activities.

Step 1 refers to 'text'. This can be any 'chunk' of content in written, spoken, or audio-visual form. And as mentioned earlier in this chapter, this text may also refer to a chunk of content which the teacher has not yet set down on paper, in a slideshow, or on video. Materials extract 4.E shows a conventional 'text' as it appears in a textbook.

Step 2 asks us to highlight key concepts in the text. For example, Materials extract 4.E shows a linear text on living things and their environment. This means the key concepts are different animals, plants, and locations.

Living things and their environment

An organism's environment is everything around it which affects the way it lives, including non-living features like climate, landscape, and soil, and other living organisms which affect its struggle for a living.

Habits and communities ──────────────────────────── **defining**

A habitat is <u>a part of the environment in which</u> a group of organisms, called a community, lives. Meadows, ponds, woodlands and sea shores are habitats. A rock pool is a habitat with a community including sea weeds, anemones, winkles, crabs, and fish.

A niche is the position an organism occupies in a community, such as flesh eating, grass eating, insect eating, or blood sucking. Foxes occupy a flesh-eating niche in Britain, whereas in Africa it is occupied by lions, tigers, leopards, etc. ──────── **explaining**

A population is a group of organisms of the same kind. A forest <u>may have</u> populations of squirrels, owls, spiders, oak trees, and bluebells. The density of a population depends on the birth and death rates of the population.

Environmental factors ──────────────── **exemplifying**

Environmental factors are those features of a habitat which affect the types of organism that can live there. They <u>include</u> the physical factors of climate, landscape, and soil, and biological factors, including all the ways in which other living things in the habitat affect each other.

Wild deciduous woodland is rare nowadays. Most has been cleared for pasture or crops, or changed into commercial conifer plantations. Some woods are dominated by oak, others by beech, ash, or, in damp soils, alder. They are home to numbers of insects and other invertebrates.

A single tree can be a habitat and each type has a different community living on it and in it. Oak tree communities include algae, fungi, mosses, lichens, gall wasps, aphids, weevils, beetles, lacewings, and moth caterpillars.

A coral reef is a habitat with one of the richest and most diverse communities on Earth.

Materials extract 4.E Linear text (adapted from Beckett & Gallagher, New coordinated science: Biology, OUP, p. 168.)

Step 3 involves looking at the general academic language in the text, which is 'invisible' in the sense that it is easily overlooked. The best way to 'find' it is simply to look for common phrases and see what thinking skill or 'function' is being demonstrated (see Table 4.14). In this case, we can identify occurrences of 'is a … which' and 'is a … with', which are structures used to give definitions. We can also identify 'may have' and 'can be', which are used to give explanations. Finally, we have 'such as', 'like', and 'include', which are structures used for giving examples. In short, the general academic language of the text is definition, explanation, and exemplification. This structure—define, explain, exemplify—is commonly found in expository texts from the social and natural science curricula.

Defining	Explaining	Exemplifying
… is part of …	Foxes occupy … whereas in …	Plural nouns
… is a … with a …	it is occupied by lions.	… including …
… is the position an … occupies in …	… may have …	… like …
… is a group …	… can be …	… such as …
… are those features which …		… refers to …
… is a habitat with …		… they include …
		… like this …

Table 4.14 Sample phrases of general academic language from Materials extract 4.E

Step 4 refers to 'procedure'. It is worth bearing in mind that steps 1 to 3 determine what the procedure will be. We may find a linear text like the one in Materials extract 4.E followed by comprehension questions in the textbook. It is highly likely that such comprehension questions accompanying the text would focus on 'defining', 'explaining', and 'exemplifying', and would therefore require students to reproduce some of the structures identified in Table 4.14.

Step 5 refers to 'embedding general academic language into activities'. A CLIL teacher using the text in Materials extract 4.E with accompanying comprehension questions would need to consider how to embed this general academic language into a reading activity. One simple way of doing this is to incorporate the language into the questions, as shown in Materials extract 4.F.

Give a definition for a niche:

A niche is the position an _____ occupies in a _____.

Give an explanation for a niche with a comparison between Britain and Africa:

_____ occupy a _____ niche in Britain, whereas in Africa it is occupied by _____.

Give two examples of a niche:

… such as _____ and _____.

Materials extract 4.F Prompts for writing about a 'niche'

Of course, there are many ways of embedding language into classroom activities, and these will be examined in detail in Chapters 5 to 7. The aim here is to present the principle of making an aspect of language explicit, visible, and accessible for learners. Without this, the parachute jump task (see Materials extract 4.A on page 72) becomes too complex to undertake. Learners are asked to produce content-specific language without being prepared for such production demands. By preparing ahead, CLIL teachers can do much to help learners on their journey towards becoming more confident in the L2.

6 *Create initial talk time*

Roth (2005), in his groundbreaking study of the role of language in native-speaker classrooms in the learning of science, suggests that science teachers should set out to achieve a convergence between the language of students and the language of science in the classroom. In Roth's words, knowing language and knowing the world go hand in hand; neither can precede the other, and they evolve together (2005, 84). Whilst Roth was referring specifically to L1, the principle he describes is also useful for CLIL classrooms. This principle is one which accepts that learners will always have some prior understanding of new learning, however rudimentary (see Chapter 7). Learners will also have some idea of what language to use to express this initial idea, however undeveloped. In the CLIL foreign language context, this initial understanding is also highly likely to involve the learners' L1. In Roth's view, we need to acknowledge the fact that learners dealing with new content need to be able to express their basic grasp of the content before they can develop their understanding further. We can then begin to look at the scaffolding and instruments we can offer learners to assist them in gradually broadening their understanding of content through the L2. As Roth says:

> Practical actions provide the conditions for the emergence and evolution of the language simultaneously with the emergence of the perceivable patterns in the material world.
> (Roth, 2005, 80)

This has fundamental implications not only for the science classroom, but also for the CLIL classroom. Both L1-only and CLIL lessons require 'practical actions' to set up the conditions necessary for learning and language to develop together. But these practical actions arguably play a greater role in CLIL lessons because they help define CLIL methodology itself. CLIL teachers make strategic decisions to use specific instruments to guide and support learners in their classrooms. The first of these 'practical actions' is to create initial lesson time for thought and talk. This leads us to consider what kind of talk is appropriate for this thinking stage.

Cummins's view of BICS and CALP is helpful here. In Chapter 3, we saw that BICS refers to the informal language of social interaction which takes place in classrooms, corridors, playgrounds, and other 'social' areas and contexts of schooling. Indeed, BICS could be described as the 'chat' of schools and schooling. Cummins (2000) suggests that it takes migrant children two to three years to learn

BICS. By contrast, CALP reportedly takes a minimum of five years to acquire. CALP is the language of learning, but it is also very much the language of exams and evaluation, and Cummins suggests it is this language which Hispanic children, for example, need to have explicitly taught to them in order for them to succeed in the US school system.

Figure 4.8 shows Cummins's cognition–context matrix, which describes four 'zones' of learning (see Chapter 3). Any form of planned learning can occur in any of these zones for any learner, and it is the job of teachers to know which learning zone is appropriate for their learners at a given point in the lesson. Cummins points out that it is useful to think in terms of sequences of learning moments when students may find themselves in any one of these zones. It is important for teachers to plan learning so that students can move from one zone to another to maximize their learning. This movement is of particular significance for CLIL. It suggests that the learning must begin with the learners and where they are before they can work towards attaining the 'institutional standard' of knowledge. Similarly, the use of the L2 must be strategically planned along this journey, so that it allows learners to move from using their 'own' language to the 'standard' language of the subject, allowing continued opportunities for BICS, but supporting the growing demand for CALP.

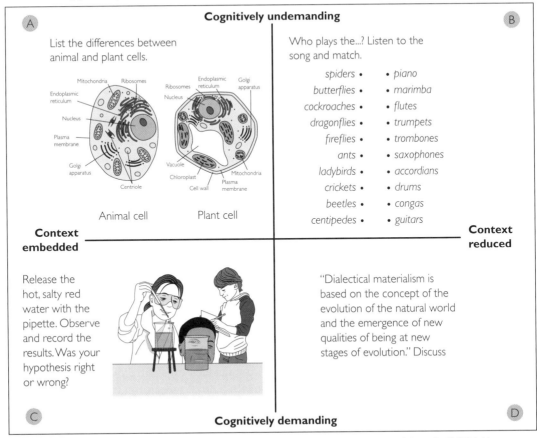

Figure 4.8 Four examples of learning in Cummins's matrix (adapted from Ball, 2014.)

The example learning moments in Figure 4.8 give us a good idea of the types of learning which fit in the corresponding zones of Cummins's matrix. Zone A has plenty of context (the illustrations of the cells) which allows learners to sort information (cognitively undemanding). Zone B provides little visual context (two lists) and has learners matching items (cognitively undemanding). Zone C has learners carrying out a practical laboratory activity which allows them to see and touch, and so context is embedded. However, they also have to predict what will happen, which is more cognitively demanding. Zone D has learners reading a quotation written in formal extended language which is distant from their everyday language experiences, and so context is reduced. Learners are then asked to discuss the quotation without using any other prompts, which is cognitively demanding.

This learning zones matrix lends itself to thinking further about the idea of including initial talk time at the beginning of a lesson sequence for learners to familiarize themselves with 'emergent' concepts. Initial talk time in a language chosen by the learners clearly fits into Zone A, as this is where cognitively undemanding and contextualized forms of learning take place. This kind of talk may have some features of BICS, but this does not suggest that talk in Zone A is exclusively BICS, since CALP is involved in any learning activity by default, and is therefore present throughout Cummins's matrix.

7 *Sequence activities from 'private' through to 'public'*

Focusing on talk over writing, at least initially, is a fundamental way of enabling learners to move at a pace which is slow enough for them to develop an understanding of the content 'in their own words' before attempting to use the 'standard' or 'school' language of learning (Roth, 2005; Gibbons, 2002). There is a need at this initial point for what is known as **'exploratory talk'** (Barnes, in Mercer & Hodgkinson, 2008), which gives learners the opportunity to 'explore' the content and, as Barnes puts it, 'talk themselves into understanding'.

Gibbons (2002) describes a clear sequence of activities which enable learners to have plenty of context. This helps them to formulate their understanding of the learning taking place and to express it in their own words. They can then move on through a series of activities, which culminate in a task that requires them to produce a piece of writing using standardized 'content language'. The key interest of Gibbons's sequence is that the initial focus is on talk in groups, which allows learners to share understanding with each other in their own 'language', i.e. their own private form of talk. This is followed by teacher talk in plenary, which allows the teacher to model the 'standard language' of the subject, whilst at the same time engaging with the learners' own self-worded contributions. This enables learners to take standard models from the teacher and/or from other students. Finally, learners produce a written version of this initial talk in the form of a report on what was done, utilizing as much standard subject language as possible. Gibbons (2002) describes this sequence of moving from talk to writing as a way for learners to take stock of what they have achieved through their own articulation of the content, before moving on to produce the written piece—the 'academic standard' of the learning. This strategic sequencing of activities, initiated by learner language, is also reflected in much of the literature on subject-specific teaching.

All of the above ideas are summarized in Table 4.15. It shows how learners move from the private and personal mode of learning to the public and subject-based. And we can see how the ideas move from being personal and informal to standardized and formal.

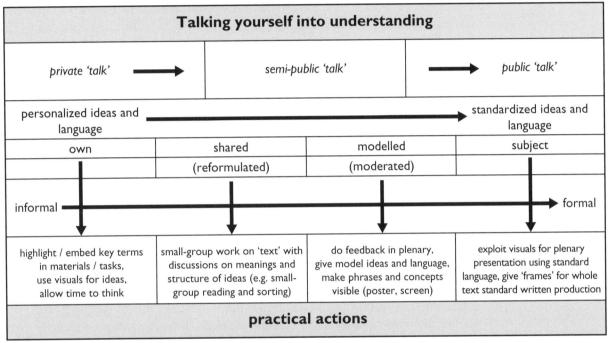

Table 4.15 *A visualization of moving from 'private talk' to 'public talk'*

Gibbons's continuum reminds us that learners coming to new learning invariably bring with them a language of their own to express this new knowledge. The challenge for teachers is to support the transition from private to public talk. Lee (2006) exemplifies the problematic contrast between the 'usual linguistic habits' of learners and textbook-based mathematics: 'You times the length by the width and you get the area.' versus 'The area of a rectangle is equal to the length multiplied by the width.' Lee refers to this latter language as 'the mathematics register' and points out that students are marked higher in course work if they use this standard conventional style. In daily life, people need everyday language to be able to access the meaning of the mathematics and its language, but in school mathematics, these words are not considered necessary in the conventional mathematical style.

Lee's example of 'personal' language versus 'public' content language has special relevance to CLIL. It is important in CLIL to sequence activities from 'private talk' to 'public talk' so that, as Lee puts it, learners can 'regenerate the missing information' in their own words. This results in a well thought-out movement from where the student is to where the school would like them to be. Perhaps most importantly for the CLIL classroom is the potential that this sequence offers for embedding a wide range of language-support instruments along the way. Specific instruments for supporting student output will be dealt with in detail in Chapter 6.

CLIL would also benefit from a modified version of Cummins's cognition–context matrix. In the matrix, language has an implicit presence everywhere along the cognition and context axes. It is not made explicit. This makes it difficult for content teachers to 'see' the language in order to make decisions about it, dismantle it, rework it into learner-friendly chunks, and build it back into lessons. To remedy this, we could add an extra visual element to Cummins's matrix for making the 'foreign language' more visible to the teacher. This would help teachers to plan sequences of learning with language challenges in mind, and in so doing give learners the support they need to make the transition from private to public language usage more easily.

This transition can also be seen from a whole-school perspective. Llinares et al. (2012) write about how language changes as children progress through each stage of schooling. They suggest that at entry to schooling aged six or seven, children are exposed predominantly to BICS (see Figure 4.9). The language of learning is the same as everyday language, and they have plenty of opportunities to communicate about their learning in their own language. As we saw in Chapter 3, as learners get older and progress through the curriculum, their learning becomes more CALP-orientated, and the language becomes more abstract and less immediate. The problem with this, as Llinares et al. (2012) stress, is that learners risk losing opportunities to talk about their own perspectives on what they are learning. This is a crucial argument where CLIL is concerned, because what we know about language learning tells us that in order to develop foreign-language skills, learners need opportunities to practise these skills. If higher school learning is predominantly CALP-orientated and limits the opportunities for learners to talk more informally, it risks reducing their opportunities for language practice.

International schools around the world, where learners are typically non-native speakers of English, frequently face this challenge. To take an example from the International Baccalaureate Middle Years Programme, a 15-year-old girl comes late into the programme, with conversational English and possibly some conceptual understanding in her L1. There is an **ELL (English language learner)** department responsible for supporting her, but it is too late to withdraw her completely for one-to-one tuition, as some schools do—particularly with later-arriving younger learners. The challenge therefore falls to the ELL department to attempt to support the student as she goes straight into content lessons taught through the medium of English. The classes lean more towards the CALP-heavy end of the continuum, and the BICS that the student is equipped with is not adequate for her to cope with the academic weight of this new curricular language. What this learner really needs is a mainstream subject teacher who can ensure that she gets opportunities to use both informal language, as well as CALP, to talk about new concepts in class.

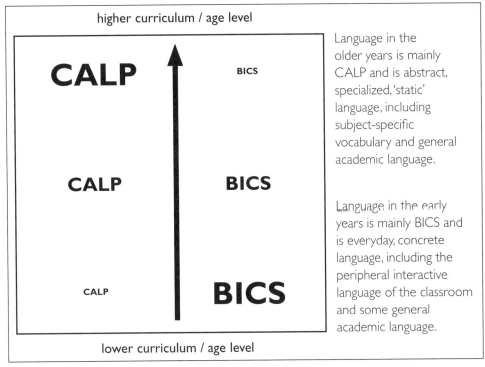

Figure 4.9 Layers of language in learning

There is one further danger associated with the predominance of CALP in the upper years of schooling. Not only do curriculum programmes which develop in this way run the risk of reducing opportunities for language skills development, but they may also move education too far from a focus on the <u>processes</u> of learning to a focus on the <u>products</u> of learning. Of course, this is not the case in all contexts. Nevertheless, the BICS–CALP dichotomy is one which requires us to be alert to the need for opportunities to use both kinds of language throughout the curriculum and age range, and to plan learners' academic language experience accordingly. In programmes which are CALP-heavy at the upper end of the school, CLIL demands opportunities for extra productive language practice. Simply put, even at the age of 18, if we want students learning science in an L2 to be able to use the language of science, they will need to be given opportunities to talk.

Summary

In this chapter, we have tried to identify and illustrate different layers of language (the subject-specific layer, the general academic layer, and the peripheral layer), the various characteristics of these layers, and their application in the CLIL classroom. The chapter has also explored the relationship between thinking and language in curriculum subjects, and the journey from BICS to CALP. The main focus of the chapter has been the presentation of seven principles regarding the types of teacher support necessary in CLIL learning contexts.

Task

If you would like to look at a practical task to explore your own practice related to the content of this chapter, see Appendix 1 (page 290).

Further reading

Cummins, J. (2000). *Language, power and pedagogy: Bilingual children in the crossfire.* Clevedon, UK: Multilingual Matters.
Chapter 3 (*Language proficiency in academic contexts*) and the explanation of BICS and CALP provide very useful background to understanding second language development in the school environment.

Gibbons, P. (2002). *Scaffolding language, scaffolding learning: Teaching second language learners in the mainstream classroom.* Portsmouth, NH: Heinemann.
An overall good read for teachers working through a second language, but Chapter 3 on sequencing learning (*From speaking to writing in the content classroom*) is particularly useful.

Llinares, A., Morton, T., & **Whittaker, R.** (2012). *The roles of language in CLIL.* Cambridge: Cambridge University Press.
Offers a description of how language and dynamic in education can change (from more active to more passive) through the school years, plus good argument for CLIL classroom practice which develops all language skills. See Chapter 1 (*Classroom registers and their impact on learning opportunity*).

Mohan, B. (1986). *Language and content.* Reading, MA: Addison Wesley.
Already recommended as a good investigation of the integration of language and content, but in addition, Chapter 2 (*A knowledge framework for activities*) gives a useful walk through example curriculum themes and the different types of thinking skills and the language needed for expressing them.

Smyth, G. (2003). *Helping bilingual pupils to access the curriculum.* Abingdon, UK: David Fulton Publishers.
Gives good argument for and examples of plotting language development through curriculum guidelines, and how this can be used in assessment. See Chapter 5 (*Learning support or language support?*) for examples of thinking skills and language plotted across curriculum subjects.

5 GUIDING INPUT

Overview

In this chapter, we will look at the CLIL teacher's role in terms of guiding learners through the demands of lesson input. 'Input demands' refer to the listening, watching, and reading skills required to complete a task in an L2. Faster spoken language usually increases the difficulty of understanding what is being said, and longer sentences with multiple clauses can make understanding written texts more challenging. These factors, and many others, can make the process of **decoding** and arriving at the correct meaning difficult for learners, particularly in a foreign language. This chapter offers a 'walk' through a series of exercise types that are particularly effective when teaching CLIL, and we will look specifically at **language-sensitive activities** which focus on developing learners' decoding skills. These activities focus on the linguistic aspects of content, whether it is lexical aspects at word level, or grammatical aspects at longer clause and sentence level. Decoding-skills activities will also highlight the various 'shapes' of subject content which enable the learner to visualize the way in which knowledge is structured.

Decoding and schemata

Good readers do two things simultaneously: they 'decipher' the symbols and the sound–symbol relationships that they represent, and then they associate this 'code' with meanings. Meanings associated with this code can be linked to background information already possessed—knowledge, experience, language—known as '**schemata**'. The dual processes of decoding and activating schemata work in unison to help good readers extract meaning from a text.

In the total-cloze activity in Materials extract 5.A, we can begin to decipher some of the text as it progresses from frames 1 to 4. In frame 2, for example, we can infer the likely grammatical classification of several missing words ('An [noun] is [verb] up of a [noun] of …'). A native speaker has an advantage, but a non-native speaker also possesses the same underlying grammatical knowledge, which can be exploited by the teacher. In the third frame, it becomes possible to apply some basic knowledge of the topic, or our 'schemata' in order to infer some quite specific vocabulary items from the topic.

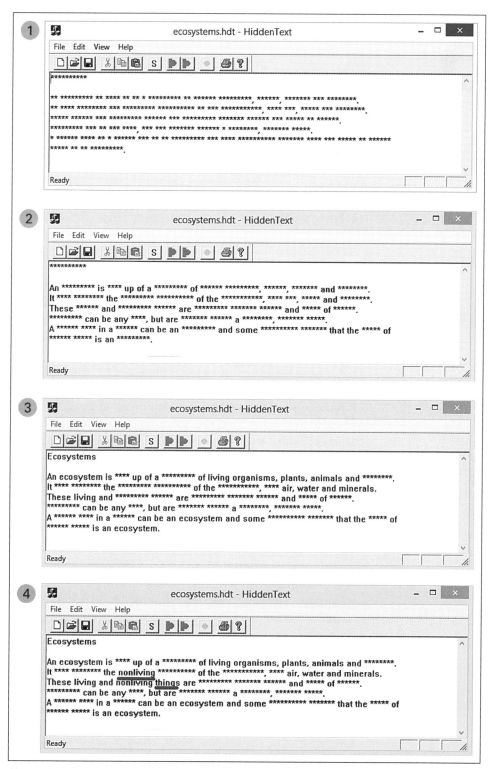

Materials extract 5.A Total-cloze software (http://www.factworld.info/en/Computer-CLIL-Materials-for-Computer)

Next, we can combine background knowledge with our decoding skills. Here, decoding refers to how words link together in sentences and how words collocate to form phrases like 'living and non-living things'. It is the abstract and idiomatic terms with very specific contextual meaning that are the most difficult to identify. However, the activity in Materials extract 5.A exemplifies how our eyes and brain work together when we confront a new text, bringing into use what we already know about the topic and our skill of inference to make sense of the text.

Like good readers, good listeners work in similar ways. Spoken language is also codified in ways that allow us to call on background information to help us with meaning. We may not be able to see the words that we are trying to process by decoding the corresponding sounds. But what we can see and gain meaning from is the context itself, and sometimes an interlocutor with whom we can interact.

Despite the differences between a written text and a spoken text, the concepts underlying the two forms tend to have the same structure, as we will show below. It is this 'shape' of content that lends itself so usefully to a CLIL approach. By exploiting the structural body of the information being presented, CLIL teachers can enable learners to use language to assimilate key ideas more easily.

Authenticity

In CLIL contexts, it is quite common for classes to use textbooks and videos on the internet intended for native speakers. All of this input may appear to be 'authentic', since it is intended for a native-speaker audience, but it may not be realistic or relevant to the NNS reader or listener. Geddes and White (1978) suggested that teachers aim for 'approaching authenticity', because in doing so, they can bring the characteristics of real-world speech into the classroom. CLIL can also offer authenticity of 'response' and 'interaction', since geographers, physicists, or mathematicians tend to be doing the same 'authentic' kind of work. In a classroom context, therefore, we can refer to activities which are authentic to the world of geography, physics, mathematics, etc. For example, where a discussion follows a text on global warming and where learners are investigating factors of life on Earth affected by the phenomenon, both the reading and the discussion can be said to be authentic to geography, because this is precisely what geographers do.

This question of authenticity is under constant debate. Widdowson (1979) argued for a consideration of the distinction between 'genuineness' and 'authenticity'. According to Widdowson, a text is genuine if it displays the language characteristics typical of the genre it belongs to. In contrast, a text is authentic if it relates appropriately to the task and the kind of interaction and response that occurs. This is a useful distinction for CLIL-based practice: as it never considers the issue of language in isolation, it can place all emphasis on the task.

'Shapes' of subject content

By its very nature, subject content is different from the kind of material characteristic of language-teaching textbooks. Although a language textbook may include a unit on global warming, the language of the unit remains the objective, rather than the concepts. It is also the language that is being illustrated through the topic which forms the basis of the assessment, not the other way round. In a curriculum textbook for science on the same topic (global warming), the focus of the learning will be squarely on the conceptual and the procedural content. While there may be some overlap of concept and language in both cases, a language learner is unlikely to be assessed on the physical processes of the greenhouse effect and global warming. A language lesson might focus on how global warming works, in order to create the context for a discussion of its effects on our daily lives. However, the assessment will be on the language of cause and effect, as opposed to the deeper scientific aspects of global warming.

The science student, on the other hand, is expected to be able to explain the processes of global warming, discuss the causes and effects of those processes, and suggest solutions to the problem. The language of the physical process of global warming will need explicit handling in the classroom. The 'shape' of the content is embedded in the illustration of the process of global warming (see Figure 5.1). The process language will be sequenced by discourse markers for each stage. The different stages will be connected in terms of their cause-and-effect relationship, represented by arrows or similar symbols, and learners of science will need to have a grasp of this cause-and-effect language for the purposes of describing the process. It makes sense for teachers to exploit the shapes and symbols for the purpose of guiding the learner through the input.

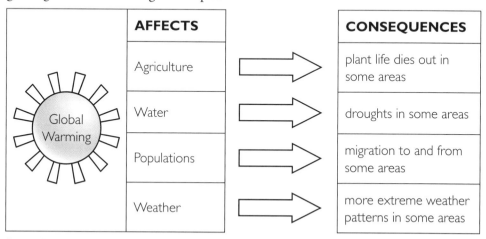

Figure 5.1 How global warming affects life on Earth

Language learners are more likely to be expected to discuss how the phenomenon of global warming affects their lives and life on Earth in general, as shown in Figure 5.2, rather than specific physical aspects of the process of global warming.

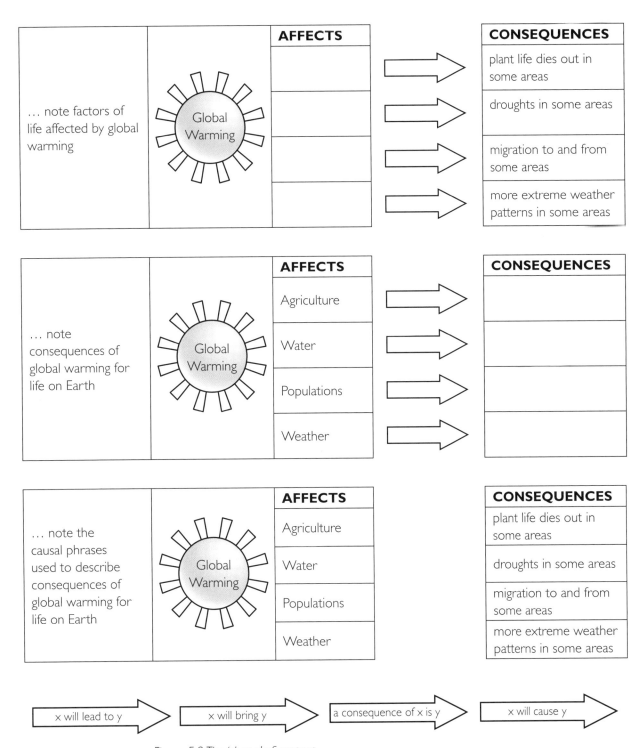

Figure 5.2 The 'shape' of content

Whereas language students need the language of causation to carry out a discussion of the effects of global warming on their lives, and some additional language to explain those effects, science students need the academic discourse of science. Here are four sentences on global warming, derived from Figure 5.1 (on page 106):

- A consequence of global warming on agriculture is that plant life dies out in some areas.
- As for water, global warming will lead to droughts in some areas.
- Where populations are concerned, global warming will cause migration to and from some areas.
- In terms of the weather, global warming will bring more extreme weather patterns in some areas.

The causes and consequences of global warming can be expressed using a flow diagram, where a cell presenting a factor of life on Earth affected by global warming is connected via an arrow to a cell presenting the consequences of global warming on this factor. This is typical of much process description in expository genre texts like the one in Figure 5.1 (see Chapter 7 of Hudson (2007) for a discussion on genre and language). Input content may be presented in written form on a textbook page, as an animation embedded within a slideshow, or as an image on a screen accompanied by a short monologue description in the style of a short lecture given by the teacher to the class. The illustration in Figure 5.2 can represent the 'shape' of the content in each case. For the purposes of guiding learners through content input, it makes a lot of sense for teachers to exploit support structures in this way. In both Figures 5.1 and 5.2, it would be very helpful for learners to be provided with the illustration to annotate when reading and note-taking, when watching the animation and listening for key information, or when following the teacher's monologue. Learners can read/watch/listen and decipher the 'code' of the text/slideshow/monologue by focusing on key aspects of content and language.

What CLIL teachers need is a familiarity with the 'shape' and organization of the content they are offering to learners on a daily basis. This 'semi-script' (Geddes & White, 1978) gives a logical, visible structure to input as a whole, summarizes key ideas, and acts as a basis for highlighting key language for the learner.

What we offer in this chapter is an inventory of content-input types from a number of subjects, with suggestions on particular structures teachers can use to help learners listen, watch, or read new input content. It is by no means a complete list, but it serves as a good starting point for teachers who are striving to familiarize themselves with the shapes of their content-area input.

An inventory of input-processing activity types

Directed activities related to texts, or **DARTs** (see Davies & Greene, 1984), refers to a concerted effort in science education to help learners deal actively with the science texts they were being asked to read. However, this principle of active reading is relevant to all subjects. The following inventory of text-based activity types is a useful checklist for teachers to use when developing active reading strategies.

It is important to differentiate between activities which require learners to focus on language and structure within a text—referred to as 'reconstruction DARTs'—and those which require learners to focus on the subject content, referred to as 'analysis DARTs' (Wellington & Osborne, 2001). The activities presented here start with a reconstruction focus at the lower word-and-phrase level and move up to whole-text processing with more content-analysis focus. There is likely to be a variety of types of interaction with text in a classroom where NNS learners are working through the medium of an L2. On the one hand, subject teachers may feel they need to focus learner attention on individual items of vocabulary or grammar within a reading text for the purpose of learning new terminology or practising common structures. On the other hand, as suggested in the introduction, it is never a good idea to offer isolated text work in a CLIL classroom only for this purpose. Wherever teachers use text material with a language focus, it should ideally occur within a sequence of other related activities which build up to a meaningful task (see Chapter 7).

Processing at the level of words and phrases

Activity type 1: Gap-fill or 'cloze'

Gap-fill activities are a good way to reinforce vocabulary that has already been encountered elsewhere. They can allow students to use the vocabulary in a variety of contexts. The exercises can be worked on in class, either individually or in pairs, or can be assigned as homework to be quickly reviewed in class the next day.

Gap-fill, or 'cloze', activities are one method of focusing on the aspects of language that teachers wish to make salient, highlighting words and phrases for a specific purpose. In Materials extract 5.B, the text focuses on the action verbs which describe process. As we have already seen in Chapter 4, academic vocabulary gets less attention than subject-specific vocabulary, and it can be useful for learners to see how these verbs work in the discourse context.

Activity type 2: Matching terms and definitions

Matching terms with definitions gives learners familiarity with the terms in context, as well as exposure to standard examples of formal subject language in the definitions. After this initial encounter with the terms, presenting them in this way again later on gives learners the opportunity to consolidate their understanding of them.

In Materials extract 5.C (on page 111), the key terms are accompanied by an illustration. The language here is more spatially represented—for example, 'either of the two bones that go from the base of the neck to the shoulders'—so that the reading becomes more strategic on the part of the student. The teacher can model one description in plenary and then ask the students to complete the rest.

Metabolism

Read the text and fill the gaps with the words and phrases from the list. There is one phrase too many.

break down	build	keep	make	obtain	collect
play some part	slow down	speed up	take place		

Your body is a chemical factory. At any moment, up to 1,000 different chemical reactions (1) _____ inside every cell. Together, these reactions are called metabolism.

They each (2) _____ in keeping you alive and well. So, metabolism is all the chemical reactions necessary for life.

Metabolism will (3) _____ when you are active and (4) _____ when you sleep. Basal metabolism is the slowest metabolism needed to (5) _____ you alive. There are two types of metabolism.

Catabolism is the breakdown of complex molecules into simpler ones, resulting in the release of energy. All living things (6) _____ energy by a type of catabolism called respiration. This uses oxygen to (7) _____ glucose sugar into carbon dioxide, water, and energy.

Anabolism is the opposite of catabolism. Anabolism uses energy from catabolism to (8) _____ complex molecules from simpler ones. For example, energy is needed to (9) _____ starch out of glucose, and proteins from amino acids.

Materials extract 5.B Gap-fill or 'cloze' activity (adapted from Beckett & Gallagher, New coordinated science: Biology, OUP, p. 90.)

Activity type 3: Matching 'heads and tails'

The 'heads and tails' activity in Materials extract 5.D (on page 112) asks learners to match beginnings and endings of sentences. It is a simple way of getting them to read at sentence level and look at the cohesive language that connects ideas. In this extract, all the sentences use the conjunction 'because', a tactic which forces students to focus exclusively on the topic content of the sentence predicates to the right.

There are other sentence structures which can be divided in this way and exploited to create a 'heads and tails' reading activity. Most sentences which are made up of two clauses connected with a conjunction, such as 'whereas' or 'while', can be adapted to this activity type. It also works with conditional sentences with 'if', or sentences with a causal verb phrase like 'leads to'. Activity type 4 (see below) matches texts, but with no accompanying sentence structure, so that learners have to construct the appropriate sentences themselves, once they have done the matching. If desired, teachers can incorporate model sentences of the subject standard within a reading-and-matching activity.

More about the human skeleton

Match the terms with their definitions. Write the numbers in the correct places.

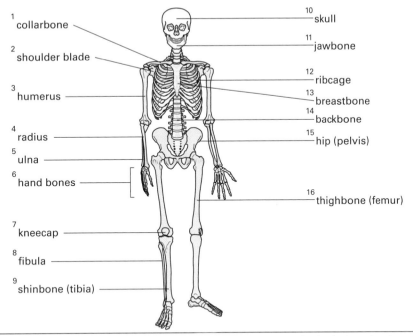

1 collarbone
2 shoulder blade
3 humerus
4 radius
5 ulna
6 hand bones
7 kneecap
8 fibula
9 shinbone (tibia)
10 skull
11 jawbone
12 ribcage
13 breastbone
14 backbone
15 hip (pelvis)
16 thighbone (femur)

	the bone structure that forms the head and surrounds and protects the brain (cranium)
	either of the two bones that go from the base of the neck to the shoulders (clavicle)
	either of the two large flat bones at the top of the back (scapula)
	the large bone in the top part of the arm between the shoulder and the elbow
	the shorter bone of the two bones in the lower part of the arm between the elbow and the wrist, on the same side as the thumb
	the longer bone of the two bones in the lower part of the arm between the elbow and the wrist, on the side opposite the thumb
	the small bone that covers the front of the knee (patella)
	the outer bone of the two bones in the lower part of the leg between the knee and the ankle
	the front part of the leg below the knee
	the bone that forms the lower jaw (mandible)
	the structure of curved bones (called ribs) that surrounds and protects the chest
	the long flat bone in the chest that the seven top pairs of ribs are connected to (sternum)
	the row of small bones that are connected together down the middle of the back (spine)
	the area at either side of the body between the top of the leg and the waist; the joint at the top of the leg
	the thigh bone

Materials extract 5.C Matching terms and definitions (adapted from Beckett & Gallagher, New coordinated science: Biology, OUP, p. 84; definitions from Oxford Advanced Learner's Dictionary, www.oxfordlearnersdictionaries.com.)

Exercise 15.4

The invention of the printing press was a very important step forward in technology. What were its results?
The sentences below have been split in half. Join together the halves that fit, and write out the complete sentences.

First half

- Monks could spend their time on other work because . . .
- Books became more plentiful and cheaper because . . .
- More people were able to own books because . . .
- More people wanted to learn to read because . . .
- There were soon more schools because . . .
- Men and women learned more about the outside world because . . .

Second half

- they were cheaper to buy
- parents realised that reading and writing were important.
- they were not needed to copy out books by hand.
- they could read about it in books.
- they could now afford to buy books, and wanted to be able to read them.
- it took much less time to produce them.

Materials extract 5.D Matching sentence 'heads and tails' (Robson, Medieval Britain, OUP, p. 80.)

Activity type 4: Matching headings to paragraphs and visuals

It is quite common for concepts to be presented with illustrations and explanations in subject-based textbooks. Materials extract 5.E helps learners consolidate key vocabulary, and it also familiarizes them with the standard language of the explanations. It is a good idea to do an activity like the one in this extract after an initial introduction to the topic involving visual input on the screen and a monologue from the teacher. This enables learners—in pairs or in small groups—to talk privately about the terms and descriptions in order to consolidate their initial understanding of the concepts.

It is quite possible to use this activity type in other ways. It would suit a computer-based activity involving learners moving items to fit them together in the correct places. It is also possible to use this activity type as a hands-on read-and-sort activity whereby learners are given cut-up images, headings, and descriptions which they must then arrange into the correct horizontal sequences.

Flooding

Draw lines to connect the headings with a paragraph and a picture.

Heavy rain	Soggy soil
Built-up areas	Steep slopes
Impermeable rock	The flat flood plain
Loss of trees	Tributaries

Flooding is mainly caused by this.
Concrete is not permeable. So rain can't soak through it. Instead it flows down the drains. Then it goes into the river. Streets flood quickly if the drains are blocked.
Trees help to prevent flooding. Roots take in water from the soil. Leaves catch rain. If you cut down trees, there may be more flooding.
The flood plain around the river is flat. When the water level rises, the river floods.
Heavy rain makes the soil soggy. If the soil is soggy, the rain doesn't soak away.
On a steep slope, rain can't soak through the ground. Instead it runs down the slope.
Tributaries increase water in the river. So it is more likely to flood.
Rain can't soak through impermeable rock. Instead, it runs over the ground.

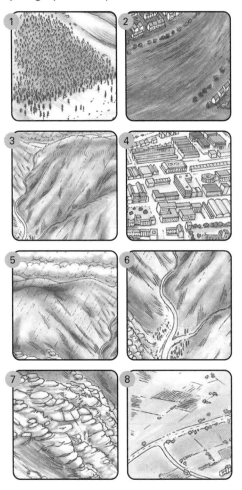

Materials extract 5.E Matching text to visuals (adapted from Clegg & Kelly, Geog.1 EAL Workbook, OUP, p 59.)

Activity type 5: Joining two lists

It is important to differentiate this activity type from Activity type 3, in which all of the sentence parts are given. This activity type, exemplified in Materials extract 5.F (overleaf), fits ideally into a lesson sequence immediately after a clear and explicit focus on the structure needed to complete the sentences in the activity. Again, it makes sense for learners to do this alone before checking in pairs, followed by a plenary feedback with the class.

Population changes

For each change in list 1, choose the likely result(s) from list 2.

1	Changes in a country
a	Everyone gets better food to eat.
b	A terrible war breaks out.
c	A deadly disease spreads.
d	There is a severe famine.
e	More hospitals and doctors are provided.
f	Birth control pills are provided.
g	More and more women get good jobs.

2	Possible results
A	Death rate rises.
B	Death rate falls.
C	Birth rate rises.
D	Birth rate falls.
E	No effect on birth or death rates.

Materials extract 5.F Joining lists (adapted from Gallagher & Parish, Geog.2, OUP, p.65.)

The next step of the activity in Materials extract 5.F asks learners to write their answers as hypothetical sentences, using the words 'if' and 'then': 'If everyone gets better food to eat, then …'. The activity focuses learners on the structure likely to be produced in this context. It lends itself to a paired speaking stage in a lesson sequence, drilling the structure. Having learners talk in pairs about possible connections between the two lists also gives them 'personal' time to sort through their ideas.

Activity type 6: Reading a text and labelling a diagram/map

This kind of **information-transfer** activity can be used effectively during the middle of a lesson sequence after initial introductions, practical presentations, and after any modelling of vocabulary or structures by the teacher and/or other learners.

In Materials extract 5.G, it is useful to think of the diagram of the respiratory system as a 'visual organization' of the key ideas in the linear text. In this way, the read-and-label activity is a type of information transfer. Activities like this help learners to select relevant phrases according to both the sense of the sentences in the text and the accompanying diagram. They can look for clues, such as repetition, paraphrasing, and location, in both of these.

The respiratory system

Read the explanations below in order to label the diagram with the words or phrases in bold. Write the corresponding numbers into the sentences on the diagram.

1   **pleural membrane**: a thin layer of skin that surrounds and protects the lungs

2   **diaphragm**: muscle between the lungs and the stomach, used to control breathing

3   **thorax** or thoracic cavity: part of the body that is surrounded by the ribs, between the neck and the waist

4   **cartilage**: the strong white tissue that is important in support and especially in joints to prevent the bones rubbing against each other

5   **larynx**: the area at the top of the throat that contains the vocal cords

6   **ribs**: any of the curved bones that are connected to the spine and surround the chest

7   **intercostal muscles**: muscles located between the ribs

8   **trachea**: the tube in the throat that carries air to the lungs

9   **alveoli** or air sacs: tiny spaces in each lung where gases pass into or out of the blood

10 **lungs**: the pair of spongy, air-filled organs in the chest that you use for breathing

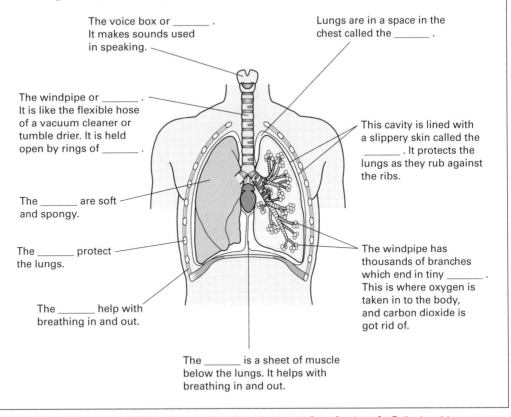

The voice box or _____ . It makes sounds used in speaking.

Lungs are in a space in the chest called the _____ .

The windpipe or _____ . It is like the flexible hose of a vacuum cleaner or tumble drier. It is held open by rings of _____ .

This cavity is lined with a slippery skin called the _____ . It protects the lungs as they rub against the ribs.

The _____ are soft and spongy.

The _____ protect the lungs.

The windpipe has thousands of branches which end in tiny _____ . This is where oxygen is taken in to the body, and carbon dioxide is got rid of.

The _____ help with breathing in and out.

The _____ is a sheet of muscle below the lungs. It helps with breathing in and out.

Materials extract 5.G Reading and labelling (adapted from Beckett & Gallagher, New coordinated science: Biology, OUP, p. 91.)

Activity type 7a: Reading and answering questions

Questions can take the simple comprehension form, with an open answer, or the multiple-choice form, with a limited number of possible answers to choose from (see Activity type 7b below). There is, of course, a role for comprehension questions in CLIL. In Materials extract 5.H, the activity has been designed to make students infer the answers by obliging them to first understand the diagram. So in question (b), learners must understand that 'married' refers to 'wife', and in (d) that Henry's son was Edward, etc. The answers required here are short, single items, but in other cases longer, fuller answers may be required. Where learners are expected to give explanations as part of their answers, there may be a need for learners to receive some additional support. This support may be in the form of model answers or word lists. Other ideas for supporting the writing of answers to comprehension questions are presented in Chapter 6.

Activity type 7b: Multiple-choice questions

In Materials extract 5.H, learners have everything they need to answer the questions on the page, and so it is entirely possible to use this type of activity as an introduction to a new topic. In Materials extract 5.I (on page 118), on the other hand, there is clearly a need for learners to understand the specific terminology used in the questions, and so this activity would need to come later in a lesson sequence. But in both cases, the activities are good for presenting standard language in context.

In Materials extract 5.I, the multiple-choice answers serve as a way of modelling standard sentences from the subject. For example, the infinitive structure ('To counter the weight of the load') follows a question with the verb 'need' (question 1). 'If' clauses are also very common in physics, particularly when questions are framed by a hypothesis (question 2). There are also specific, low-frequency vocabulary items such as 'counterbalance', 'load', and 'movable'. (See Chapter 7 for more discussion on embedding language in activities, and Chapter 6 for specific examples.)

Activity type 8: Reading a text and filling in a chart/table

Materials extract 5.J (on page 119) shows an example of an information-transfer reading activity. This type of activity requires learners to read in order to transfer key information from a linear text to a form of diagrammatical organization— in this case, a table. In order to be helpful, the table or chart must in some way summarize or categorize the contents of the text. (See Chapter 7 for more on what we call the 'text–task relationship'.) The activity in this extract makes sense in a lesson sequence where learners have already been presented with background information on food groups in some form, for example via video, slideshow presentation, animation, **realia** show-and-tell, etc. The completed table offers a summary of the key ideas and information, and a logical follow-up step would be to have learners working in pairs on spoken output. This may take the form of preparing to present one row of the table to the rest of the class.

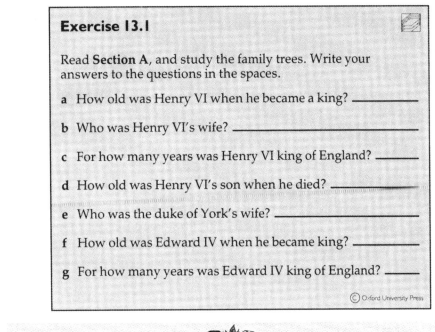

Exercise 13.1

Read **Section A**, and study the family trees. Write your answers to the questions in the spaces.

a How old was Henry VI when he became a king? _____

b Who was Henry VI's wife? _____

c For how many years was Henry VI king of England? _____

d How old was Henry VI's son when he died? _____

e Who was the duke of York's wife? _____

f How old was Edward IV when he became king? _____

g For how many years was Edward IV king of England? _____

© Oxford University Press

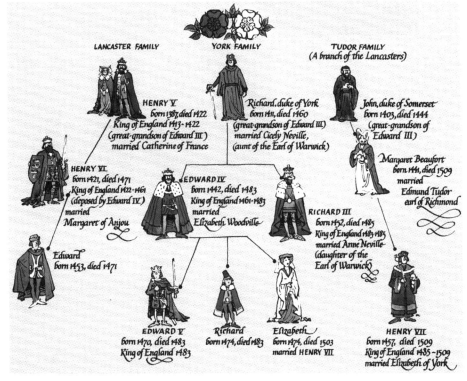

Materials extract 5.H Reading and answering questions (Robson, Medieval Britain, OUP, pp. 65–66.)

Moments

The diagram below shows a model crane. The crane has a movable counterbalance. Read the questions and choose the best answer from those given.

1 Why does the crane need a counterbalance?

   a To counter the weight of the load

   b To combine the weight of the load

   c To collect the weight of the load

2 Why does the counterbalance need to be movable?

   a If it is movable, different loads can be carried.

   b If it is movable, unlimited loads can be carried.

   c If it is movable, only heavy loads can be carried.

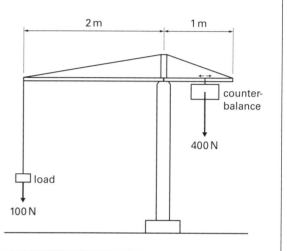

Materials extract 5.I Multiple-choice questions (adapted from Beckett & Gallagher, New coordinated science: Physics, OUP, p. 52.)

Activity type 9: Reading a text and sequencing sentences

Asking learners to put jumbled sentences from a text into the correct chronological order helps them to see and understand connections between the ideas in the text. In Materials extract 5.K (on page 120), the sentences are accompanied by an original text which learners must read in order to make decisions about the correct order of the sentences. This kind of reading helps learners think about whole-text coherence. The original text uses cohesive devices which also facilitate the linking of the steps in the sequence. Some examples of these devices are: 'but', 'at once', 'while', 'as soon as', 'again', 'by the end of the day', 'just two months later'.

The read-and-sequence activity in Materials extract 5.K (on page 120) would come after an introduction and towards the middle of a lesson sequence. Focusing on the events leading up to the Battle of Hastings gives learners a summary of important factors, whilst at the same time presenting standard structures for describing similar historical narratives. These structures may then be actively used for output production later in the lesson.

Types of food and their composition

Fill in the table by reading the following text.

The five types of food are carbohydrates, proteins, fats and oils, minerals, and vitamins.

Carbohydrates: These are sugary and starchy foods such as sweet fruits, honey, jam, bread, cakes, potatoes, rice, and spaghetti. Carbohydrates are the main source of energy for living things. One gram yields about 17kJ of energy. Most carbohydrates are converted by the body into glucose before they are respired. Plants store large quantities of starch in their seeds and in storage organs like potato tubers. In animals, the main carbohydrate food reserve is glycogen, which is similar to starch. Animals can store only limited amounts of glycogen. When this limit is exceeded, any excess carbohydrate is changed into fat or oil, and is then stored in the body.

Fats and oils: These are also called lipids, and include butter, lard, suet, dripping, and olive and cod-liver oil. These are important sources of energy because 1g of lipid can yield up to 38kJ of energy when respired. But they are less easily digested than other foods, which reduces their energy value a little. Fats are very important food reserves in animals and plants, firstly because each gram contains twice the energy of other foods, and secondly because layers of fatty tissue, especially under the skin of animals, insulate the body against loss of heat.

Proteins: The most important sources of protein are meat, liver, kidney, eggs, fish, and beans. These foods supply the raw materials livings need for growth, and for repair of damaged and worn out tissues. Proteins are not usually respired for energy, but when this happens they can yield up to 17kJ of energy per gram. Proteins are digested into chemicals called amino acids. There are about 26 of these, but only ten, called the essential amino acids, are needed by humans. Our bodies can make the rest. Animal proteins contain all ten essential amino acids and so are called first-class proteins. No plant protein contains all the essential amino acids, so they are called second-class proteins. But all ten can be obtained by eating a wide variety of plant foods. A vegetarian diet can be extremely healthy because it does not usually contain much fat, oil, sugar, or salt, and is high in dietary fibre.

Vitamins: Vitamins have no energy value but are essential for growth and health. Some are needed in very small amounts—less than one millionth of a gram a day. Vitamins take part in vital chemical reactions in the body, usually in conjunction with proteins.

Minerals: You require about 15 different minerals in your diet. Like vitamins, they have no energy value, but are essential for health. Most essential minerals are supplied by a diet of meat, eggs, milk, green vegetables, and fruit.

Food group	Source	Benefits

Materials extract 5.J Reading a text and filling in a chart/table (adapted from Beckett & Gallagher, New coordinated science: Biology, OUP, pp. 120–121.)

The Battle of Hastings

Read the text and put the sentences into the correct sequence by adding numbers.

A south wind blew in the English Channel on 29 September 1066. It took a fleet of little ships across the sea from France to England. They were packed with knights, archers, and horses. Duke William of Normandy was on his way to England.

King Harold of England was waiting with his army in Sussex (look at the map). But then he heard that the King of Norway had invaded the north of England. Harold marched his men north at once, and defeated the Norwegians in a battle near York.

While Harold was in the north, Duke William and his army landed in Sussex. As soon as Harold heard the news, he rushed south again. But he moved too fast for some of his men. He reached Sussex with only half his army.

The English and the Normans met in battle near Hastings on 14 October 1066. It was a long, hard fight, which the Normans won. By the end of the day, Harold and all his bodyguards lay dead. Just two months later, William was crowned king of England. We now call him William the Conqueror.

___ King Harold rushed south.

___ Duke William and his army landed in Sussex.

___ King Harold heard that the King of Norway was invading the north of England.

___ Harold and his bodyguards died.

___ Harold defeated the Norwegians near York.

___ William was crowned King of England.

___ The English and Normans fought a battle at Hastings on 14 October 1066.

___ William of Normandy crossed to England on 28 September 1066.

___ The Normans won.

___ Harold marched his men north.

___ He lost half his army.

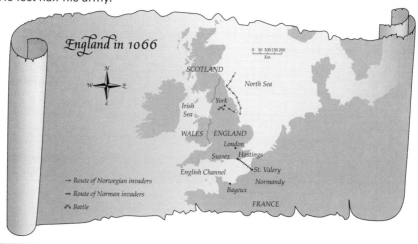

Materials extract 5.K Reading a text and sequencing sentences (adapted from Robson, Medieval Britain, OUP, p. 4.)

Activity type 10: Reading a text and sorting cards

In textbooks, a lot of subject content is presented in linear text form for learners to read and answer questions. A CLIL approach tends to exploit the very structure of the ideas in the text for the purpose of supporting the learners' reading of the text by breaking it down into smaller component parts (see Mohan (1986) on the 'knowledge framework'). A read-and-sort activity lends itself to the initial small-group discussion stage of a lesson sequence. This would involve groups discussing the content and reaching a consensus on how to sort the information into the categories provided. This small-group discussion is a very important stage which enables learners to formulate their own initial understanding of the concepts they are being asked to consider.

It is a simple step to turn any text into a read-and-sort activity once you have identified a generic structure in the ideas—a structure reflected in the categories of the three columns in the example in Materials extract 5.L (overleaf). This text describes alternative forms of energy and their advantages and disadvantages, which lend themselves to tabular organization. Teachers can write out any text in separated, tabular form, prepare a sorting sheet (with or without the headings, as students could be asked to provide the headings), then print off the table and chop up the cards. Learners then work in small groups, discussing the content of the cards and agreeing on how to arrange the information into the table.

Activity type 11: Reading and making notes

Activities where learners read and make notes provide a transition from lower-level word- and phrase-focused activities to 'content analysis'. In this way, learners move on to the stage of production work. The notes taken from the reading shown in Materials extract 5.M (on page 123) would lend themselves to preparing to speak or write on the topic at a later stage in the lesson sequence.

As with the card-sorting activity, the main ideas in Materials extract 5.M (on page 123) lend themselves to a certain type of structuring which can be seen in Materials extract 5.N (on page 124). In this case, the structure provides a note-taking frame where the information patterns of the texts can be reduced to partial-sentence gaps. Learners scan the 'Glaciers at work' text and complete the sentences.

Content analysis of whole texts

The later activity types outlined above require learners to process content by organizing key ideas. Several of the activity types employ a generic content structure as a basis for supporting learners through the reading activity. Activity types 8 and 10 both use tables for abstracting and presenting the characteristics of certain phenomena. Activity type 9 uses a chronological sequence which could be accompanied by a timeline or a flow diagram, with each event plotted in a particular order. Activity type 11 offers a note-taking frame, which follows the way the ideas are presented in the original text.

Alternative energy sources

Read the texts and arrange the cards into the table.

Alternative energy sources	Description	For	Against
Wind energy **Hydroelectric energy**	Giant wind turbines turn electrical generators. Wind turbines can be placed in a large group called a wind farm.	Renewable energy source.	Aerogenerators large, costly and noisy, with relatively low power output. Not enough wind in many areas.
Tidal energy **Wave energy**	Rivers fill a lake behind a dam. Fast-flowing water from the lake turns generators.	Renewable energy source.	Few areas of the world suitable.
Solar energy **Nuclear energy**	A dam is built across an estuary. A lake behind the dam fills up at high tide, and empties at low tide. Fast-flowing water turns generators.	Renewable energy source.	Very expensive to set up; few areas suitable.
Geothermal energy **Biomass energy**	Generators are driven by the up and down motion of waves at sea.	Renewable energy source.	Difficult to build successfully.
	Mirrors and panels are used to capture the Sun's radiant energy – usually heat.	Renewable energy source.	Continuous sunshine needed.
	Radioactive materials naturally release heat. A nuclear reactor speeds up the process. The heat is used to generate electricity.	Small amounts of nuclear fuel give large amounts of energy.	Nuclear radiation extremely dangerous. High safety standards needed. Waste materials from power stations stay radioactive for thousands of years.
	Water is heated by the hot rocks which lie many miles beneath the Earth's surface. The heat in the rocks comes from radioactive materials naturally present in the Earth.	Renewable energy source. Huge quantities of energy available.	Deep drilling very difficult and expensive.
	Fast-growing plants, or biomass, used to make alcohol. Alcohol used as a fuel, like petrol.	Renewable energy source.	Huge land areas needed to grow plants; this may upset the balance of nature.

Materials extract 5.L Reading and sorting (adapted from Pople, New coordinated science: Physics, OUP, p. 69.)

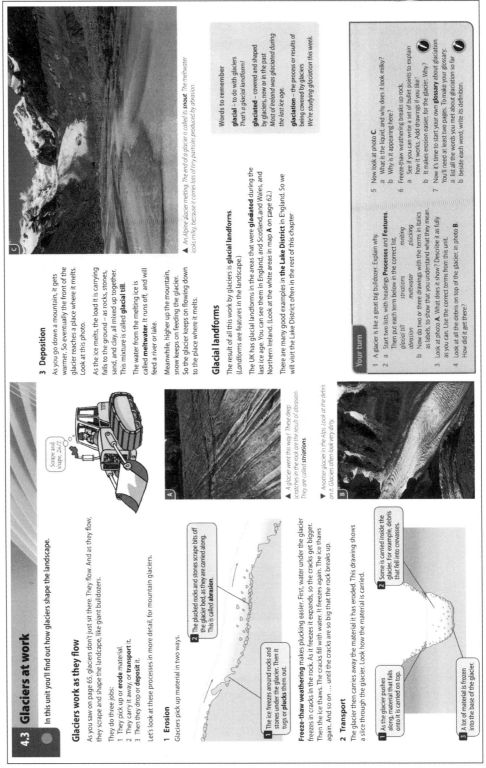

Materials extract 5.M Reading and making notes (Gallagher et al., Geog.1, OUP, pp. 66–67.)

The work of glaciers

Read the section on 'Glaciers at work' and make notes in the frame below.

1 Erosion

   i)   The glacier plucks ....

   ii)   Abrasion is where ....

   iii)   Freeze–thaw weathering helps by ....

2 Transport

   The glacier carries ....

   i)   .... on top of the glacier.

   ii)   .... in the crevasses.

   iii)   .... in the base of the glacier.

3 Deposition

   The glacier melts as it ....

   As the glacier melts, ...

   Glacial 'till' is ....

   Meltwater is ....

Result

   The result of all this work by glaciers is ....

Materials extract 5.N Reading and making notes activity

Concept mapping

We saw a concept map—'The human organism'—in Chapter 4 (see Materials extract 4.B on page 77) which presented learners with a summary of the key vocabulary items and general academic language for the topic. Similar to text maps or knowledge maps (O'Donnell et al., 2002), the advantage of concept maps like these is that they generate an overview of the key notions and language in a given area, which are not always evident or visible to learners.

The concept map is useful for processing input content. In a context where learners are faced with a linear text or teacher monologue, an incomplete concept map (as opposed to the complete version in Materials extract 4.B) allows the learners to focus on specific aspects of the input, with a view to completing the visual.

Buzan (1996) offers learners the 'mind map' and a range of tools which the user can manipulate to develop 'radiant thinking' and personalize a summary of content being learned, using not only structure and shape but also colour, images, and sound. It is important to point out the difference between giving learners a pre-prepared generic structure and asking them to produce their own personalized mind map. Learners need ample opportunity to create their own visualizations of content, especially in the later stages of a learning sequence. This is a fundamental strategy for developing effective thinking skills and **graphic literacy** (Cortazzi et al., 1998). But at the earliest stage of a sequence, the structure offered is generic for the whole class, and is based on the size and shape of the original content, not on learner preferences.

Presenting a 'standard' diagrammatical representation of content at the beginning of a lesson allows teachers to be sure that everyone is starting from the same point, particularly if such a concept map is presented in plenary. Personalized mind maps, however, are precisely that—personal—and although one mind map may be ideal for one learner, it is unlikely to be a valid 'visualization' of content for another, let alone for an entire class of learners with individual learning styles and preferences. Standardized input diagrams, visuals, and frames are useful at initial stages of lesson sequences because they get everyone started together, whereas personalized mind maps are more applicable to later stages, when each learner's understanding of a concept has developed further.

Tables

A widely used organizational structure in education is the table. Tabular information represents 'the attribution of characteristics to phenomena' or 'attribution thinking' (Burgess, 1994). Tables, or grids, present different phenomena, types, objects, or items in each column, with the attributes or criteria of these in the header row.

Materials extract 5.O shows a table listing types of metals and their relative reactivity with oxygen. A simple yet interactive listening–reading activity would involve learners working in pairs to sort text cards with the descriptors into the correct places in a blank version of the table (see Materials extract 5.P overleaf).

Metal	Behaviour when heated in air	Order of reactivity	Product
Sodium	Catches fire with only a little heating. Burns with a bright yellow flame	most reactive	Sodium peroxide, Na_2O_2 a pale yellow powder
Magnesium	Catches fire easily. Burns with a blinding white flame		Magnesium oxide, MgO a white powder
Iron	Does not burn, but the hot metal glows and gives off yellow sparks		Iron oxide, Fe_3O_4 a black powder
Copper	Does not burn, but the hot metal becomes coated with a black substance		Copper oxide, CuO a black powder
Gold	No reaction, no matter how much the	least reactive	————

Materials extract 5.O Metals and their reactivity (Gallagher & Ingram, New coordinated science: Chemistry, OUP, p. 66.)

Once the texts have been sorted, the learner pairs listen to a teacher monologue on the topic and check their tables. This would give learners ample exposure to formal, full, spoken descriptions based on the shorter form in the tables, for example: 'Sodium is the most reactive of the metals and catches fire with only a little heating. It burns with a bright yellow flame. Sodium peroxide is a product of the reaction.'

Metal	Behaviour when heated in air	Order of reactivity	Product
		most reactive	
		⬆	
		least reactive	

Materials extract 5.P Blank table for completion

The language in such tables (see Materials extract 5.Q) often includes an unusual number of adjectives/adjectival phrases ('fixed', 'regular', 'random', 'close together', 'far apart', 'strong', 'weaker') and nouns/noun phrases ('volume', 'shape', 'container', 'particles', 'pattern', 'contact', 'position', 'forces', 'a solid') to express the characteristics of the different phenomena. The verbs are predominantly stative, with 'be' or 'have' preceding them. Comparison language is explicit in cases where two phenomena are described in relation to each other (for example, in Materials extract 5.Q: 'Forces between liquid particles are weaker than in a solid'). Even where comparisons are not explicitly made, they remain implicit in the differing information ('Particles are close together'/'Particles are far apart'); and the language may need to be scaffolded for the learners, depending on the production requirements of the activity (see Chapter 6).

Solid	Liquid	Gas
Has a fixed volume and shape	Has a fixed volume but can take the shape of the container it is placed in	Can be of any volume and can take the shape of the container it is placed in
Particles are arranged in a regular pattern	Particles are random	Particles are random
Particles are in contact with each other and vibrate about a fixed position	Particles are close together but not all are touching each other Particles move slowly and randomly past each other	Particles are far apart Particles move around quickly and randomly
Forces between particles are strong	Forces between particles are weaker than in a solid	There are no forces between particles

Materials extract 5.Q Adjective density in science discourse (Kauser & O'Donoghue, Oxford content and language support: Science, OUP, p. 80.)

Generally speaking, tabular information and other diagrams of content in textbooks tend to be offered to both illustrate and summarize a subject area, often using reduced descriptions of a range of phenomena. Making active use of the tabular structure when processing reading, listening, or viewing experiences helps learners to both organize and assimilate the content. Mohan's (1986) knowledge framework offers teachers an approach to planning learning through an investigation and exploitation of different thinking skills. Mohan suggests that the planning of learning should be developed around 'knowledge structures' of LOTS and HOTS, accompanied by relevant graphics 'as a centre of organization' (1986, p.34). This can be seen in Table 5.1 for 'Description'.

DESCRIPTION		
Thinking skills	**Visuals**	**Language examples**
observing labelling describing comparing contrasting	tables diagrams pictures plans drawings maps	stative verbs adjectives relative clauses quantifiers articles prepositions of place adverbs of comparison
Key question words: **compare, contrast, differentiate, describe, state, identify**		

Table 5.1 Three elements in description (Cortazzi et al., 1998.)

Flow diagrams

Flow diagrams represent events related in time or by cause and effect. Cycles, chains, loops, processes, and instructional language are all forms of 'flow thinking' (Burgess, 1994). Sequencing words and phrases like 'first', 'second', 'third', 'after that', 'next' are frequently omitted from flow diagrams, as are action verb phrases and passive structures.

The grammar omitted from the flow diagram in Materials extract 5.R (overleaf) can be found in this fuller description of the information presented:

> Plants and animals die and are subsequently decomposed by putrefying or decay bacteria. This decomposition in turn releases ammonium compounds into the soil. At the same time, animal droppings and urine also release ammonium compounds into the soil. Next, nitrifying bacteria change these ammonium compounds into nitrates. The nitrates and ammonium are then absorbed by plant roots. Plant protein is produced as a result, and the protein is again eaten by animals.

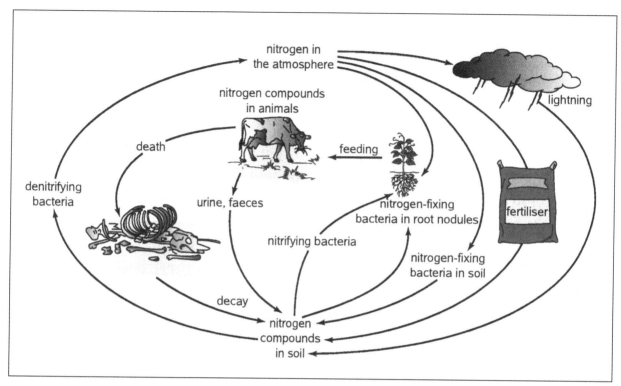

Materials extract 5.R The nitrogen cycle (Kauser & O'Donoghue, Oxford content and language support: Science, OUP, p. 78.)

A number of sequencing discourse markers are used in this causal description of the nitrogen cycle: 'subsequently', 'in turn', 'at the same time', 'also', 'next', 'then', 'as a result', 'again'.

Other examples include the water cycle and the carbon cycle. Flow diagrams are also commonly used to represent man-made processes in textbooks, for example to represent the process of how electricity is made (see Materials extract 5.S).

The numbering in Materials extract 5.S is very useful for learners, as it helps them to follow each stage of the information. A simple reading or listening/watching frame with the same numbers and short sentence starters would enable learners to read or listen/watch and complete the description of the process of generating and delivering electricity to homes.

Historical events also lend themselves to flow-diagram visualization, particularly if there is a causal relationship between the events being described. A timeline is similar in structure and can help learners visualize and process chronological text-based input. The steps in solving a mathematical problem can also be represented by numbered cells and arrows in a flow diagram. A maths teacher giving an initial demonstration of a solution could use a flow diagram whilst talking through the steps to help learners visualize the process and guide them through the demonstration. It also gives the teacher the opportunity to 'anchor' key terms and concepts in the diagram which learners will need later when feeding back results from their own work.

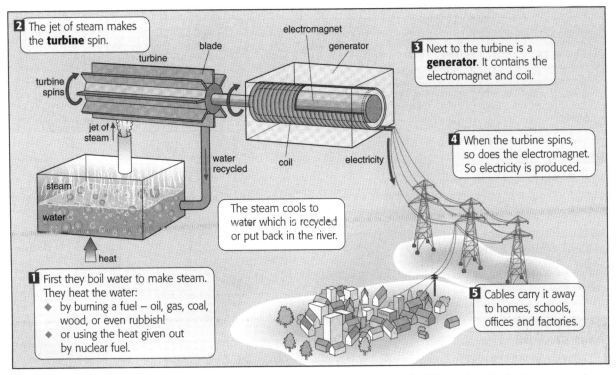

Materials extract 5.S How electricity is made (Kauser & O'Donoghue, Oxford content and
language support: Science, OUP, p. 16.)

Tree diagrams

Tree diagrams are used for classifying, grouping, and building hierarchies. 'Hierarchy
thinking' (Burgess, 1994) relates ideas in terms of super- and subordination.
Academic subjects frequently present ideas to learners using tree diagrams when
learners are expected to understand that 'x belongs to y' or that 'a is a member of b'.

The tree diagram in Materials extract 5.T (overleaf) presents tabular information
within a large tree-like structure. When phenomena are described in terms of
the groups they belong to, it makes sense that they should have aspects of their
characteristics given in order to help differentiate them from other phenomena. In
this example, learners can benefit from having the structure to support them while
listening to and watching the teacher introduce the topic with slides on a screen
at the front of the class. An incomplete tree diagram/table could also be given to
learners for them to fill in.

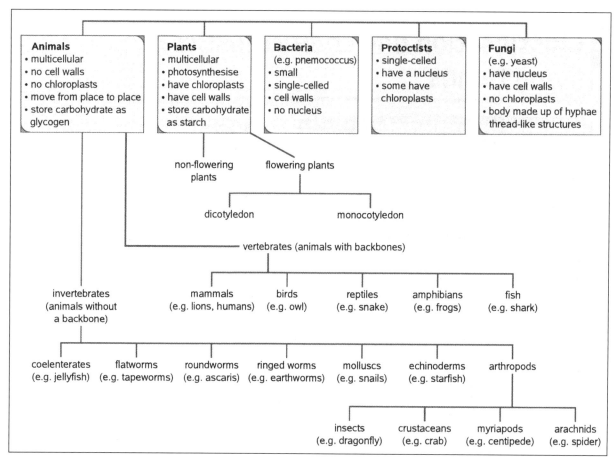

Materials extract 5.T The classification of organisms (Kauser & O'Donoghue, Oxford content and language support: Science, OUP, p. 16.)

Note-taking frames

Activity type 11, 'Reading and making notes' (see Materials extract 5.M on page 123), presented a frame in which learners were asked to read and note down key information based on a reading text related to the topic of glaciers. This note-taking frame derived its structure from the way the content was organized on the original page in the textbook. This is only one way of exploiting content structure for the purpose of producing a support frame for learners to make notes.

Some teachers use lesson plans and notes for organizing their own work in the classroom. Their notes may contain brief headings and pieces of information organized in a simple and logical way that will enable them to make use of these notes while talking to a class. Teaching notes such as these lend themselves to the further creation of note-taking frames for learners. Teachers can produce the notes with headings, bullets, numbers, and other symbols or diagrammatical representations of content and give these to the learners to help them read, watch, or listen to lesson input.

In Chapter 4, we saw how a linear text about diet and disease could be restructured to produce a series of flow diagrams which could then be used to create a sequence of activities (see Figure 4.7 on page 91).

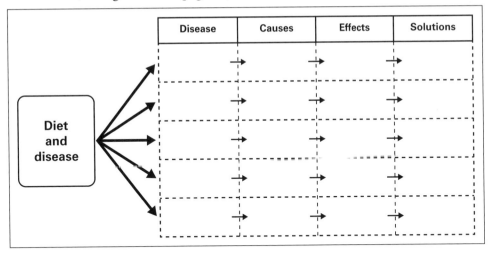

Figure 5.3 Generic structure for 'Diet and disease' text

Figure 5.3 shows how this structure could also be used as a note-taking frame, whereby learners are presented with a linear text in its full, unaltered form and asked to read and note down the key information in the correct cells. It is also useful for situations when the teacher is talking to the class about diet and disease in plenary, perhaps using visuals on the screen, and the learners are given the instruction to listen, watch, and make notes in their frames.

If a structure is not immediately visible, an experienced CLIL teacher could create one which logically represents the content in the input, be it listening, watching, or reading. Slideshow presentations are one medium CLIL teachers could use if they are interested in exploiting generic content structure for guiding learners through watching/listening activities in their subject.

Slideshow input, like the one shown in Materials extract 5.U (overleaf), offers a simple frame to be given as a handout to learners watching and listening to a presentation on a specific planet. Producing scaffolded instruments like this is very supportive for learners, who only have to filter out redundant content to focus on the information needed to fill in their note-taking frames.

My planet	Location	Atmosphere
What is the origin of the name of the planet?	Where is the planet located? How far is the planet from the Sun?	What is the atmosphere of the planet made up of?

Temperature	Make up	Extra information
What is the range of temperatures on the planet?	What is the planet made up of?	Did you find any interesting additional things about the planet?

Materials extract 5.U Note-taking frame on the planets

Illustrations

Finally, frames produced by the teacher, based on the structure of the content, bring us to the visualization of content already available for use—namely illustrations in textbooks or those drawn on the classroom board or projected on a screen.

Illustrations like the one in Materials extract 5.V offer a basis for the text frame underneath it which can be used for note-taking. Notes may include a focus on the action verbs in the text, as they are a significant aspect of the process language in this content. The text may be presented for reading and note-taking on the illustration, or in combination with a teacher monologue, making use of the illustration and following up with a reading and note-taking activity.

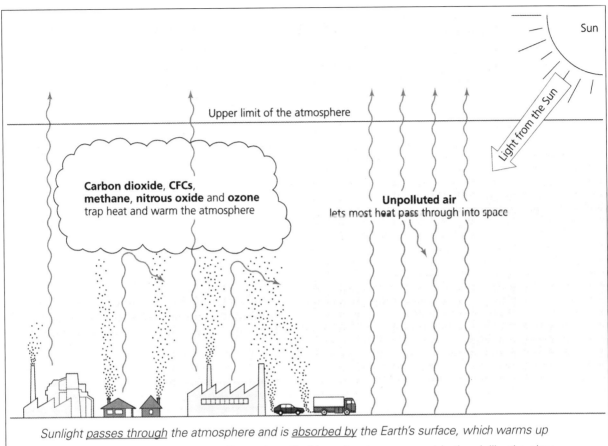

Sun

Light from the Sun

Upper limit of the atmosphere

Carbon dioxide, CFCs, methane, nitrous oxide and **ozone** trap heat and warm the atmosphere

Unpolluted air lets most heat pass through into space

Sunlight <u>passes through</u> the atmosphere and is <u>absorbed by</u> the Earth's surface, which warms up and <u>radiates</u> infrared (heat) energy. But carbon dioxide and water vapour <u>act</u> in the air like the glass in a greenhouse, <u>trapping</u> and <u>absorbing</u> some heat, which <u>warms</u> the atmosphere. This natural global warming <u>provides</u> an essential source of heat for living things. Without it, the world would be freezing at minus 17°C and life would probably not exist.

Materials extract 5.V Illustrations supported by text frames (Beckett & Gallagher, New coordinated science: Biology, OUP, p. 200.)

Summary

This chapter has presented an inventory of task types for guiding learners through the demands of input content. For organizational purposes, the activities began at word and phrase level, and then moved to whole-text processing. We have considered the skills of decoding and activating background knowledge, and we also looked at how a CLIL approach can best offer development in these skills, using the activity types in the inventory. We have also seen activities that highlight 'shapes' in subject content. These shapes enable learners to visualize the way in which knowledge is structured, and exploiting shapes in the design of activities helps reduce the overall complexity of input so that learners can arrive at meaning more easily.

Task

If you would like to look at a practical task to explore your own practice related to the content of this chapter, see Appendix 1 (page 290).

Further reading

Burgess, J. (1994). Ideational frameworks in integrated language learning. *System, 22,* 309–318.
A short, clear, and convincing rationale for using diagrams of thinking for teaching language.

Cortazzi, M. et al. (1998). Seeing through texts: Developing discourse-based materials in teacher education. *The English Teacher, XXVIII,* 39–68.
Gives a rich range of examples of generic structures in text, and argues for training teachers in visualization techniques for their work with content materials. It also summarizes a number of visual approaches to reading texts.

Geddes, M., & **White, R.** (1978). The use of semi-scripted simulated authentic speech and listening comprehension. *Audio-Visual Language Journal, XVI,* 137–145.
Describes what semi-scripts are, and argues why they are one of the best ways of bringing authentic speech into the language classroom.

Hudson, T. (2007). *Teaching second language reading.* Oxford: Oxford University Press.
A very good basic text on theory and practice of second-language reading.

Lynch, T. (2009). *Teaching second language listening: A guide to evaluating, adapting, and creating tasks for listening in the language classroom.* Oxford: Oxford University Press.
A very good text for preparing listening experiences in the classroom.

6

SUPPORTING OUTPUT

Overview

> Talking gets students to think, and thinking is needed for writing.
> (Zwiers, 2008)

This chapter looks at supporting CLIL learners in in the output skills of speaking and writing. There is an underlying principle here, as suggested in the quotation above, that CLIL practice is typically focused on the move from speaking to writing—a move already discussed to some extent in Chapter 4. The opposite can also be true, of course: written production might in some cases provide a safer and more guaranteed framework for speaking. So although we will consider these two skills separately in this chapter, there is a high degree of symbiosis. We will look first at speaking, then at writing, with the aim of helping subject teachers to see the range of activities available and how they might adapt them to their own contexts. The aim is to provide a set of tools to help teachers with the ongoing process of matching support with activities, according to specific learner needs.

Speaking

In language teaching, the function of speaking is accepted as a natural feature of the classroom. Unless learners begin to express themselves orally in the target language, there remains a feeling in both teacher and student that something is awry—that little progress is being made. The same might be said of written production, but learners first pick up confidence through speaking, through beginning to express their opinions and personalities in a foreign language. Such feelings of confidence are powerful, and generations of language learners have attested to the positive effect they have on their learning.

However, bilingual education and CLIL have also given us a further perspective on speaking and its function in the subject classroom. When students are learning history in a foreign language, do history teachers view 'talk' in the same way as their language counterparts? It is less likely that they view speaking as a natural feature of the classroom, since their major concerns are conceptual. CLIL, with its natural tendency to encourage a more learner-centred methodology, brings speaking to the fore, putting Swain's (1985) 'output hypothesis' into practice. Broadly speaking,

Swain's hypothesis, derived from her observations of bilingual education, was that learners are not convinced that they understand a concept until they have expressed it in their own words. This is a crucial observation in terms of the relationship between self-expression and cognitive development. In line with this idea, Clegg also remarked:

> Talking about something which one is learning is important, because it is when we express a new concept linguistically that we gradually develop it. The concept may be partly developed in our minds, but until we start to communicate it linguistically, we don't know how clearly—or unclearly—it is formed.
> (Clegg, 2002a)

If we accept these principles, then CLIL teachers need to encourage oral interaction in their classrooms. This raises the issue, of course, of how to create the 'affective conditions' in classrooms for this to happen; in other words, conditions that make learners feel comfortable enough for such interaction to take place. Primary school teachers rarely have problems in this regard, but at secondary level, students tend to be more self-conscious, and the materials they are studying through the L2 might not seem immediately geared towards encouraging discussion or opinion. Studying the Carlist Wars on a Friday afternoon in the heat of late June in Spain is not an ideal scenario for animated discussion. The content of the subject syllabus cannot be manipulated in the same way as that of a language syllabus, in which topics of general interest can be cherry-picked and used to frame the underlying linguistic objectives. But we can design our materials to help (see Chapter 7), and we can make use of activity types that help students to engage, whatever the concept and time of day.

Speaking activity types

There are, of course, many types of speaking activity, but those which tend to work in CLIL practice are the following:
- Individual talk (for example, digital slideshow presentations, show and tell, delivering a report)
- Open and closed question-and-answer sessions (from teacher to class, and from student to student)
- Speaking in pairs (for example, discussions, sharing information, interviewing each other)
- Speaking in small groups (for example, discussions, making group decisions, finding solutions to problems as a group)
- Role-playing specific subject-related scenarios (for example, dialogues on specific themes)
- Speaking within a small group and then sharing information with members of other groups (for example, 'jigsaw reading and speaking')
- Speaking as a whole class (for example, plenary discussions, searching for information from class peers, surveying the class)
- Reading aloud (for example, information transfer or giving instructions).

Language teachers reading the above list might ask for a further consideration of the distinction between 'accuracy' and 'fluency', since speaking activities tend to be orientated towards one or the other. Murphy (1991) offers a useful discussion of how accuracy and fluency speaking activities can be mapped onto each other, but in CLIL, a fluency activity will still need to be scaffolded and supported. The key question for CLIL teachers is the scope of language support required for each activity. So in addition to talking about accuracy and fluency, we might talk of moving from activities which are 'more scaffolded' to 'less scaffolded' as learners develop more independence and become able to communicate more effectively and autonomously.

Language support types

The following list provides some tools for scaffolding language support. We will look at each of these in more detail later on (see *Language support in practice*).

- full scripts
- models
- brief pre-activity language practice
- word lists
- information gap
- jigsaw tasks
- sentence starters
- substitution tables
- annotated visuals
- questions without answers
- speaking frames
- notes to speak from

Making decisions about language support

Equipped with the tools listed above, an inventory of activity types (see Chapter 5), and the collection of language support strategies found in this chapter, teachers can begin to build language-supported speaking activities based on their students' specific needs. Figure 6.1 (overleaf) offers an example range of language support options for the activity type 'individual talk'.

It is in the scaffolding of speaking activities that the work of the CLIL teacher becomes most apparent. Hayes-Jacobs (2006) writes of the need to allow learners to use their own language first when communicating about new content, and then go on to gradually support their production of the 'formal' language' of the subject. This can depend on the lesson sequence stage and the language level of the learners, of course, but what appears to be needed are initial activities which give learners the freedom to explore concepts in their own language, before they go on to do activities which scaffold learner production of the formal standardized language of the subject. The crucial point about CLIL is that language support can never be excluded, since it is by definition a methodology which involves the learning of content through a foreign language. In such contexts, strategic and planned scaffolding is the key.

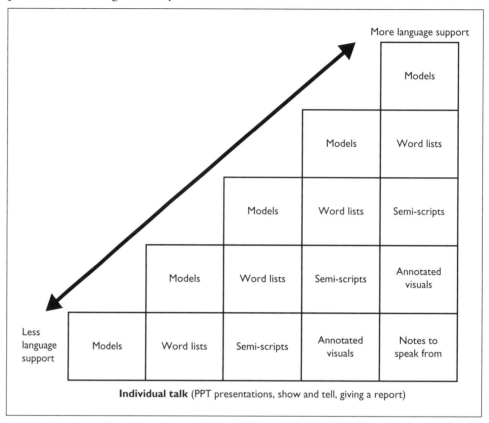

Figure 6.1 Range of language support options for individual talk

Language support in practice

Full scripts

Full scripts refer to complete pieces of text which are provided for the purpose of supporting writing or speaking or both. They can be used to expose students to the standardized language of the subject being learned. Instruction sheets, which are usually written in formal, concise, and subject-specific language, lend themselves to scripting. During an experiment, for example, learners will be reading and following precise instructions (see Materials extract 6.A). Learners can be instructed to work in pairs and take it in turns to read aloud the scripted instructions, directing their partner who is handling the practical work. Later on, when students are asked to write up their notes on the experiment in the form of a laboratory report—explaining the steps they took, the equipment they used, the hypotheses they made, the tests they carried out, and the results they recorded—the instruction 'script' will be very useful as a source of standard language to support this specific activity.

Melting and freezing

1 Dip the ice cube in water and place it on a plate.

2 Lay the string across the top of the ice cube.

3 Sprinkle salt onto the ice cube. Make sure you sprinkle the salt near to the string.

4 Watch the clock for 15 seconds.

5 Take hold of the ends of the piece of string.

6 Slowly lift the string. The ice cube should be attached to it.

Materials extract 6.A Instructions 'script' for carrying out a science experiment

Models

In CLIL lessons where teachers are presenting new knowledge, learners can find it helpful to have key ideas and language strategically highlighted and repeated for them, both in oral and written form. Production can be encouraged, with scaffolded support later in a lesson sequence. This standard language can also be highlighted as part of a listening activity in initial introductory stages. As we saw in Chapter 5, labelling visuals as part of listening and watching activities gives learners the opportunities to note down key phrases for later use. This key language may include noun phrases, and also action verbs, sequencing phrases, and other related aspects of key CALP discourse.

Brief pre-activity language practice

A more explicit technique than modelling involves students reproducing examples of target phrases and sentences as a precursor to carrying out an activity. This may include students being given a spoken or written example sentence and then being asked to create a similar sentence using a different prompt, as with the key language of cause and effect that was mentioned in Chapter 5:

x causes *y* to be -ed.
x causes *y* to [infinitive verb].
x causes a [noun phrase] of/in *y*.
x causes a [noun phrase].

These standard structures can be exploited for practising oral production in specific content topic areas in preparation for further activities:

Global warming causes sea levels to be raised.
Global warming causes sea levels to rise.
Global warming causes a rise in sea levels.
Global warming causes a sea-level rise.

This kind of practice sets learners up with examples of standard language for use later in independent speaking and writing work.

Word lists

Offering learners access to key words and phrases in context (see Materials extract 6.B) can help them begin to speak on a new topic. This key language can consist of the different parts of sentences that the students are being asked to produce, such as subject nouns, verbs, and object nouns.

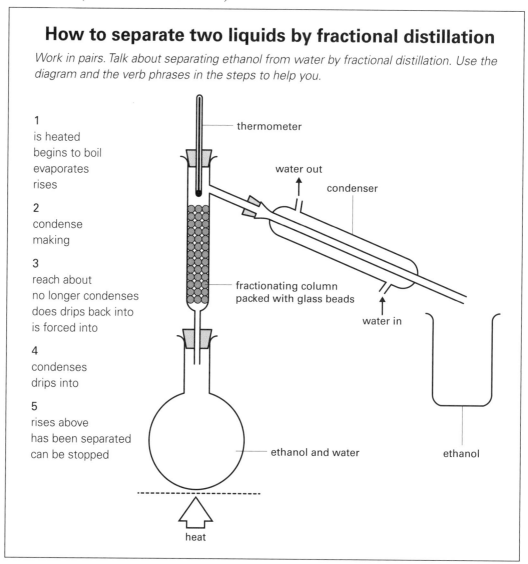

How to separate two liquids by fractional distillation

Work in pairs. Talk about separating ethanol from water by fractional distillation. Use the diagram and the verb phrases in the steps to help you.

1
is heated
begins to boil
evaporates
rises

2
condense
making

3
reach about
no longer condenses
does drips back into
is forced into

4
condenses
drips into

5
rises above
has been separated
can be stopped

thermometer

water out

condenser

fractionating column
packed with glass beads

water in

ethanol and water

ethanol

heat

Materials extract 6.B Contextualized key language (adapted from Gallagher & Ingram, New coordinated science: Chemistry, OUP, p. 22.)

In Materials extract 6.B, learners have been given numbered word lists to help them talk through the process of separating two liquids by fractional distillation. This activity occurs after the learners have watched a demonstration of the experiment and have had the relevant standard language introduced to them in a comprehensive description provided by the teacher during the experiment.

What about these old gadgets?

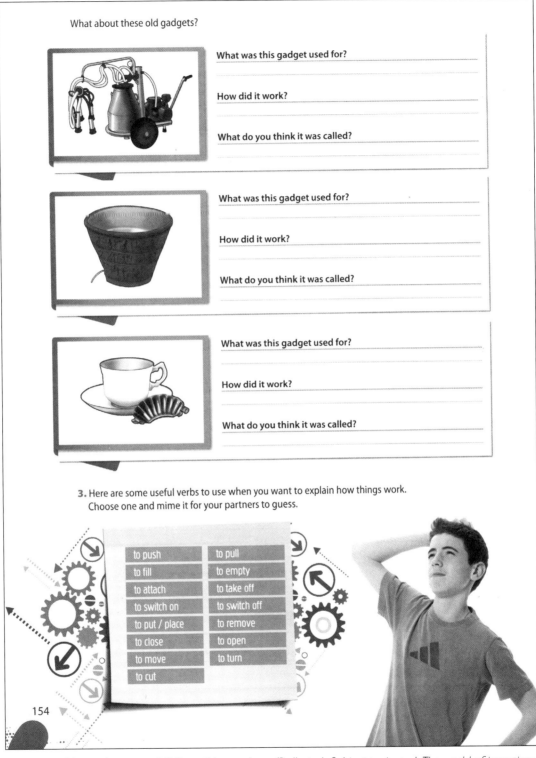

What was this gadget used for?

How did it work?

What do you think it was called?

What was this gadget used for?

How did it work?

What do you think it was called?

What was this gadget used for?

How did it work?

What do you think it was called?

3. Here are some useful verbs to use when you want to explain how things work. Choose one and mime it for your partners to guess.

to push	to pull
to fill	to empty
to attach	to take off
to switch on	to switch off
to put / place	to remove
to close	to open
to move	to turn
to cut	

154

Materials extract 6.C Describing gadgets (Ball et al., Subject projects 1: The world of inventions, Ikaselkar, p. 154.)

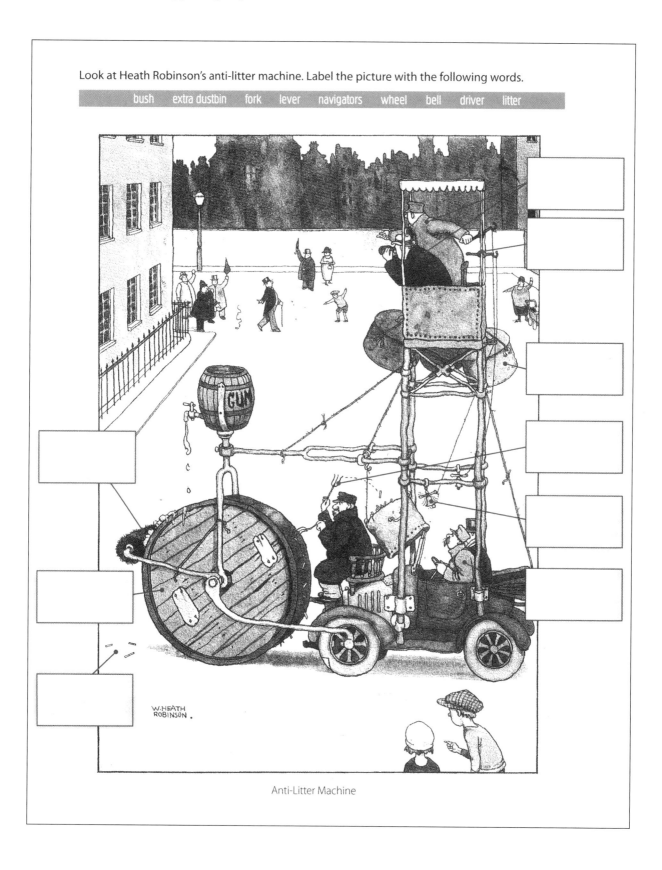

Look at Heath Robinson's anti-litter machine. Label the picture with the following words.

bush   extra dustbin   fork   lever   navigators   wheel   bell   driver   litter

Anti-Litter Machine

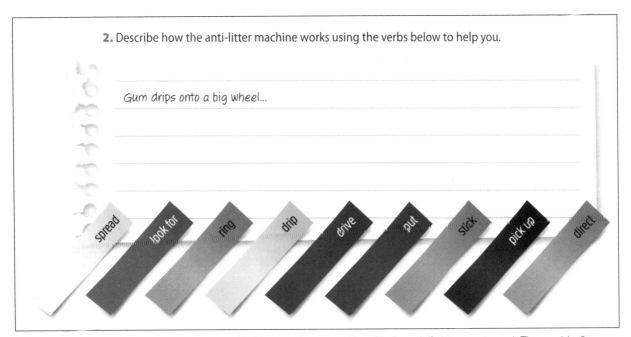

2. Describe how the anti-litter machine works using the verbs below to help you.

Gum drips onto a big wheel...

spread look for ring drip drive put stick pick up direct

Materials extract 6.D The anti-litter machine (Ball et al., Subject projects 1: The world of inventions, Ikaselkar, p. 155.)

Learners watch and follow this description, making notes according to the teacher's instructions. At a subsequent stage, students work together in pairs to begin reconstructing the description using the action verbs provided. The step-by-step process followed in the lesson further supports learners in clearly laying out the structure of the description.

In the first step of an exercise sequence, shown in Materials extract 6.C (on page 141), learners use a structure with three clear frames to produce speculative descriptions of three eccentric gadgets, followed by a mime activity featuring action verbs useful for explaining processes.

In the second step of the exercise sequence, shown in Materials extract 6.D, an anti-litter machine must first be labelled with the necessary nouns before learners can attempt to describe how the machine works to each other, in pairs. Verbs are provided at the bottom of the page to help them, along with a simple present-tense model for the beginning of the process. The teacher can remind learners to insert the sequence markers ('first', 'then', 'next', etc.), since they are necessary but hardly the main element of the total linguistic and cognitive challenge here. The three-frame structure has a clear benefit in contextualizing key words: the first step activates background knowledge and language; the second step contextualizes noun phrases with an illustration; and the third step presents verb phrases to help learners produce their own description.

How to stop rust

Text A: How to stop rust.

Talk to your partner to fill in the missing information from your text.

1 **Paint.** Steel bridges and railings are usually painted. Paints that contain lead or _____ are mostly used, because these are especially good at preventing rust. For example, 'red lead' paints contain an oxide of lead, Pb3O4.

2 **Grease.** _____ and _____ are coated with grease or oil.

3 **Plastic.** Steel is coated with plastic for use in garden chairs, bicycle baskets and dish racks. Plastic is cheap and can be made to look _____.

4 **Galvanizing.** Iron for sheds and dustbins is usually coated with _____. It is called galvanizing iron.

5 **Tin plating.** Baked beans come in 'tins' which are made from steel coated on both sides with a fine layer of tin. Tin is used because it is _____ and non-toxic. It is deposited on the steel by electrolysis, in a process called tin-plating.

6 **Chromium plating.** Chromium is used to coat steel with a shiny protective layer, for example on car bumpers. Like tin, the chromium is deposited by electrolysis.

7 **Sacrificial protection.** Magnesium is more _____ than iron. So, when a bar of magnesium is attached to the side of a steel ship, it _____ instead of steel. This is called sacrificial protection, because the magnesium is sacrificed to protect the steel.

Text B: How to stop rust.

Talk to your partner to fill in the missing information from your text.

1 **Paint.** Steel bridges and railings are usually painted. Paints that contain lead or zinc are mostly used, because these are especially good at _____ rust. For example, 'red lead' paints contain an oxide of lead, Pb3O4.

2 **Grease.** Tools and machine parts are coated with grease or oil.

3 **Plastic.** Steel is coated with plastic for use in _____, bicycle baskets and dish racks. Plastic is cheap and can be made to look attractive.

4 **Galvanizing.** Iron for sheds and dustbins is usually coated with zinc. It is called galvanizing iron.

5 **Tin plating.** Baked beans come in 'tins' which are made from steel _____ on both sides with a fine layer of tin. Tin is used because it is unreactive, and non-toxic. It is deposited on the steel by _____, in a process called tin-plating.

6 **Chromium plating.** Chromium is used to coat steel with a shiny _____ layer, for example on car bumpers. Like tin, the chromium is deposited by _____.

7 **Sacrificial protection.** Magnesium is more reactive than iron. So, when a bar of magnesium is attached to the side of a steel ship, it corrodes instead of steel. This is called sacrificial protection, because the _____ is sacrificed to protect the steel.

Materials extract 6.E Information-gap speaking from a text (adapted from Gallagher & Ingram, New coordinated science: Chemistry, OUP, pp. 88–89.)

Information gap

A similar way of offering learners standard language through talk is by giving them gapped 'bodies of information' to speak from whilst interacting in pairs. In the example given in Materials extract 6.E, learners speak with a partner to find the information missing from their own text. **Information-gap** speaking activities can be used at most stages in the lesson sequence involving key vocabulary, but work particularly well as a warm-up to introduce new words. They bring authentic purpose to communication by getting learners to elicit the missing words from each other.

With paired information-gap speaking activities, it can be useful to spend some time focusing on question forms with learners. In Materials extract 6.E, Text A, learners will need to ask 'Which paints are used?', 'Paints that contain what are used?', or similar structures. As this example suggests, information-gap activities can be employed with any content which lends itself to producing two versions of the same input content. Also, Materials extract 6.E shows text being used exclusively, whereas in Materials extract 6.F, the illustrations accompany the descriptions and help the listening partner to situate the missing information in the text.

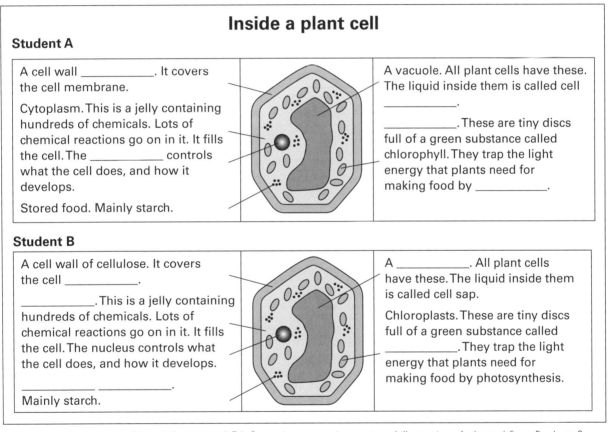

Materials extract 6.F Information gap using text and illustrations (adapted from Beckett & Gallagher, New coordinated science: Biology, OUP, p. 19.)

Graphs, charts, flow diagrams, timelines, and other graphic organizers can be turned into paired speaking activities. It can be particularly rewarding when used to support tasks in which learners exchange personal information. For example, when learners carry out survey work related to their own lives, it enables the exchange to be based on real and meaningful information, which lends a more authentic feel to the activity.

Comparing fitness

Student A

Part 3 Caring for our health

1 This bar chart shows the level of fitness of our class.

Level of fitness shown as number of students

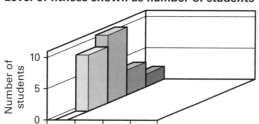

Level of fitness shown as % total of students

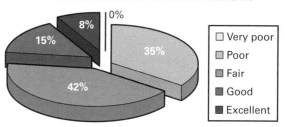

2 In our class timetable, we have lessons where we exercise 2 times a week for a total of 120 minutes.

3 Out of school, the number of students and the type and frequency of exercise are as follows:

Frequency of exercise	Number of students	Type of exercise
Never	5	No activity
Twice a week	4	Dance
Three times a week	9	Gym

Student B

Part 3 Caring for our health

1 This bar chart shows the level of fitness of our class. (Add a scale to the vertical axis.)

Number of students					
	Very poor	Poor	Fair	Good	Excellent
	Level of fitness				

2 In our class timetable, we have lessons where we exercise _____ times a week for a total of _____ minutes.

3 Out of school, the number of students and the type and frequency of exercise are as follows:

Frequency of exercise	Number of students	Type of exercise
Never		
Twice a week		
Three times a week		

Materials extract 6.G Information-gap speaking using personal data (adapted exchange material from Science across the world, Association for Science Education.)

In the example shown in Materials extract 6.G, two classes in the same school carried out an investigation into their levels of fitness. The classes then exchanged their results, and the teacher used the data to set up communicative activities in the classroom. Materials extract 6.G requires Student B to ask Student A for information about the data regarding levels of fitness in the partner class. This particular task has learners working in pairs, asking for and giving information about the numbers of students with different levels of fitness in the class, as well as information about the frequency of the exercise undertaken. Student B must ask 'What percentage of the class/How many students are Excellent?' and similar questions to fill in the missing information. This kind of shared survey data should again be considered within a sequence where learners go on to do a comparison between data from their own class and the results collected by the partner class.

Jigsaw tasks

Another information-gap speaking task is one which is known as a **jigsaw task**. In this type of group task, learners are each given the role of 'expert', but only in one part of the topic being studied. In the lesson, learners are given a letter—A, B, C, or D—and are told to get together with other students of the same letter group ('A's with 'A's, etc.). Group A is given text A, group B is given text B, etc. and these groups are then instructed to collect key information for their part of the investigation and to have a discussion in their 'expert' groups to arrive at a consensus regarding the information. This information could be collected from reading texts, graphic data, internet sources, or any other type of information related to the topic. An example is shown in Materials extract 6.H.

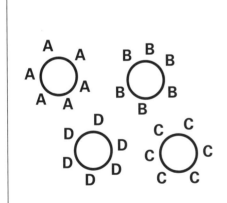

Tissue types

Type of tissues	Kinds	Structure	Functions	Position within organs
A Epithelial				
B Connective				
C Muscular				
D Nervous				

Materials extract 6.H Jigsaw task

In this particular example, the class is studying 'Types of tissue in the human body' and the teacher has decided to do the 'jigsaw' task in order to help the learners read and speak about the topic. All the learners are instructed to find their particular group's information in their textbooks and are given the table shown in Materials extract 6.H for this purpose. Group A is investigating epithelial tissue, group B connective tissue, group C muscular tissue, and group D nervous tissue.

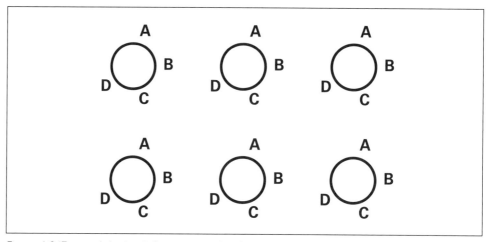

Figure 6.2 'Experts' sharing information with other 'experts'

Following a signal from the teacher, the students form new groups so that each group has one representative from each expert group. At this stage, the experts share information with their new group members (see Figure 6.2).

Depending on the general language level of the class, teachers can also decide which functional aspects of the task to support, for example the types of question required in the sharing phase. Scaffolded examples could be displayed in class, ranging from formal ones such as 'What are the functions of connective tissues?' to the more natural 'OK—nervous tissue. What kinds?'.

A follow-up to this stage would be to put the students back into their expert groups and to ask them to compare the information they have collated. Then at the next stage of this lesson, teachers could provide language support in the form of writing frames, for the purpose of preparing accurate, paragraph-based descriptions of the different tissue types.

Sentence starters

Another form of support is to give learners the beginnings of sentences to help them answer questions or speak on a given topic. The sentence starters may also be presented with a word list of key vocabulary for the learners to choose from when compiling their complete sentences.

In Materials extract 6.1, learners are given sentence starters to help them talk through a description of how a simple motor works. Again, this would preferably come at the moment just after learners have watched a demonstration of a simple motor in action, accompanied by a teacher-led explanation of the process. The sentence starters could also be arranged so that students perceive patterns in the way that the sentences might continue. For example, 'The poles of the magnet …' will require some sort of verb phrase, as will 'The coil is free to …'. Teachers can also demonstrate here whether the verb phrase is likely to be passive or active, depending on the nature of the action itself. The fact that the language used to describe processes often involves a combination of passive and active structures makes it a good example to use in order to help learners develop their own CALP-related awareness.

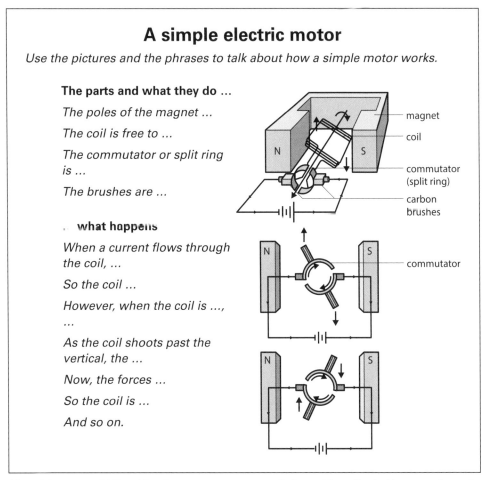

Materials extract 6.I Speaking from sentence starters (adapted from Pople, New coordinated science: Physics, OUP, p. 164.)

Substitution tables

The substitution table, deliberately disinterred from the early periods of language teaching, can be useful for CLIL-related purposes. Substitution tables can be used for single- or multiple-sentence construction and for producing longer texts in paragraph form. They can also be used to support longer written output and as part of whole-chunk output support in the form of a speaking or writing frame.

In mathematics, learners are frequently asked to carry out calculations orally, as in Materials extract 6.J (overleaf). In a CLIL mathematics classroom, one way to help learners do this is to create substitution tables which model standard solution-giving sentences, and which describe calculations in full. Having this language visible while learners are working, for example on a handout, on the screen or board, or on wall posters, helps to familiarize them with the language by absorbing it from the classroom environment.

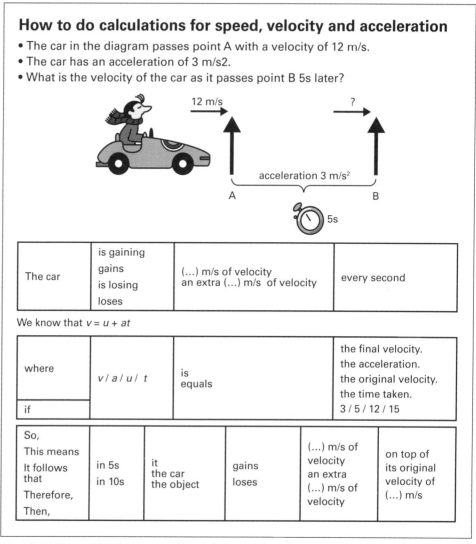

How to do calculations for speed, velocity and acceleration

- The car in the diagram passes point A with a velocity of 12 m/s.
- The car has an acceleration of 3 m/s2.
- What is the velocity of the car as it passes point B 5s later?

The car	is gaining gains is losing loses	(...) m/s of velocity an extra (...) m/s of velocity	every second

We know that $v = u + at$

where	$v\,/\,a\,/\,u\,/\,t$	is equals	the final velocity. the acceleration. the original velocity. the time taken.
if			3 / 5 / 12 / 15

So, This means It follows that Therefore, Then,	in 5s in 10s	it the car the object	gains loses	(...) m/s of velocity an extra (...) m/s of velocity	on top of its original velocity of (...) m/s

Materials extract 6.J Substitution tables 1 (adapted from Pople, New coordinated science: Physics, OUP, p. 21.)

In Materials extract 6.K, a complete description of mitosis is presented in one table. This works because the sentences are all structured in the same way. In this lesson, learners work together in pairs, following the instructions for simulating mitosis with paper and clips, whilst using the substitution table to produce their own descriptions. Again, this should be seen as a stage which follows a teacher-led presentation or a recorded animation, meaning the students have already explored mitotic cell division by listening, watching, and working with descriptive text to put the original description into the correct order. At the point described here, the learners are working on rebuilding the description and then practising it themselves by using the materials listed in the 'Instructions for mitosis simulation'. As a follow-up, teachers could ask a pair of students to present their description and simulation to the class.

Topic: Explaining mitosis

Instructions for mitosis simulation

Start with eight strips of paper, four plain strips and four coloured strips. These represent the *chromosomes*.

1 Take two A4 sheets of paper placed together to make a rectangle. This represents the *cell*.

2 Place two plain and two coloured strips (chromosomes) onto the cell.

3 Then add 'copies' to each strip and connect them with a paper clip to give a chromosome. The paperclip represents the *centromere*.

4 When the chromosomes line up along the centre of the cell, place your strips along the join in your two pieces of paper.

5 As they start to separate, pull off the paperclip and put it on one side.

6 Move the strips to the opposite ends of the cell.

7 Pull the two sheets of paper apart to represent *the cell division*.

8 Move the strips to the middle of the sheets of paper to represent two new cells.

Use the language below to help you give your explanation:

(NB The sequencing phrases in the first column are all in the correct order, and the first sentence has been done for you.)

Sequence	What	Action	What
To begin with,	the parent cell	are pulled	four chromosomes
Before the process of cell division starts,	(we have) two daughter cells	has	a full copy of the original chromosomes
			along the middle of the cell
		duplicate	
In the next step,	cell division		one copy of each strand going to each side
and then,		each with	so that each has two strands
	the chromosomes		
		line up	to the opposite sides of the cell (poles)
	the chromosomes		
Now,		occurs	
	the pairs of chromosomes		
and		split at the centromere	
Finally,	the strands of chromosomes		

Materials extract 6.K Substitution tables 2

Annotated visuals

A very simple yet effective way of supporting learner talk is to provide visuals which have been annotated with key language. These visuals can be given to the learners ready-made as handouts or can be constructed by the learners themselves. This technique lends itself to guided input activities such as 'listen and label', which could be followed by a supported output activity, for example one where learners watch and make notes, share the information orally, or peer-check the accuracy of what they have written. Later still, the checked visuals can be used as scaffolds for student monologues in plenary.

Materials extract 6.L is from a lesson on chemical reactions and is used to guide learners as they listen to a teacher, or a recorded description, explain the formation of acid rain. During the description, learners are asked to label the illustration with the key action verbs used at each stage of the process. These ('are released', 'are emitted', etc.) can be seen alongside the illustration. During the description, the teacher can make liberal use of stress, intonation, and repetition to highlight the key phrases the learners need to note down on their illustration. Once the description is over, the teacher asks the learners for the phrases they noted down and indicates where the elicited action verbs fit in the acid rain formation process by pointing to the relevant parts of the illustration on a screen.

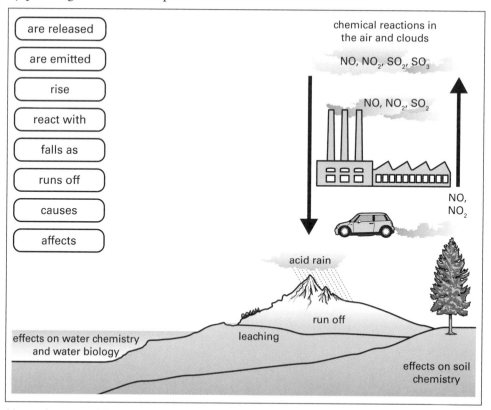

Materials extract 6.L How acid rain is formed (adapted from Science across the world, Association for Science Education.)

The next step in the lesson requires the learners to work in pairs and attempt to recreate the process description, taking turns to describe it to each other while the teacher walks around, providing support when needed. Finally, two pairs of learners are asked to take the role of the teacher and come to the board, with one pair pointing through the illustrated process and the other talking through the description. The illustration serves as a semi-script for the teacher to follow in delivering a standard account of the process of acid-rain formation. It is also exploited as a frame to guide learners through the listening and note-taking parts of the lesson. Lastly, the annotated illustration embeds key language and acts as a scaffold for learners to support their own reproduction of the process. A transcription of two learner descriptions is shown below.

Chemistry: How acid rain is formed

(One student stands at the screen.)

T1 Here we go.

S1 Gases are released from car exhausts and factories and they went up to the clouds, there they react with, um, water in the clouds and fall down as acid rain, and the acid rain runs off the hills, and leaching of the sea, or rivers and affects the chemistry of salts in the river.

T2 Very good.

T1 Yes, that was nice, thank you very much. Perhaps the second pair can have a go now …

(The second student comes to the screen.)

S2 Um, the gases are released from cars or factories and arise into the sky. There, they are, they react with the water in the clouds and then they fall down, it falls down as acid rain. It runs off, it runs off the hillside and is leaching into the river and there it affects the water and soil chemistry.

T1 Thank you very much.

In subjects that make widespread use of visuals for illustrating processes, it makes good sense to exploit them for making language more salient. The illustration can be seen as a bridge between the standard language of the subject and the learners' own language. It is a small step from here to providing a writing frame for the purpose of supporting learners in writing a formal description of the process at a later stage in this lesson, or as homework. This 'formal' frame signifies a logical step in the transition from 'personal talking' to 'formal writing'.

Questions without answers

There are many communicative activities which lend themselves to supported speaking in a CLIL classroom. One example is shown in Materials extract 6.M (overleaf). Originally called '**question loops**', this activity type requires learners to ask a (scripted) question in the form of an incomplete sentence, then listen for the correct answer. This involves the entire class listening, searching, and reading out their assigned scripted sentences. It is essentially the same as the sentence 'heads and tails' activity type, but conducted orally. One student begins the round by reading the beginning of the sentence they have been assigned. Then the student in possession of the remaining part of the same sentence reads their text, which includes the beginning of another sentence, and the process continues until the loop arrives back at the first student. This activity combines syntactic processing with conceptual logic. Both the language and the content demands must be met for the listening students to realize that they have the 'tail' clause.

Topic: Observations and reactions

A car's exhaust pipe will rust faster	
A catalyst is a substance that changes the rate of chemical reaction	if the car is used a lot.
A reaction goes faster	but remains chemically unchanged itself.
Drenching with water	when the concentration of a reactant is increased.
Enzymes are proteins	prevents too much damage from spilt acid.
Food cooks much faster in a pressure cooker	which act as biological catalysts.
Hydrogen peroxide decomposes	than in an ordinary saucepan.
In fireworks, powdered magnesium is used	much faster in the presence of the enzyme *catalase*.
In this country, dead animals decay quite quickly.	rather than magnesium ribbon.
Magnesium powder reacts faster	But in Siberia, bodies have been found fully preserved in ice.
Rate is a measure of the change	than magnesium ribbon, with dilute sulphuric acid.
The more sweet things you eat,	that happens in a single unit of time.
The reaction between manganese carbonate and dilute hydrochloric acid speeds up	the faster your teeth decay.
The reaction between sodium thiosulphate and hydrochloric acid	when some concentrated hydrochloric acid is added
Zinc and dilute sulphuric acid react much more quickly	takes a very long time if carried out in an ice bath.
Zinc powder burns much more vigorously in oxygen	when a few drops of copper (ii) sulphate solution are added.
	than zinc foil does.

Materials extract 6.M Question loop (adapted from Gallagher & Ingram, New coordinated science: Chemistry, OUP, pp. 126–147.)

To create these loops, type out sentences on a specific topic in a table with two columns. There should be one sentence for each student in the class, or at least one sentence per pair. Split the sentences down the middle, at a convenient syntactic point. Put the second half of the sentences in the second column so that it is placed with the first half of the following sentence. Put the second half of the last sentence with the first half of the first sentence (see Materials extract 6.N). Print out the sheet in large print and cut up the strips. Hand out one strip to each student.

A car's exhaust pipe will rust faster	than zinc foil does.
A catalyst is a substance that changes the rate of a chemical reaction	if the car is used a lot.
A reaction goes faster	but remains chemically unchanged itself.

Materials extract 6.N A cutting from the printed question loop 'Observations on reactions'

Information-search activities, an example of which is shown in Materials extract 6.O (overleaf), take this interaction a step further by requiring learners to get out of their seats and ask classmates for information, as instructed by the teacher or on a card given to them. Each interlocutor must listen to the question and provide the information if they have it. A key difference here is that the language is only partially scripted.

In the 'Planets' example, there are a series of four information cards, each with one item of information missing. There are also prompts helping learners make questions and answers. These information-search activities can be constructed to fit a wide variety of content types, and teachers are encouraged to make their own based on the content they are teaching. A template with a structure for 'Two things you know' and 'Two things you want to know' is given in Materials extract 6.P (overleaf), with a few examples inserted. Add questions and answers, terms and definitions, or similar items to a template like the one shown. Print out the sheet so each learner receives a card with two questions and two answers.

With the template structure shown, learners are guaranteed not to find all the answers to their questions with one single person, and must ask at least two people to find all the information they need.

Mercury	Venus
Position: nearest to the Sun	Position: second closest
Distance from the Sun: _____	Distance from the Sun: 108,200,000 km
Temperature: varying –184°C to 427°C (–300°F to 800°F)	Temperature: _____
Mass: 3.30 x 10^23 kg	Mass: 4.869 x 10^24 kg
Atmosphere: almost none	Atmosphere: very thick, poisonous
Core: partly liquid iron	Core: iron
Named after: Roman winged messenger and escort of the dead	Named after: Roman goddess of love
Other: fastest moving planet	Other: has volcanoes
Saturn	**Uranus**
Position: 6th	Position: 7th
Distance from the Sun: 143,350,000 km	Distance from the Sun: 287,200,000 km
Temperature: varying –170°C (–274°F)	Temperature: –200°C (–328°F)
Mass: _____	Mass: 8.683 x 10^25 kg
Atmosphere: Hydrogen	Atmosphere: _____
Core: rocky	Core: molten rock
Named after: Roman god of agriculture	Named after: Greek god of the sky
Other: famous for its rings	Other: has belt of 11 faint rings

Question help

What is the location of …? / Where is … situated?
What is the distance of … from the Sun? / How far is … from the Sun?
What is the temperature / mass / atmosphere / core of …?
What is the atmosphere / core made up of …?
What does the atmosphere / core consist of …?
What is the planet … named after? / Where does the name … come from?
What else can you tell me about …?

Answer help

… is located / found / is situated
The distance between … and the Sun is … / The distance of … from the Sun is …
… has a temperature of … / from … to … / … varying between … and … / ranging from … to …
… has a mass of … point … times … to the (power of) … kilos
… has a (very thick / thin / poisonous) … atmosphere (made up of …)
… has a core made up of … / which is made of … / consists of …
… is named after
It is also … / It also has … / It also …

Materials extract 6.0 Information search

Q1	What important organs do the ribs protect?	Q3	
Q2	What does the skeleton support?	Q4	
A7	Arteries take blood away from the heart.	A5	
A10	Muscles help the body to move and stand.	A8	
Q5		Q7	What takes blood away from the heart?
Q6		Q8	
A2	The body is supported by the skeleton.	A1	The ribs protect the heart and lungs.
A9		A11	
Q9		Q11	
Q10	What helps the body to move and stand?	Q12	
A3		A6	
A12		A4	

Materials extract 6.P A template for creating an information-search activity

Speaking frames

Speaking frames take the structure from a body of content and break it down into sections, headings, and prompts. The prompts may include some of the supporting techniques suggested earlier in this chapter, such as word lists, sentence starters, and gapped sentences—all placed within the structure of the larger frame.

In Materials extract 6.Q, learners are asked to talk about four principal problems, sequenced numerically. They are given prompts (mainly noun phrases) to help them cover the main ideas, as well as action verbs to help them construct full sentences.

The problem with fertilizers

First …	tasteless,	are often
	nutrients,	are low in
	fresh,	don't stay
	risk of disease	may be contaminated
		collect in
		have been linked with
Second …	run off into rivers,	get washed out of
	algae growth,	end up in
	no light,	grow so well that
	oxygen starvation	die because
		feed on … using up
Third …	nitrates in drinking water,	can then pass through
	health problems	end up in
		have been linked with
Lastly …	balance of nature,	upsets
	weeds and insects,	encourage
	wildlife, humans	attract more
		ends up using lots
		kill
		are bad for

Materials extract 6.Q Speaking frames (adapted from Gallagher & Ingram, New coordinated science: Chemistry, OUP, pp. 160–163.)

The example shown in Materials extract 6.Q would be located at a later stage of a lesson sequence, when learners have had plenty of topic input from a variety of sources and media. At this stage, students work in pairs to create descriptions.

Note that there is still room for them to make use of their own language. The example would work well in co-ordination with a guided presentation that learners are asked to make on the topic. Speaking frames help learners practise their talks, and again signify a milestone on their journey towards producing standard subject language.

Notes to speak from

In the same way that teachers prepare notes to help them run a lesson successfully, notes can provide valuable support for the CLIL learner. In Chapter 5, we saw how a summary of content was used to guide learners as they watched a slideshow on the planets. The same summary could be used as helpful scaffolding to help learners prepare and talk through their own presentation on a planet of their choice. An example of this is shown in Materials extract R.

Planets

My Planet

Insert a picture illustrating where the name of your planet comes from.

Explain the origin of the name of your planet.

... is named after ...

Location

Insert a picture illustrating the location of your planet in relation to other planets in the solar system.

Say where your planet is.

Say how far your planet is from the Sun.

... is found ...
The distance from ...
to the Sun is ...

Atmosphere

Insert a picture illustrating the atmosphere of your planet.

Say what the atmosphere of your planet is made up of.

The atmosphere of ... is
made up of ...

Temperature

Insert a picture illustrating the temperature of your planet.

Say what the range of temperatures is on your planet.

The temperature ranges
from ... to ...

Make up

Insert a picture illustrating what your planet is made up of.

Say what your planet is made up of.

... has a core which is
made up of ...

Extra information

Insert an illustration for any extra information you can find about your planet.

Present any interesting additional things you found about your planet.

It is also ...
It also has ...

Materials extract 6.R Notes to speak from

The speaking frame for 'Planets' is similar in principle to the ones described in the previous section. The sections of the presentation frame are organized with headings. The scaffolding includes a selection of adjective, verb, and noun phrases to help learners create their own descriptions of their chosen planet, which they then present to the class.

Moving on to writing

Why ask students to write? According to Clegg:

> Unlike talk, in which concepts soon 'fly away', writing allows us to hold incomplete concepts, so that we can operate on them through modifications in written language, and push the refinement process much further than we can through talk. So writing is *par excellence* a thinking process. And teachers need to guide their learners to become experts in the process of writing and thinking in their subject. This means that subject teachers need to understand the organization of written discourse and the cognitive value of learners organizing their ideas in writing, and offer their students opportunities to practise this in the classroom.
> (Clegg, 2002a)

Nevertheless, it is difficult to talk about writing as a skill which fits comfortably into all areas of the curriculum. Whereas speaking activities can be adapted to fit diverse parts of learning programmes, writing is conditioned more by the demands of subject-specific genres. Subject teachers incorporate speaking into their classes by default, through the regular occurrence of teacher–student dialogue—an interaction pattern which we have added to in the previous section. However, it is more difficult for subject teachers to envisage an equally wide range of writing activities as standard classroom methodology. Certain subjects—mathematics, for example—do not immediately fit the profile of a writing-rich subject area. In this respect, the range of CLIL-based writing support needs to be more subject-specific and led by the forms and shapes of writing particular to the subjects themselves, rather than by a variety of different forms of interaction.

Llinares et al. (2012) write of students being 'apprenticed' in curriculum writing. 'Apprenticeship' is a good metaphor for students being trained in the forms of writing they come across in a given subject, as it suggests a move from less formal to more formal structured writing, following given patterns found in specific subject areas.

Writing across the curriculum (Lewis & Wray, 1998) is a rich resource for CLIL teachers looking for ideas on producing 'frames' to help students develop their subject-based writing skills. Lewis and Wray advocate a selective use of writing frames. Of course, it must be remembered that the authors are largely presenting techniques for work with L1 learners. In a CLIL context, the idea of the scaffold, represented by the frame, should be considered in its Vygotskian form (1986), whereby the support is offered to enable L2 learners to move from the '**zone of proximal development**' (**ZPD**) to beyond, where greater autonomy lies. In other words, learners move to areas of learning that would be difficult for them without the provision of additional scaffolding. In this respect, writing support in CLIL is both valid and necessary, up to the point where learners no longer need it.

What we are advocating, therefore, is an approach which provides subject-specific scaffolding for writing (the range), over a period dictated by the writing support needs of learners studying through an L2 (the scope).

The range of writing in CLIL

There are four broad genres of writing in the school curriculum: descriptive, narrative, expository, and persuasive. In the same way that these genres make up the majority of reading experiences for learners, they also constitute the staple diet for writing.

Important for a CLIL-based approach to writing is a consideration of the specific nature of these genres within a given subject. History tends to be descriptive, narrative, and persuasive, with less in the way of expository writing. On the other hand, science tends to have learners writing expository and descriptive texts but fewer persuasive and narrative ones. Mathematics is light on writing altogether, though this can depend on specific contexts and their curricular approaches. Where writing is involved, it tends to be expository, with some descriptive writing. Geography, with its more **transversal** content, can offer a wide range of writing experiences for learners.

The scope of writing in CLIL

In addition to looking at the range of writing in a subject class, it is necessary to examine the scope, or the size and shape, of the individual writing support provided. There are a number of ways teachers can provide writing support, some of which we have encountered already as language support types in the section dealing with speaking (see page 135). These include simple techniques such as spoken or written teacher prompts, or models of structures provided on the board or on handouts. The key to supporting writing in CLIL is to structure lesson sequences so that they culminate in written production which meets the formal language expectations of the subject.

The following forms of writing support can be given for the butterfly visual shown in Figure 6.3.

All the items above help CLIL learners to write about the life cycle of the butterfly. The key decision the teacher has to make is the extent of support the learners need, a decision which will be conditioned by the lesson objective. In a CLIL lesson where learners have followed an exposition on the life cycle of a butterfly, and have had the opportunity to discuss the visual in pairs, the next step would seem to demand a more formal 'fixing' of the concepts by having the learners formulate a text using the scaffolds shown above. Other support strategies follow below.

Sentence-level support

Sentence starters

Sentence starters can serve as prompts for CLIL learners who often encounter difficulties at the initial stage of text formation. This is a natural problem for a non-native writer, since discourse conventions, often alien to learners, tend to cluster around introductions and resolutions. Sentence starters, or opening gambits, can also provide cohesion at any point in the text, with simple

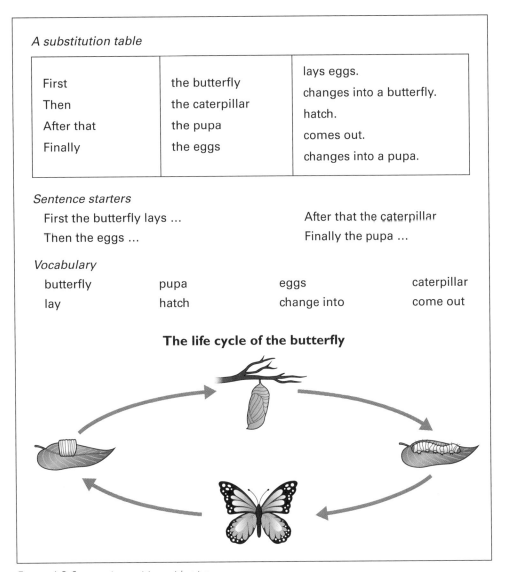

A substitution table

First	the butterfly	lays eggs.
Then	the caterpillar	changes into a butterfly.
After that	the pupa	hatch.
Finally	the eggs	comes out.
		changes into a pupa.

Sentence starters

First the butterfly lays ...

Then the eggs ...

After that the caterpillar

Finally the pupa ...

Vocabulary

| butterfly | pupa | eggs | caterpillar |
| lay | hatch | change into | come out |

The life cycle of the butterfly

Figure 6.3 Supporting writing with pictures

discourse markers such as: 'firstly', 'secondly', etc. being easy items to employ. It is common in subject textbooks for units of work to be followed by questions which refer to content covered in a given unit, such as: 'Describe two ways in which animals can disperse fruits and seeds. Give an example of each.'

Sentence starters and word lists can be given to offer support for writing the answers to the above question (see Materials extract 6.S overleaf), where all students need to do is transform the infinitive into the *-ing* form, for example 'by carrying away'.

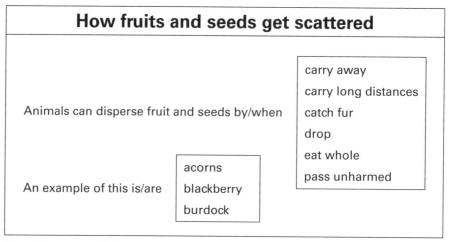

Materials extract 6.S Sentence starters and word lists

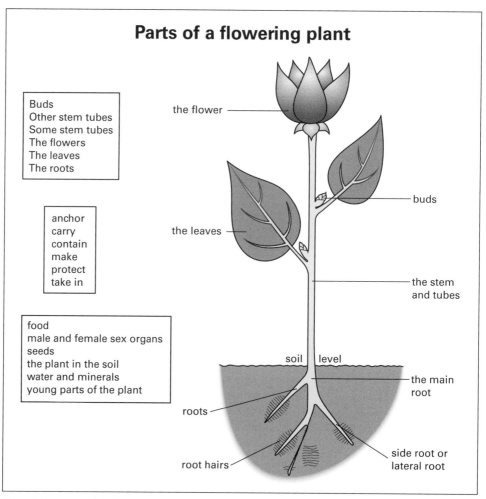

Materials extract 6.T Sentence starters and word lists with illustrations (adapted from Beckett & Gallagher, New coordinated science: Biology, OUP, p. 70.)

Sentence starters and word lists with illustrations

Textbook illustrations are frequently used to present key terminology, by illustrating definitions, explanations, and characteristics of subject phenomena. An example is Materials extract 6.T, where the learning objectives involve the parts, structures, locations, and functions of flowering plants. It can be useful to exploit the visual with accompanying sentence starters and word lists to scaffold the learners' written production.

Substitution tables

Substitution tables focusing on single-sentence writing provide a lot of support for lower-level language students who are able to make decisions about the content, but may need extra help in putting the sentences together. The key principle with a substitution table is that while it is possible to make errors in the content, they can be constructed so that it is impossible to make a linguistic error, freeing up the cognitive aspect and removing some of the language pressure. As shown in Figure 6.4, creating a substitution table is a straightforward process.

---

1 Start with a text:

'Nobody knows exactly how our climate will change. Some places may get drier and have year-round increases in temperatures of up to 4°C. Other places may become several degrees cooler. Stormy weather may become more common. Glaciers and icebergs may start to melt and never form again. Whatever happens, climate change will affect people as well as the natural world. But there are things that we can do to slow down the changes and to minimize any negative consequences.'

2 Identify core sentences in the text:

Some places may get … and have year-round …

Other places may become …

Stormy weather …

Glaciers and icebergs …

3 Select key structures and organize them into a table.

Some places Other places Stormy weather Glaciers and icebergs	may	become more common. get drier. become several degrees cooler. have year-round temperatures up to 4°C hotter. start to melt.

Figure 6.4 Creating a substitution table

If necessary, remove structures which do not fit in the table, or add others which you consider useful. In Table 6.1 (overleaf), the noun and adjective phrases can be altered to suit the experimental context. This particular substitution table plays a role during a lesson in which students are learning how to write up their laboratory work in a science report.

We thought	candles butter margarine ice cheese chocolate	would melt	in	cold cool warm hot boiling	water.
But it/they melted					

Table 6.1 A substitution table for writing up a tested hypothesis

It is worth bearing in mind that the input text for creating a substitution table does not necessarily have to come from a textbook. Frequently, content teachers come up with input texts themselves, and creating a substitution table from these involves writing down the script on paper to identify the key structures that learners need to make their own.

Paragraph-level support

Substitution tables can be constructed to support longer paragraph writing. The principle is the same as with producing a sentence-based substitution table, and it involves teachers working through a section of text to find the language necessary for the learners to be able to write on a given topic. By way of example, let us look at Figure 6.5, which shows the topic 'Comparing planets', following the three-step approach outlined above.

Even though there are no discourse markers used for comparison in the text itself, it would also be useful for budding NNS scientists writing about planets in English to be given conjunctions such as 'whereas' or 'but'. These can be incorporated into the substitution table as shown in the right-hand column. Note that the teacher has decided to omit information about size and movement, choosing to focus on atmosphere, distance from the Sun, and temperature.

Whole-text support

Writing frames are full-length structures used to support the writing of longer texts. They combine some or all of the techniques described above (sentence starters, word lists, and substitution tables). Persuasive texts can be seen throughout the curriculum, and a common aspect of these texts is the language of cause and effect. An example of this genre and a writing frame support can be seen in Materials extract U (on page 166). This example offers a whole-text structure in the frame, with section headings, sentence starters, and a word list.

1 We select a text:

Comparing planets

Mars is called the 'red planet' because iron materials in its soil make it look red. It has a very thin atmosphere, which is mainly carbon dioxide. It is smaller than the Earth and is further from the Sun. Mars is the fourth planet from the Sun. The temperature on Mars is never higher than 20° Centigrade. At night it usually falls below −120° Centigrade.

Venus is our nearest neighbour but is very unlike the Earth. It has a heavy atmosphere of carbon dioxide which traps the heat. Its temperature is about 480° Centigrade all the time. There are two interesting things about Venus. Firstly, it rotates from east to west. The only other planet that does this is Uranus. Secondly, Venus takes 243 days to rotate on its axis but only 225 days to orbit the Sun. So its day is longer than its year!

Like our moon, Mercury has no atmosphere. It is the smallest planet and the one closest to the Sun. Its temperature during the day is 510° Centigrade. But at night the temperature falls to −170° Centigrade because there is no atmosphere to trap in the heat.

2 We identify key structures:

  Mars has a very thin atmosphere …
  Venus has a heavy atmosphere …
  Mercury has no atmosphere.
  Mars is the fourth …
  Venus is the nearest …
  Mercury is the closest …
  The temperature on Mars is (never higher than) …
  The temperature on Mars usually falls below …
  The temperature on Venus is about …
  The temperature on Mercury falls to …

3 We create our substitution table:

Mars Mercury Venus Earth	has	a very thin a heavy no	atmosphere	(but) (whereas)
	is	the fourth planet from the nearest planet to the closest planet to	the Sun Mars Venus Mercury Earth	
The temperature on	Mars Venus Mercury Earth	is is about is never higher than usually falls below/to	20°C 480°C 510°C −170°C −120°C at night during the day all the time	

Figure 6.5 Substitution table for comparing planets

Write about air pollution.

Causes
Pollution is caused by …

Consequences
Polluted air can cause …
It also …

Pollutants
The main pollutants are …
They are produced by …

Carbon monoxide
This is …

Hydrocarbons and nitrogen oxides
They produce …
… irritates … and …

These words will help you:
coal
oil
natural gas
burning
respiratory infections
lung cancer
allergies
gasoline
car
engine
colourless
odourless
poisonous
ozone
nose
throat
eyes
water

Materials extract 6.U Writing frame for 'Air pollution'

A second example is given in Materials extract 6.V and offers a frame devoid of key content phrases. The focus in this case is on the general academic language inherent to the text type—namely 'cause–effect–solution'—and it relies on learners knowing or finding the key content language themselves.

Content is frequently presented in summary form in textbooks, for example in a table. The idea that the CLIL learner can easily produce a full version of the text using the summary is questionable, because the general academic language necessary to transform the format is largely invisible. The example in Materials extract 6.W, accompanied by a further writing frame in Materials extract 6.X (on page 168), can help to support extended writing on vitamins, their properties, their associated food types, and the consequences that arise from their shortage in our diet.

Pollution from fossil fuels

What pollutants are produced from fossil fuel burning?
(Give names)

Where do you mainly find these pollutants?
When ... burn, ..., ... is produced.

... escapes ...

... all contain ...

These are an indirect result of ...

This is also a by-product of ...

It is formed in ...

... come from ...

What are the dangers/consequences of these pollutants?
It is poisonous.

... is known to cause ...

It can cause ...

... can affect ...

... damages ...

... these attack ...

What can be done?
... can be fitted with ...

... energy efficiency ...

... alternative fuels ...

... legislation ...

Materials extract 6.V Writing frame for 'Pollution from fossil fuels' (adapted from Gallagher & Ingram, New coordinated science: Chemistry, OUP, pp. 190–191.)

The main vitamins and minerals you need

Substance	Where you find it	Why you need it	Shortage can cause
Vitamin C	Oranges, lemons, grapefruit, green vegetables, potatoes	For healthy skin and gums, and to heal wounds quickly	**Scurvy.** Gums and nose bleed. The body bleeds inside.
Vitamin D	Milk, butter, eggs, fish, liver (also made by skin in sunshine)	For strong bones and teeth	**Rickets.** The bones become soft and bend.
Calcium	Milk, eggs	For strong bones and teeth	**Rickets.**
Iron	Liver, spinach	For making red blood cells	**Anaemia.** The person is pale and has no energy.

Materials extract 6.W Example of a content summary table (Beckett & Gallagher, New coordinated science: Biology, OUP, p. 119.)

The main vitamins and minerals you need

Name of vitamin
You get ... from ...
... can be found in ...
... is found in ...

What vitamin is for
It is needed/important/essential for ...
... is needed for ...
You need it for ...

Consequences of shortage
A shortage/lack of ... can cause/lead to ...
Not getting enough ... can cause/lead to ...
If you don't get enough ..., it can cause ...

Materials extract 6.X Accompanying writing frame (adapted from Gallagher & Ingram, New coordinated science: Chemistry, OUP, p. 119.)

The extent of support that teachers give to enable learners to reproduce content in their own words, without disregarding the standard language requirements of the subject, differs from context to context. CLIL teachers, however, will always need to give learners initial time to think about new subject knowledge and the opportunity to express their understanding of it in their own words. Learners will also need the chance to talk about these initial ideas in pairs and/or small groups to be able to gauge their understanding alongside that of their peers. Writing frames like these come at a stage in the learning process when learners have managed to produce 'first drafts' of new content and language.

Another example, shown in Materials extract 6.Y, is a fully supportive writing frame which has been organized into headed sections with sub-headings. There are gapped sentences accompanied by a key vocabulary list. All the possible information and structures learners could possibly need to write about the functions of the liver has been provided for them. Teachers may decide to give only the section headings as a writing prompt. Or they may decide to provide the headings and the gapped sentences, or just provide the gapped sentences and the word list.

Jobs done by the liver				glucose
Storage	Glycogen Minerals Vitamins	It stores … It changes this … when … It stores …, as well as … needed to make … It stores …	glycogen, the body, minerals, copper, potassium, iron, red blood cells
Extractions/ reactions	Amino acids Poisons	It takes the … out of …, and changes … into … It takes some … from … and makes them … These … come from …	vitamins A, B and D, goodness, amino acids, urea, kidneys, poisons
Production	Digestion Clotting	It makes …, which is needed for …	germs, alcohol and drugs, fibrogen, blood
By-products	Heating	These and many other … produce …, which the … to keep …	wounds, heat

Materials extract 6.Y Writing frame for 'Jobs done by the liver' (adapted from Beckett & Gallagher, New coordinated science: Biology, OUP, p. 131.)

Composition and text structure

With regard to the more traditional 'composition', the task shown in Materials extract 6.Z (overleaf) occurs, as we have been emphasizing, at the very end of a lesson sequence. Nevertheless, the conceptual knowledge gathered must be combined efficiently with the procedural and linguistic dimensions in an explicit fashion in CLIL. Here, in the context of the topic of human geography, students consider a range of solutions, report which they think are the most feasible, and then (in step 3) write a composition about the solutions to population growth. Step 3 suggests how this might be done, but with emphasis on the structure of the text, as opposed to the language. At this stage, and at this level, the inherent language is assumed. The structural aspects of this type of text, however, are not.

Consider these 'solutions' that have been tried in the **past** for problems of excessive population growth.

1.- Write down in your notebook the solutions that you think are a good idea.

a) Enforced (obligatory) sterilisation (of women) after birth of first child. (China & India)
b) Free contraception and family planning advice. (Nigeria)
c) One-family one-child policy. (China)
d) Raise the age of marriage for women to 21. (Bangladesh)
e) Tax concessions (pay less tax) to childless couples (China)
f) 'Fertility reduction' treatment for women   (Bangladesh)

2.- Be prepared to justify your decisions to your teacher.

3.- Write a short composition, the first part about the **consequences** (of population growth), the second part about some of the **solutions** that you have read about, and some that you may have thought about yourself. It should have **at least** three paragraphs:

1° = Introduction + consequences
2° = Some of the solutions, and why they were/are good or bad
3° = Some kind of conclusion.

Materials extract 6.Z Population growth in human geography (Beobide & Ball, Geography 3, Ikastolen Elkartea, p. 159.)

Support based on the gradual sequencing of language is also crucial in guiding accurate but more extensive writing. In Materials extract 6.ZZ, learners are introduced to the purely descriptive aspect of data reports in a unit on 'Health', which will eventually require them to:

- gather data
- describe results
- draw conclusions
- give advice.

Here, students fill in the gaps using the bar chart as their source of information. Later in the sequence, they will be expected to use the language and structures embedded in the model to comment more freely on a variety of data sources regarding the health of their own classmates.

3. Look at the bar chart showing the calories of 100 grams of different types of food.

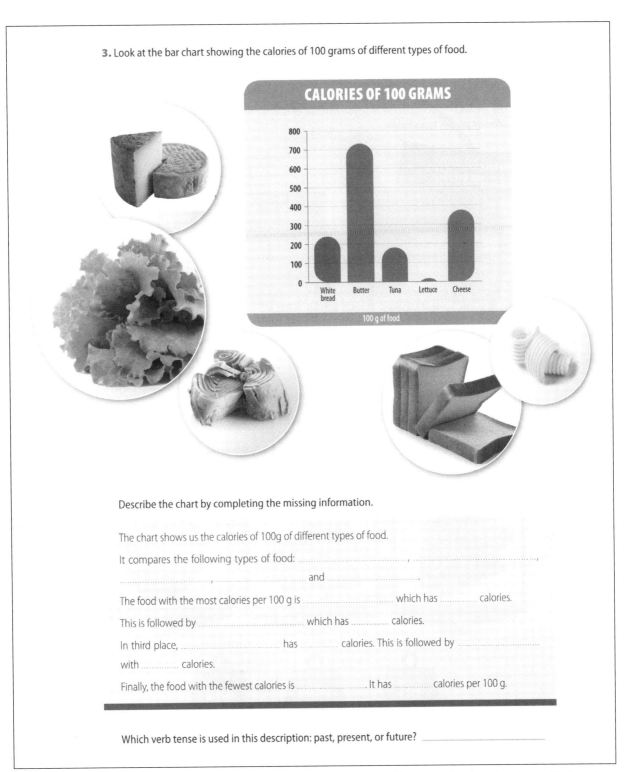

Describe the chart by completing the missing information.

The chart shows us the calories of 100g of different types of food.

It compares the following types of food: ...., ...,

................................, ... and ....

The food with the most calories per 100 g is .... which has .... calories.

This is followed by .... which has .... calories.

In third place, ... has .... calories. This is followed by ....

with .... calories.

Finally, the food with the fewest calories is .... It has .... calories per 100 g.

Which verb tense is used in this description: past, present, or future? ....

Materials extract 6.ZZ Embedding contextualized language for data description (Ball et al., Subject projects 2: Healthy U, Ikaselar, p. 100.)

Summary

This chapter has looked at a range of instruments for teachers to use when preparing output activities for their own classes. There is an underlying principle that learners need opportunities to assimilate and express new knowledge in their own words. Initial talk time allows them to carry out this essential process. At the same time, it can be useful to look at the scope of speaking and also writing support in terms of the range, or 'shapes', of content, as each follows a specific organizational structure, depending on the subject and genre of text. With a little practice, CLIL teachers can develop useful skills for preparing support for activities where learners speak or write which corresponds to their specific subject area.

We have emphasized that one of the key challenges for CLIL teachers aiming to provide support is to actually 'see' this support in the original content item. The content item may be a visual, a text, a talk, or any form of content to be presented to the learner in a lesson. What CLIL teachers need to be aware of is the key structures they would like their students to be able to produce, either in spoken or in written form. Another issue highlighted in this chapter is the 'scope', or the type and amount, of support to give. Once CLIL teachers have identified the key structures in a content item, the next step is to prepare these structures in a form appropriate to the students' level and the activity in hand.

Task

If you would like to look at a practical task to explore your own practice related to the content of this chapter, see Appendix 1 (page 292).

Further reading

Hayes-Jacobs, H. (2006). *Active literacy across the curriculum: Strategies for reading, writing, speaking, and listening.* Larchmont, NY: Eye on Education.
The whole book offers useful advice on developing language in the curriculum, but also gives a very clear argument for schools joining up parts of the curriculum and teachers sharing information for the purpose of developing learner language. See Chapter 7 (*Mapping active literacy*).

Lewis, M., & **Wray, D.** (1998). *Writing across the curriculum.* Reading, UK: University of Reading.
A useful collection of non-fiction writing frame templates to guide and support learners, with some background information on producing your own writing frames.

Mercer, N., & **Hodgkinson, S.** (Eds.) (2008). *Exploring talk in school: Inspired by the work of Douglas Barnes.* SAGE Publications: Kindle edition.
A basic but thorough argument on developing learning through talk in all subject areas of the curriculum. The whole book is packed with great ideas, but Barnes's Chapter 1 (*Exploratory talk for learning*) is a must-read.

7

DESIGNING MATERIALS FOR CLIL

Overview

This chapter looks in detail at the ways in which we can help students to learn through interacting with clear and supportive teaching materials. The bulk of the chapter consists of the description and analysis of seven principles for materials design in CLIL. The chapter does not deal with the adaptation of materials as such, but most of the design principles mentioned will also help teachers in this regard. Prior to illustrating the set of potential guidelines, we will consider some of the issues surrounding the design of didactic materials, and in this particular case, those materials that are destined to be used by non-native speakers learning through an L2.

Time and inspiration

In the educational world in general, the first thing to point out with regard to the writing and design of classroom materials is that many teachers find neither the time nor the inspiration to undertake it, at least to any substantial degree. In terms of the time issue, it is obvious that any teacher, experienced or inexperienced, managing a 20-hour-plus weekly timetable with its attendant preparation and marking demands, administrative duties, and possible responsibility as a class tutor, will justifiably look upon the need to create a custom-built course for the academic year as one demand too many. Creating effective materials requires time and attention, and full-time professional authors are paid to do just that. As proof of this, the shelves of bookstores in most developed countries groan under the weight of textbooks, with publishers offering the consumer (institutions, teachers, students) a wide range of choice, often planned and written under the consensus-based auspices of national curricula. Parallel digital versions also exist, which include extra resources to extend learning opportunities, and extra applications and tools to facilitate classroom management. In the end, unless a national or regional government prescribes a specific textbook for schools to use, the material that teachers choose comes down to a matter of personal choice. Sometimes the decision is made by the individual subject teacher, sometimes by the head of department, or preferably as the result of dialogue between all those concerned.

The textbook may be extremely effective, but it is nevertheless worth bearing in mind that its contents are the result of the perspective and inspiration of a third party in whom teachers are obliged to invest a considerable amount of trust.

Personal investment

Teachers will all recognize the basic feeling of security that a trusted textbook provides, and will often base their eventual preferences on criteria such as how well the book engages and motivates students. Since the thematic content is normally determined by the wider curriculum, teachers will often judge a book on its procedural content: 'That new textbook I was talking about has got some really great activities for the science research unit. It's really useful on a Friday afternoon!'

Nevertheless, any teacher who has been given the time and opportunity to create (and then use) their own materials in the classroom will attest to the enormous influence this process can have on their personal and professional development (Allan, 1997). Just as personal investment in a task enhances student learning, the writing of materials and the insights this provides can be invaluable for teacher development (Roberts, 1998). Some teachers are better at designing materials than others, but all teachers can be trained to produce something that works—and the satisfaction of seeing their own materials in action (whether original or adapted) can be enormous.

CLIL, with its organic growth and its (up to now) concomitant lack of a clear set of guiding principles, has in many cases obliged teachers to create custom-built materials. Necessity has all too often been the mother of invention in CLIL, and it would be misleading to pretend that this has always been a positive phenomenon. When teachers set out on their particular CLIL journeys, the various demands involved can be considerable. If they are also obliged to adapt or even create their own materials, it can be an exhausting experience.

Publishers have often been slow to step into the breach, usually because of the expense involved in publishing for niche markets. This has compounded the difficulties for individual schools and regions, who could have benefited from clear published models to help support CLIL initiatives. To respond to the growing demand for materials, subject-based books are sometimes imported from their country of origin and used in CLIL classes. But this type of publication has rarely proved useful in CLIL contexts. In fact, directly imported material, originally designed for native speakers and often written with no consideration of language support, can often bring about disastrous consequences. Similarly problematic is the widespread practice of taking subject-based books from a country's national curriculum and simply translating them into the L2. Although it is not always the case, these books may lack the perspective on language salience that CLIL attempts to engender, and their design principles will have remained unaffected by the type of considerations that experienced CLIL authors have taken on board.

Guidelines and criteria for CLIL

Mehisto (2012a) wrote some useful guidelines with regard to the criteria that teachers might consider when taking on the challenge of writing CLIL-based materials. Although some of the criteria he lists relate exclusively to general educational practice, the ten 'principles', as Mehisto calls them, offer good insight into the key characteristics of effective CLIL materials, and prioritize a useful set of considerations. The following five (numbered according to Mehisto's own list) seem to have the most exclusive focus on CLIL:

Quality CLIL materials …

1 make the learning intentions and process visible to the students.
2 systematically foster academic language proficiency.
5 help create a safe learning environment.
6 help foster co-operative learning.
9 foster cognitive fluency through the scaffolding of content, language, and learning skills.

We will refer to this list of criteria in relation to our own set of principles for CLIL materials design. However, the seven principles to be analysed and exemplified all derive from particular learning situations which arise from the practice of CLIL. It follows, therefore, that when we look at any activity in a CLIL textbook, it will reflect a certain learning theory. In the most basic of senses, this means that it will involve some sort of language support. This is something that can never be subtracted from CLIL-based discourse or practice.

CLIL-based materials also serve as fixed references, as examples of the principles that they illustrate and reflect. Good materials, or 'quality' materials, to borrow Mehisto's phrase, are the best 'teacher-trainers', whether they have been written by the teacher or not. We will explore this notion further in Chapter 10, but for now it suffices to observe that good materials can always be physically present—on the shelf, in a bag, on the staffroom table—whereas it is impossible for a good teacher-trainer, however influential in person, to always be around. And with the passing of time, a trainer's influence inevitably becomes more vague, more abstract. Good materials, on the other hand, are always within easy reach.

Seven principles

Some of the seven principles to consider when designing materials for use in CLIL-based contexts (see Table 7.1 overleaf) have already been mentioned in this book. For example, the three dimensions of content (item 2 in Table 7.1) and the 'adjusting of the volume' of any one of these dimensions were first explored in Chapter 3. In Chapters 5 and 6, we explored notions inherent to the guiding of input and the supporting of output (item 3). The notion of 'scaffolding' has also been covered, and the importance of thinking in sequences (item 7) underpins many of the other principles. Others have been less discussed, but here we are simply trying to provide clear 'snapshot' examples of each principle. By doing so, we wish to illustrate the connections that unite them all, and which contribute to the overall picture of what constitutes good CLIL practice.

Seven principles for CLIL materials design	
1	The primacy of 'task' (the text–task relationship)
2	Prioritizing the three dimensions of content
3	Guiding input and supporting output
4	Scaffolding and embedding
5	Making key language salient
6	The concept of 'difficulty' in didactic materials
7	Thinking in sequences

Table 7.1 Seven principles for CLIL materials design

1 *The primacy of 'task' (the text–task relationship)*

Before we can really explore this first notion in any detail, it is necessary to define the word 'task' satisfactorily.

What is a 'task'?

The initial problem with defining what a 'task' is stems from the similarities in meaning that this word shares with the terms 'activity' and 'exercise'. A further problem resides in the fact that these three terms are often used interchangeably in informal educational discourse. However, on closer examination of the meaning of 'task', Lee, for example, attributes a short list of components:

> A task is (1) a classroom activity or exercise that has (a) an objective attainable only by the interaction among participants, (b) a mechanism for structuring and sequencing interaction, and (c) a focus on meaning exchange; (2) a language-learning endeavour that requires learners to comprehend, manipulate, and/or produce the target language as they perform some set of work plans.
> (Lee, 2000)

The implication of this is that if an 'activity' or 'exercise' does not include these components, it cannot be considered a 'task' as such. It seems a reasonable way of making the distinction between the three terms. For the purposes of CLIL, Lee's definition of a task could be summarized thus:
- A task is goal-orientated
- A task requires interaction among learners
- A task requires the interaction to be 'sequenced' (i.e. to have identifiable stages)
- A task requires a set of 'work plans'.

If we agree with Lee's definition, then the online example shown in Materials extract 7.A is clearly not a 'task'. There is nothing wrong with it, in essence, but it requires neither interaction, nor sequencing, nor a set of work plans. It could be considered 'goal-orientated', but only in the very basic sense of contributing (in the medium-term) to the learners' understanding of the function of the present perfect. There is no other apparent purpose, other than the general aim of developing the learners' linguistic repertoire.

Choose either the present perfect or the past simple to go into each sentence. Use contractions where possible, but only for negatives: haven't, didn't, *etc.*

1 'This is my house.' 'How long have you lived here?'
   'I (live) here since 1997.'

2 He lived in London for two years and then he (go) to Edinburgh.

3 When I left school, I cut my hair and (wear) it short ever since.

4 Shakespeare (write) a lot of plays.

5 My brother (write) several plays. He has just finished his latest.

6 I (not see) him for three years. I wonder where he is.

7 He (not smoke) for two weeks. He is trying to give it up.

8 Chopin (compose) some of his music in Majorca.

9 'When (he/arrive)?' 'He arrived at 2 o'clock.'

10 I read his books when I was at school. I (enjoy) them very much.

Materials extract 7.A Online task (www.esl-lounge.com)

There are several reasons why Lee's definition of 'task' works well from the perspective of a CLIL materials designer. Firstly, if there is a 'goal'—namely a reason beyond the mere mechanical execution of an exercise—learners might be more motivated to carry it out. This seems like a reasonable supposition. CLIL has no necessary monopoly on being 'interesting', but a motivated student is always more likely to engage and therefore to learn. Similarly, 'interaction among learners' is necessary for the reason we have already stressed, which is the importance of learners producing language in their own words in order to learn concepts. And in a CLIL classroom, the more varied the interaction, the better. The 'sequencing' of this interaction is then a form of scaffolding—a way of making the process more evident to learners, and supporting the different types of language demands that will occur at the different stages of the task. We illustrated this notion in Chapter 2 (see page 38). Finally, 'a set of work plans' reads like the basis for a sequence of activities enriched by an authentic purpose. When learners are aware, right from the start, of the nature of the task at the end of a learning process, and they are interested in getting there and carrying out that task, the process is much more likely to be an enjoyable one, for both teachers and learners.

The text–task relationship

We first encountered this phrase in Chapter 2, as an example of one of the characteristics which one might expect to encounter in the CLIL classroom. The suggestion was that CLIL students, whether in primary, secondary, or tertiary education, would benefit from being given a clear understanding of the task—of knowing exactly what they have to do with a given text. Indeed, we went slightly further than this and proposed that the 'text' should be secondary to the task—that the task should be the true driver of the learning process, and that the text (whether written or spoken) should be subservient to the task, as the means to an educational end.

This only seems obvious when we consider the traditional tendency to phrase instructions along the lines of 'Read the text and answer the questions that follow'. In such cases, the 'text–task' relationship may be clear, but the text is in fact exercising a kind of tyranny on the learning process, as if it were always the most important element. This can be seen in the way instructions are traditionally worded in a way which seems to ask learners to focus exclusively on the text before even knowing what the task involves. But surely it is the task—effectively what students actually do with the text—that should be driving the process?

The ubiquitous text-led instruction in the paragraph above, which can be found in most typical assessment and classroom texts, is not necessarily 'wrong', of course. Generations of learners have been schooled on it. But it has certain problems, particularly when looked at in the context of the CLIL classroom.

In Materials extract 7.B, which is aimed at young secondary school CLIL students, no reason is given for reading the text, nor is there any instruction that might orientate the students by highlighting the potential difficulties of the process they are about to carry out. However, students can assume (correctly) from the title that they are to learn about the 'layers of a forest'.

The Layers of a Forest

If you want to find a cool place in summer, even when it's hot, then the forest is a good place. The tops of the trees protect us from the sun, like an umbrella. This is called the 'tree layer'. Various trees can be found at this level, such as beech, oak, birch and ash. Pine trees can also be found, and spruce. The middle layer is called the 'shrub layer', and it is not as tall as the tree layer. Examples of vegetation at this level are hazelnut and hawthorn shrubs, and there are also young trees. The next layer down is called the 'herb layer', and the plants here are bracken, grass and ferns – none of which need much sunlight. It can be quite dark down at this level, and there might be a moss layer on the forest floor, underneath the herb layer.

Answer the following questions:

1   According to the text, how many layers are there in a forest?
2   Which is the highest layer?
3   Which layer receives the most sunlight?
4   What is the layer called where young trees grow?
5   Write down in a list all the layers of a forest.
6   Which is the layer which receives the least sun?

Materials extract 7.B Layers of a forest

Of course, these questions may form part of a longer sequence which requires students to do lots of interesting things. We cannot be sure, but we can probably deduce from the text that it is introductory, and that for the students, this is new conceptual territory—namely the 'layers' that make up a forest, their relative positions, and their separate characteristics.

The main problem with this activity lies in the assumption that the students come to this environmental science class with zero knowledge of the topic. The fact that this text is probably an introduction to the topic is no excuse for ignoring the likely pre-existing knowledge, or 'schemata', that students are likely to have, simply from having lived in the world for the 12 or so years prior to this activity. For example, the question 'How many layers do you think there are in a forest?' might be a much better way of starting the lesson, before reading the text. Assuming we can convince students that the topic is worth considering in the first place, a quick pair-work brainstorm on how many layers there might be, and what they might be called, would be much more useful for students studying this topic in an L2. Let us look at the reasons why this might be the case.

1 It 'fronts' the task. Students know immediately what they have to do.
2 It is inductive. It does not simply transmit information to the students. It asks them to think first.
3 It suggests that the teacher values the students' capacity to think.
4 It will require some interaction among students, preferably in the L2.
5 It will encourage students to think about the technical vocabulary before encountering it.
6 It gives a reason for reading the text. It thus makes the activity 'task led'.

Also, for the purposes of interaction, the teacher could provide some simple scaffolds for the reporting-back stage, for example: 'We think there are X layers. We think they're called …' The simple act of involving students before they read the text creates all sorts of communicative opportunities which are otherwise lost by the limitations of the original design.

To conclude, the 'text–task' relationship underlying the 'layers of a forest' example is a relatively flimsy one, whose good intentions may be compromised by the basic design. To be fair, as we mentioned in Chapter 2, the traditional linear text as the sole source of input is now much less common since the internet serves as a quick and easily accessed source of target-language material. Nevertheless, whatever the form of text input, the issue of the quality of the text–task relationship still holds.

'Fronting' student involvement

In Chapter 2, we showed the example of how completing a 'mind map' in technology drove the reading of a text, and not vice versa. Similarly, the task in Materials extract 7.C, called 'Odd word out', is from a 'soft'-CLIL textbook in Spain for 13-year-olds, from a unit called 'Healthy U'. The task is from the introductory phase, and is the second of more than 50 tasks that are carried out over a period of almost three months.

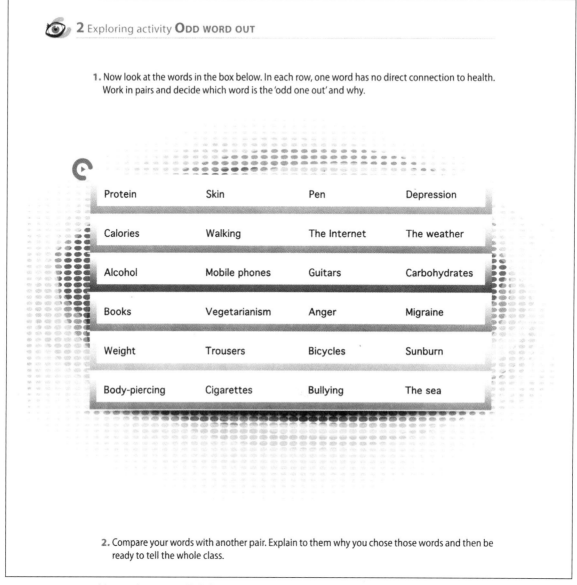

2 Exploring activity **ODD WORD OUT**

1. Now look at the words in the box below. In each row, one word has no direct connection to health. Work in pairs and decide which word is the 'odd one out' and why.

Protein	Skin	Pen	Depression
Calories	Walking	The Internet	The weather
Alcohol	Mobile phones	Guitars	Carbohydrates
Books	Vegetarianism	Anger	Migraine
Weight	Trousers	Bicycles	Sunburn
Body-piercing	Cigarettes	Bullying	The sea

2. Compare your words with another pair. Explain to them why you chose those words and then be ready to tell the whole class.

Materials extract 7.C Odd word out: fronting the task (Ball et al., Subject projects 2: Healthy U, Ikaselkar, p. 100.)

In this example, instead of providing students with a list of the contents they are to study, the task simply requires them to divide into pairs and work out which word from each row is <u>not</u> connected to what they are going to study. It matches Lee's definition of a task, and it 'fronts' the student action, or intervention. It requires interaction—first in pairs and then between pairs—and there is no reason why it cannot be carried out in the L2. The teacher's principal role is to set up the task. Only at the end of the process are they required to help confirm the answers. Most importantly, the 'text' is <u>subservient</u> to the task, and the relationship between the two is much more likely to be clear to the learner.

2 *Prioritizing the three dimensions of content*

We first illustrated this notion of the three dimensions in some detail in Chapter 3 (pages 52–54). There, we suggested that the word 'content' contains more complexities than has previously been explored in CLIL discourse, and that language, among other things, is also 'content'. We thus challenged the idea of CLIL as a 'dual-focused approach' and offered teachers a three-dimensional model, focusing on this wider notion of content. We said that any activity or task could be defined as the teaching of 'conceptual content, by means of procedural choices, using specific language derived from the discourse context'. We also suggested that the teacher could control the inevitable interplay between these three dimensions by adjusting the relative volume of each, according to the demands being made. We illustrated this by means of the 'mixing desk' metaphor from a music studio.

We added that all three dimensions could be described as 'content', and that the interplay between them defines CLIL practice. The concepts are ultimately understood by doing something, using a certain type of discourse. We suggested that teachers in CLIL-based contexts might use these three dimensions as both planning tools and classroom priorities, according to how they see the demands of any particular objective. We have also tried, so far, to use this model as a theme for this book, and to offer it as a simple working framework for CLIL.

Materials extract 7.D (overleaf), the 'Europe Quiz', provides a further example of the three dimensions with regard to materials design. The example is taken again from 'soft'-CLIL content for teenagers, used in this case for the English-language syllabus as part of a unit entitled 'Europe: United in diversity'. Once again, the task is introductory, but the unit is designed to take up roughly 40 hours of class time. As the title indicates, the aim of the unit is to teach enough content about Europe to illustrate both its similarities and its differences, which means the unit is likely to be quite concept-heavy—certainly as substantial as a similar 'hard'-CLIL unit in geography. There is no reason why the task could not appear in a CLIL geography syllabus. Perhaps the difference for a geography teacher would be the obvious highlighting of the 'three dimensions'.

Concept, procedure, language

Conceptually speaking, the task shown in Materials extract 7.D contains a mixture of facts and notions regarding Europe, some of which students will know and some of which they will need to speculate upon. The questions are multiple choice, and read out by the 'expert' peer-interlocutor who knows the answer (it is ticked—see Materials extract 7.D). The conceptual (outcome) objective is therefore to acquaint students with some examples of the type of content they will be asked to deal with during the unit.

Procedurally speaking, the task requires students to interact. This interaction involves speaking, but of a fairly easy nature because the students read from a script—a 100% scaffold, you might say. They must also listen carefully to the multiple-choice options, and respond accordingly. In the 'sit-down' phase (step 2),

2 Introductory activity **EUROPE QUIZ**

How much do you know about Europe?

1. Do the 'walkabout' multiple choice quiz with the rest of your class.

  • Take your card and ask a classmate your question.

EUROPE QUIZ

0

What is the capital city of the Czech Republic?

  • Budapest
  • Riga
  • Prague ✓

  • Then your classmate will ask you a question from his/her card.
  • When you've both asked and answered the questions, exchange cards and find someone else to ask.
  • Keep asking, answering and exchanging cards until your teacher tells you to STOP!

2. Now, do the 'sit-down quiz'. Fill in the gaps with just one word.

  a) Mount Elbrus is the **highest** mountain in Europe.

  b) Switzerland is famous .... watches and clocks.

  c) The Volga is the .... river in Europe.

  d) Mount Etna is Europe's .... active volcano.

  e) In Istanbul, you can eat your .... in Europe, then walk to Asia for lunch.

  f) Cristiano Ronaldo was .... on the island of Madeira.

  g) Basque is the .... language spoken in Europe.

  h) Helsinki is the .... city of Finland.

  i) BMW cars are .... in Germany.

  j) London is the capital city with the highest .... in Europe.

3. Check with a partner.

4. Now share your answers with the whole class.

Materials extract 7.D The Europe quiz (Ball et al., Subject projects 2: Europe: United in diversity, Ikaselkar, p. 10.)

the students then attempt a gap-fill on the basis of their 'new' knowledge, an activity which obviously requires them to read and (minimally) write. They are then encouraged to check answers with a partner before finally sharing in plenary.

Linguistically speaking, the task focuses mainly, although not exclusively, on the superlative form. Indeed, half of the questions in step 2 (b, e, f, h, i) focus on other language issues, such as the passive and dependent prepositions. The superlative is featured because the facts in the quiz are intended to be of an 'interesting' nature, and interesting facts often require superlative forms. The superlative form therefore occurs naturally in this conceptual/procedural context. In addition, quiz-based discourse often requires the passive voice. Also, the dependent preposition in question 2b will recur substantially in this unit, because the unit goes on to focus on multiple features of Europe—physical, cultural, and economic. So here, the structure is simply being embedded into the larger sequence (the unit).

The mixing desk

Returning to the 'mixing desk' metaphor from Chapter 3, the four steps of this task constitute an objective which is determined by its position in the unit's overall sequence. For example, to describe this cluster of tasks and activities in terms of a conceptual objective would surely be a mistake. The students are not expected to 'learn' this content; they are merely being introduced to the type of content that will be covered during the unit. So the conceptual 'volume' is turned down.

The procedural content is surely more important, and would probably constitute the objective. The students are being asked to interact, think about, and discuss (in the sit-down stage) the content, but it is the process and not the product of learning that takes precedence here. So the procedural volume is turned up.

The linguistic content is also important, but it is only the tip of the iceberg. The tasks and activities are hinting at what is to come, and providing some support for future challenges, as the complexity of the unit inevitably increases. The objective of the activity cluster is only partly linguistic, and like the conceptual content, it serves as a vehicle that carries the procedural weight. At this stage of the sequence, this is what students should expect. They know that things will change as they progress further into the sequence and the volume of the conceptual and linguistic dimensions gradually begins to increase.

Any one of the three dimensions, therefore, can be the priority. It is simply a matter of the teacher making a coherent decision, or of respecting the decision already taken by the author of the materials. As we have already noted, it is the conscious interplay between these three dimensions that most clearly characterizes good CLIL practice.

3 *Guiding input and supporting output*

These closely related notions have already been explored substantially in Chapters 5 and 6, but they are also key factors to consider in relation to materials design. In many ways, we could say that they are (or should be) one of the most important considerations of any paradigm of education, not just of CLIL. All learners must ultimately acquire the output tools that permit them to express themselves, both orally and in writing, and they must also be able to acquire the input skills that enable them to read and to listen effectively. These are lifelong skills whose basic building blocks, once in place, can then serve as a basis for coping with increasingly more challenging material.

Nevertheless, both CLIL and EAL have helped to awaken a growing consciousness of the fact that we can neither assume learners understand content input automatically, nor simply expect them to magically develop CALP-based powers of expression, and this has led to a greater focus on subject-based literacies. It has also engendered a strong sense of how we enable input—and foster output—in NNS educational contexts. It should go without saying, of course, that we are also concerned with the quality of that input and output.

Supporting speaking and dialogic talk

With regard to output, the example we used in Materials extract 7.C (on page 180) to illustrate the principle of task primacy is also useful here. In that activity, students were asked to decide on the odd word out, and then to justify their choices to their partners. A certain linguistic level is assumed, since no scaffolds have been provided for the task. However, the action 'justify their choices to their partners' can be interactively awkward, even in the L1. What natural functional language would students use, assuming they were actually interested in justifying and comparing? We could avoid potential problems by scaffolding some structures, writing them on the board and encouraging students to use them, but this can be slightly artificial. So instead, the second instruction asks students to 'explain to them why you chose those words and then be ready to tell the whole class'. In other words, the comparison is carried out not by comparing, as such, but by a process of self-justification, which seems more natural. These rough explanations can then be slightly refined before they are aired in plenary. This would give students more confidence, and enable a wider range of students to contribute publicly.

This example of students learning by interacting with each other is what Alexander (2008) calls '**dialogic talk**', and it has as much importance in the CLIL classroom as it does in any other educational context. Notice, however, that it is the materials that are stimulating the inter-student dialogue here, not the teacher. Classroom management will obviously help, but what is eventually said will depend on the students themselves.

In 'hard' CLIL, such speculative dialogue is equally important, and it tends to occur at the orientation phase of a sequence. Materials extract 7.E shows a 'hard' CLIL task about industry for the 14- to 15-year-old age range in the Basque Country, focusing on the small industrial town of Beasain, some of whose features students must try to guess, working in pairs. In order to speculate, students require very little language, since most of the questions are of the 'either/or' variety. Nevertheless, the concepts are not easy ones. Acknowledging this, question 2 asks the students to check their answers against the official data, and question 3 asks them to explain why they got some of the questions wrong. However, because the linguistic demand of hypothesizing in the past is quite high, the author provides some scaffolds, one with a past conditional ('we thought there would be') and the other with a modal structure ('maybe most of'). The student output is therefore supported, but only after the initial student intervention.

Have a look at the following questions based on some social data of Beasain. Work in pairs.

1.- Read the questions and write the guesses in your notebook.

   a) Beasain is an industrial town. Would you expect more **women** or more **men** in the total population? *"I would expect to be more......."*

   b) Industrial towns attract 'migrant' workers from other areas of the country. Would you expect more **women** or more **men** migrants in Beasain?

   c) What percentage of the total population of Beasain do you think is 'migrant'?

   d) Would you expect the unemployment figure (percentage) to be higher or lower than for example Castrelo de Miño?

   e) In 2010 the average unemployment figure in Spain was 20 % of the active population. What do you think the figure was for Beasain?

   f) In which sector do you think most people are employed in Beasain: In agriculture, industry and building, or services?

   g) In terms of percentages, would you expect a higher or a lower **inactive** population in Beasain than in Castrelo de Miño?

2.- Now look at the following data to work out whether your guesses were accurate or not in some of the categories. If you were wrong, write the correct answers to the side of your guesses, then draw a line through your guesses to indicate that they were wrong.

3.- Find two of the guesses that were wrong, and before your teacher asks you about them, **try to justify why you guessed as you did**. The guess may have been a good one! Write down a sentence with your partner and be ready to use it when you teacher asks for the answers.

For example:

*"For Number 1, **we thought there would be** more men than women in the total population, because in an industrial town more of the workers are men."*

4.- Be ready to speculate on the reasons why you were wrong.

For example:

"For Number 1, maybe most of the active population is married, and belongs to families? Maybe industry attracts families, not single workers?"

Materials extract 7.E Beasain: Getting students to talk (Beobide & Ball, Geography 3, Ikastolen Elkartea, p. 60.)

From this example, we can see that it is not always necessary to provide the language up front, as if students were unable to think and speak without preparation. Notice, too, how the 'post-task' scaffolds clean up the student language and focus on the accuracy that is likely to have been absent in the speculation stage. Students are actually being asked to write the justifications in question 3, demonstrating the increasing focus on accuracy that can accompany the transition from speaking to writing.

PPP in reverse

In the end, what is the best way to get students talking about difficult things? In CLIL, by reversing the old 'PPP' notion (presentation, practice, production) and treating learners as if they have something to say, 'supporting output' is surely facilitated. In Materials extract 7.E, the students produce, practise, present, then produce again, this time more accurately. The output is guided here by prioritizing the process, which in turn helps the learners to assimilate the concepts, using functional language which supports the technical language related to the specific topic. The students are encouraged to be wrong. In fact, in this task, it is better to be wrong, because it generates more language, and crucially, more thinking. The students are learning about industry, but the procedural dimensions of this task are somehow much greater. As a social scientist would surely say, one of the main functions of geography is to help people think and analyse (in the case of Beasain, through talking). Here, the series of tasks ably supports these cognitive purposes.

Supporting writing

We have already seen examples of how to support writing in previous chapters, but in relation to the general principle of supporting output, we are more focused on how the materials themselves can assist in the development of this crucial skill. As with the 'industry' example in Materials extract 7.E, the skills of speaking and writing are often intertwined, or occur along a continuum. Also, as mentioned in the previous chapter, subjects require different types or genres of writing, which have specific writing conventions. So how can materials design principles in CLIL help us to support writing, in all its subject-based diversity?

On a purely sentence-based level, Materials extract 7.F shows how two simple scaffolds can cover considerable conceptual ground. The scaffold to the left uses the verb 'to stop'; and, like similar verbs of negative assertion such as 'prevent', 'prohibit', and 'ban', it requires a gerundive structure. The scaffold to the right, however, only requires an infinitive structure. The entire range of inventions for which humanity is responsible can be delineated by these two scaffolds, within the conceptual framework of 'needs', a key consideration when talking about inventions and technology. Here, students can confine themselves to the six that most interest them, but in terms of supporting output, this is an accuracy-based exercise. The volume of the linguistic dimension is turned up high.

With regard to guiding students in the correct use of more subject-based discourse, Materials extract 7.G (on page 188) shows just the final part of a three-stage experiment about water density and temperature. As in Materials extract 7.F, scaffolds are provided to enable students to write their conclusions, but there is a wider range of structures, and the language itself is more formal, suggestive of the conciseness required when writing scientific conclusions.

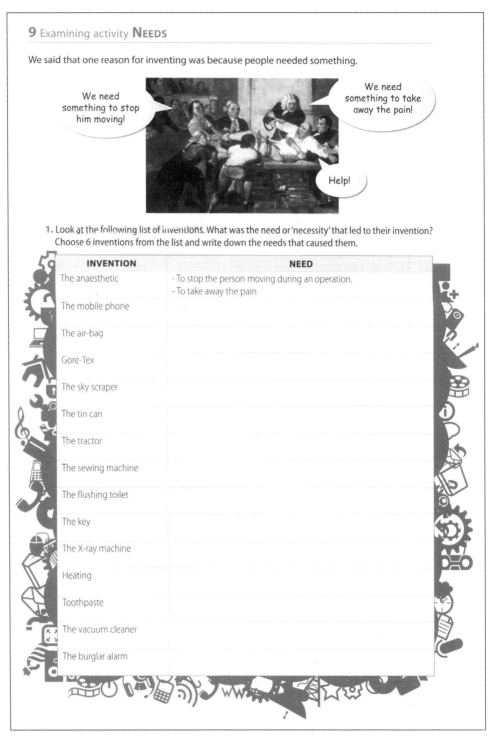

9 Examining activity **NEEDS**

We said that one reason for inventing was because people needed something.

We need something to stop him moving!

We need something to take away the pain!

Help!

1. Look at the following list of inventions. What was the need or 'necessity' that led to their invention? Choose 6 inventions from the list and write down the needs that caused them.

INVENTION	NEED
The anaesthetic	- To stop the person moving during an operation. - To take away the pain
The mobile phone	
The air-bag	
Gore-Tex	
The sky scraper	
The tin can	
The tractor	
The sewing machine	
The flushing toilet	
The key	
The X-ray machine	
Heating	
Toothpaste	
The vacuum cleaner	
The burglar alarm	

Materials extract 7.F Providing simple language scaffolds to support conceptual development (Ball et al., Subject projects 1: The world of inventions, Ikaselkar, p. 152.)

Water density

Fill another of the small containers with hot water. Add a drop of green food colouring and a teaspoon of salt. You are going to release some hot, salty green water into a glass of normal cold water.

What do you think will happen?

Now release the hot, salty green water into the glass.

Was your hypothesis right or wrong?

What conclusions can you draw from the experiments? Write three

sentences. You will need some of the language from the box.

	Right	Wrong
Hyypothesis 1		
Hyypothesis 2		
Hyypothesis 3		

- From the experiments we can conclude that ...
- When hot water mixes with water at normal temperature ...
- When salty water ...
- Salty water is denser than ...
- Cold water goes to ...
- Hot water goes to ...

Materials extract 7.G Water density and temperature (adapted from Ball et al., Subject projects 1: The secrets of the oceans, Ikaselkar, p. 39.)

To give an example of more extensive writing, the report on two towns shown in Materials extract 7.H is demanding for a variety of reasons. It is basically a research project, but once students have gathered the data, they must organize it and structure it into a written report, with the proviso that they can only emphasize four aspects, listed in step 4 of the task. To help them, the instructions suggest that these be structured in a certain order, and in step 5, examples are offered of words and structures (in bold) which would be appropriate to use for a written report in this discourse context. Since the groups are comparing and contrasting, they must use contrastive language. But this language then sub-divides into various types—namely discourse markers ('On the other hand'), conjunctions ('whereas'), causal language ('could be due to'), and other formal markers which help to introduce topics or paragraphs ('regarding', 'with reference to'). Teenage learners do not use these structures spontaneously, either in the L2 or in their L1, so support is provided here. But the students still have to think and act for themselves.

Now, using the information from the previous activities, you will write a **short report** comparing data on two towns.

To do the report you have two alternatives:

1.- You can do as we suggest and try to compare Castrelo de Miño with Hellin. You have already seen some data for these towns, but you may need more. Some suggested sites are: www.ine.es, www.infoagro.com, www.magrama.gob.es.

2.- You can choose two different locations from the ones above, but make sure first that you can obtain the information about population, working sectors and unemployment. The towns can be similar in size, but there should be some differences, geographically- speaking. Try to use towns from different provinces, or if from the same community, from different landscape areas.

3.- Whichever alternative you choose (Castrelo de Miño and Hellin or two different ones), you must compile a 'report' of **2/3 pages** to later communicate to your classmates. You can work in groups of 3. The report must have a **brief introduction** where you locate the areas to compare. Then define them with respect to:

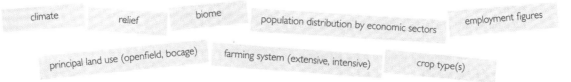

climate   relief   biome   population distribution by economic sectors   employment figures

principal land use (openfield, bocage)   farming system (extensive, intensive)   crop type(s)

4.- In order to structure the report, the **main sections** should be these five below. You can read more details looking at the check-list.

- Differences (in the aspects from point 3 above)
- Similarities (in the aspects from point 3 above)
- Significant differences (in the aspects…)
- Possible reasons for significant differences
- Conclusion

5.- In the report use **contrastive** language. Here are some examples.

"**Regarding** the climate of the two towns, we found some significant differences. For example, **whereas** the main feature of Castrelo de Miño's climate was **X**, the climate of Hellin was…"

"Looking at the unemployment rates **we can see that whereas**…"

"**With reference** to the two towns' principal agricultural activities…"

"**On the other hand,** Castrelo de Miño's land structure consists of…"

"**Similarly,** Hellin's…"

"We think that this significant difference **could be due to**…"

Materials extract 7.H Supporting extensive writing: research project (Beobide & Ball, Geography 3, Ikastolen Elkartea, p. 30.)

Guiding input

The two main types of input refer to the skills of reading and listening. These, along with watching, were formerly described as the 'passive' skills, but we now know that, in cognitive terms, an 'active' reader and listener benefits more. Nowadays, learners are generally required to read and listen purposefully, particularly in educational contexts. In CLIL, the more evident the purpose is made, the better, and so the combination of 'active + purposeful' is a very positive development.

Reading

With regard to reading, the demands on learners increase year by year, in terms of text length, the amount of technical language, and the complexity of the related activities. Written texts themselves, as we have noted, differ across subjects, but the social sciences, for example, are generally regarded as 'text heavy'. This could be a reason for CLIL programmes to avoid them or to embrace them—the latter because of the linguistic richness that they offer. Obviously, we would prefer to consider any content type appropriate for CLIL, but bearing in mind the 'text–task' relationship discussed earlier, it is surely more important to consider how we can facilitate understanding, without compromising the conceptual level of the objectives.

The very appearance of a text such as 'Proletarian ideologies' in Materials extract 7.1 can be intimidating for an NNS learner, despite the helpful use of subtitles, occasional bold font, and the two photographs of the topic protagonists. The first related task below the text, however, feeds students the content-obligatory CALP related to 'liberalism' and only asks them to supply the vocabulary for the socialist/communist ideologies. 'Anarchism' is then dealt with in the second step of the task.

The support for the reading derives from several techniques:

1 The table for step 1 'breaks down' the content into two manageable halves (first the proletarian ideologies, then anarchism).

2 The fact that the table provides the liberal ideas implies that the objective here is focused more on the new concepts (learners have already studied the liberal revolutions).

3 The table reflects the binary (opposite) nature of these ideologies. Once again, this breaks down the conceptual weight of the text.

4 The language for each column is complex, but narrowly limited to the particular historical discourse of the binary opposites. Some of the words are in the text (for example, 'classless'), but others students must work out for themselves ('non-privileged', 'egalitarian', 'communal society', etc.).

The reading here is carefully co-ordinated with the tasks, with the key language made salient. And complex though its concepts may be, the text is made more comprehensible by the guided nature of the tasks. However, the students must nevertheless both understand the text and eventually produce the correct terms. They are encouraged to be 'active' throughout. This means the conceptual and linguistic demands remain high, whilst the procedural demand is lowered.

... / ...

Friedrich Engels (1820-1895)

Proletarian ideologies: Unions and Socialists

Socialists (from the word 'Society') believed in certain principles. But basically, they believed in solidarity (proletarians working together to improve conditions) and an egalitarian society in which everyone had equality of opportunity – or the same chances to live a decent life. They believed in a classless society, where economic ideas would serve everybody, not just a few.

Communists (from 'Community'). The German philosopher, Karl Marx, went further than socialism. He believed that Liberalism was 'false liberty', and thought that the famous '*Declaration of the Rights of Man*' of 1789 was focused too much on the individual. The individual had **liberty**, but to do what? Marx thought that many bourgeois factory owners (especially) had used liberalism to make themselves very rich, and exploit the proletariat. This was not 'liberty' for Marx. He wanted society to be 'communal' and controlled, not individualised. Only in this way could people be 'free'. He thought that eventually, the proletariat would dominate the bourgeoisie (Proletarian's dictatorship) and then control the means of production (the factories). Based on these ideas, Lenin led the

Russian Revolution of 1917, applying communist theory to practice.

Anarchism

The Anarchists differed from the communists in that they rejected all types of authority – the State, the Church, and political parties. This is why there was never an official 'Anarchist Party', and no organised groups or associations. The anarchists, guided by Bakunin, believed that politics as practised by the State was simply a form of economic oppression. To end this, they believed in 'free association', in which society would organise itself from the 'bottom up', not from the 'top down'. For an anarchist, freedom was only possible if people were permitted to choose their own relationships – personal, professional and political.

Mikhail Aleksandrovich Bakunin (1814-1876), the founder of the anarchist movement.

In places where industrialisation occurred very late, or where there were many rural proletarians (like in Spain), the anarchist movement was very important. There were different ideas and sub-groups, and some of them employed violent terrorist-type methods, especially during periods of economic crisis.

Here are some activities related to ideology.

1. Below you will see various opposite ideas to the philosophies of socialism and communism. From the previous texts, extract the word or phrase that opposes the idea expressed below. The first one is done for you.

Liberalism	Socialist or communist idea
Working alone, to improve your life	Working together
Individuality	Solidarity
Privileges	
Class-based society	
Wealth for the minority	
A society of individuals	
A 'free' society	
The bourgeoisie control the proletariat	
The bourgeoisie control the production	

Separate the following characteristics into Communist or Anarchist. If the ideas belong to both ideologies, put them into the 'Ideas In Common' column.

Classless Society; Proletarian control; State-owned economy; Internationalism; Disappearance of the State; State-owned property; Disappearance of private property; Society organized by 'free association'

IDEAS IN COMMON	DIFFERENT IDEAS	
	Communism	Anarchism

Materials extract 7.1 'Proletarian ideologies': Breaking down text-based demands (Beobide & Ball, History 4, Ikastolen Elkartea, p. 71.)

The reading task in Materials extract 7.J (from the same sequence as Materials extract 7.I) also tries to break down the concepts by dropping the procedural demand whilst maintaining strong conceptual and linguistic dimensions. The factory owner is fictitious, but his subsequent complaints are immediately framed by the three concepts in the instruction: Money, Hours, and Working Conditions. Students know instantly that these concepts are what they need to focus their attention on. They must read the text and decide which of Sir Ivor Swissbank's complaints to add to the diagram below the text. As such, the reading remains subordinate to the task, whose successful completion will cover almost all the facts required for this often complex topic.

Read the text below by a (fictitious) factory owner, complaining about workers' demands. When you have read it, look at the diagram below. It contains all the aspects of the three main issues of Unionism and workers' demands: *Money, Hours, Working Conditions*, From the text, add the aspects (in note form) that are missing to the three issues.

Copy the diagram and write next to the arrows the specific details that are missing. One aspect of 'Money' is already done for you. Write in the others.

Sir Ivor Swissbank (Factory Owner)

The problem with these union types is that they want too much! They already have very good conditions indeed. I can't understand their problem! After all, we are providing work for them. What more do they want? Well, I'll tell you what they want.

The 'representative' came to me yesterday with a list of demands which were absolutely ridiculous. Of course he talked to me about wages and about establishing a minimum one. That is impossible, of course. Then he started talking about wage structure. 'Wage structure''! I told him. 'What does that mean'? And he told me that wage structure meant that every year I should give the workers higher wages – give them more money. Ridiculous again! Then he started talking about something different – about the terrible noise in the factory and other things related to this. 'What other things?' I asked him. 'This factory is very comfortable!' I told him. But he told me that the workers wanted holidays, and also sickness benefit – so that if they were ill and could not work I would have to pay them. Pay them for not working? Ridiculous! He also said that they wanted protection from the machines, because they were very dangerous. Well, I'll think about that one.

I thought he'd finished, but no…! He then started telling me about the time that they spent in the factory. He said that there should be a stipulated maximum, such as 8 hours. 'Not enough' I replied. But he continued talking about the topic of breaks. 'Breaks?' I shouted. 'You mean you want the workers to stop working every hour and rest? What a ridiculous waste of time. What about productivity?' I asked him. He also said that women and children should work less hours than men. Well, I'll consider that one, I suppose.

He finished by talking about money again, of course. How about 'productivity bonuses'? he asked. And something else – oh yes – establishing 'hourly rates of pay' so that they could know how much they would earn. 'Hourly rates?' I shouted. Preposterous! They'll want to own the factory next!

Money   ⟶   A minimum wage.

Hours   ⟶

Working Conditions   ⟶

Materials extract 7.J Sir Ivor Swissbank: Breaking down text-based demands (Beobide & Ball, History 4, Ikastolen Elkartea, p. 72.)

In the same way, gap-filling exercises like the one in Materials extract 7.K (overleaf), more typical of language textbooks, can be used for the resolution stage of a history sequence, by simply organizing the activity around the vocabulary items that carry the most conceptual weight.

Listening

For many years in language teaching, listening was often practised for its own sake. Listening exercises could be tortuous to do, often due to poor acoustics, disembodied voices, topics unsupported by meaningful content, but above all the quite reasonable question uppermost in the student's mind of 'Why am I doing this?'. Listening exercises rarely, if ever, reflected authentic pragmatic discourse, and hardly ever led to anything other than the checking of answers.

In CLIL, the listening 'text' should be used, as with reading texts, to do something else. This conforms to the aforementioned idea of the text–task relationship. It is hardly a novel observation that people generally listen in order to do something. We can listen for pleasure, of course, but even the traditional end-of-term film can be a disaster if it is too complex linguistically, meaning all students experience is meaningless noise. It is always useful to have something concrete to do with a listening text, a principle that is even more important now that teachers can draw on such a wide range of media. However, the media themselves, attractive though they may be, will guarantee neither understanding nor interest if there is no mediation by the teacher.

Besides, the problem in CLIL is rarely one of a lack of content or a lack of authenticity. The problem with an official syllabus is often that there is too much content, which we need to break down and make digestible for NNS learners. Materials extract 7.L (on page 195) shows the tasks following the one described in Materials extract 7.K. The topic is 'Fishing', from a geography syllabus for Spain. The listening is long and detailed, and so a variety of techniques have been used to lend the exercise some coherence and logic.

The tasks in Materials extract 7.L include a 'pre-listening' stage (step 1), a 'whilst listening' stage (step 2), which only requires students to answer questions on the first half of the dialogue, and an 'after listening' stage (step 3). This final stage checks the first half only—a good idea to make sure that everyone is on the right track—before asking students to listen to a shorter second half of the interview and answer questions which are of a slightly different type from the ones in step 2.

Step 1 'embeds' some of the low-frequency vocabulary inherent to this particular topic ('trawlers', 'canning') so that students have a list to check off as they listen to the dialogue. Notice students will have dealt with these words already, so this stage simply requires them to judge the words in terms of their relevance to the topic. They then move on to step 2 and answer the questions, seven of which involve choosing between two given options. This means students have to listen carefully, but no production is required. So the procedural demand of the text itself is

The beginnings of the Workers' Movement were in England, with the creation of the Trade Unions. To analyse the reasons for their creation, and the objectives that they came to fulfil, try to fill in the ten gaps in the following text. Work with a partner. Some suggested words are below the text.

The emergence of Trade Unions

Trade Unions were officially formed in the 19th century in _____(1)_____. Their formation coincided with the development of the new ____(2)____ class which had appeared during the Industrial Revolution and which had become a significant factor in 19th century society. Many of the more militant workers realised that they had to protect themselves from possible ____(3)____ by their employers. When the Industrial Revolution began, many workers suffered very ____(4)____ conditions both at work and at home, but no-one seemed to care very much. So workers began to ____(5)____ themselves and make demands for better conditions. They tried, for example, to ____(6)____ the amount of hours worked. They also tried to improve ____(7)____ and working ____(8)____ in the factories. At first, they were considered to be trouble-makers and ____(9)____, and many employers tried to silence them. The employers, who formed the new and prosperous bourgeoisie, knew that the more that they exploited their workers, the higher their ____(10)____ would be.

organise   wages   exploitation   conditions   radicals

reduce   proletarian   profits   Britain   poor

Materials extract 7.K Gap-filling exercise: Focus on key terms (Beobide & Ball, History 4, Ikastolen Elkartea, p. 68.)

considerably reduced. The final part (step 3) can even be done after the listening has finished, and discussed in pairs or in small groups. The questions should certainly be read out to students before the final part begins.

The CLIL geography task in Materials extract 7.M (on page 196) is an example of a very different type of listening, which simply uses a series of statements from a fictitious congress on emigration from the developing to the developed world and asks students to agree or disagree (on a scale of 0 to 10).

Students obviously cannot see the statements, but two of the six are:

Speaker A   In my opinion, it's really stupid to allow too much immigration to our developed world. Many of those poor countries have just not organized their economies very well, and that is basically their problem. They should stay there and work harder at improving their own countries, instead of coming to ours.

Speaker B   The world belongs to everyone. We are all brothers and sisters, and there should be no frontiers. The more we live with people from other cultures, the happier and more understanding we become. If people are poor, if people are looking for new opportunities, we should help them to realize their dreams.

Now you are going to listen to a dialogue between a retired English fisherman and a radio presenter.

1.- **Before you listen**, write down in your notebook the words that you think will not be key vocabulary on the programme. Compare them with another pair.

Nets   Trees   Crew   Hunt
Trawlers   Captain   Tippex   Pocket
Radar   Trip   Tennis   Ice   Fleet   Catch
Canning   Anchovies   Squirrels   Inshore   Brave   Bonuses   Cars

2.- Now, try to answer the questions for the first half of the listening only.

a) Was his boat a *company*, a *business*, or a *factory*?

b) Did *he* work on the freezer trawlers? | Yes | No |

c) Who handles the fish on land? Mention 3 types of people.

d) Who is the most important person for the fishermen?	The Owner.	The Captain
e) The owners always agree to the terms of a fishing trip.	True	False
f) The Captain never loses money on a trip.	True	False
g) Most of the crew earn the same basic money.	True	False
h) The prices on land always stay the same.	True	False

i) Two types of fish are mentioned. Which are they?

3.- Check your answers with either the teacher or your partner, then try to answer the following questions based on the second half of the listening.

a) Fishing is more dangerous now than before.	True	False

b) Write down 3 things that he considers to be dangerous.

c) What is a fisherman's biggest enemy?

d) Mention one thing that he considers to be positive about being a fisherman.

Materials extract 7.L Supporting a complex audio text (Beobide & Ball, Geography 3, Ikastolen Elkartea, p. 51.)

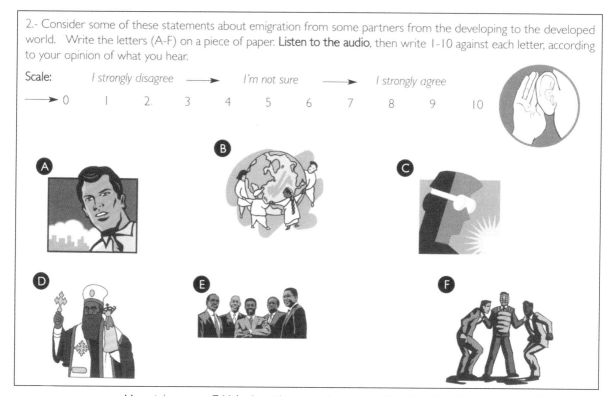

2.- Consider some of these statements about emigration from some partners from the developing to the developed world.   Write the letters (A-F) on a piece of paper. **Listen to the audio**, then write 1-10 against each letter, according to your opinion of what you hear.

Scale: *I strongly disagree* ⟶ *I'm not sure* ⟶ *I strongly agree*

⟶ 0   1   2   3   4   5   6   7   8   9   10

Materials extract 7.M Audio with opinion-based task (Beobide & Ball, Geography 3, Ikastolen Elkartea, p. 160.)

The exercise eventually serves as a stimulus for the 'resolution' task shown in Materials extract 7.N. As such, the activity helps to develop the skill of listening, but its main objective is to extend students' understanding of the concept of underdevelopment.

4 Scaffolding and embedding

On the most basic level, 'scaffolding' is an explicit form of language support, whereas 'embedding' is more implicit. With scaffolding, the materials writer is saying, 'Look: this is the language you need here, at this juncture, for this purpose.' This language could be academic or it could be functional. It does not matter; the language is being made salient. With embedding, the materials writer simply weaves the key language, or some of it, into the flow of the sequence of tasks or activities. The idea is that learners pick up this language (and the concepts expressed by it) whilst engaged in the tasks because the key language is literally 'embedded' in the learning material. But the design of the tasks is such that teachers might not need to make the language so salient in class, at least in the initial phase of the sequence.

The notion of embedding stems from classic primary school materials design, whereby textbooks introduce concepts using a drastically scaled-down field of discourse, to then recycle key vocabulary and structures in subsequent chapters or

3.- Now, work in pairs and write a 'Resolution', based on the issues you have seen concerning population. Write a minimum of six, and a maximum of ten. Write your own words, and don't copy exact sentences from Q1. You can use the ideas, but you need **resolution language** (see example below).

At the end of a congress, the participants publish a 'resolution', as a list of 'action points'.

5th World Congress on Population. Madrid, Spain

1.- More resources must be provided for the education of women in the developing regions.
2.- . . .

Materials extract 7.N 'Resolution' task (Beobide & Ball, Geography 3, Ikastolen Elkartea, p. 161.)

units. Learners see the key vocabulary and structures often, in a variety of contexts, and eventually begin to use them naturally. At the same time, however, it is inevitable that other learning materials—and indeed teachers themselves—will be providing more explicit forms of support, possibly by scaffolding certain language items to ensure that the key ones are noticed. This explicit approach might seem to correspond more to the conscious process of learning an L2, as opposed to the subconscious acquisition of the L1—to cite Krashen's (1988) more classic learning-acquisition distinction—but in truth the two techniques of scaffolding and embedding work in tandem.

This is most certainly the case in CLIL. In fact, it might be said that the effective practice of CLIL depends on a constant balancing of scaffolding and embedding techniques. How explicit do we need to make things? To what extent can we rely on the effectiveness of the embedded material to do the work for us? These are an interesting questions to consider, and, like the 'three dimensions' already referred to, an awareness of the demands of any one classroom moment, or of any one lesson sequence, enables teachers and materials writers to plan their practice and materials accordingly.

Scaffolding

A very simple example of CLIL-based scaffolding is shown in Materials extract 7.O (overleaf). Taken from a music sequence for lower-secondary NNS learners, it can be seen from the orientation phase of the sequence that this interactive information-gathering task deliberately limits the language to the objective, avoiding any kind of 'collateral' possibilities. The objective is made explicit by the instruction 'Ask your classmates about their musical abilities', and the procedure is carefully controlled and the exact language is provided. It may seem a rather mechanical exercise, but the adverbial phrases required to describe the range of musical abilities on any given instrument are not necessarily transparent or available to these learners. So although the materials writer has taken no chances here, there is still scope for the language to be used for more complex purposes later in the sequence. The main purpose, however, is for the learners to establish a sort of linguistic base camp.

Materials extract 7.0 Information-gathering task (Ball et al., Subject projects 1: We've got talent!, Ikaselkar.)

Embedding

The three activities in Materials extract 7.P, from two consecutive pages of a textbook, ask students to match the six short texts to the graphs (step 2). However, the culmination of the sequence is a writing activity (step 3), which involves students writing a short description of their local climate. A good description would include some of the vocabulary and structures inherent to this type of writing. Examples of this very special meteorological text type are provided by the short texts, in which the inherent structures are embedded—for example 'situated in/on', 'between the months of …', 'dropping to minus 4', 'July is the hottest month', 'where the temperatures average', 'it lies on', 'the heaviest rain', 'but especially in the summer months'.

This is a typical CALP-infused sequence, in which the language is both dense and formal. Students are not expected to learn every possible expression within this field of discourse, but the embedded language and the accompanying activities, which are challenging but not impossible, will guarantee the retention of some of this language. But at no point has the materials writer said 'Now use some specific words and phrases from the texts to write about your local context'. The objective is implicit, and the learners' relative success or failure to achieve this outcome can be judged according to the assessment criteria that individual teachers choose to use. We will look at assessment criteria in Chapter 9, but for now, the example serves to contrast embedding techniques with those of scaffolding.

A simpler example from primary science, shown in Materials extract 7.Q (on page 201), gives learners the steps and resources required to carry out the experimental process 'Observe materials melting'. Designed for native speakers of English, it is nevertheless a good example of the 'embedding' form of language support being used. Although the entire procedure is based on a limited series of verbs, these verbs are crucial for any type of scientific procedure which involves making observations and drawing conclusions. The verbs ('observe', 'repeat', 'record', 'check', 'plan') are, in the purely scientific sense, the very point of the whole procedure. The materials ('ice', etc.) are simply the vehicles for each step of the procedure, the conceptual objective of which is to understand at what temperature each material melts. During the process, learners will pick up more language—some of it technical, some of it not (for example, 'Ice melts at …', 'What can you see now?', 'ceramic bowl')—but the crucial language (i.e. formal verbs of process) is embedded, and will undoubtedly be recycled in subsequent chapters.

5 *Making key language salient*

This principle relates closely to the previous one of scaffolding and embedding. Once again, there is agreement between this materials design principle and CLIL-based learning theory. Both Gibbons and Cummins have argued in various publications (e.g. Gibbons, 2000; Cummins, 2002) that ensuring the salience of language issues should be a central part of standard educational practice, regardless of whether the learners in question are being taught in their L1 or an L2.

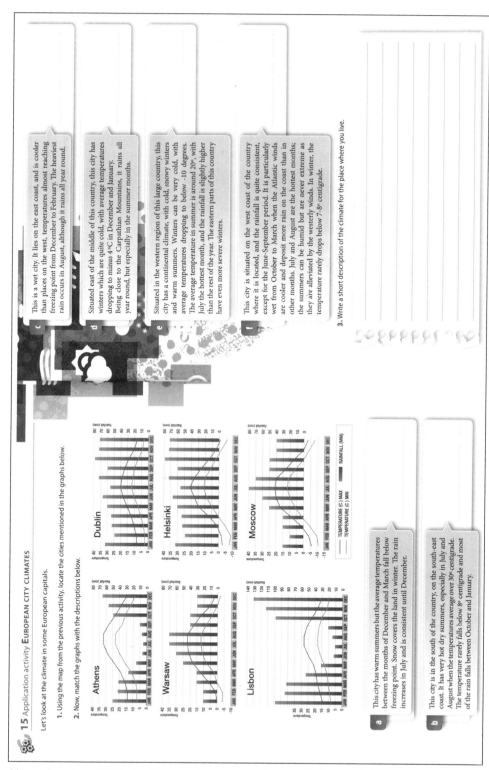

Materials extract 7.P Embedding key language in the text (Ball et al., Subject projects 2: Europe: united in diversity, Ikaselkar, pp. 28–29.)

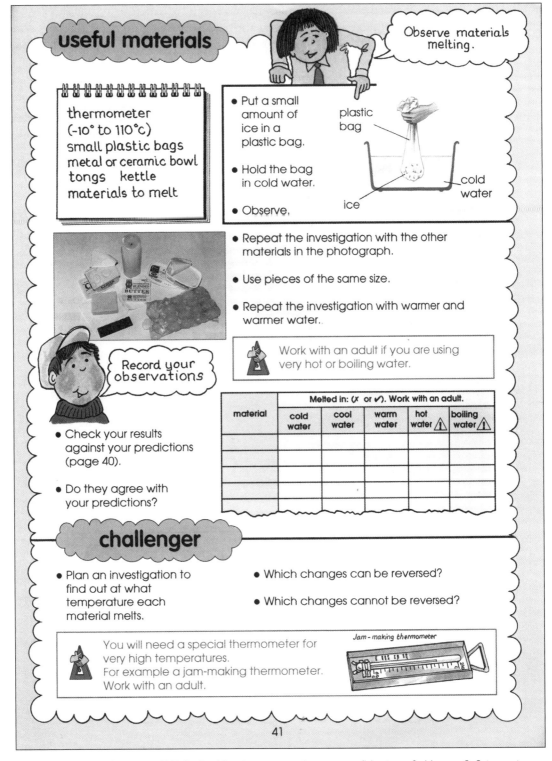

Materials extract 7.Q Embedding in steps and resources (Harrison & Moorcroft, Science in action Book 3, Folens, p. 41.)

Nevertheless, it depends what we mean by 'salience'. As the discussion on scaffolding and embedding above has briefly demonstrated, good, conscious materials design can help to provide this salience, without teachers being constantly obliged to step out of the conceptual flow in order to put on some sort of 'language hat'. Indeed, within CLIL practice, this is often the aspect which worries subject teachers the most. In 'hard' CLIL especially, subject teachers feel that they have quite enough on their plates without the constant need to focus the learners on the language too. It is a slightly contentious point, but the more training CLIL teachers receive, the more aware they become of the issues, which in turn helps them to convey these issues in a meaningful way to their learners. But if the materials can do some of the work for them, then so much the better.

... / ...

The Suez Crisis began when the Egyptian leader *Nasser* decided to nationalise the Suez Canal Company in 1955. This caused problems for Great Britain and France, because the canal had become the major 'gate' for Europe's booming oil industry. Britain also owned 45% of the company. Also, the new state of Israel, (whose history we learnt last year) – and whose relationship with Egypt was very bad – also wanted to use the canal.

Egypt was becoming friendly with the Soviet Union and China, and had bought arms cheaply from both. A coalition of French, British and Israeli troops invaded the northern canal zone and fought with Egyptian soldiers. The USA criticised the invasion and was afraid it would provoke the Soviets into fighting for the Egyptians. After US pressure, in 1957 the war ended, and the UN sent in a peace-force (UNEF – United Nations Emergency Force) to protect the area. The English Prime Minister, *Eden*, was forced to resign, the French pulled their troops out of NATO, and the Egyptian leader Nasser became a hero from the more militant Arab perspective.

The Hungarian Uprising took place almost simultaneously. Hungary was part of the Soviet bloc, but after the death of Stalin the nationalists in Hungary saw a chance to free the country from the Soviets and to regain control. The nationalists rose up in October against the 'puppet' government, and installed their own communist leader, *Imre Nagy*. The USA announced that they would not support the uprising, so Khrushchev realised that he could act without beginning another major superpower conflict. When Nagy announced that he would allow free elections and take Hungary out of the Warsaw Pact, the Soviets sent in soldiers to brutally suppress the revolution and maintain Hungary's position in the Soviet Union.

LANGUAGE MATTERS

Doing the Dozen!

Make sure you remember...

Geo-political
Blockade
Demilitarised
Containment
Censorship
Proxy
Deterrence
Bi-polarisation
Superpower
Détente
Buffer (zone)
Escalate

Soviet tanks in Budapest (1956)

Materials extract 7.R Doing the Dozen! (Beobide & Ball, History 4, Ikastolen Elkartea, p. 192.)

This principle of making key language salient is relatively easy to demonstrate. In Materials extract 7.R, from a CLIL history textbook, the author has inserted the section 'Language Matters' to the side of a text which covers various events and issues related to the Cold War and the post-World War II global situation. However, 'Doing the Dozen!' refers to 12 key terms that have featured in the previous 15 pages of the textbook. They are all good examples of CALP terminology, relate closely to this particular field of historical discourse, and are therefore central to any understanding of the causes, events, and consequences of the Cold War. Without them, any discussion of the topic would be disabled, particularly at assessment level. The language provides the 'frame' for the central concepts, and certain morphological elements—present in words such as 'geo-political', 'demilitarised', and 'bi-polarisation'—often carry useful clues such as prefixes which should help learners unpick the meaning.

Teachers can use 'Doing the Dozen!' in various ways, but the idea of the section is basically to recap, by explicitly integrating the conceptual content and the accompanying language. For example, in pairs, Student A takes the first six terms, and Student B the second six. Student A picks one of their six words and defines it to Student B, who must try to identify it from the list—and then vice versa until all the terms have been covered and the students are sure they understand the concepts. If the students defining the terms do not understand them, they will have a difficult time with this task. Bearing this in mind, teachers could give students some preparation time to look back through the book and work on their six terms before the information-gap task begins. The key language is therefore made salient, but the student is in command of the process.

In Materials extract 7.S (overleaf), the first step of the task involves matching six short texts to the generic terms provided below, each of which is made salient by the very nature of the task. To further consolidate the concepts, step 2 requires students to match the key geographical words listed in the table to their opposites, which are embedded in the texts. So 'steep' is paired with 'flat, low-lying' in text 1, and 'urban' with 'rural' in the same text. The word 'wealth', however, has its antonym in text 6, and will therefore require strategic reading to locate. Once the students have completed the two steps, the key language will have been made salient.

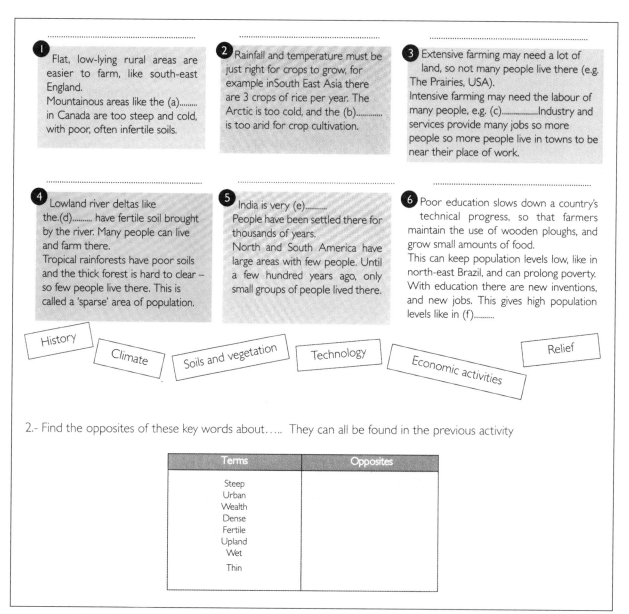

1. Flat, low-lying rural areas are easier to farm, like south-east England.
Mountainous areas like the (a)......... in Canada are too steep and cold, with poor, often infertile soils.

2. Rainfall and temperature must be just right for crops to grow, for example inSouth East Asia there are 3 crops of rice per year. The Arctic is too cold, and the (b)............ is too arid for crop cultivation.

3. Extensive farming may need a lot of land, so not many people live there (e.g. The Prairies, USA).
Intensive farming may need the labour of many people, e.g. (c)................Industry and services provide many jobs so more people so more people live in towns to be near their place of work.

4. Lowland river deltas like the.(d).......... have fertile soil brought by the river. Many people can live and farm there.
Tropical rainforests have poor soils and the thick forest is hard to clear – so few people live there. This is called a 'sparse' area of population.

5. India is very (e)...........
People have been settled there for thousands of years.
North and South America have large areas with few people. Until a few hundred years ago, only small groups of people lived there.

6. Poor education slows down a country's technical progress, so that farmers maintain the use of wooden ploughs, and grow small amounts of food.
This can keep population levels low, like in north-east Brazil, and can prolong poverty. With education there are new inventions, and new jobs. This gives high population levels like in (f).........

History   Climate   Soils and vegetation   Technology   Economic activities   Relief

2.- Find the opposites of these key words about….. They can all be found in the previous activity

Terms	Opposites
Steep	
Urban	
Wealth	
Dense	
Fertile	
Upland	
Wet	
Thin	

Materials extract 7.S Strategic reading for key language (Beobide & Ball, Geography 3, Ikastolen Elkartea, p. 152.)

As the history activity in Materials extract 7.T demonstrates, even standard comprehension questions on a text from a previous activity can be supported by focusing on the language–concept relationship. Questions 1, 2, 4, and 6 focus on single words, question 3 on part of a sentence, and question 5 can be answered with reference to a single term. Even question 7 will relate the objectives of nationalism to limited and specific terms.

Try to find the answers to these questions in the previous text:

1. According to the text, what is the opposite of 'liberal'?
2. When talking about political systems, which word in the second paragraph describes the politics of a State when is controlled completely by one Government?
3. Quote the part of the sentence which tells you that the liberals won the final Carlist War.
4. Which word tells you that the new education system was obligatory?
5. Which kind of society was immigration creating?
6. Which word (one) means the opposite of 'political centralism'?
7. List the three objectives of the nationalist movements appeared at the end of 19th century.

Materials extract 7.T Supporting comprehension questions by focusing on language (Beobide & Ball, Geography 3, Ikastolen Elkartea, p. 116.)

6 *The concept of 'difficulty' in didactic materials*

Why are some things more difficult than others? In a broad philosophical sense, the answer to this question is usually the rather ironic 'It is difficult to say', largely because difficulty lies on a continuum, but also because the perception of whether something is 'easy' or 'difficult' is often subjective, and conditioned by individual variables and circumstances. What is difficult for one person is not necessarily difficult for another.

However, if we ask a monolingual English speaker to read a German newspaper, the English speaker will undoubtedly find this a difficult task. Why? The answer must be that the newspaper was not intended for them. But in a scholastic or educational context, everything with which we provide the learner—and here we are talking about didactic materials—is intended for the learner. It follows, therefore, that aside from the natural considerations for different abilities that exist in any one classroom, it is not the materials themselves that are 'easy' or 'difficult' but rather the tasks that we as educators assign to them. What are we asking the students to do? If a physics teacher acknowledges the fact that the theory of relativity is generally a complex topic for students to understand, then it is up to that teacher (or materials designer) to decide how to deal with the theory and break it down so that the students stand a chance. It is never a question of simplification. There are many ways and means to facilitate understanding.

This notion is hardly exclusive to CLIL, but the assimilation of concepts in a foreign language is usually one of the main topics of conversation that surround CLIL practice on a daily basis. Often it is related to the subject. Maths, for example, is often viewed as too 'difficult' for CLIL purposes, and physical education is considered too unchallenging, linguistically speaking, to merit a place in the CLIL curriculum. These views may be valid, but only if the decisions are based, at the very least, on the three dimensions of content that we have proposed in this book. This is true of any individual topic in any individual subject. If a topic is perceived as 'difficult' by students, then what do they really mean? The truth is that they probably found the topic difficult on a conceptual, procedural, and linguistic basis—a 'triple dose' of difficulty. The only thing we can do, as materials writers or teachers, is dismantle the topic with regard to the three dimensions, and find a way to make it more digestible for students. In a broad sense, good CLIL does this all the time. In a narrower sense, we need to see which dimensions we can manipulate for the purpose of making topics accessible to students—and it not always the linguistic dimension. In fact, more often than not, it is the procedural dimension that determines the comprehensibility of a concept, as we have already seen. The idea that it is simply the text, or the language employed, that determines comprehensibility is dangerously misleading.

In a sense, this entire book deals with the issue of 'support', and so here we simply need to consider some obvious examples. We dealt with the 'text–task' relationship in Chapter 2, and in this chapter we have talked about the 'primacy' of task. The relationship between these notions and the discussion of 'difficulty' is a particularly intimate one.

It seems appropriate at this point to return to physics, traditionally seen as a difficult subject. The text in Materials extract 7.U was produced by an eight-year-old studying in a CLIL context.

On the theory of relativity

Einstein stated <u>that the theory</u> of relativity belongs <u>to the</u> class of 'principle <u>theories</u>'. As such, it employs an analytic method. <u>This</u> means <u>that the</u> elements which comprise <u>this</u> <u>theory</u> are not based on hypothesis but on empirical discovery. <u>The</u> empirical discovery leads <u>to</u> understanding <u>the</u> general characteristics of natural processes. Mathematical models are <u>then</u> developed which separate <u>the</u> natural processes into <u>theoretical</u>-mathematical descriptions. <u>Therefore</u>, by analytical means, <u>the</u> necessary conditions <u>that</u> have to be satisfied are deduced. Separate events must satisfy <u>these</u> conditions. Experience should <u>then</u> match <u>the</u> conclusions.

<u>The</u> special <u>theory</u> of relativity and <u>the</u> general <u>theory</u> of relativity are connected. As stated below, special <u>theory</u> of relativity applies <u>to</u> all physical phenomena except gravity. <u>The</u> general <u>theory</u> provides <u>the</u> law of gravitation, and its relation <u>to</u> other forces of nature.

Materials extract 7.U Einstein for eight-year-olds (adapted from en.wikipedia.org/wiki/Theory_of_relativity.)

The text is difficult, in both conceptual and linguistic terms, particularly for an eight-year-old NNS of English. However, the child was not a precocious genius, but merely responding to the instruction 'Underline all the words beginning with the letter "t"'. It is a good activity for an eight-year-old, who is still at the early stages of reading in the L1. The child has responded appropriately to the procedural demands of the task. This is an extreme example, perhaps, but it proves the point that it is not necessarily the text itself, but the procedural nature of the task we apply to it that determines whether learners will find it manageable or not. In CLIL, therefore, we might be so bold as to say: 'There is no such thing as an easy or a difficult text; there are only easy or difficult tasks.'

7 *Thinking in sequences*

In Chapter 2, we dedicated some time to the consideration of this principle, and so here we only need a brief consolidation of it. Indeed, almost all the examples in this chapter can be viewed under the umbrella of this principle, and its overarching nature makes it an ideal conclusion to our analysis of the seven principles of materials design for CLIL.

One of the main points we made in Chapter 2 was that tasks (and activities) in CLIL should not be seen in isolation, but as part of a larger sequence. We said that in educational and conceptual terms, there is always a 'before' and an 'after'. Students never approach a task with no knowledge whatsoever about its content, and there must always be a reason for engaging with the task itself. The reason for engaging with the task forms the logic of the 'after' stage of learning. Also, with regard to language, we noted that the stage of a sequence determines the nature of the discourse. Teachers and students can use radically different language at the beginning and at the end of a sequence, even though they are still working on the same concept.

'Narrative structure' in CLIL classes

The language features of classic narrative structure—namely orientation, complication, and resolution—are useful to consider here as they help us to understand the impact of sequence. All educational events follow a similar structure. A single lesson will contain these three 'moves' as a minimum, as indeed will a sequence of activities or lessons. When designing materials, these moves are central to almost all of the considerations of how to make materials effective. If the language is too complex, or too 'CALP' in the orientation phase, learners may become frustrated and lose the motivation to continue. They should therefore come to expect the bulk of the key language to be worked on in the complication phase. This makes sense in L1 sequencing too, but in CLIL it is a non-negotiable part of the methodology.

The resolution phase usually includes the assessment, and perhaps some tie-up work beforehand. It would be very unusual to introduce new language at this stage; in fact, it would be illogical and counter-productive. We will look in more detail at assessment in Chapter 8, but here it seems sufficient to say that tasks at the resolution phase will have certain identifiable features. The verb 'discuss' is recognized universally as resolution-type instruction. It may be the process verb used in the instruction for an essay, or it may be a production task that is resolving a shorter sequence of activities. But it is rarely associated with the introduction of a concept.

Summary

In this chapter, we have proposed and then illustrated seven principles to be considered when designing materials for CLIL practice. We have attempted to further exemplify the notions explored in Chapters 5 and 6, and suggested that the design and use of materials by CLIL teachers, although time-consuming, can be a powerful factor in professional development. We have also suggested that materials reflect an underlying learning theory, and that as training exemplars, they are always present.

Task

If you would like to look at a practical task to explore your own practice related to the content of this chapter, see Appendix 1 (page 292).

Further reading

Chadwick, T. (2012). *Language awareness in teaching: A toolkit for content and language teachers*. Cambridge: Cambridge University Press.
A short but highly practical book which offers strategies for identifying and then supporting academic language in subject teaching. Its three sections—'Classroom', 'Coordination', and 'Exams'—also offer practical advice regarding implementation and assessment.

Dale, L., & **Tanner, R.** (2012). *CLIL activities*. Cambridge: Cambridge University Press.
A very comprehensive and detailed resource book for both subject and language teachers involved in CLIL. Its main sections focus on input ('Guiding understanding'), on academic language, and then on the production-based skills of speaking and writing.

Grandinetti, M., Langellotti, M., & **Ting, T. Y. L.** (2013). How CLIL can provide a pragmatic means to renovate science education—even in a suboptimally bilingual context. *International Journal of Bilingual Education and Bilingualism, 16,* 354–374.
A very interesting and innovative article which explores a number of themes pertinent to CLIL, such as higher-order thinking skills, how good practice in CLIL can stimulate better science teaching, and moreover how interesting and well-planned teaching material can motivate students of all levels of ability.

Tomlinson, B. (Ed.) (2011). *Materials development in language teaching, second edition*. Cambridge: Cambridge University Press.
A series of articles by various authors, all experienced in the craft of materials writing for foreign-language students. The book is not about CLIL as such, but contains a wealth of advice, much of it applicable to materials design in general.

8

ASSESSMENT IN CLIL

Overview

This chapter situates CLIL-based assessment within the standard agreed framework available to all educational models, and then moves on to a consideration of how the special nature of CLIL affects some aspects of this framework, particularly with regard to the content–language issue. We will analyse how the process-led tendencies of CLIL prioritize the practice of continuous/formative assessment, and look at the issue of language 'risk' in CLIL-based summative testing, identifying the ways in which we can guarantee fairness for learners who are being assessed in a language other than their L1. The three-dimensional content framework of 'concept, language, procedure' will again be used to help teachers to identify and then balance the assessment demands made on learners. For language teachers in particular, we will also suggest solutions to the problem of assessing conceptual content when the primary focus of their role is on teaching and examining linguistic objectives. In addition, the chapter will look at competences, and how they seem to fit naturally into a CLIL-based framework of learning and assessment.

Assessment versus evaluation

These terms are often used synonymously, especially by speakers of Romance languages. But it is important to distinguish between them. **Evaluation** is the systematic appraisal of merit, value, and significance against a standardized set of criteria. So you can evaluate a course using a questionnaire, for example. Assessment, on the other hand, is the documentation of knowledge, skills, attitudes, and beliefs, usually carried out in a way that is measurable. So according to this definition of assessment, you can assess students on a course by means of a test, or on the basis of something else that they have done—something that is observable.

Types of assessment: formative and summative

Before we can discuss assessment within a CLIL framework, we need to remind ourselves of the standard concepts of assessment in the wider educational field.

Overall, there are two main types of assessment: summative and formative. In summative assessment, the focus is on assessing what learners have achieved at a specific point in time. It is often associated with end-of-year/end-of-term testing, it best represents the notion of 'assessment <u>of</u> learning', and it is evaluative.

Formative assessment, on the other hand, is more associated with ongoing, **continuous assessment**. It is linked to the notion of 'assessment <u>for</u> learning', in that it is more diagnostic, and usually takes place during a course. It also includes within its broader remit practices such as self-assessment, peer assessment, and performance assessment. **Portfolio assessment** is also formative, and involves learners maintaining a dossier of samples of work produced throughout the year.

Formative assessment can be seen as a gradual information-gathering process for students (by a process of dialogue and feedback with the teacher) in order to perform more effectively in eventual summative assessment events. Viewed in this light, formative assessment can appear subservient in its role, preparing students for the next summative event—the next hurdle in their ongoing academic development. However, the potentially subordinate nature of formative assessment does not entail a downgrading of value but rather a recognition of the universality of summative marks or grades which eventually come to certify a student's performance. This remains the prevalent means of assessment. But as we shall see later in this chapter, the distinction between these two types of assessment is often unclear and perhaps unnecessary. Moreover, we will also see that summative assessment, particularly in CLIL, can assume a variety of more interesting guises.

Neither type of assessment is 'better' than the other, because they both serve a slightly different purpose, and the final course 'mark' that a student obtains can be a combination of both continuous and summative assessment. The weighting, in percentage terms, could be 50:50, 90:10, or any other combination, of which students should be aware. We will return to this notion of weighting later in the chapter, since it has implications for CLIL practice.

The various types of assessment are summarized in Table 8.1.

Assessment and teachers

One of the most awkward truths about general education is that although teachers worldwide test their students on a regular basis, and examinations continue to form the basis for this universal practice of assessment, few teachers are actually trained to write exams. This is not a criticism—it is just an observation of the current state of things. Many teachers get it right in the end, through a process of trial and error, but we could rightly argue that no learner should ever really be subject to such processes of trial and error! But in defence of teachers, writing good tests and exams is difficult, and that is just in the non-CLIL, native-speaker sphere of education. Once we turn to CLIL, the issue takes on yet another layer of complexity.

Formative/ continuous assessment	• Ongoing and developmental assessment • Provides information about learners' understanding • Helps them to identify problems by giving feedback on what they need to do to improve, possibly (though not necessarily) in order to perform better at the next summative event
Summative assessment	• An end-of-year/end-of-course test • Measures learners' overall achievement of course objectives • Usually non-continuous
Performance assessment	• The observation of a range of classroom tasks to assess how well learners perform against a set of explicit criteria
Peer assessment	• Learners provide feedback to their classmates on their work, often guided by explicit (and comprehensible) assessment criteria
Self-assessment	• Learners monitor their own progress • They decide how well they are doing/have done • They identify the aspects that they need to work on
Portfolio assessment	• A collection of learners' work gathered over a year/ course which shows evidence of their subject knowledge, skills, and development

Table 8.1 Types of assessment

Continuous assessment is also difficult to do well. Unlike summative testing, it is far from universal, and many teachers are not even given the opportunity to try it out. Certain national systems, suspicious of less objective means of assessment, reduce continuous or formative methods to the bare minimum, meaning they do not influence the 'final mark'. In other contexts, continuous assessment is often seen as too time-consuming, requiring constant vigilance from teachers and co-operation from students, not to mention agreement on how to manage the process across the entire school curriculum. If it is to work, everyone involved has to be convinced and committed. This is not always easy to achieve.

Objectives, outcomes, and criteria

The word 'observable' is crucial to this chapter, because we are talking about assessment and not about evaluation, although there can be some overlap. With regard to assessment, then, we cannot talk about this topic unless we also mention objectives. We briefly looked at objectives in Chapter 3 in relation to our initial discussion of the word 'content'. We concluded that it is impossible to divorce the content of a valid lesson from its objective, or the contents of a syllabus from its longer-term aim.

Similarly, therefore, it is impossible to assess students without reference to clearly stated outcome objectives. An 'outcome' is a visible, observable result. In any type of assessment, the objective must refer to something that we can observe in a student's behaviour or performance. So if a history objective states 'To identify the causes and consequences of World War I', then it is a valid objective, because it is possible to observe whether students can truly 'identify' these things.

Notice, too, that the kind of objective stated in the above paragraph, with its infinitive structure 'To identify …' and its explicit outcome, has the appearance of a conceptual objective. But we can also have procedural objectives—a significant member of the three-dimensional content group. During the process of identifying the causes and consequences of World War I, students might take part in a short debate to evaluate certain aspects of the related issues. The students could reasonably be assessed on their debating ability, if the history teacher considers it to be an important skill for a budding historian to develop. A debate could even form part of the summative assessment, although the objective would need to be reworded. We will return to this later in the discussion of assessment through the three dimensions, but as we shall also see, procedural objectives are very close to what we are beginning to label as 'competences'.

However, objectives are not sufficient by themselves. We also need assessment criteria to complement and reflect the outcomes that we want learners to manifest. In a mathematics test, the criteria may simply be 'the answers'. Students must provide these single, closed answers and the teacher (the marker) simply records how many of these responses are correct. But in a history essay entitled 'Were the American colonists justified in waging war and breaking away from Britain?', the answers are not so clear. Add to this the fact that the question appears to be soliciting students' opinions, and it becomes clear that the criteria for judging this essay fairly are far more complex. This is true enough in an L1 educational context, but in a CLIL syllabus, we would need to be very clear indeed about what constitutes a satisfactory response, and we would need to take into account the special nature of assessing students who are using a language other than their L1.

'Soft' CLIL: is it a problem?

In the context of this brief discussion of objectives, we will need to revisit the issue of 'soft' CLIL, and the problem of its overall aims. If it is really 'language led', then the assessment measures will need to reflect this. Therein lies the problem, so far unresolved in the field of CLIL, of exactly how far language teachers should go in their content-based remit. If they go too far and make the lesson look—to all intents and purposes—like a subject lesson, then why merely assess the language? Teachers would reply that they are paid to teach a linguistic syllabus, despite the importation of more 'content'. We will deal with this later in the chapter, but it is a crucial issue, and one which suggests that it may be a misconception to describe 'soft' CLIL as 'language led'. If we import conceptual and procedural content into our language lessons, then what are we going to do with them? Disguise or ignore them and hope that students will not notice when they come to be assessed on language only? They would be right to protest if that were the case.

Formative assessment and CLIL

The task-based nature of formative/continuous assessment and the wider variety of classroom interaction that it requires inevitably make it a more comfortable candidate for assessment in CLIL. Didactic units tend to be longer, there is more conceptual sequencing, there is more group work, and there is a greater choice of formats for the presentation of work. This increases the possibilities for teachers to work out schemes of ongoing assessment that take procedural- and process-orientated objectives into account. For example, do teachers use group work because they like the atmosphere it creates, or because they need the students to form groups of three in order to play distinct roles and work on different aspects of a complex task together? In the latter case, teachers can assess the group work. Has Student A done what he/she was supposed to have done? Has Student B been 'co-operative'? Has Student C spoken mainly in English in the group phase? These competences can all be assessed. As such, there could be a short summative test on the content studied at the end of each term, but it might only represent 20 per cent of the final mark. The end-of-term test need not dominate that same period's activities nor impinge unfavourably on the class atmosphere. So if CLIL appears to favour an increase in formative/continuous assessment, we will need to look carefully at the ways in which we can do this.

CLIL and conventional assessment: interfaces and differences

In standard assessment, there are two central issues that must always be considered. We could call these 'core notions'. These two core notions are **validity** and the 'washback effect'.

Validity

This basically refers to the need to test, or assess, the same content that we have taught. So if students have been working on World War I during the term, they would be surprised (and indignant!) if the end-of-term test were to be about World War II. A crude example perhaps, but that is basically what is meant by the notion of validity.

To borrow from the three-dimensional framework again, a less basic example of validity would be to consider procedural content as well as conceptual and linguistic content. So if teachers have been fostering certain subject-specific procedural skills in their students, those students would quite reasonably expect those same skills to figure significantly in the assessment measures, as opposed to others which have been relatively neglected.

The 'washback effect'

> Concern has long been voiced about the power of tests to affect what goes on
> in the classroom, the educational system, and society as a whole; the so-called
> "washback effect".
> (Alderson & Wall, 1993)

What these authors mean is that in education, teachers will tend to 'teach to the
test', which sounds fine if we are talking about validity. It is not fine, however,
when the nature of the assessment begins to affect the way students behave.

If we have dedicated the school year to competence-based performance tasks,
process-led group work, research tasks, and student-centred activities in general,
it would be counter-productive to base most of the infamous 'final marks' on a
battery of summative tests. It is easy to consider these tests valid, because they
cover the conceptual, procedural, and linguistic content of the course, but they fail
the students in terms of the 'spirit' of the overall educational approach adopted. If
students are not rewarded for the work done during the term, then next year they
are unlikely to co-operate; or, if they do, they will co-operate reluctantly. This is
the washback effect, and it can have crippling consequences on both teacher and
student morale. In CLIL-based contexts, as we shall see, the increase in process-
led approaches necessitates a careful rethink of the features and weighting of the
overall assessment measures.

Content or language?

This is a question often asked by CLIL practitioners who are starting out on their
journeys: 'What do we assess: content, language, or both?' This is a reasonable
question, given that the term 'CLIL' emphasizes both content and language, as if
they were equal partners, deserving equal attention. The statement that 'CLIL is
a dual-focused educational approach in which an additional language is used for
the learning and teaching of both content and language' (Mehisto et al., 2008) has
given rise to the natural corollary that this might also be true of CLIL assessment;
that it is 'dual focused'. However, nothing could be further from the truth. CLIL-
based assessment is very much focused on the 'content', although we have been
careful in this book to define the multi-layered meaning of that word. In 'hard'
CLIL particularly, we cannot talk about assessing the language. It makes no sense,
given the likely subject-based objectives and overall aims.

However, we can consider the language aspect. This is not the same as saying we
should 'assess' it directly. Indeed, a good competitor for the CLIL acronym is
'LEST'—Language Enhanced Subject Teaching (Ball & Lindsay, 2010)—whose
message is also that language forms a part of the overall considerations, in the
context of assessment. Can students show evidence of conceptual understanding or
not? Do students have the linguistic tools and repertoire to do this? Therein lies the
issue, because assessment in a CLIL-based setting is inevitably complicated by the
added factor of language.

The teacher designing the unit will know what he or she wishes to teach and what the overall purpose of the CLIL module is. Therefore the answer to the 'language or content' question is determined by the relative priority within those objectives.
(Coyle et al., 2010)

Coyle et al. mean that a teacher setting a test can adjust the linguistic demand according to the way the 'unit' has been taught. We would argue that the priority should always be the content, but as Coyle et al. suggest, the assessment can also consider language features if the teacher deems it appropriate. A student could probably pass an exam without producing much CALP, but would be unlikely to figure among the higher scorers. This is how it should be, particularly in those cases where the teacher has made the key vocabulary and structures salient, worked on them, and even explicitly asked for their presence in the exam. In a very simple sense, this is surely a good example of content–language integration. The language remains the vehicle, but its judicious and appropriate use in an exam context will earn the student higher marks.

We could argue that this is also true of L1 assessment, although to a lesser extent. For this reason, it must be re-emphasized that in 'hard' CLIL, where the objectives are content-led, we are testing content, not language. However, even in 'soft' CLIL, which is language-led, we could still argue that it is the conceptual content that should be tested, and not the language. The language is still the 'vehicle' carrying the content. Without using appropriate language to express the concepts, students will probably encounter difficulties, and so it is the function of both the teacher and the materials to make the language–content relationship salient. If this is done, the assessment procedure is likely to be fair.

Language demand/risk

This discussion of the content–language relationship leads us inevitably to the central issue of CLIL-based assessment, namely language demand, or language risk. In basic terms, this refers to the permanent tension between learners' conceptual knowledge and their language level. In other words, students learning in the L2 will always know more than they can express. In CLIL-based contexts, where students are faced with a much greater level of input (and possibly output) demand, where the texts are authentic and often not designed for L2 readership, the language factor must be taken into account in assessment, and particularly (although not exclusively) in the test design and assessment criteria. Why? Because language must not be a factor which obstructs the ability of students to express the concepts or demonstrate the skills and attitudes that constitute the outcome objectives of the course.

This attention to language risk can be managed in two ways. The first way, within a classic summative testing framework, is through the conscious design of test items that vary the language-risk factor, combining these design principles with appropriate assessment criteria. For example, the test item in Materials extract 8.A (produced for a CLIL project in the Middle East) was designed for teacher-training purposes, to demonstrate the concept of language demand/risk. Here, the original test item is defined as 'low risk', as the accompanying notes indicate.

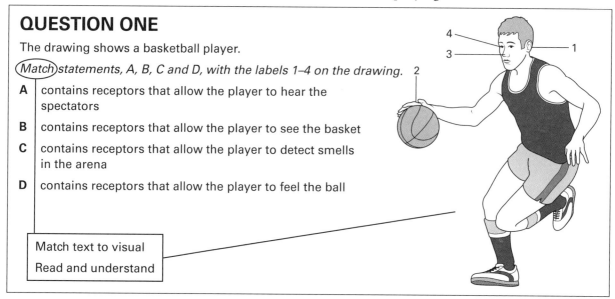

QUESTION ONE

The drawing shows a basketball player.

Match statements, A, B, C and D, with the labels 1–4 on the drawing.

A | contains receptors that allow the player to hear the spectators

B | contains receptors that allow the player to see the basket

C | contains receptors that allow the player to detect smells in the arena

D | contains receptors that allow the player to feel the ball

Match text to visual

Read and understand

Materials extract 8.A Low language risk/demand in test type

We could go further and identify some important reasons for defining this as 'low risk'. The linguistic demand is fairly minimal, principally because students are not obliged to produce any language. The demand is only at the level of comprehension, and this merely involves understanding the light procedural demand (matching by labelling), understanding the four sentences and fulfilling the conceptual demand, itself facilitated by the clarity of the visual and the repetition in the four sentences of the same syntactic structure: 'contains receptors that allow the player to …' Even if this rather academic structure were to challenge students, the presence in each sentence of the active verbs 'hear', 'see', 'detect', and 'feel' ensures that the demonstration of understanding is unlikely to be obstructed.

Nevertheless, we are reluctant to give the impression, with the above example, that the job of CLIL teachers is to somehow make things easy for the students. This is not the case at all. Good testing requires a range of demands, and as long as we are conscious of this principle, students will feel they are being assessed fairly. We could probably say that the following principles correctly summarize the factors that must be taken into consideration:

- What is the 'linguistic demand' (e.g. in science or history)?
- What is the relationship between the text and the task?
- What is the relationship between the graphic (diagram, graph, etc.) and the task?
- What is the task? Does it involve mainly reading or writing?
- How 'open' or 'closed' is the task?

The graph below shows the cases of measles in the United States, 1994–2014
(New Journal of Medicine)

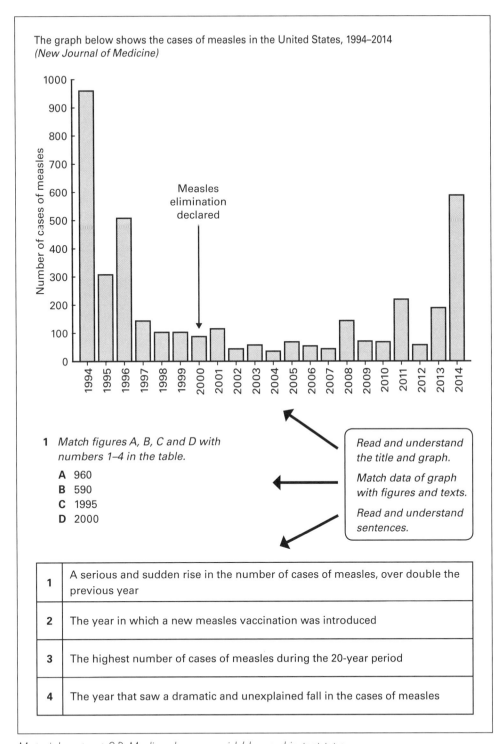

1 *Match figures A, B, C and D with numbers 1–4 in the table.*

A 960
B 590
C 1995
D 2000

Read and understand the title and graph.

Match data of graph with figures and texts.

Read and understand sentences.

1	A serious and sudden rise in the number of cases of measles, over double the previous year
2	The year in which a new measles vaccination was introduced
3	The highest number of cases of measles during the 20-year period
4	The year that saw a dramatic and unexplained fall in the cases of measles

Materials extract 8.B Medium language risk/demand in test type

To understand these principles through a further example, consider Materials extract 8.B. The demand here is higher, not only due to the conceptual level of the content and the more complex nature of the visual, but also due to the formality and range of the particular CALP-rich discourse. The test item is clearly more complex, but the language risk is still not 'high' but rather 'medium', again due to the fact that no written production is required.

As a final example, the demands of the exam question shown in Materials extract 8.C for a CLIL student studying industrialization in history in Spain are completely different from those of the previous cases described.

Represent on a diagram the population growth of these countries, using the data below. Then comment on the main points, comparing percentage growths of the individual countries.

POPULATION GROWTH (EUROPE 1088–1910)				
	1800	**1850**	**1900**	**1910**
The Netherlands	2,200,000	3,100,000	5,100,000	5,900,000
Great Britain	10,900,000	20,900,000	36,900,000	40,800,000
France	26,900,000	36,500,000	40,700,000	41,500,000
Spain	11,500,000	15,500,000	18,600,000	19,900,000
Germany	24,500,000	31,700,000	50,600,000	58,500,000

Materials extract 8.C Exam question: multiple demands (Beobide & Ball, History 4, Ikastolen Elkartea, p. 62.)

This test item has two stages. The first involves the transformation of the data into diagrammatic form (the format and type of the diagram is left to the student), and the second asks students to 'comment' on the data, 'comparing' the growths of the five countries.

It is immediately clear that teachers marking this test item will require a series of clear assessment criteria, agreed upon beforehand and written down explicitly, in order to guide their judgement of the work. These criteria must reflect the range of skills students need to answer this question—but what are these skills? Below, we can see the skills the students need to demonstrate for Materials extract 8.C and begin to work out the possible assessment criteria that might derive from them.

1 Are students able to choose an appropriate graphic form with which to represent the data, and do students then represent the data correctly?
2 Are students able to comment on the data, and what does this require?
    a The written commentary requires students to initially decide on what 'the main points' are. For example, the countries that experienced the greatest and the least growth over the 110-year period must figure in the commentary (the Netherlands versus Great Britain, for example). If students fail to do this, then their understanding of the concepts here will be questionable.

b Students need to understand the conceptual point of the data, i.e. that industrialization affected the population growth of developing countries differently. Students must also know the factors which affected this phenomenon.

c Students must structure the commentary, fronting the salient data and then including, but not over-emphasizing, less significant data. This structuring will require the use of general CALP, including discourse markers such as 'The most important', 'regarding', 'in terms of', 'firstly', etc.

d Students will need to use the language of contrast and comparison, of percentages, of percentage growth, and will need some of the inherent CALP vocabulary which relates specifically to this period in history and to these particular concepts (industrialization and its effect on population growth) Students will also need to use the language of cause and effect.

The assessment guide needs to incorporate the above criteria in order to be reliable and valid, and the assessment of the exam question in Materials extract 8.C cannot be left to the subjective judgement of the marker. In 'hard' CLIL, the linguistic criteria in 2c and 2d are obligatory in order for students to show their understanding of the main conceptual content, indicated by 2a. Once we understand the high language risk/demand of this innocent-looking question, we can begin to appreciate the implications for CLIL-based test design. Notice, also, that the most obvious 'history skill' here is contained within 1 above—namely choosing the graphic form and representing the data correctly. Nevertheless, once we consider the range of demands made by the exam question, it becomes obvious that it is the linguistic demand that requires the most attention from both the students and the marker. However, when we say 'linguistic demand', it is also clear that the demand is indeed a history-related skill: interpreting and comparing data, identifying similarities and differences, and explaining the causes for such similarities or differences all contribute to the discourse of history.

As Llinares et al. (2012) tellingly remark, 'using grammar and vocabulary effectively is deeply implicated in the quality of their [the CLIL students'] performance'. We would conclude, therefore, that the marker will need to consider these language features in a way which means their relative presence or absence affects the final mark. This does not mean 'subtract one mark for bad spelling' but rather that a percentage of the total marks for this question will depend on students employing, as efficiently as possible, a range of comparative structures and language to describe cause and effect, and demonstrating that they can structure the text, however basically. This is not assessing the language as such, but rather acknowledging that it is impossible to answer this question without some mastery of these particular grammatical structures. This is the essence of CLIL, and its most important message. The language must support and reflect the particular discourse field. At some point when answering the test item above, students must attempt to write something along the lines of 'The population of the Netherlands grew more slowly over this period than the population of Great Britain. This was due to …'.

We can award the higher marks to students who use this language more accurately and appropriately, but we are not 'assessing language' as such. We are assessing its use, in its obligatory context. We do the same in L1, but we are much less aware of it.

Llinares et al. (2012) regard this salience of language demands in CLIL assessment as a necessary part of general CLIL practice: 'The language CLIL learners need to use must be brought out into the open as an explicit component of the tasks they do.'

Assessment and the three dimensions

The three dimensions of content (see Chapter 3) are also useful in the context of assessment because they enable teachers to 'adjust the volume' of any of the three content types (concepts, procedures, language) in the classroom. This can also be done in an exam or in a more informal assessment situation. Clearly, if a test demands high levels of all three content types, then it is difficult. This is perfectly valid, of course, but teachers can then consider how to adjust the volume of each element of the test that makes demands on students.

In CLIL, if the language demand is not supported by procedural and conceptual decisions/adjustments, then we may be judging students unfairly, as we saw in the previous section. The conceptual content cannot be compromised, of course, and it must be learned as efficiently as in the L1, or else the whole CLIL venture is pointless. But by considering the assessment tools from a three-dimensional perspective, it is often easier to judge students fairly.

In Materials extract 8.D, which features question types taken from school-based summative examinations in CLIL classrooms for different age levels, the language 'risk' is easy to identify. For example, Question 1 makes very little language demand. However, by considering the other two dimensions, we can confirm that this is a suitable question type (although perhaps a little too easy).

Notice that these test questions cannot be considered 'easy' or 'difficult' on a one-dimensional basis alone. We have already considered this issue in Chapter 7, in which the point was clearly made that the nature of the task determines the difficulty of a text. The advantage of working in CLIL is that it enables us to view academic tasks from these various perspectives, so that when we assess CLIL students in an exam, we can judge the language risk by considering it in relation to the conceptual and procedural demands.

The conceptual demand in the examples in Materials extract 8.D derives from the topic being tested. What is it about? What do students need to know? The procedural demand refers more to what students have to do. What actions do they need to carry out in order to fulfil the demands of the question? These procedures might be cognitive skills or simply test-based procedures. In Question 1, for example, students must read and understand the question and the instruction, select appropriately from a list (cognitive skill) by ticking the correct animals (test procedure).

Question 1

Which of these animals is likely to live in a desert?

Tick the ones you think they are.

- polar bear
- dolphin
- starfish
- lion
- jerboa
- camel
- lizard

Conceptual demand = low (1)

Procedural demand = low (1)

Language demand = low (1)

Question 2

Read the short text which accompanies the diagram, then answer the questions that follow.

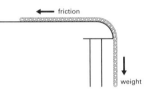

The diagram shows a chain hanging down over the edge of a table. Two of the forces on the chain are: the weight of the part of the chain which is hanging over the edge; friction between the chain and the table.

a The chain is not moving. What does this tell you about these two forces acting on the chain?

b The chain is moved slightly to the right. It begins to slide off the table. What does this tell you about these two forces now?

c Describe how the size of each force (the weight and the friction) changes as the chain slides off the table.

d How does the speed of the chain change as it slides off the table?

Conceptual demand =

Procedural demand =

Language demand =

Question 3

The plastic bottle has lemonade in it. Write in the boxes to show the parts which are:

a solid

b liquid

c gas

One has been done for you.

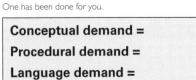

Conceptual demand =

Procedural demand =

Language demand =

Question 4

Complete the table.

Opposite idea	Socialist or communist idea
Working alone, to improve your life	Working together
Individuality	Solidarity
Privileges	
Class-based society	
Wealth for the minority	
A society of individuals	
A 'free' society	
The bourgeoisie control the proletariat.	
The bourgeoisie control production.	

Conceptual demand =

Procedural demand =

Language demand =

Question 5

Some students wanted to find out how well three different solvents—cooking oil, methylated spirits, and water—would dissolve a number of solutes. Some of the steps in their investigation are shown in the list below but they are not in the correct order.

Write them in the correct order.

A They wrote down their results.

B They put 20 cm³ of one of the solvents in two beakers. They repeated this with the two other solvents.

C They collected the equipment that they needed.

D They stirred the mixtures.

E They added some salt to three beakers containing the different solvents. Then they added some margarine to three more beakers containing the different solvents.

Conceptual demand =

Procedural demand =

Language demand =

Materials extract 8.D Test questions: three-dimensional assessment

The language demand can relate to several aspects of tasks, as we have seen throughout this book. For example, again in Question 1, students must understand the language of the question and the instruction, and recognize the animals in the list. These are low-level reading strategies (if we agree that the question and instruction are fairly transparent), but the main point with regard to 'language risk' is surely that students are not required to produce any language at all. Neither is any of the language particularly 'academic'.

However, several of the examples are less straightforward. Question 2, as you will immediately see, is more demanding on all three levels.

Read through the examples. The box below each of the questions, inserted for the purposes of this chapter, is a three-dimensional 'demand' box. As you read the questions, think about them on a 'demand' scale of low to high, but in terms of the language, concepts, and procedures involved. A score of 1 indicates low demand, and a score of 5 indicates very high demand. The suggested levels of Question 1 have been done for you. There is a table on page 229 with some suggested answers.

By identifying these relative demands and the interplay between them, we can allocate marks more accurately to the individual questions. Question 2 clearly requires a more careful and more detailed allocation of marks, because the language demand is such as to make it a major factor in the students' ability to succeed. To simply award one mark for each question on the basis of its conceptual accuracy (Question 2, a–d) can only be justifiable on a course which has not made the required language salient.

In Question 4, it might be possible to show understanding without the best words/ phrases for the slots, but a student who supplies 'A society of people working together' for the opposite of 'A society of individuals', although employing a decent paraphrase and deserving of a mark, has not achieved the same as a student who supplies the phrase 'A collective', the content-obligatory term for this slot.

In Question 5, the three demands are fairly equal, and none too complex, so we can focus on a much simpler mark scheme to reward the correct order. In general, this considered 'weighting' of marks seems fairer when conducted under the auspices of the three dimensions.

The various types of formative assessment

We have mentioned formative/continuous assessment already, although not in the same detail as the summative type. We said, however, that CLIL lends itself more naturally to formative-type assessment, because of the greater emphasis in CLIL courses on performance, on students 'doing things'. This can sound rather facile unless we look more carefully at what we mean by 'doing' things. In CLIL, as we have seen, the reduction of teacher-centred, transmission-based learning has generally led to an increase in the volume of student action, or student 'intervention'—a good word to describe what committed CLIL practitioners have noticed about their classrooms. This being the case, we need our assessment procedures to both reflect and support it.

'Backward' design

One of the main consequences of a syllabus which emphasizes student action is the prevalence of performance-based productive assessment events, usually occurring—although not exclusively—at the end of a didactic unit. In 'hard' CLIL, such units can last for several months, a factor which can radically change the assessment procedures employed by teachers, who need to monitor student progress on a regular basis. Students also need to know that they are more or less on the right track, given the amount of content that needs to be assimilated.

This has led to the development of **'backward' design** as a method of assessment (Wiggins & McTighe, 1998), which was also explored by Ribe and Vidal (1993) in their influential book *Project work*, published on the cusp of the appearance of the CLIL acronym. Backward design also lends itself to a more competence-based approach, but first we need to see an example, this time from 'soft' CLIL. Materials extract 8.E (overleaf) is taken from a unit on music in an English textbook, aimed at 12-year-olds in a CLIL-based multilingual curriculum. It is a strong example of backward design, and it offers an interesting insight into the sometimes complex relationship between formative/continuous and summative assessment.

The unit, called 'We've got talent!', consists of more than 40 tasks, divided into three content-based modules. With English timetabled four times per week, this unit can last for up to ten school weeks. The entire unit is based on its culmination, called a **'complex integration task'** (Aldasoro, 2013). Students are made aware of this task during the initial phase of the unit (see Materials extract 8.E). In the initial 'planning activity', after some orientation exercises on certain music-related concepts, students are asked to think about the procedural implications of the task they will perform in two months' time. What will they need to do?

When students have done this, they are then asked to consider the conceptual implications of this eventual performance. What will they need to know? (See Materials extract 8.F on page 225).

Moving on to the complex integration task at the end of the unit, the checklist in Materials extract 8.G (on page 225) represents a final reminder for students. It may not look like much, but it actually incorporates the entire conceptual, procedural, and linguistic sweep of the unit.

8 Planning activity **'WE'VE GOT TALENT' MUSIC CONTEST: PLANNING**

What are we going to do at the end of this unit? Hold a music contest at your school, of course!

DON'T MISS!!!

WE'VE GOT TALENT!

FRIDAY, 12th DECEMBER
LIVE in the School Auditorium

Be there for:
THE BEST GROUPS!
THE BEST AUDIENCE!
THE BEST JUDGES!

WHAT?

1. What will you have to do? Here are the main things you will need to do for the contest. Put the sentences into the correct columns *of the table.*

a) Introduce yourselves 'live' on stage

b) Adapt a song

c) Form a group of 3 or 4 persons

d) Record a video of your group's autobiography

e) Perform the song that you have adapted

f) Be the jury for another group's performance

g) Be the audience for the performance

BEFORE WE PERFORM AND JUDGE	WHEN WE PERFORM AND JUDGE

Materials extract 8.E A planning activity (Ball et al., Subject projects 1: We've got talent!, Ikaselkar, p. 14.)

2. So what do you have to do to prepare for the contest?
The modules of this unit will help you prepare for the contest. Look through the unit and identify the main topics of each module.

3. Write down in which module you will find the following topics.

UNIT TOPICS	WHICH MODULE?
Musical genres	Module 1
Opinions on performance	
Autobiography of a music group	
Good performances	
Music groups	
Elements of music	
Recording and editing a video	
Musical instruments	
Adapting a song	

Materials extract 8.F The conceptual elements of musical performance (Ball et al., Subject projects 1: We've got talent!, Ikaselkar, p. 15.)

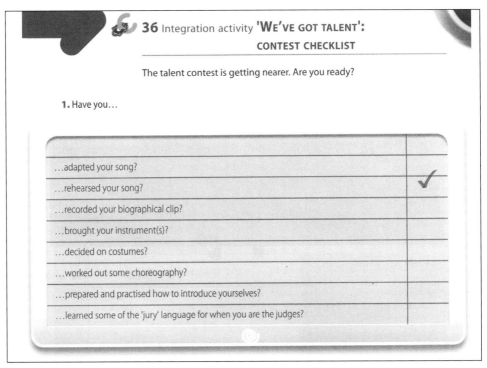

36 Integration activity **'WE'VE GOT TALENT'**:
CONTEST CHECKLIST

The talent contest is getting nearer. Are you ready?

1. Have you…

…adapted your song?	
…rehearsed your song?	✓
…recorded your biographical clip?	
…brought your instrument(s)?	
…decided on costumes?	
…worked out some choreography?	
…prepared and practised how to introduce yourselves?	
…learned some of the 'jury' language for when you are the judges?	

Materials extract 8.G Checklist (Ball et al., Subject projects 1: We've got talent!, Ikaselkar, p. 55.)

The content of the unit is subsequently checked in more detail in the post-performance self-assessment activity (see Materials extract 8.H), but even judging by just the previous basic demands, it is clear that this unit has covered a substantial amount of content. The actual self-assessment activity makes students aware, in case they missed anything, exactly what they have been learning by summarizing the content of the unit in detail. It has been good fun, but this is the 'hard' end of 'soft' CLIL, and as such, the content is taken seriously.

Notice, too, how the three sub-activities that constitute the overall complex activity in Materials extract 8.H are a strong example of content–language integration, but in the three-dimensional sense that we have emphasized throughout this book. Task 1 is mainly conceptual. Task 2 is more linguistic (the language and structure of biographies) and procedural, with digital competences to the fore. Task 3 is again more linguistic, but with the focus more on language functions, in this case how to give opinions, emphasizing the use of music criteria and polite modal forms. All of these are, of course, worked on throughout the unit.

Formative to summative: four issues

The 'We've got talent!' unit described above demonstrates exactly why we need formative/continuous assessment. If we think that CLIL can help us to motivate students to develop a positive attitude towards content, and help them to simultaneously improve their performance in the vehicular language, then we cannot simply abandon them to the cold process of summative assessment after ten weeks of engaging and motivating them with content. Entertaining though 'We've got talent!' appears to be, the complex final task is really a summative test. It is the culmination of almost three months' work, integrating a wide variety of skills and examining the following competence:

> 'The student selects the music and the images appropriate to the parameters of the situation and integrates them into a musical montage, gives information about the authors or participants of this musical montage, and assesses montages performed by others.'

With regard to how we assess, there are several options open to those in CLIL-based practice; but first we need to be aware of the issues involved. As we will see, in terms of assessment methodology, there is no necessary distinction between assessing 'hard' and 'soft' CLIL. Let us examine four of these issues related to CLIL assessment with reference to the 'We've got talent!' unit.

38 Self-assessment activity REFLECTING ON MY WORK IN THE UNIT

You've finished the task! But how well do you think you did it? Complete the table below.

	FOR THE TALENT SHOW, I...	I MANAGED WELL	I DIDN'T MANAGE VERY WELL
TASK 1	chose the appropriate genre		
	chose the clothes and choreography for the genre		
	changed the musical elements of the song		
TASK 2	wrote the group's autobiography		
	organized the information into the categories of an autobiography		
	used the appropriate verb tenses		
	used the appropriate pronouns		
	created an autobiographical video of our group		
	put together the images and the sound of the video		
	used the video editing program properly		
TASK 3	gave my opinion about my colleagues' performances		
	used polite language		
	justified my opinion using the things I have learnt in the unit		
	used the correct adjectives		
	used opinion language		

Materials extract 8.H End-of-unit self-assessment activity (Ball et al., Subject projects 1: We've got talent!, Ikaselkar, p. 57.)

1 Length

The unit is long. This is because it contains a substantial amount of content. If the final (summative) performance earns students the majority percentage share of the marks, then they will need to receive staged feedback leading up to this final performance. If the students were actual musicians, this would surely also happen. In the 'We've got talent!' unit, therefore, each module contains a self-assessment check and a peer-assessment activity to consolidate the conceptual content encountered so far (see Materials extract 8.I).

These formative activities (the peer-assessment activity is perhaps better described as a 'task', according to Lee's definition in Chapter 7) do not necessarily earn students any marks, but they help them to see where they stand in relation to some of the demands that will be made in the (distant) final assessment. If students choose to tick 'Well' for all the content objectives listed, and peers have endorsed this, a poor final performance is still possible. But students would have little cause to complain about their final mark.

2 Process and product

The length of the unit suggests that we might also prefer to distribute the marks in a way that better represents the process, rather than simply the product. This process–product dichotomy (Bruner, 1960) has for some time represented the core of educational philosophy, and in truth it is probably more of a continuum than a dichotomy. Here, to represent the process, the 'We've got talent!' unit uses a series of simple staged 'integration' tasks (as opposed to the final complex integration task), which appear at the end of each module and either 'retrieve' the inherent content or actually work on the preparation of the final complex task. In Materials extract 8.J (on page 230), students must retrieve the concept of genre by choosing one of the songs to adapt (which they will go on to use in the final performance) and then adjusting the musical elements to fit this genre-based choice. The instruction 'Practise your new version' in step 4 will inevitably involve peer (and possibly teacher) feedback. But a mark can be awarded for this work.

3 Formative or continuous?

If we award marks for these staged checks and retrieval tasks, then we are arguably just applying a series of smaller, summative assessment procedures. It also invites the question of whether there is a difference between the terms 'formative' and 'continuous', despite the fact that they tend to be used synonymously. Assessment theory tends to assert that 'formative' cannot be graded (i.e. awarded marks), since its function is to advise, not to test. It is prescriptive but ungraded. The word 'formative' itself suggests this, but 'continuous' does not. It remains an unclear area, but 'continuous' suggests that learners are being continually assessed throughout the process, and that the summative stage is simply one part of this more gradual, more accumulative assessment. The opposite of 'continuous' may therefore be 'non-continuous', not 'summative' (see Figure 8.1 on page 233).

19 Self-assessment activity CHECKPOINT

Now it's time for you to check up on what you have learned.

1. Complete the following table.

IN THIS MODULE, I HAVE BEEN LEARNING TO...	IN WHICH ACTIVITIES?	HOW WELL CAN I DO THIS?	
		WELL	NEED MORE PRACTICE
...identify the musical genre when I hear different pieces of music, e.g. *opera, heavy metal*, etc.			
...identify the basic elements of music when I hear different pieces of music, e.g. *instruments, harmony*, etc.			
...match written definitions with the musical elements.			
...classify musical instruments into different types, eg. *aerophone, idiophone*, etc.			
...describe musical instruments including information, e.g. *where they come from, what they are made of, how they are played*, etc.			
...describe instruments using expressions, e.g. *It is an idiophone instrument. It comes from Africa. It is made of wood. It is played with the fingers.*			
...change some of the basic elements of a song, e.g. *rhythm, lyrics*, etc.			

2. Ask your partner what he/she has written in the third and fourth columns.
If he/she has not done some of the activities very well, can you help?

Materials extract 8.1 Self- and peer-assessment activity (Ball et al., Subject projects 1: We've got talent!, Ikaselkar, p. 34.)

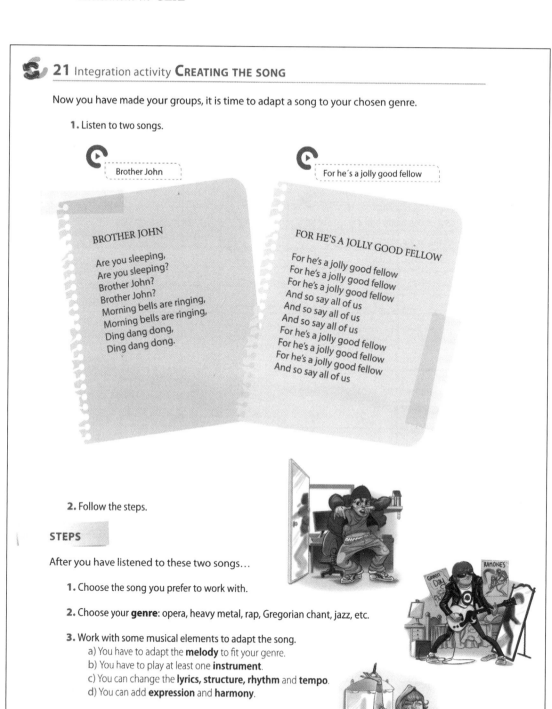

21 Integration activity **CREATING THE SONG**

Now you have made your groups, it is time to adapt a song to your chosen genre.

1. Listen to two songs.

Brother John

For he´s a jolly good fellow

BROTHER JOHN

Are you sleeping,
Are you sleeping?
Brother John?
Brother John?
Morning bells are ringing,
Morning bells are ringing,
Ding dang dong,
Ding dang dong.

FOR HE'S A JOLLY GOOD FELLOW

For he's a jolly good fellow
For he's a jolly good fellow
For he's a jolly good fellow
And so say all of us
And so say all of us
And so say all of us
For he's a jolly good fellow
For he's a jolly good fellow
For he's a jolly good fellow
And so say all of us

2. Follow the steps.

STEPS

After you have listened to these two songs…

1. Choose the song you prefer to work with.

2. Choose your **genre**: opera, heavy metal, rap, Gregorian chant, jazz, etc.

3. Work with some musical elements to adapt the song.
  a) You have to adapt the **melody** to fit your genre.
  b) You have to play at least one **instrument**.
  c) You can change the **lyrics, structure, rhythm** and **tempo**.
  d) You can add **expression** and **harmony**.

4. Practise your new version.

Materials extract 8.J Retrieving concepts: integration activity (Ball et al., Subject projects 1: We've got talent!, Ikaselkar, p. 36.)

It is unnecessary to delve too deeply into this issue here, since we are simply trying to propose the best and fairest ways to assess learners in CLIL-based contexts. However, CLIL is not exempt from the universal requirement of certification in assessment, whereby we measure students' performances in relation to some pre-defined national standard. Is it unfair, therefore, to award marks to students during the process, when common sense tells us that they are still in the practice phase, still inexpert in relation to the assessment objectives?

There are two answers to this question. The first is that we are trying to focus learners on the importance of the process, not simply the end result. This is good for the purpose of differentiation, because weaker students get the chance to shine in other areas of performance, and good for the purpose of motivation, because when students see that it is not simply the final test that counts, they are more likely to engage in lessons, and more likely to see the logic in intervening and working hard. This type of continuous assessment does not 'give away' marks any more easily, but it surely focuses learners more coherently on the multiple aspects of the content that affect their progress. In CLIL, learners need to know that they are meeting the required standards. Their natural concern that their language level might somehow be preventing them from doing this means they will need constant reassurance to the contrary. In the 'We've got talent!' unit above, three months is a long time to wait to find out whether you have 'passed' or not.

The second answer to the process question is to look at the aspects of classroom performance that we wish to assess. What is interesting here, especially with regard to more competence-based practices, is that with process-based assessment we can focus on different areas of performance, often called '**meta-disciplinary areas**'. These are also known as 'general competences'. For example, in the European Parliament's list of eight 'key competences for lifelong learning' (2006), the competence 'Learning to learn' is meta-disciplinary. It belongs to no particular academic discipline, but is common to all of them. The same can be said for 'Sense of initiative and entrepreneurship'. However, in the same list, the competence 'Mathematical competence and basic competences in science and technology' is clearly not meta-disciplinary.

If we take the competence 'Learning to learn' seriously, and wish to incorporate it into our curriculum, then how can we do this unless we make students aware of it and its components? To simply use summative assessment to achieve this, although valid, now seems akin to a dereliction of duty, especially when working with CLIL. 'Learning to learn' is made up of many components: listening and responding to feedback, self-assessment and self-awareness, working cooperatively in groups, understanding how to organize learning, etc. Can we award marks for these sub-competences? The answer is surely 'yes', because even the most cursory glance at the unit 'We've got talent!' highlights the obvious link between the meta-disciplinary competences and the observable actions that students must eventually be assessed on. In Materials extract 8.G (on page 225), all the demands have been required of students along the way, and all of them have involved co-operation, planning, consensus, and thought. Whilst it remains true that we can judge these requirements on the final summative assessment day, it seems almost illogical to do so. Surely—and in CLIL especially—we can and should allocate some marks to the process?

4 Certification and assessment

Nevertheless, there is a difference between certification and assessment. This is because, ultimately, we need to know if learners can 'fly solo'. The checklist requirements in Materials extract 8.G (see page 225) can all involve group awareness and co-operation, but in competence-based theory and in CLIL, learners must also be able to act alone. This individual proof of competence is what certifies that students have reached the pre-defined standard.

Of course, this also depends on the nature of the competence being examined. Like objectives, competences must be observable. In the case of 'We've got talent!', the competence (see page 226) and its attendant skills and content can be assessed using four types of measurement. We have seen three so far:

1 short summative assessments, in the form of simple integration tasks
2 continuous assessment of meta-disciplinary competences
3 final summative complex integration task.

We may feel that these are enough to assess students with. We may feel that students' individual contributions to these largely co-operative tasks have been sufficiently observable during the process for us to award an objective mark based on these three measurements.

The missing measurement—certification of the competence in an individual situation—can be tested by requiring students to respond to all of the demands made in the competence statement. For example, the final component of the competence 'assesses montages performed by others' is a good content–language integration exercise. The test item in Materials extract 8.K (based on a real video clip) measures students' ability to do this, but individually.

Your American friend Todd has sent you a video of his band. He is the singer, and he wants to know your opinion about the band and the video.
- Watch the video.
- Write down your opinion about his band and the video. Use your knowledge of music to justify your opinion.
- Use Audacity to record your opinion about Todd's band, then video and email the message to your teacher.

Materials extract 8.K Item to test competence individually

The matrix shown in Figure 8.1 is helpful as a way to sum up this section. The vertical line represents the type of assessment, whereas the horizontal represents frequency. The elements in each quadrant are taken from the discussion so far, and from examples derived from the unit 'We've got talent!'.

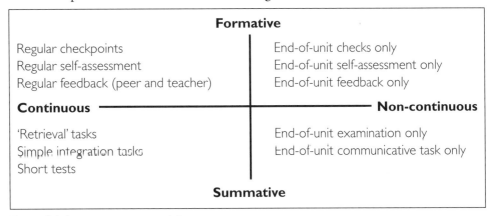

Figure 8.1 Assessment type and frequency

The matrix, through its vertical axis, indicates the objective of the assessment type. Is the objective to prepare for or to arrive at the certification of an objective (summative) measurement, or is the objective of a more formative nature? (see Figure 8.2).

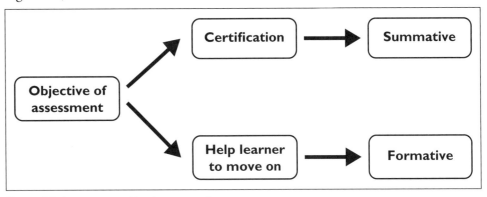

Figure 8.2 Assessment objectives according to type

Through its horizontal axis, the matrix also indicates the likely pedagogic orientation, or the learning theory, behind the assessment (see Figure 8.3 overleaf). This is because the frequency at which we assess indicates our likely beliefs about how students best learn. In terms of the matrix, 'bottom-right' teachers will assume things about their students that teachers who locate themselves to the 'top-left' and 'bottom-left' do not. All positions within the matrix could be valid, but the crucial point is that they represent differing learning theories.

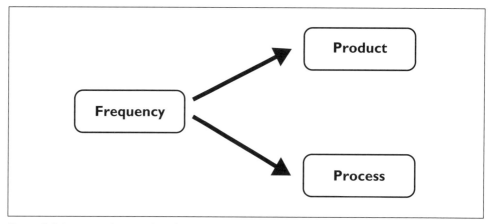

Figure 8.3 Learning theory related to assessment frequency

CLIL and competences

There is no automatic connection between CLIL and competence-based education, but as we have already stated, the future of education is competence-orientated and CLIL would seem to have an important role to play. Why is this?

One obvious reason is the tendency of CLIL teachers to extend their methodological repertoires, sometimes out of necessity, but more often due to the fact that their approach becomes less teacher-centred. It is difficult to maintain an efficient CLIL classroom environment based on the transmission of knowledge by the teacher alone. Besides, the nature of knowledge no longer seems to allow for such a limited, one-directional view of learning interaction. As a result of this, learners do more. CLIL lends itself to a more student-centred approach because both teacher and learner are more aware of the inadequacy of mere transmission. The result seems to be a greater proliferation of more performance-based communicative activities. These are natural terrain for competences.

Situations

The term 'competence' is problematic, and subject to different variations when incorporated into educational curricula. However, we can usefully state, for the purposes of this chapter, that a competence is a cluster or aggregate of abilities, knowledge and skills—all of which relate to one another. These enable a person or an organisation to perform effectively in a job or situation.

The first key factor here is that abilities, knowledge, and skills are all described as elements subordinate to a competence. In effect, they are its components (see Figure 8.4). The second key factor is that a competence, as described here, can only exist within a situation (Roegiers, 2000). In other words, a situation is required in order for a person to demonstrate (through an action or a series of actions) a given competence, and in assessment terms, to demonstrate the characteristics of the competence required.

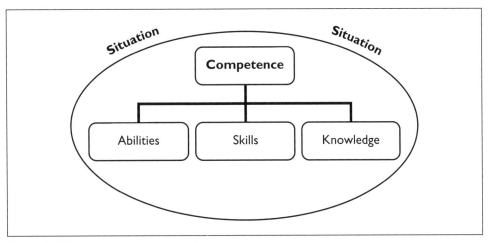

Figure 8.4 Situation, competence, and components

In the school context, situations in which students can demonstrate competences in an authentic way can be difficult to come by. However, even within the relatively limited parameters of the classroom, we can provide valid frameworks for competence-based action. The internet has generated a greater raft of possibilities for teachers, enabling genuine communication not simply with other schools but with public and private institutions, who can be persuaded to respond authentically. Students can make real suggestions, real complaints, and provide real data. There is much less need now for students to feel that school is a place where hypothetical actions are undertaken, for a hypothetical future.

Nevertheless, situations do not need to be particularly extensive or serious to be valid settings for the measurement of a competence. They just need to be coherent and they need to be real for the students. So, for example, in 'We've got talent!', the situation is simply as shown in Materials extract 8.L.

We've got talent!

Your school is organizing a talent show for your fellow students where you can all show your talent as performers. You will also act as a jury and judge your classmates' performances in the show.

In order to participate in the talent show, you need to carry out the following tasks:

1 Before the show:
   a Send your teacher a presentation video of the group.
   b Choose a song and adapt it.

2 During the show:
   a Introduce your group and the song you're performing.
   b Perform the song.

3 Judge your classmates' performances using the music criteria and contents you've been working on through the unit.

Materials extract 8.L Situation for 'We've got talent!'

The four elements of a 'situation'

Of course, this is an example of 'soft' CLIL, and so the fact that the school is holding the talent show in English makes sense—in scholastic terms—because English is important both at school and in the future of these non-native-speakers' daily lives, and it also important to be able to perform well in front of a peer audience. However, a competence-based action, in an assessment situation or otherwise, also requires four further obligatory elements. These are <u>actor</u>, <u>recipient</u>, <u>objective</u>, and <u>medium</u>.

These four elements are very useful for both curricular planning and CLIL teachers. They enable both 'soft' and 'hard' CLIL teachers to build a coherent framework for any didactic unit they need to teach. If the summatively assessed end product is a subject-specific competence (or set of competences), then the four elements make the planning of a communicative task (as in 'We've got talent!') much clearer.

The actor–recipient–objective–medium relationship is indivisible. For example, if a student (the actor) is addressing an audience of class peers (the recipient) by means of a PowerPoint presentation (the medium), because he or she wants to persuade them that his or her suggestion to reduce carbon emissions at school is the best (the objective), then he or she must understand that the combination of these elements conditions both the language and the manner of presentation. Imagine an entirely different set of demands, using the same four elements: if two students (the actors) are addressing the local town council (the recipient) by means of an email (the medium) because they want to improve their town's image on a local tourist-board English website to attract more visitors of their own age (the objective), then they will need to use entirely different content and language from the previous example.

Both scenarios must be framed by a situation, which tends to form the 'why' of the whole venture. In the first situation, the students are trying to help save the world. In the second, they are trying to alter the image—and thus the tourist intake—of their town, to their own and the town's benefit. Learners respond better to these situations, and they can drive the content of any syllabus.

Competences and language

Importantly, CLIL-based practice also enables us to see more clearly the link between competences and language. This is probably the key to why CLIL has become so popular, and why it should continue to play a significant role in education.

We mentioned earlier in this chapter that one of the alternative acronyms to CLIL is LEST (Language Enhanced Subject Teaching—see page 237). In some ways, it conveys a clearer message than the CLIL acronym, because it emphasizes the supporting role language plays in the content–language partnership. It is possible that the 'dual focus' of the CLIL acronym is muddying the waters, because teachers are never quite sure which of the two components they are supposed to be emphasizing. Whilst it is true that in this book we have been stressing that CLIL is about the learning of 'content', we have also been at pains to point out that language is also precisely that—content. We cannot have it both ways, of course, but from successful CLIL practice we have drawn the conclusion that language objectives tend to retire into the background. CLIL is not language teaching as such, and we have seen from the summative assessment section (see page 211) that language is only assessed in its role as the tool of expression, as the conduit of academic discourse.

This can also be true of 'soft' CLIL, whether or not we persist in associating it with the phrase 'language led'—which is a phrase we have questioned. This is a counter-intuitive point for language teachers, but it may represent the future. The more students 'do' with language, the more it seems to make sense to them. The archives of CLIL schools around the world are filled with student feedback that attests to this claim.

If we accept this claim, it has significant implications for how we envisage the role of language in the future. As a subject in its own right, or as a meta-disciplinary tool? In this final section of our consideration of CLIL-based assessment, let us look at the position of language vis-à-vis the competence scene in general. We need proof that what Graddol (2006) said about English—that it is no longer a mere language but a 'core skill'—is true of languages in general.

The three bases of competences

Although the terminology can differ across countries, it can be useful to see competences as shown in Figure 8.5 (overleaf). On the left are the three basic elements which drive and condition our behaviour as humans. On the right, there are five meta-disciplinary competences that feature either wholly or partly in a variety of European curricula (Garagorri, 2010). These meta-disciplinary competences, sometimes called 'general' competences, are derived from natural behavioural responses to the demands of the three elements to the left. We could add others, but the relationship is the important thing to note here.

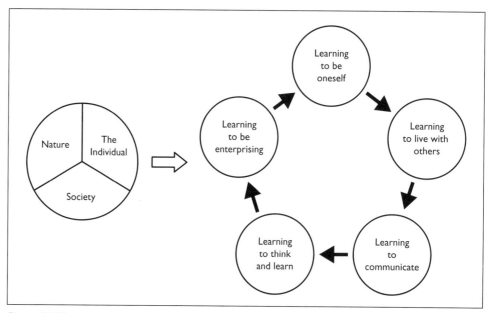

Figure 8.5 The three bases of competences

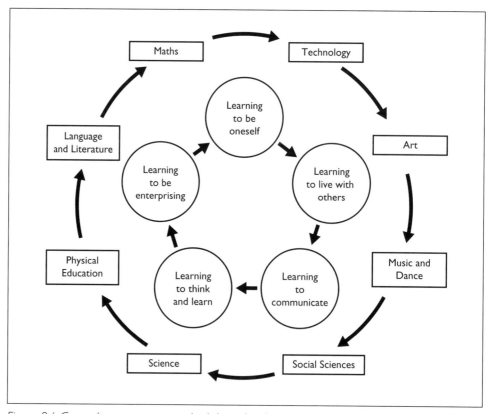

Figure 8.6 General competences worked through subject areas

Moving on to school and academic life, we find that the general competences can be worked through subject-specific areas, as we can see in Figure 8.6.

Finally, and most importantly, if we look again at Figure 8.6, we can see that the only truly transversal element common to all of these competences is actually <u>languages</u>.

Why, therefore, would we assert that CLIL is the best medium for conveying this message? Perhaps because the learning route becomes more like the one shown in Figure 8.7 when CLIL takes over from exclusively content-based approaches.

Using language … through different content … to develop competences.

Figure 8.7 The CLIL learning route

If subject teachers find the 'three dimensions' of content useful, for planning and/ or assessment purposes, then the route shown in Figure 8.7 highlights even more clearly the significance of language.

The previous example of the four elements of a situation can be paraphrased as follows: 'The student (the actor) addresses an audience of class peers (the recipient) by means of a PowerPoint presentation (the medium), to persuade them that his or her solution to reduce carbon emissions is the best (the objective).' From this, we can see that the subject teacher, in order to assess this presentation, will need to consider first and foremost the coherence of the conceptual content: are the proposed solutions scientifically sound and feasible? Beyond that crucial assessment criterion (at the head of the list below, in italics), covering the subject-specific content, what other considerations come into play? Without knowing the exact weight and direction of the teaching unit that led to this description, we can see that the linguistic components are various:

To what degree are the solutions scientifically sound and feasible?
- What forms of address should the speaker (actor) adopt?
- What opening gambits should they use?
- How formal should the register be, to a peer audience?
- How should the presentation be structured?
- Which discourse markers should indicate the stages of the presentation?
- How should the text be organized on the PowerPoint slides?
- How should the speaker use that text to address the audience?
- What aspects of persuasive language should they use?
- How convincing is their use of intonation?
- How fluent is their delivery?
- How well do they include the specific language (CALP) inherent to this topic?
- How well do they employ conditional 'if' clause structures?

When we look at this list, we can see that language is by far the dominant component of the student's performance. This is the case, of course, because we have required the student to perform, and this type of scenario is now commonplace in schools. However, when students are required to use an L2, the linguistic demands stand out much more than they might in the L1 classroom, precisely because so many of the elements would come fairly naturally to a native speaker. This is not to downplay their general importance in L1 contexts, but they simply cannot be ignored in CLIL-based assessment. Indeed, they form its very core. This is not a contradiction of the claim made earlier in this chapter that we must assess 'content' first and foremost. Remember that we tried to reshape the issue by suggesting that language is in fact a form of content, and that by making it more salient, we support the procedural (and conceptual) objectives.

With the backward-planning scheme that we also suggested earlier (see page 223), all these demands can be taught, and then practised using checklists and simple integration activities or tasks until the final, summative assessment day.

'Boxing weights'

Marks can be awarded along the way, as we have said, but in the summative test (in this case, the PowerPoint presentation), teachers must also 'weight' the criteria fairly, according to the importance that they have given them during the teaching unit.

A useful metaphor here is that of boxing weights. Just as boxers are categorized into heavyweight, middleweight, and lightweight groups, we can view the various components of a competence in the same way, with heavyweight being the most important component teachers want to prioritize. So, for example, if a science teacher has worked on how to organize the PowerPoint presentation, how to structure a scientific text (in this medium), and which key features of topic-specific discourse they were expecting to see, then these criteria would figure in the heavyweight column of Table 8.2. Similarly, depending on the explicit weight the teacher has given to the criteria, the other columns might be filled as shown.

Heavyweight	Middleweight	Lightweight
• Proposes sound and feasible scientific solutions • How to organize text in a PowerPoint presentation • Scientific text structure • Inclusion of topic-based CALP	• Discourse markers • Fluency of delivery • Persuasive language	• Formality of register • Forms of address • Opening gambits

Table 8.2 'Boxing weights' for the summative assessment of a process

If the teacher was satisfied that the 'boxing weights' reflected the teaching and learning that took place during the unit, then they could go on to distribute the marks accordingly. The heavyweight section could be awarded 60 per cent, the middleweight 25 per cent, and the lightweight 15 per cent. The exact weighting of the three sections is flexible; it might depend on the nature of the topic and on how easily identifiable the assessment criteria are. Apart from the fact that the mark for the mastery (or otherwise) of the scientific content must always figure in the heavyweight column, the boxing weights permit a CLIL teacher to see more clearly the contribution of the language-related components of the competence.

Here, in a very observable way, we can see how both the language and the conceptual content are vehicles for supporting and developing the competence. We said the same in our original 'three-dimensions' discussion in Chapter 3, but now the procedural content that we mentioned then looks very much like the core element of the competence. To illustrate this with a concrete example: a student trying to propose a solution to global warming might suggest reducing carbon emissions, and rightly so. However, if the student cannot persuade people clearly and coherently to agree, and fails to articulate the proposed solution successfully, his or her mark will not be as high as it could have been.

Rubrics and band scales

It also goes without saying that this assessment analysis, using the 'boxing weights' above, is based largely on spoken performance. The written considerations, in this case, are subservient to the spoken ones, although they could be important as cues and as a structural basis for the oral delivery of the presentations. But whether this task is principally a written or an oral task, we would still need to consider the weighting of the demands and even contemplate situating them within some form of **rubric**, using band scales. Examples of rubrics are not difficult to find for most subjects (see www.rubrics4teachers.com), and although no detailed rubric is exactly the same, in the case of certification we always need tools, such as band scales, to be able to measure the scale or degree of the communicative performance. We need to know what separates a pass from a fail, for example.

We suggested that the previous 'heavyweight' criteria from Table 8.2 could constitute 60 per cent of the total mark, thereby reflecting the relative importance of the language skills and scientific knowledge involved. Nevertheless, due to the diverse and three-dimensional nature of the criteria (text structure, CALP, scientific accuracy, ICT considerations), a CLIL teacher would still need to know how to judge the scale of achievement of each of these items. If this is 'hard' CLIL, then 'Are the solutions scientifically sound and feasible?' represents a criterion that can be either fully or partially achieved. It is not an absolute criterion. 'Scientific text structure' might be easier to spot, at a glance, and the 'topic-specific CALP' can be listened for during the presentation–or judged by reading an accompanying text that the teacher might have requested for this unit of work.

It is difficult (and possibly unwise) to suggest detailed rubrics for this type of task. They are complex to write, and teachers are busy enough. There are plenty of examples and advice on the internet, should teachers wish to try their hand at writing one. As shown in Table 8.3, the bands could simply be expressed with scaled adverbials, in what is known as a 'holistic' rubric.

Criteria	3	2	1	0
Proposes scientific solutions	Soundly	Adequately	Incoherently	Not at all
Organizes text in PowerPoint	Efficiently	Adequately	Poorly	Not at all
Structures scientific text	Perfectly	Adequately	Poorly	Not at all
Includes topic-based CALP	Fully	Adequately	Seldom	Not at all

Table 8.3 Holistic rubric

The combination of the specified assessment criteria, the boxing weights, and a simple rubric seem enough to guarantee that students are being fairly judged in terms of the stated competence—a scientific competence whose components include clear examples of linguistic and procedural content. The rubric allows the person marking to calculate a score for the 'heavyweight criteria' which will represent 60 per cent of the total mark. Further rubrics can be devised for the middle- and lightweight criteria if need be. In the end, teachers will know if the assessment measures at their disposal have been adequate to measure the competence of students performing in a foreign language.

An 'analytic' rubric, part of which can be seen in Table 8.4, places the qualitative criteria and accompanying scores along the top row and then literally 'analyses' them in the columns, according to the demands and objectives of the tasks. These can be complex to construct, due to the gradation of each component of the objective and the language that the rubric writer needs to employ in order to accurately describe the differences. However, once written, they can serve as a powerful and accurate measure of the skills being assessed.

Table 8.4 shows an example written for a CLIL class's presentation on 'Unconventional energy sources'. Three criteria have been abstracted from the more extensive rubric to show how different skills and competences can be assessed together. The first is related to the subject-based demand of 'identifying relevant information from various sources'. The second relates to the discourse of the topic and to the adjustment of the language (in the presentation) to a peer-group audience, and the third is 'meta-disciplinary'.

Criteria	Excellent 5	Good 4	Satisfactory 3	Almost satisfactory 2	Unsatisfactory 1
Student identifies relevant information from various sources	Student identifies relevant information from at least four sources of at least three different types.	Student identifies relevant information from at least three sources of at least two different types.	Student identifies relevant information from at least two sources (possibly of the same type).	Student identifies relevant information from one source.	Student doesn't identify relevant information from any sources of information.
Student uses new language related to energy and environment in simple sentences	Student uses correctly all the new words and expressions related to energy and the environment in simple sentences.	Student uses correctly at least 15 new words and expressions related to energy and the environment in simple sentences.	Student uses correctly at least ten new words and expressions related to energy and the environment in simple sentences.	Student uses correctly at least four new words and expressions related to energy and the environment.	Student does not use correctly any of the new words or expressions related to energy and the environment.
Co-operative work; active listening and interaction	Student contributes with information and work of high relevance to prepare presentation. Always focuses on task.	Student contributes with information and work of relevance to prepare presentation. Focuses on task most of the time.	Student contributes with some information and work to prepare presentation. Sometimes focuses on task.	Student contributes with one or two pieces of information and work to prepare presentation. Rarely focuses on task.	Student doesn't contribute with any information and work to prepare presentation. Never focuses on task.

Table 8.4 Analytic rubric for a CLIL science presentation

Transparency

It is essential that these criteria of assessment are shared with students, and that they know exactly what they mean and what implications they have on their own actions. The acronyms **WALT (We are learning to …)** and **WILF (What I'm looking for …)** are useful right down to young learner assessment. They are not exclusive to CLIL, but are useful messages for all forms of performance-based learning. They have also proved popular because they are easy to share with quite young children, helping them to understand and verbalize learning objectives in a less abstract manner. WALT and WILF can be drawn as characters, and their messages put up on posters on the classroom wall.

Finally, if teachers are concerned with the transparency of the assessment process, then the process itself might usefully be summarized with the broad categories of measurement represented by the inner circle in Figure 8.8 and some of the measurement tools and considerations represented by the outer circle. Here, the clockwise progression of the obligatory (inner) considerations should be reflected by the appropriate choices from the outer components.

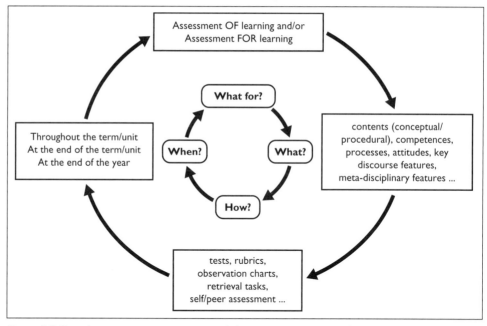

Figure 8.8 Broad assessment categories and their measurement tools

Summary

In this chapter, we have attempted to analyse how teachers in a CLIL context can assess their students, from a technical and an ethical point of view, since we have established that language itself must not be an obstacle, but rather a vehicle for the demonstration of understanding. We have applied the three-dimensional model of content to CLIL-based assessment, and suggested that CLIL-orientated practice provides a fertile terrain for continuous or formative assessment, with conceptual knowledge and language often at the service of procedural, skills-based tasks that form the basis of competences. Finally, we have tried to show how language is the only truly transversal component common to all subject areas and competences.

Task

If you would like to look at a practical task to explore your own practice related to the content of this chapter, see Appendix 1 (page 292).

Further reading

Ellis, R. (2003). *Task-based language learning and teaching*. Oxford: Oxford University Press.
Although only two of the chapters are specifically focused on assessment and evaluation, and although the book is not concerned with CLIL directly, it is nevertheless an excellent analysis of how task-based approaches—intimately related to good CLIL practice—provide a clearer framework for considering performance-orientated assessment.

Hönig, I. (2010). *Assessment in CLIL: theoretical and empirical research*. Saarbrücken: VDM Verlag Dr Müller.
An interesting research study from Vienna University on how assessment is carried out in CLIL schools, based on data from a sample of teachers. The research contradicts the notion that CLIL subject teachers do not assess language as such, raising questions as to the complex issue of balancing the testing of content and language.

Kiely, R. (2014). *CLIL—the question of assessment*. www.unifg.it/sites/default/files/allegatiparagrafo/20-01-2014/kiely_r._clil_assessment.pdf
A useful discussion regarding accountability in CLIL assessment, particularly with reference to the relative lack of evidence that CLIL students perform as adequately as their L1 peers in terms of subject learning.

Serragiotto, G. (2007). Assessment and evaluation in CLIL. In D. Marsh & D. Wolff, *Diverse contexts—converging goal* (pp. 271–283). Frankfurt am Main: Peter Lang.
A useful discussion of the gap between theory and practice in CLIL assessment. Drawing on the Italian context, the article suggests that more consensus is required as regards CLIL assessment, and that a shift from summative testing to more formative measures would benefit CLIL in general.

9

MANAGING CLIL IN SCHOOLS

Overview

In this chapter, we will look at the main issues which schools need to address in order to manage CLIL effectively. CLIL programmes are whole-school matters: they involve the school as an institution and its various stakeholder groups, including learners, parents, and teachers. For this reason, CLIL programmes need to be managed at the whole-school level as well as enacted in the classroom. Several aspects of the programmes need to be directed by management policy. The school will, for instance, need to choose a subject and find a teacher. It will then have to decide on a course structure; for example, a part-CLIL short-term course which teaches only part of the subject in L2, or a full-time long-term course which teaches the subject entirely in L2 for a year or more. The school will also need to decide which learners are right for the CLIL programme and at what age they should start. Assessment procedures have to be agreed upon, and teaching materials procured. Any collaboration between teachers—for example between subject and language teachers—has to be planned in a structured way. Thought must be given to the development and dissemination of good CLIL pedagogy. Stakeholder groups may have to be consulted, and the project as a whole is likely to need guiding by policy developed with the help of senior management.

Subjects

A school embarking for the first time on a basic CLIL programme needs to choose a subject, or indeed a selection of subjects. This choice may depend on several very practical things. For example, a teacher with sufficient fluency in L2 may be available; this is often a key criterion. Alternatively, a suitable subject may emerge because, if taught in L2, it will attract learners. Science, for example, may attract some older learners because they want to pursue the subject in higher education and are aware that it is taught partly in the L2 at the university of their choice. Some subjects are initially attractive because they seem easier to teach in L2; sometimes highly contextualized and visual subjects may appeal for this reason, such as art. It may also be that attractive L2-medium materials are readily available for a given subject: materials can give strong support to both learners and teacher and may help a school to decide on a subject. With collaborative programmes (see

'Course structure' below), a good professional partnership between a language and subject teacher may be a deciding factor which also gives the programme a good start.

Course structure

Once a subject has been chosen, the length of the programme and the hours per week need to be determined. Here, it is crucial to distinguish between very different types of CLIL programme. Some programmes are short-term and only partly taught in the L2. They are often 'language-led', i.e. they are chosen as much for their assumed language-learning value as for their capacity to develop subject knowledge, and as such are often run in collaboration with a language teacher. A programme of this kind may be offered as one lesson per week out of, say, three, and for a limited period—for example, a 25-week module. This kind of course may be preferred by a school which is less sure whether it wants to offer a long-term, full-time, L2-medium subject programme, with all that this entails in terms of teacher language ability, learner motivation, parental commitment, etc. It may, for example, be chosen to suit a subject teacher who is enthusiastic about CLIL but who is not wholly confident in the L2 and could not teach the subject full time for a long period in a way which maintains high subject standards. In this sense, a 'soft' CLIL programme is crucially a lower-risk programme: for example, learners who do not learn—or a teacher who does not teach—quite as well as they would if working in L1, can be confident that what is 'missed' in an L2-medium lesson can be covered in the next L1-medium lesson. Part-CLIL programmes are being pursued, for example, in Austria, where legislation implemented in September 2013 requires Technical High Schools (**Höhere Technische Lehranstalten**, often abbreviated to **HTLs**) to teach at least 72 hours of the curriculum to Year 3 students through English. Schools are left to decide how they meet this requirement, depending on criteria such as teacher language ability, resources, etc. Some may do it fairly intensively over two months; others may choose to spread the hours out over the academic year. Part-CLIL programmes of this kind sometimes lay emphasis on the collaborative input of a language teacher, to support both the learners and the L2-medium subject teacher. As such, the collaborative structure within which the two teachers will work has to be agreed upon.

If the school is thinking of implementing a long-term, full-time CLIL programme within which the subject will be taught only in the L2 for a year or more, i.e. a 'subject-led' programme, it will need to be sure that it has a teacher who has good enough language ability to teach the subject. This teacher may, however, need help with CLIL pedagogy (see 'Continuous professional development' on page 255). The school will also have to give thought to learner language ability (see page 251), materials (see page 256) and assessment (see page 252 and Chapter 8). This is a much higher-risk kind of CLIL programme in that it will have to ensure levels of subject achievement which are equal to or better than the levels that the learners would have achieved in their L1. The need to maintain school and national subject standards means the decision to adopt this kind of CLIL programme is not one a school will take lightly.

CLIL programmes are sometimes characterized by their relationships with other programmes and initiatives being run by the school. They may, for example, be accompanied by a language course aimed at supporting learners' levels of L2 ability. They are also sometimes marked by the use of two languages in the classroom, and they may involve collaboration between subject and language teachers both in and outside the classroom. Figure 9.1 (overleaf) shows a set of possible CLIL programme options which serve a variety of purposes.

Options 1 to 4 show collaborative relationships between subject and language teachers. Options 1 and 2 show how a CLIL course may be accompanied by a language-booster course, to be attended by students either before entry, during the course, or both. In option 1, the L2 teacher offers a general-purpose course, and in option 2 a course in which the language is tailored to a greater or lesser degree to the needs of the subject. Option 1 is common in schools where learners are considered to be in need of somewhat higher levels of L2 ability in order to enter a CLIL course. Option 2 is not common in schools, partly because L2 teachers do not normally have an adequate command of subject-specific language. These courses are, however, more common in L2-medium further and higher education, especially in courses in language for specific purposes. However, in some countries—for example in Bulgaria—it is common for learners embarking on full-time CLIL programmes to complete a whole pre-CLIL language-booster year in which language courses, both general purpose and subject specific, take up a considerable proportion of curriculum time.

Options 3 and 4 are common in collaborative language-led programmes in which language teachers work together with subject teachers. In option 3, there are two teacher languages in the classroom: the subject teacher does not have sufficient L2 fluency to teach in the L2, and so the language teacher teaches in support of the subject teacher, sometimes focusing on the subject, sometimes on the language. This is a less common structure than option 4, whereby both teachers work exclusively in L2. Collaborative teaching involving two teachers in the same classroom is more costly than having one teacher in the classroom and may therefore only occur sometimes within a collaborative CLIL programme.

Collaborative options like 3 and 4 are common in Italy, for example, where it may sometimes be difficult to find a subject teacher with sufficient L2 ability to teach the subject alone, as in options 1, 2, or 7. Many such collaborative ventures in Italy have proved to be relatively successful in terms of subject and language development, motivating learners, and enriching both subject and language teachers.

Options 5–7 show 'subject-led' programmes, in which subject teachers work on their own. Option 7 is by far the most common kind of programme. However, options 5 and 6 do occur. In option 5, oral work takes place mainly in the L1 while reading and writing are done in L2. This kind of programme tends to be literacy-orientated and may occur in subject contexts in which reading material tends to be in the L2 (often English). Option 6 is rare, but can occur where subject teachers are less fluent than their students in oral L2—perhaps in higher classes—but are comfortable listening, reading, and writing in the language. Option 7 is common, especially in subject-led programmes in countries where both teachers and learners can be expected to have fairly high levels of L2 ability. It may or may not be accompanied by option 1.

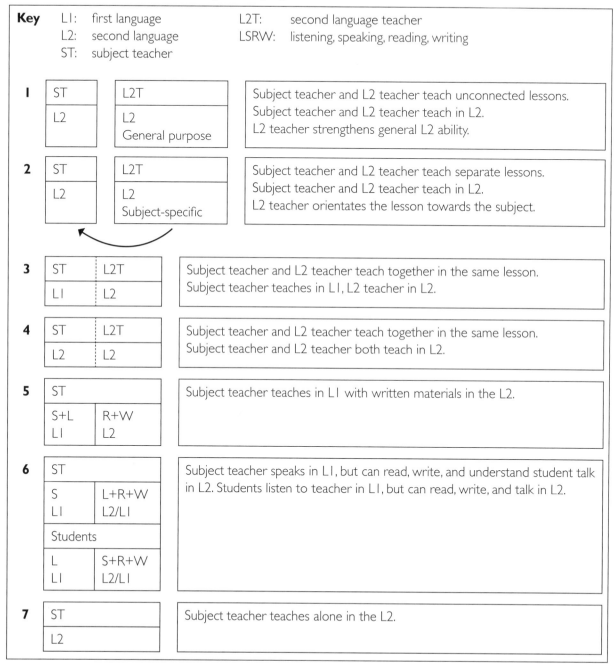

Key	L1:	first language	L2T:	second language teacher
	L2:	second language	LSRW:	listening, speaking, reading, writing
	ST:	subject teacher		

1

| ST | L2T |
| L2 | L2 General purpose |

Subject teacher and L2 teacher teach unconnected lessons.
Subject teacher and L2 teacher teach in L2.
L2 teacher strengthens general L2 ability.

2

| ST | L2T |
| L2 | L2 Subject-specific |

Subject teacher and L2 teacher teach separate lessons.
Subject teacher and L2 teacher teach in L2.
L2 teacher orientates the lesson towards the subject.

3

| ST | L2T |
| L1 | L2 |

Subject teacher and L2 teacher teach together in the same lesson.
Subject teacher teaches in L1, L2 teacher in L2.

4

| ST | L2T |
| L2 | L2 |

Subject teacher and L2 teacher teach together in the same lesson.
Subject teacher and L2 teacher both teach in L2.

5

| ST | |
| S+L L1 | R+W L2 |

Subject teacher teaches in L1 with written materials in the L2.

6

ST	
S L1	L+R+W L2/L1
Students	
L L1	S+R+W L2/L1

Subject teacher speaks in L1, but can read, write, and understand student talk in L2. Students listen to teacher in L1, but can read, write, and talk in L2.

7

| ST |
| L2 |

Subject teacher teaches alone in the L2.

Figure 9.1 Forms of CLIL provision

Teachers

When considering teaching a subject in L2—especially a full-time, long-term course as in option 7—a teacher needs to think about two main capacities: L2 ability and CLIL pedagogical ability. As far as language ability is concerned, teachers have to feel confident enough that they can teach their subject in L2. This means thinking about the subject-specific and general academic aspects of the subject language (see Chapter 4), and also about the language of teaching. In other words, can they do what they want to do pedagogically speaking in the L2? In some countries, especially those where the L2 may be in fairly widespread social use, there are many teachers whose L2 ability is sufficient. In others, however, such teachers may be scarce.

In addition to considering their own L2 ability, teachers must also think about learner L2 levels. What if teachers are fluent enough in the L2 themselves but cannot make themselves understood by the learners, or encourage expression in the L2? The most L2-fluent teacher can feel very incompetent when working with learners with intermediate or fairly low abilities in the L2. If this is the case, the subject teacher needs training in the specialist pedagogy necessary for these contexts, which we describe in Chapters 5 and 6. This pedagogy can reduce the language demands of subject teaching and support both the cognitive and language abilities of learners. When considering teacher professional development to support a CLIL programme, it is often the language level of learners which the school will take into account. This may lead it to offer training to subject teachers not so much in the L2, but in CLIL pedagogy.

Learners

Students need sufficient ability in the L2 to be able to learn a subject in it. It is hard to say what this means. Learning new subject content and new language skills simultaneously tends to become ineffective below a given level of L2 ability, as learning becomes too slow and cognitively too demanding. Above this level of L2 ability, and with good CLIL pedagogy (see Chapters 5 and 6), it is possible to maintain levels of both subject and language development which are at least adequate and may even be superior to L1-medium subject teaching. It is likely that this L2 ability level differs according to certain criteria. It can vary, for example, between individual learners. A learner with good subject knowledge and motivation for the subject can cope with lower levels of L2 ability. Conversely, a learner with good language levels can handle higher subject demands. It can also vary between subjects: some subjects are less visual, more text-dependent, and less context-embedded, in Cummins's (2000) terms (see Chapter 4). Learners would therefore need high L2 ability to cope. Others may be easier for students to deal with in L2 because they involve a lot of visual or physical content, such as art or PE. And as we have just discussed, the likelihood of learners coping in L2-medium lessons can depend on the teacher: those with good CLIL strategies will be able to teach their subject more easily to learners with low L2 ability. We will deal with this topic further in Chapter 10.

Schools have options on how entry to CLIL programmes should be determined (Mehisto, 2012b). Some schools may wish to select learners for entry to CLIL programmes on the basis of measured L2 ability. Others may reject this as too exclusive a procedure. Some schools may wish to offer language-booster courses to prepare students for entry (see page 249). A school may well also take the view that it can only offer a CLIL programme to learners who are still developing their L2 abilities if it employs a subject teacher with good CLIL pedagogical skills who can raise the language skills and subject knowledge of learners at the same time.

Under certain circumstances, CLIL courses can be offered to learners with very low L2 ability. This happens, for example, in lower primary schools where young learners begin L2-medium subject lessons without having had time to develop their L2 ability very much at all. However, with good CLIL pedagogy on the part of subject teachers, their levels of L2 ability can be raised fairly quickly; and it is worth noting that in these cases, they have a whole school career ahead of them in which to develop this L2 ability.

Assessment

Assessment is a key whole-school matter for several reasons. Firstly, it is a complex matter, as Chapter 8 has shown, and appropriate expertise needs to be found amongst staff. Assessment in CLIL tends to be a weak point: not enough practitioners know enough about how to make it both fair to the learner and reliable as a means of establishing subject knowledge levels which are comparable with levels measured in the L1. In addition, separate CLIL courses running in the same school—and also between schools—need to use similar measures, to avoid discrimination between cohorts. Appropriate procedures for designing assessment tools and grading test performance have to be agreed upon. Measures also need to be seen amongst learners, teachers, and parents to have the same standing and reliability as L1-medium assessment tools—and to be equally challenging. Where national public examinations are concerned, schools may need to reach agreement with the education authority over the format of national CLIL-medium examinations. In Bulgaria, for example, learners undergoing the language-booster year (see 'Course structure' on page 248), go on to do two years of curriculum subjects in that language but then, for the last two years of school, go back to having Bulgarian as the medium of instruction for the curriculum and are ultimately assessed in Bulgarian in the school-leaving exams.

CLIL pedagogy

Teaching in an L2 requires a specialist pedagogy. It is not the kind of pedagogy which a teacher would normally use when teaching in L1 or acquire in initial teacher education. We have described CLIL pedagogy in detail in Chapters 5 and 6. Naturally, low ability in the MoI makes it difficult for learners to comprehend curricular concepts because they are so preoccupied with simply trying to understand the language. So the essential aim of CLIL pedagogy is to amplify the content of lessons so that learners with low ability in the MoI can nevertheless make sense of what the teacher is saying. It uses a range of means of increasing the chances that learners will understand—for example, the style of teacher talk, the use of visuals, listening and reading support tasks, etc. It also involves ways of supporting the learner during speaking and writing activities, so that attention needs to be paid less to the construction of sentences and more to the construction of subject knowledge. These teaching strategies are often fairly new to subject teachers, and so they may experience a steep learning curve when they start teaching their subject in L2. Depending on the level of L2 ability of their learners, many will welcome help.

Schools can provide this in several ways. First, they may be able to offer some form of **continuous professional development (CPD)** (see page 255). Second, they can work co-operatively with another, possibly more experienced, school (see page 262). Third, they can structure collaboration within a school between CLIL teachers who are all trying to do similar things in their classrooms. Teachers might all be struggling, for example, with getting learners to talk about subject concepts in L2, either in pairs, groups, or in whole-class plenary sessions. Teachers used to working in L1 will probably not know how to deal with this problem, and would therefore benefit from discussing possible solutions with each other. They may similarly be wondering, for instance, how to assess subject knowledge in L2 (see Chapter 8). A forum in which these kinds of discussions can take place would undoubtedly be welcomed by teachers: they would be able to share their views on what works, and could extend each other's skills and repertoires by collaborating with each other. A school can therefore help teachers with their professional development by establishing this forum and giving it a measure of official recognition. It may well also be the case that the school wants to evaluate over time—perhaps formally—its progress towards building CLIL capacity amongst its staff. This would involve helping teachers to develop and monitor their professional CLIL capacity by instituting an official forum in which pedagogical strategies are fleshed out and then developed in classroom practice. We will return to this question of monitoring progress in 'Monitoring and evaluation' on page 260.

Language teaching

As we have seen earlier in this chapter, a school may want to orientate part of its language teaching toward CLIL programmes, in order to help both learners and teachers in those programmes to develop the language of learning. Some language teachers welcome this: they may feel that it expands their professional horizons and leads them into interesting new territory. Other language teachers, however, may baulk at the prospect.

They can have good reasons for this. Language teachers are not normally trained to deal with the language of the subject. They are trained largely to teach the language of social intercourse. Learning what CALP is (see Chapter 4) may be very new for them. Similarly, many feel that they are not familiar with certain curricular subjects, and doubt their ability to work within a subject whose content they do not fully understand. It is an understandable reaction; but the experience of many CLIL teachers (and minority-language support teachers who are in the same boat) is that you do not need to understand the subject completely in order to support learners who are learning it through L2. Your expertise is the language of the subject and the language of learning, not the subject concepts themselves; those are the domain of the subject teacher. In addition, however, some language teachers may feel unsure about the whole idea of collaboration at this level with a subject teacher—and especially, for example, collaboration within the same classroom. Finally, it is not at all uncommon for language teachers to feel that the subject teacher is encroaching on their territory: the latter is, after all, working in the language being taught by the language teacher, and perhaps showing success in increasing learner fluency. Language teachers may also become worried that 'their' language is being taught by a subject teacher who makes a lot of language errors. All this could lead some language teachers to feel that CLIL might undermine their professional status, especially since there is often talk amongst education authorities that CLIL can 'kill two birds with one stone'. Language teachers could reasonably ask what this might this mean for their professional future.

Again, this fear is normally easy to lay aside: the introduction of CLIL does not normally mean that conventional language teaching in a school is reduced. Indeed, it often means that the professional opportunities for language teachers are enhanced. However, it can happen that in some schools, CLIL is introduced through a secondary subject department, without reference to the language staff. This is a situation which is likely to offend language teachers, and it would be understandable if they viewed CLIL from the sidelines with suspicion. A school which does this is making a major mistake; the involvement of language staff in the planning and delivery of CLIL programmes is another reason why CLIL needs to be managed at a whole-school level.

It should also be pointed out that if a school wants to direct some aspects of its language teaching provision towards supporting CLIL, it might have to do more than involve a member of the language staff. It may also need a slightly altered language syllabus which incorporates either CALP or elements of language specific to a subject. And this would need to be reflected in the language materials. Subject- or CALP-related language syllabuses and materials are scarce in CLIL programmes. They may be found to some degree in minority-language support programmes, in which language-support teachers may have been working on the language needed to support minority-language users within subjects. However, even here, both syllabuses and materials are rare. Support staff tend not to have access to professional materials; they make their own, perhaps rather hurriedly, as and when they are needed to support a mainstream subject lesson. For this reason, fully developed language programmes led by language teachers specifically in support of a subject are not common (though they do exist—for instance, in the Ikastola schools in the Basque country). It is more common for language support to CLIL to be of a general-purpose nature: for example, a language-booster course may be offered (see page 249). Only when a language teacher is working closely together with a subject teacher—for example, when teaching collaboratively in the same classroom, or perhaps within the framework of a whole pre-CLIL year of teaching language through subjects—does the language teacher become more closely and fruitfully familiar with the specific language demands of a subject.

Occasionally, if expertise exists, it may be possible for the school to offer CPD to the language teacher. If local (or more distant) expertise exists, language teachers may be able to follow a course which gives them insight into how to support both learners and subject colleagues within a CLIL programme. Similarly, they may be able to acquire this kind of expertise through a partnership with another local school which has built up this experience over time.

In addition, language teachers can sometimes have further roles within CLIL programmes. They may find themselves called upon to offer support courses to subject teachers outside school time to help them upgrade their language skills. They may also find themselves involved in co-ordinating a CLIL programme across the school, using their capacity as cross-subject language specialists. They may, in rarer circumstances, find themselves working on cross-curricular language development initiatives involving not only the CLIL team, but also members of staff who are interested in developing CALP skills across the school as a whole (see page 257).

Continuous professional development

We have mentioned that schools may require help from providers of CPD to run CLIL programmes, and we will look at this in detail in Chapter 10. Schools may need this help in the planning and/or delivery of a CLIL programme, as they become more familiar with their professional support needs. CLIL provision (at least in Europe) is not well supported by services offering teacher-education expertise, though there are some exceptions, such as in Germany or Switzerland, where CLIL teacher education is available in both INSETT and ITE. Normally, however, pedagogy tends to be developed from the bottom up within individual schools, and it is not easily accumulated by INSETT or ITE providers. Nevertheless, schools may be able to benefit from receiving CPD support, whether it is supplied by university-based providers or training institutions who are either local or more distant. The focus of this support may be on a range of aspects of CLIL, from programme planning through to classroom strategies and the language demands of specific subjects. Similarly, the focus may be on the needs of both subject and language teachers. Perhaps more usefully, a provider of CPD in CLIL may be able to offer school-based support: in other words, it could work with one particular school, investigating and providing for its very particular CLIL requirements, in terms of specialist expertise—for example in assessment—or of the needs of particular members of staff.

Professional development may also be available to a school via twinning arrangements—indeed, in the absence of CPD provision, such development opportunities may be both easier to find and more relevant. A school which has already developed CLIL expertise, often by trial and error, contains a lot of professional experience—sometimes more than an independent training provider can offer. A school which is planning a CLIL programme for the first time can gain a great deal of support by working collaboratively with a more experienced school, through inter-school visits, classroom observations, and more formal CPD sessions. It can also receive further support once it has gained some CLIL experience and is ready to look into specific aspects of CLIL in more detail. It often happens that the more experienced school also develops its own CLIL expertise further by being forced to make its experience clear to the partner institution.

Finally, there is an ever-increasing number of online courses available to support CLIL teachers. The CLIL Essentials course offered by the British Council is a case in point.

Resourcing

CLIL programmes need resourcing, and one key type of resource is textbooks. A few subject textbooks exist which are specifically designed for CLIL programmes— see, for example, those published by Cornelsen in Germany (e.g. history and geography) or by Oxford University Press in Spain (e.g. natural and social sciences)—but by and large, textbook publishers do not feel the CLIL market is large enough to invest in. In the case of system-wide L2-medium education, for example in Africa, they simply publish as if learners were native speakers (Peacock, 1995). This means subject teachers who work in L2 often have to rely on textbooks published for native speakers. Selecting an appropriate textbook of this kind means balancing subject appropriateness against language accessibility. Textbooks which are right for their learners in terms of subject depth and detail may be linguistically too demanding, whereas a textbook which learners can read more easily may be insufficiently demanding in conceptual terms. A CLIL subject teacher using a textbook written for native speakers will often need to take a specific pedagogical approach to help their NNS learners make sense of it.

A school will need to be involved with the procurement of materials for CLIL classes: for instance, they will need to fund the purchase of textbooks, which they may also need to monitor in terms of their use and usefulness. In the absence of textbooks, many CLIL teachers have to produce their own materials; and it is sometimes claimed that this accounts for a large percentage of the time CLIL teachers spend on a lesson. Making materials often requires that subject teachers use skills they may not have; and a lot of CPD time in CLIL is given over to the production of materials which provide language support. Online sources of subject content are often what teachers use as the basis for their own materials—but again, these need to be adapted for CLIL purposes.

Because many CLIL materials are made by teachers, they find it useful to share them, and many CLIL programmes run websites both to share materials made by teachers within the programme and to provide users with a directory of other

CLIL materials websites (See References for examples). Schools which run CLIL programmes are interested in the availability of both teacher-produced and online CLIL materials, and this is often one focus of CLIL management policy.

Other language programmes

CLIL programmes will not be the only programmes in a school in which language and subjects are brought together. In any European school, there are likely to be others, the main two candidates being language support for minority learners and cross-curricular language programmes in the L1.

In most European schools, there will be groups of migrant and/or immigrant learners. They may either be learning in an L2 and speaking another language at home, or they may be second- or third-generation immigrants who suffer from educational disadvantages caused by various factors, including the fact that the learners' families themselves may have low levels of education. These learners may also have the additional disadvantage of belonging to a low-status minority community. Many schools have units staffed by specialists in second-language learning and in language–content integration whose job it is to provide both learners and teachers with the support they need. This support may come in the form of helping learners to develop their L2 CALP and deploy it effectively in mainstream subject classrooms. It may also involve helping teachers to find ways of facilitating this CALP development process, often at the same time as working to maintain the L1 abilities of the learners – especially in the early years. In some countries, this support is underfunded and poorly developed. In others where there are good traditions of offering minority-language support, such support units will contain staff with much more expertise in language–content integration than CLIL teachers. It is often the case that these two groups of teachers with very similar skills and interests work in the same school but do not liaise with each other. It is probably rare to find instances in which they pool their resources and expertise and work collaboratively towards a common goal. Minority-language support programmes also operate at a whole-school level—for reasons similar to those which we listed earlier in this chapter with regard to CLIL programmes. Here, therefore, there is often a great deal of scope for senior management as well as individual members of staff to engage in collaboration.

The other type of initiative which is sometimes found in schools, and which relates to language–content integration, is a cross-curricular language programme in the L1. Some schools take the concept of CALP in L1 seriously: they take the view that cross-curricular language skills are necessary for successful learning, that these skills are better 'taught than caught' (i.e. that all learners will not necessarily just pick them up), and that schools should teach them explicitly in the L1. Many L1-medium CALP initiatives of this kind take the form of, say, a beginning-of-term one-week study-skills programme, or ongoing lessons in language-related study skills. These may be taught by an L1 specialist or by subject teachers who integrate the skills into their subject teaching. A widely accepted proposition in the field of education in L2 (Cummins, 2000) states that learners who have developed good CALP in their L1 will be able to transfer some aspects of this to learning in their L2, and that this will make L2-medium learning easier as a consequence. Schools which explicitly develop good L1 CALP are thus likely to be better at providing both CLIL and mainstream support for minority learners in the subject classroom. Conversely, many learners who come across CALP skills being taught explicitly for the first time in CLIL lessons will, as we mentioned in Chapter 3, be aware that they are basic cross-curricular skills which they should have been taught in L1 long ago.

CLIL is therefore likely to be related to other bodies of expertise operating elsewhere in the school and making similar use of whole-school management processes in order to do so. The school would do well to manage CLIL programmes in such a way as to maximize the positive effect of sharing experience and expertise between these programmes and minimize the repetition of similar management structures.

Stakeholders

Several groups of stakeholders are involved in the development of CLIL programmes, including education authorities, parents, teachers, and learners. A further important reason why CLIL is an issue for whole-school management is that the interests of all these stakeholders need to be taken into account; and conflicting interests need to be reconciled in ways which are often not necessary with other school subjects and programmes.

Education authorities

Education authorities are often interested in CLIL. They tend to believe that CLIL can generate certain educational rewards which have been claimed for it (see Chapter 2), and may be encouraged in this belief by government or EU policy. Some provide policy, resources, funding, and CPD services. They may also run large-scale CLIL programmes in schools—the education services in Catalonia, Madrid, and Lombardy are cases in point. There is sometimes a tendency for authorities to accept arguments for CLIL rather unthinkingly, without reference to published evidence, or an in-depth consideration of the resourcing which CLIL programmes need and the financial implications of this. Nevertheless, where an education authority supports CLIL programmes, it tends to be a major force in their development and maintenance. In other contexts, it may be the school which plays the leading role in offering the CLIL programme, in which case it may need to convince a less-informed education authority that what it is doing is worth supporting. Either way, schools running CLIL programmes need to find ways of talking to and negotiating with their controlling authority.

Parents

Schools offering CLIL programmes also need to interact with parents. Indeed, it may be the parents who initially influence the establishment of the programme. In some parts of Europe, parents are aware that CLIL is an established way of learning, that it may have strong adherents amongst politicians and academics, and that in some contexts, high learning success is claimed for it. In the same way that in Canada, for example, middle-class English-speaking parents are keen to have their children educated in French in immersion schools, educated parents in some parts of Europe (for example in Finland) can be a key driver of the development of CLIL programmes in secondary schools. In other countries, it may be the school which is convinced of the value of CLIL and which needs to persuade less-informed and perhaps sceptical parents of the benefits of the programme. This is especially the case with 'hard', subject-led CLIL programmes in which the learner intends to pursue a whole subject full-time in the L2. Parents may need to be convinced of the admittedly somewhat counter-intuitive claim that learners can sometimes achieve better levels of subject knowledge by learning in L2 than in L1. Regardless of the circumstances, schools running CLIL programmes need to find good ways of communicating with parents, either to show that they are responsive or to act as persuaders, and this will involve using their established means of home–school communication.

Teachers

Teachers are crucial to the success of CLIL programmes. A teacher who is both good at teaching the subject and good at doing so in L2 is very valuable to a school. Schools which want to offer CLIL programmes need to ensure that these teachers feel rewarded, that their skills are valued, and that they get at least some of the resourcing they request. CLIL programmes which are run by teachers who are largely responding to pressure from senior management rather than following their own interests are unlikely to be successful. In some cases, the teachers themselves will want to offer the programme and may, in the first instance, need to 'sell' it to a sceptical senior management team. For these reasons, relationships between school management and CLIL teachers often require more care than those which exist for less complex subjects.

Learners

Finally, the most important stakeholders are the learners. They must in one way or another thrive in a CLIL programme. If they do not thrive on an individual basis, the programme is not for them; if a whole cohort fails to thrive, something is clearly wrong at another level, perhaps with the teacher or the way in which the programme was designed. It is crucial that learners make their own decision as to whether they want to take part in CLIL, particularly if they want to embark on a full-time programme.

Of course, selection criteria (see page 252) may apply. Moreover, parents will have their views, and so will teachers. The latter may well have an opinion on whether or not a learner has sufficient subject ability or language ability to make a success of a CLIL programme. But this may not correspond to the way the learners themselves feel. Some learners may want to participate, even though their teachers feel that they will not thrive in the programme. Other learners may be unwilling to participate, despite teachers feeling strongly that they would benefit from it—especially if they were counselled appropriately both before and during the programme. Schools must recognize that all of the above stakeholder groups have views on CLIL programmes, and they will need to establish ways of interacting with them—and mediating between them when necessary. In the section 'Whole-school management structure in CLIL' (on page 262), we will look at structures which schools could put in place to manage the expectations of these groups, as well as the other whole-school aspects of CLIL programme management which we have discussed.

Monitoring and evaluation

Like all education provision, CLIL programmes vary in their quality. Indeed, when we look beyond CLIL to consider other forms of L2-medium education in the wider world, and especially in developing countries, what often strikes us is that education authorities simply do not understand what learning and teaching in L2 involves (Djité, 2008). In Europe, the picture is very different. Here, management of education by authorities tends to be familiar and effective, school self-monitoring is common, and CLIL programmes enjoy a good deal of success. Nevertheless, as we have previously pointed out in this book, CLIL is by no means a fully understood concept. We are gradually coming to know what it is and how to do it. Very often, we are learning from the bottom up: schools engage in CLIL and find out in the process how it might be made to work. Education authorities may well encourage and support CLIL, but sometimes they do not know how it works half as well as the schools who are doing it. In addition, we differ in our views of what constitutes success. Different types of CLIL programme have different aims and need to be measured according to different criteria. Even from school to school, stakeholders may not agree on what constitutes good practice and what represents a quality outcome. For these reasons, standards have so far been hard to define, and practice in evaluation is not yet well established.

What might a school have to think about if it wants to monitor its CLIL practice? It could firstly be concerned with whether evaluation is carried out internally or externally: for instance, will an education authority want to inspect a CLIL programme as part of the routine school inspection? There are probably few established inspection regimes for CLIL programmes in European countries, simply because inspection agencies have not yet built up sufficient levels of expertise in CLIL standards. However, as countries develop expertise, good evaluation practice begins to emerge. In the Netherlands, bilingual education is monitored by a national agency (the European Platform), which introduced the

'Standard for Bilingual Education' (European Platform, 2013b) to define the levels of quality against which bilingual schools are measured. This includes, for example, the proportion of the school curriculum delivered in L2, levels of learner language ability and subject achievement, pedagogy, staffing, and materials. Schools are inspected at the early stages of their development as bilingual institutions, as they mature, and also as they work to sustain levels of performance over time. Similarly, in Austria, within the framework of further education, technical high schools (HTLs; see page 248) support CLIL. A national working group (the 'Bundes-AG CLIL') consists of representatives from every province in the country. In every HTL implementing CLIL, a senior member of staff who oversees CLIL implementation in the school reports to their regional representative on the national working group. In this way, the HTLs in Austria are constructing a national system for collecting data on, and providing support to, CLIL operations in further education.

A school will also want to monitor its own performance internally (Mehisto, 2012b), particularly as its various stakeholder groups will have their own interests in this. Teachers, learners, and parents will all be eager to know what the standards are of both subject knowledge and language. The school management team may be anxious to demonstrate the achievement of targets to both parents and education authorities. In addition, they may be interested in cost-effectiveness, in the value of the resources they invest—for instance, in CPD and teaching materials. And they may also be interested in the relative effectiveness of CLIL pedagogies. The 'Course structure' section of this chapter (see page 248) outlines the way in which a school management team could work to support and monitor the progress of its CLIL programme. It may construct a plan to guide the initiation and development of its CLIL programme; this is likely to include targets against which achievement in the programme is measured. The school might want to know, for example:
- about levels of subject achievement
- about levels of learner language ability
- about teacher levels of CLIL pedagogy
- about teacher levels of language ability
- whether pedagogy is effective
- whether materials are appropriate
- whether training is effective
- whether assessment is appropriate
- whether learners are appropriately entered for CLIL programmes
- whether parents are kept well informed and are satisfied
- whether any liaison with other schools is effective.

In order to be in a position to monitor progress on such quality issues as these, the school will need the appropriate expertise, an evaluation tool, and people who can do the monitoring. A school can buy in expertise from a national body, a local authority, a university, or an INSETT provider if it is available. For example, in the Netherlands, the European Platform can provide its members with such expertise. In other countries, associations of subject teachers or more informal self-supporting groups of schools and individuals may hold forums to share expertise.

However, such expertise is only likely to be available in more 'mature' contexts where it has been built up over time; many schools will, at present, not have access to it and will have to generate their own expertise through trial and error, by noticing what works and what does not.

Formal instruments for internally monitoring the quality and development of CLIL programmes are also, at present, likely to be scarce. An example of such an instrument appears at the end of this chapter (see Table 9.1 on pages 264–265). Schools also need people who can carry out this internal monitoring. Members of senior management may or may not have the relevant expertise, and it is often the CLIL teachers themselves who have to monitor their own and their colleagues' work. This requires a degree of trust amongst the teachers, and a formal structure within which such evaluation can take place. This structure is best established by means of school policy.

Whole-school management structure in CLIL

Collaboration between teachers in CLIL programmes can be an informal, bottom-up process: teachers work with each other if they get on well and if the enterprise is professionally interesting. However, this form of collaboration is often unplanned and can be unreliable. In order to manage a programme with the range of whole-school implications such as those we have been discussing in this chapter, a school ideally needs a formal management structure at the level of senior management, as well as a development plan. A school with ambitious CLIL plans will wish to instigate formal administrative frameworks which set out the purposes, means, and requirements of the collaborating parties and may even acknowledge this contractually. School policy on CLIL development will require collaboration to take place and will set out objectives and performance indicators which aim to raise subject achievement in clearly specified ways.

Whether a school has a development plan or a management structure in place often depends on the extent to which school development planning is common in the local educational context. By and large, development planning is not yet common in CLIL programmes. Such plans, however, do exist and it is worth looking at how they work. Sometimes the most relevant planning structures and processes exist in minority-language support programmes. Formal collaborative planning agreements of this kind are common—for instance, in the EAL sector in the UK, where they go by the name of 'partnership teaching' (Bourne & McPake, 1991). Within these arrangements, a whole-school plan is developed which requires mainstream subject and EAL teachers to collaborate in order to support EAL learners, both in separate provision and within the mainstream subject classroom. The plan asks teachers to 'set goals', 'experiment', 'evaluate', 'disseminate', and 'review'. EAL development across the school within these parameters is guided and monitored by an appropriate management team.

A CLIL management committee would consist of an appropriate member of senior management, together with two or three members of staff, elected by their peers if appropriate, and including a CLIL teacher and a language teacher. The committee would meet on a specified number of occasions throughout the year and draw up a school development plan for CLIL. The plan would specify, for example: exact, achievable targets for the number of learners the school wishes to be engaged in learning CLIL subjects; the levels of examination achievement the school aims to reach in CLIL subjects; the number of staff the school wishes to include in the CLIL programme; and the amount and type of materials it believes to be necessary for teaching and learning CLIL subjects. The plan would also include milestones for achieving these targets and a procedure for monitoring and reporting on them. Amongst other things, the committee would:

- compile and provide outline guidance to CLIL staff, specifying the characteristics of high-quality teaching of subjects in L2. It would expect CLIL teachers to follow this guidance
- specify how the school will make progress towards attaining quality targets in classroom practice
- provide guidance to CLIL staff, specifying how learners are to be assessed in CLIL subjects, especially in respect of appropriate forms of assessment (see Chapter 8)
- specify how examination standards in CLIL subjects are to be comparable with standards in subjects taught in the L1, and how learners are to be enabled to take public examinations in CLIL subjects
- be able to advise on the purchase of high-quality teaching materials for teaching subjects in L2
- determine the extent to which collaboration between teachers outside the classroom should be paid for. Teachers in CLIL projects tend to collaborate out of goodwill, but in the long run that is not sustainable. A good school will, if possible, pay for formal teacher collaboration, even if only nominally.

The committee may need a formal instrument for measuring the extent to which the school is developing towards its CLIL targets. In the same way, inspectors may need a similar instrument to assess its progress. Inspection of CLIL programmes is very much in its infancy, as is in-school monitoring of CLIL targets. However, Table 9.1 (overleaf) shows a sample instrument which could be used to monitor development towards targets in this way.

Target	Stage 1	Stage 2	Stage 3	Stage 4
1 Learner achievement in CLIL subjects	Learners achieve on average lower levels of CLIL subject knowledge than if they were learning in L1.	Learners achieve on average similar levels of CLIL subject knowledge to those they were achieving in L1.	Learners achieve on average higher levels of CLIL subject knowledge than those they were achieving in L1.	Learners achieve on average high levels of CLIL subject knowledge.
2 Learner L2 ability	Learners have on average low levels of L2 ability.	Learners have on average developing levels of L2 ability.	Learners have on average good levels of L2 ability.	Learners have on average high levels of L2 ability.
3 School planning structure for CLIL	Senior management is not aware of the planning requirements for raising achievement in CLIL.	Senior management has an initial awareness of the planning requirements for raising achievement in CLIL.	Senior management is fairly well informed about the planning requirements for raising achievement in CLIL.	Senior management is fully informed about the planning requirements for raising achievement in CLIL.
	No management structure for raising achievement in CLIL exists, and no planning responsibilities are allocated.	An initial management structure for raising achievement in CLIL exists, and some planning roles are being carried out.	A functioning management structure for raising achievement in CLIL is in place, and most planning roles are being carried out.	A management structure for raising achievement in CLIL works effectively, and all planning roles are being carried out.
	No plan exists for raising achievement in CLIL.	An outline plan for raising achievement in CLIL exists.	A partial plan for raising achievement in CLIL exists.	A fully developed plan for raising achievement in CLIL exists.
	No targets have been set for raising achievement in CLIL.	Few targets have been set, few are monitored, and few are being achieved.	Some targets have been set, some are monitored, some are being partially achieved.	Comprehensive targets have been set and are effectively monitored. Many are being achieved.
	Staff are not involved in planning for CLIL development.	A few staff are involved in planning for CLIL development.	Many relevant staff are involved in planning for CLIL development.	All relevant staff are fully involved in planning for CLIL development.
	No collaboration between staff on CLIL development takes place.	Minimal collaboration between staff on CLIL development takes place.	Fairly regular collaboration between staff on CLIL development takes place.	Collaboration between staff on CLIL development is widespread and routine.
4 CLIL teacher L2 ability	CLIL teachers have on average low levels of L2 ability.	CLIL teachers have on average developing levels of L2 ability.	CLIL teachers have on average good levels of L2 ability.	CLIL teachers have on average high levels of L2 ability.
	The school is not aware of levels of CLIL staff language ability.	Levels of CLIL staff language ability are known.	Levels of CLIL staff language ability are known and occasionally monitored.	Levels of CLIL staff language ability are known and regularly monitored.
	Language development plans for staff do not exist.	Outline language development plans exist for some staff.	Language development plans exist for all appropriate staff.	Detailed, monitored language development plans exist for all appropriate staff.

Target	Stage 1	Stage 2	Stage 3	Stage 4
5 Teacher ability to teach their subject in L2	CLIL teachers have low levels of skill in teaching their subject to learners with low L2 ability.	CLIL teachers have developing levels of skill in teaching their subject to learners with low L2 ability.	CLIL teachers have good levels of skill in teaching their subject to learners with low L2 ability.	CLIL teachers have high levels of skill in teaching their subject to learners with low L2 ability.
	The school is not aware of levels of CLIL staff pedagogical ability.	Levels of CLIL staff pedagogical ability are known.	Levels of CLIL staff pedagogical ability are known and occasionally monitored.	Levels of CLIL staff pedagogical ability are known and regularly monitored.
	Professional development plans for staff do not exist.	Outline professional development plans exist for some staff.	Professional development plans exist for all appropriate staff.	Detailed, monitored professional development plans with targets exist for all appropriate staff.
	CLIL staff are not taking courses in teaching their subject in L2.	Some CLIL staff are taking courses in teaching their subject in L2.	Most CLIL staff who need it are taking courses in teaching their subject in L2.	All CLIL staff who need it are taking courses in teaching their subject in L2.
6 School-based training	CLIL teachers are not receiving any school-based training in teaching their subject in L2.	CLIL teachers are receiving occasional school-based training in teaching their subject in L2.	CLIL teachers are receiving regular school-based training in teaching their subject in L2.	CLIL teachers are receiving regular school-based training in teaching their subject in L2 and are offering training to other schools.
7 Teaching materials	Materials for teaching CLIL subjects do not exist, or are of poor quality.	Materials for teaching CLIL subjects are of acceptable quality.	Materials for teaching CLIL subjects are of good quality.	Materials for teaching CLIL subjects are of high quality.
8 Selection	No formal arrangements exist for defining learner entry to CLIL programmes.	Outline arrangements exist for defining learner entry to CLIL programmes.	Good arrangements exist for defining learner entry to CLIL programmes.	Detailed and effective arrangements exist for defining entry to CLIL programmes.
9 Assessment	No agreement exists between staff for assessment in CLIL.	Outline agreement exists between staff for assessment in CLIL.	Good agreement exists between staff for assessment in CLIL.	Detailed and effective agreement exists between staff for assessment in CLIL.
10 Orientating L2 teaching to CLIL	L2 teachers are not orientating their subject to CLIL.	Some L2 teachers are orientating their subject to CLIL where relevant.	Most L2 teachers are orientating their subject to CLIL where relevant.	All L2 teachers are orientating their subject to CLIL where relevant.
11 Liaison with parents	No liaison takes place with parents over participation in CLIL programmes.	Outline arrangements exist for liaison with parents over participation in CLIL programmes.	Good liaison takes place with parents over participation in CLIL programmes.	Close and effective liaison takes place with parents over participation in CLIL programmes.
12 Liaison with other schools	The school does not collaborate with other schools for sharing expertise in CLIL.	The school occasionally collaborates with other schools for sharing expertise in CLIL.	The school regularly collaborates with other schools for sharing expertise in CLIL.	The school is a local leader in good practice in CLIL and provides training to other schools.

Table 9.1 An instrument for monitoring development towards targets for schools offering CLIL programmes

Summary

This chapter has looked at CLIL from the viewpoint of managing a CLIL programme. We have considered what school management teams and groupings of CLIL teachers need to think about in terms of what goes on both inside and outside the classroom. This concerns a range of stakeholders, such as the students (who may need selecting and assessing), the teachers (who need appointing and perhaps training, and who need to collaborate), the parents (who need to be informed and sometimes reassured), and the school management team (which needs to oversee, develop, and evaluate). It also concerns the programme (which needs to be designed and resourced). Because CLIL tends to grow from the bottom up, in many countries CLIL management is still a work in progress, but good practice is accumulating.

Task

If you would like to look at a practical task to explore your own practice related to the content of this chapter, see Appendix 1 (page 294).

Further reading

Clegg, J. (2014). *Teacher collaboration in CLIL.* Macmillan OneStopEnglish. www.onestopenglish.com/clil/methodology/articles/article-teacher-collaboration-in-clil/157768.article
A short overview of the ways in which subject and language teachers can collaborate in CLIL projects. More useful articles on CLIL can be found at www.onestopenglish.com/clil.

Kelly, K. (2014). *Ingredients for successful CLIL.* British Council Teaching English. www.teachingenglish.org.uk/article/keith-kelly-ingredients-successful-clil-0

Kelly, K. (2015). *COOP CLIL: Collaboration between language teachers and subject teachers.* www.teachingenglish.org.uk
The first article by Kelly provides a short but comprehensive overview of questions to do with the management of CLIL projects. The second offers a view of the possibilities for collaboration in the Austrian HTL CLIL programme. See www.teachingenglish.org.uk/clil for more useful articles on CLIL.

Mehisto, P. (2012). *Excellence in bilingual education: A guide for school principals.* Cambridge: Cambridge University Press.
A rare example of a whole book devoted to issues of management of CLIL programmes at whole-school level.

Pavesi, M., Bertocchi, D., Hoffmanova, M., & **Kazianka, M.** (2001). *Teaching through a foreign language.* TIE-CLIL. www.ub.edu/filoan/CLIL/teachers.pdf.
A short introduction to CLIL, but including chapters on management issues and also a chapter on teacher education.

10 TRAINING TEACHERS FOR CLIL

Overview

In this final chapter, we will look at the issues surrounding the provision of training for CLIL teachers. Due to the range of contexts in which CLIL operates, it is difficult to propose a generic training model, but relatively easy to identify basic training needs. Within these parameters, we can propose a set of options. In the previous chapter, we considered the wide range of issues regarding the implementation of CLIL programmes, issues which eventually fall into the narrower remit of teacher training. We use the word 'narrower' in the sense that if we consider CLIL to be a methodology, then its parameters must be identifiable. We now need to limit the practice of CLIL to a set of teacher and learner behaviours that we recognize and which we can organize within a training framework. The corollary of this statement is to also say that we can close the door on certain practices that we do not consider representative of CLIL. This chapter, therefore, will consider the issue of CLIL-based teacher training in this light. What do CLIL teachers need to know? Which learning theories are they likely to agree with or be persuaded to consider? What useful models already exist? What are the differing needs of language and subject teachers, and can these be reconciled within a working model?

CLIL teacher variables

Before we can talk about CLIL training, we need to explain what we mean by a 'CLIL teacher'. As we now know, they come in various guises. We have the 'hard' CLIL proponent, who is a subject teacher, and the 'soft' CLIL proponent, who is a language teacher. These types fit well into the framework of secondary and tertiary education, but in primary education the frontier is less clear—teachers may have originally trained in a particular field but have subsequently become more general practitioners. Also, in secondary education, we have seen that language teachers can also (if the national system permits it) be trained to work in different subject areas. It all depends on the country and the system.

Training variables

With regard to standard teacher training for school systems, all countries provide a form of what is called 'initial', or pre-service, training. This ***ab initio*** period can vary from one year to four, depending on the scope of the training and the qualification it confers. All countries also provide some form of in-service teacher training (INSETT), which comes under the umbrella of continuous professional development (CPD) and may be compulsory or voluntary, depending on the system. The resources and educational budgets available to individual countries will condition these variables, although training can also be provided by private, government-approved institutions. For tertiary education, particularly universities, the picture is far less clear. To teach in a university has rarely required any *ab initio* teaching qualification, although some countries offer ongoing methodological training—more as a result of the growth of CLIL and English-medium education than of any government-led reforms which have been introduced since the **Bologna Process** was initiated in 1999 to seek ways of standardizing the European tertiary education system.

To prescribe or not to prescribe?

A significant factor relating almost exclusively to CLIL settings is that its practising teachers are unlikely to have received any initial CLIL-focused training whatsoever, but rather to have taken up the practice after they had qualified or been teachers for some years. This can cover a wide range of experience, from a newly qualified teacher to one approaching retirement, and has certainly been true of the first phase of CLIL, dating from the acronym's birth in 1994. The second phase of CLIL, loosely identifiable as the post-millennial period, has seen a growth in publications, research, ICT influence, and national government-led initiatives in CLIL. However, it has still not seen a significant growth in pre-service training programmes. Instead, CLIL has depended on a growing number of trainers, themselves a product of the first 'bottom-up' phase, when teachers themselves were developing early CLIL. In the beginning, although it borrowed from previous and existing approaches, CLIL simply grew and developed organically. No top-down provision, in the form of legislation, could ever really have shaped it.

The subsequent exponential growth of CLIL has enabled it to develop loose parameters undisturbed by much prescription, although, as we have argued in this book, this period is surely coming to a close. According to Coyle (2009), 'What is certain is that there is no single model for CLIL and that for approaches to be effective, they have to be contextualized, evaluated, and understood in situ and "owned" by all those involved.'

This may have been true until recently, but a new phase of CLIL is beginning, not simply because competences have burst onto the educational scene but also because of the parallel incorporation into the labour market of more and more students who have experienced a plurilingual mode of education. Students who left a CLIL school in 2015 (the publication year of this book) and who decided to study a pedagogy-related degree at university would surely be surprised if their course neither mentioned CLIL nor included some provision in its direction. If this is true, and teachers are now looking for more prescriptive CLIL guidance, then for their students' sake we have an obligation to provide it.

Teacher language levels versus methodological awareness

We often produce exhaustive lists of student competences, both subject-specific and meta-disciplinary, without ever stopping to ask if teachers themselves are competent in nurturing a learning environment in which students can achieve their utmost potential. Before we enter the wider terrain of teacher competences, therefore, it is worth considering the basic question that is always asked of those teaching subjects in CLIL. How competent must a CLIL subject teacher be in the LoI to be considered qualified for the job?

Before we attempt to answer this thorny question, there is another to consider. Is it fair and correct to distinguish between the (allegedly) required language levels of teachers working in primary, secondary, and tertiary education? The question is often asked because it is widely seen to be the case that as the cognitive level of study increases, so too does the language demand for both teacher and learner. However, this argument only takes CALP into consideration. For example, a primary teacher will also need high levels of BICS and functional classroom language to conduct a successful lesson with younger children in the L2.

Regardless, the rule would seem to be that the higher the teacher's level of language ability the better. There are a couple of problems with this rule, however. The first is that it can bring about unwanted consequences. One of them is legal, whereby educational ministries set the language bar too high because they feel publicly obliged to do so. The ambitious decision by the Italian government in 2013 to introduce some degree of obligatory national CLIL provision at upper-secondary level inevitably raised the question of what minimum levels of language competence would be required of the teachers. The Italian government was immediately faced with the old conundrum: pitch the level too low—for example, B1 on the **Common European Framework of Reference (CEFR)** — and you risk triggering a barrage of criticism concerning the lowering of standards. Pitch the level too high (for example, C1 on the CEFR) and you risk excluding the very teachers who have been responsible for the organic development of CLIL so far in that country. The added problem is that educational ministries are rarely acquainted with the fact that to move from B1 to C1 requires a lot of time (and money). If CLIL had been bound by these principles in its first phase, it would never have got off the ground.

The second problem with this rule of stipulating language levels is that it conveys the mistaken impression that teacher language levels are somehow the principal measurement of a CLIL teacher's competence. This may seem to contradict our insistence in this book on the importance of language, of the importance of making it salient to students, and of the concomitant need for subject teachers to be more aware of the impact of language on cognition. So what is the answer? What is more important for the CLIL teacher: methodology or language ability?

The answer is surely that both are important, but that up to now in CLIL, methodological concerns have been paramount. This is why CLIL has continued to grow and contribute to the professional development of practising teachers. There is plenty of evidence of this. The road ahead, however, will have some twists and turns, largely because the growth of CLIL-based practice will be accompanied by more state control and top-down legislation, which will need to be properly informed. To shed some light on this problem, let us consider Figure 10.1.

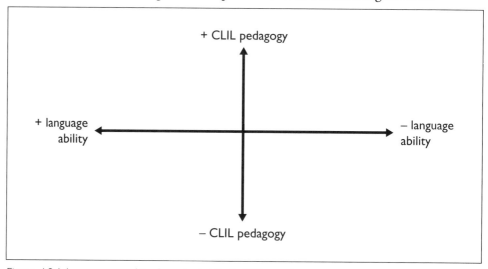

Figure 10.1 Language and pedagogical skills in CLIL teachers

If there is an ideal quadrant to aim for, it is clearly the top-left one. High levels of ability in both language and pedagogy should guarantee success. In contrast, the bottom-right quadrant should be avoided, for obvious reasons. However, the extreme points of these two quadrants, if we consider them as the opposing ends of a continuum, have not been typical of the CLIL movement so far. Teaching effective CLIL, as with any other methodology, takes time; and so it was unlikely—certainly in the early days when CLIL was dominated by English—that a perfectly honed workforce of 'top-left' teachers would appear. Even in those countries where the L2 was commonly used and spoken (for example English in Scandinavia), the pedagogical awareness required to practise CLIL was not automatically present. There is no magical or necessary connection between the two attributes, language and pedagogy. As such, what we need to consider now in order to establish a baseline are the other two quadrants. We also need to ask ourselves the fairly simple question: which teacher is more likely to be successful? The teacher in the top-right quadrant or the teacher in the bottom-left one?

In our experience, it is in the top-right quadrant where we will find teachers whose pedagogical awareness can compensate for their lack of linguistic assets.

On the other hand, the teacher in the bottom-left quadrant, with a low level of CLIL pedagogy but a high level of language ability, will often struggle. This point echoes the story of the history teacher in Spain from Chapter 2 (see page 21) who sought advice on how to improve his English level ahead of his first CLIL venture. The trainer's advice ('Just don't talk so much') was neither meant to belittle the importance of teacher talk nor intended to minimize the positive effect on teacher confidence that fluency can confer. Rather, it was meant to highlight the far greater importance of pedagogical awareness and learner-centred approaches.

It follows, therefore, that it is often a waste of time and money to separate language improvement from CLIL training. The best CLIL training courses include both elements. It is true that teachers need some kind of minimum level of language to benefit from such courses, but it is extremely rare for a subject teacher at CEFR levels A1 or A2 to be considering teaching CLIL to any meaningful degree in the short term. Such teachers would indeed need to attend language-booster courses to then be considered for the '**looped course**' (whereby the CLIL language is picked up as a by-product of a training course which focuses principally on pedagogy) at some approximate future date.

The future of teaching and learning

Predicting future changes on the basis of current circumstances has never been easy. As Henry Ford tellingly remarked, 'If I had asked the people what they wanted, they would have said faster horses.'

How can we best prepare today's schoolchildren for an increasingly fast-moving and dynamic society? Until quite recently, standard public education was conservative and slow-moving, following on from the education acts that gradually guaranteed free state education for most of Europe's population. It reflected the more gradual pace of change that took place over the post-industrial period, preserving practices and traditions that were based on a high degree of consensus. People, as Henry Ford remarked, were fairly sure about what they needed—whether they were right or not. However, now that the pace of change has accelerated so dramatically, no such consensus exists. The enormous impact of the internet and the digital revolution has made us realize that educational legislation no longer determines the shape of society but is instead forced to react to changes taking place elsewhere. Today's whiteboards are tomorrow's museum pieces.

It is an extremely exciting time to be involved in education, but a challenging one too. How can we educate children for the future when we cannot even predict what they will be doing in ten years' time? All that we can predict for certain is that the skills needed by the present generation of children will be fundamentally different from those that we have valued and nurtured for so long. The other equally telling certainty for teachers interested in CLIL to bear in mind is that the future is surely a multilingual one. How can we best train our teachers, given this future scenario? What skills will they need to foster?

According to the Maastricht Communiqué (2004), with particular reference to vocational training, those skills are:

- problem-solving skills
- coping effectively with change
- communicating with peers and clients.

This is further expanded upon by the statement that '[as] firms and sectors compete on innovation, and as globalization creates turbulence in traditional markets, new skill and competence requirements emerge. They have to be identified and considered in reforms of initial and continuing training curricula' (Cedefop/Maastricht, 2010). In step with these notions, we have already stated that the future will be 'competence led', echoing the message outlined in the EU's *Key competences for lifelong learning—a European framework* (2006). If the road ahead is competence led, then it will also need to be learner centred. As we saw in Chapter 8, it is impossible to measure competences without the observation of actions framed within authentic situations. These actions are performed by the learner and facilitated by the teacher. The transmission model of education is unlikely to survive in this new educational habitat, and CLIL has already given us some clues about how to prepare ourselves for this changing landscape.

A new hybrid teacher?

In 1986, Mohan wrote, 'In subject matter learning we overlook the role of language as a medium of learning, and in language learning we overlook the fact that content is being communicated.' If, as Bullock (1975) stated, 'All [subject] teachers are teachers of language', then it seems equally useful—at the other end of the continuum—to expect all language teachers to incorporate more conceptual content into their lessons, as Mohan implies. If all language teachers begin to consider themselves content teachers, then instead of maintaining the divide between the language and subject worlds, we will begin to build bridges between them. We have already seen the possibilities of shared and collaborative practices in Chapter 9, and so once the bridges have been established, the resulting practitioner will surely become a more 'hybrid' teacher, whose expertise is no less specialized, but instead specialized in a broader sense. The language teacher can benefit from all three dimensions of content (those of concepts, procedures, and language), not just one (language). The subject teacher benefits, too, by becoming more aware of the language dimension, and becoming more adept at making the role of language more salient in the classroom.

If we were to imagine how these 'hybrid' teachers might behave, and what attributes and skills they would possess, we might describe a broad profile as shown in the list below. They are all behaviours that stem from the sort of beliefs and practices we have been discussing throughout this book.

- The teacher guides input and supports output.
- The teacher scaffolds language and learning.
- The teacher never assumes that the student understands.
- The teacher's methodological repertoire widens.
- The teacher varies the forms of interaction in the classroom.
- The focus of the teacher's assessment reflects a greater concern with 'process'.
- The teacher recognizes that academic language consists of different types of subject-specific discourse.
- The teacher understands that education requires a journey from BICS to CALP.
- The teacher makes the role of language (in cognition) more salient.

We could add further behaviours to the profile, but the above list is sufficient to provide a snapshot of the sort of content that is needed for a CLIL training course, whether initial or in-service.

There is no doubt that a CLIL teacher needs a specific type of training that goes beyond the formation of a foreign-language teacher or a subject teacher—one which prepares teachers for what Wolff (2012) has called 'language-sensitive content teaching'. We can now add, with a nod to Mohan, 'content-sensitive language teaching'.

Good practice

The list above relates traditionally (in CLIL terms) to subject teacher concerns; but obviously, in a new hybrid framework, the distinction between the subject and language teacher begins to look a little less clear—for good reasons. Nevertheless, all teachers are theoretically bound to a code of good practice. And whereas no teacher, however disillusioned, walks into class with the intention of doing things badly, there is always room for improvement. We can always aspire to do things better, whether it is CLIL-related or not. For this reason, any discussion of training needs to confront the notion of good practice.

The problem is that one teacher's idea of good practice is not necessarily the same as another's. Culture and social context tend to condition these beliefs, and discovering absolutes in this area can be philosophically complex. Time, too, leaves its mark on proceedings, and what seemed like good practice 50 years ago can now seem primitive. A useful way to approach the notion of good practice is to consider the story of 'Mrs Smith'.

This true story is based in an inner-city state secondary school in London in the late 1970s. The school had a large first-generation intake of Bengali speakers, and was struggling on a minimum diet of ESL provision. An inspector was called in to advise on the situation, particularly regarding truancy problems. While talking to the head teacher, the inspector was told of the worrying case of a Bengali-speaking girl who was persistently absent from school, but only on certain days of the week. The inspector, turning the issue around, asked on which days the girl did attend school. The head teacher replied that she tended to turn up on Tuesdays and Thursdays, and that these two days coincided with lessons taught by a teacher whom we will call 'Mrs Smith'. Interested by this information, the inspector asked if he could observe Mrs Smith teaching, in order to see what it might be that encouraged the girl to attend on those days. The head teacher agreed, and the inspector took notes during a short period of observation.

In terms of her personal profile, Mrs Smith spoke several languages, but not Bengali. However, there were a variety of reasons for her success in encouraging the girl to feel that her classes were a safe environment for a non-native speaker of English to be in. The notes the inspector took on Mrs Smith's lessons are listed below:

1 Clear lesson frames ('The lesson will begin with X and will end with Y.')
2 Clear instructions on how to complete the class tasks
3 Frequent comprehension checks
4 Clear, loud voice with marked intonation and pitch
5 Warm encouragement
6 Repetition
7 Clear, syntactically simple sentences
8 Visual aids
9 Rich classroom environment
10 Constructive criticism of students' work
11 Clear, orderly explanations and sequencing of processes ('First we see this, then we see the other, and finally the result we see is …')
12 Vocabulary made comprehensible by explanation, visuals, and reformulation (i.e. saying things in a different way)
13 Students given time to answer
14 Different types of question asked
15 Full involvement of students
16 Time limits for group tasks set
17 Appropriate L1 use.

Although we could add more, the list reads like a solid set of strategies for any teaching paradigm that must take the needs of NNS learners into consideration. Apart from the fact that we can immediately relate Mrs Smith's methods of classroom management to most of the issues raised and analysed in this book, it is also interesting to note—from a teacher-training perspective—how each of the 17 strategies falls into one of the three classic categories of effective teaching:

• affective (emotional)
• management (organization)
• language (teacher talk, student talk, importance of language in cognition).

There is plenty of evidence to suggest that learners respond to teachers who are aware of these three categories (Cullingford, 1995). They are relevant to all educational contexts, but particularly significant in those where the learner is deprived of the safety-net of the L1. Rogers wrote:

> The educational situation which most effectively promotes significant learning is one in which (a) threat to the self of the learner is reduced to a minimum and

(b) differentiated perception of the field is facilitated.
(Rogers, 1951)

Although, as a psychologist, Rogers was most concerned with the affective aspect of human management, it is nevertheless clear, from Mrs Smith's behaviour, how an emotionally aware teacher naturally involves the other related aspects of good practice, namely management and language. It would be perfectly valid to introduce a training course on CLIL with the story of Mrs Smith, and then to ask the trainees to categorize the items in the list in a table such as the one shown in Table 10.1 below. Although some of the behaviours could fit into more than one category, most of them fit clearly into one of the columns. Then once they have completed the task, practising teachers could be asked to what extent they think they use the various techniques that derive from each category.

Certain items on the list may require clarification, for example item 8 ('Visual aids'). In the late 1970s, these were much more limited than they are nowadays, but were still significant in science-related subjects where realia could be used to support comprehension. Item 17 ('Appropriate L1 use') could not refer to the use of Bengali by the teacher, since Mrs Smith did not speak it, but rather refers to the judicious use of awareness-raising questions such as 'How do you say this in your language?' Indeed, the sudden awareness that the learners will not automatically understand gives rise to the techniques derived from these items in the inspector's list. It is interesting, too, how many of the techniques seem to derive from good primary school practice (items 3 to 10)—a point so often made by experienced CLIL teachers.

The task in Table 10.1 is partially completed for the purposes of this book; as already mentioned, some of the items could be included in more than one category, but the 17 items refer principally to teacher intention, not necessarily to how students perceive them. Item 7 ('Clear, syntactically simple sentences') may indeed make students feel happier, but the principal concern of the teacher is clarity. Item 5, however, would seem to have affective intentions.

Affective	Management	Language
5	1	7

Table 10.1 Task to assign examples of good practice to their appropriate categories

Suggested answers are on page 299.

Requirements for CLIL teachers: the three *savoirs* model

The above discussion leads us conveniently on to another useful framework for the training of CLIL teachers. As noted in *The European framework for CLIL teacher education*:

> Teachers undertaking CLIL will need to be prepared to develop multiple types of expertise, among others in the content subject; in a language; in best practice in teaching and learning; in the integration of the previous three; and in the integration of CLIL within an educational institution.
> (Marsh, Mehisto, Wolff & Frigois, 2010)

Indeed, when reading literature related to CLIL teacher-training, the requirements can at times seem both exhaustive and exhausting, although they are intended as standards, or exemplars. They do, however, refer primarily to teacher 'competences' (see *The CLIL teacher competences grid* (Bertaux et al., 2010)), suggesting observable performance-based behaviours. The three *savoirs* model (based on the French verb *savoir*, meaning 'to know') helps to make these multifaceted demands a little less daunting, by placing them in three clearly differentiated frames. (Note that the following descriptions have some information omitted, partly to reduce the lists, but also to help guide the end-of-chapter task (see page 296).

Savoir

The first requirement, *savoir*, is related to teacher knowledge, the most evident meaning of *savoir*. In this category, teachers need to know about the following aspects of CLIL practice:

- Theories/principles of teaching and learning
- Assessment and monitoring, including the requirements and range of assessment approaches (formative and summative)
- The subject and the pedagogy of the subject
- The statutory curricula
- CLIL (definition, key elements, benefits, difficulties)
- Literacy, numeracy, ICT skills (how to use these to support teaching and wider professional activities)
- Achievement and diversity (how to personalize/adapt for other speakers, special needs).

Savoir-faire

The second requirement, *savoir-faire*, is related to the 'how' of teaching. In this category, teachers need to be able to do certain things, which can be divided up into five components: plan, teach, assess, create a learning environment, and collaborate.

Plan

- Design effective learning sequences
- Plan for all students and all learning styles
- Write and/or adapt material
- Design good visual aids
- Determine student language levels and needs
- Design opportunities to develop literacy, numeracy, and ICT skills
- Integrate language into subject-area planning
- Identify the language needed to ensure efficient classroom management, student comprehension, rich language and content input, and rich student language and content output
- Anticipate the need to support comprehension of written material or other documents
- Analyse content in terms of language needs
- Select material and activities in view of learners' oral production
- Identify language components needed for both written and oral production, and create or adapt materials for this purpose.

Teach

- Use a range of strategies and resources (including e-learning), taking diversity into account and promoting inclusion
- Select ICT strategies and resources, and create learning experiences that use ICT to organize, research, interpret, communicate, and represent knowledge
- Build on prior knowledge, develop concepts and processes, enable learners to apply new knowledge and skills to meet learning objectives
- Use language effectively for introducing new concepts, explaining, questioning, etc.
- Support content learning in CLIL language classes and language learning in CLIL content classes
- Use a repertoire of strategies for scaffolding language use and supporting learners' language production
- Decide if and when to use 'translanguaging'
- Correct effectively.

Assess

- Plan and make effective use of a range of assessment, monitoring, and recording strategies
- Provide timely, accurate, and constructive feedback on learners' attainment, progress, and areas for development
- Support and guide learners to reflect on the learning process.

Create a learning environment

- Establish a purposeful and safe learning environment conducive to learning

- Provide challenging learning experiences where students can use higher-order and critical thinking skills
- Establish a clear framework for classroom discipline to manage learners' behaviour constructively and promote their self-control and independence.

Collaborate

- Work with partner teachers to plan, team-teach, share knowledge and resources, and standardize assessment procedures
- Understand language competences for CLIL, including BICS, CALP, class management, and language for teaching and learning.

Savoir-être

The third requirement, *savoir-être*, refers to professional attributes such as disposition and attitude. In this category, teachers must understand learner needs, and know how to respond to them by displaying appropriate behaviours related to classroom values, relationships, and attitudes.

- Have high expectations of learners
- Demonstrate positive values, attitudes, and behaviour
- Communicate effectively and work with others
- Allow for personal professional development
- Reflect on and improve practice
- Be open to, but constructively critical of, innovation
- Contribute to learning communities and other professional networks
- Act on advice and be open to coaching/mentoring.

The three *savoirs* might form a daunting list, but they should not be interpreted as requiring a CLIL teacher to be super-human. Teachers possess more skills than they often realize, and it is only when we come to list them that they appear unrealistic, because they are so numerous. Teacher competence should also be seen within a continuum, and less-experienced practitioners obviously need time and opportunity to develop such a substantial repertoire. Nevertheless, the list can enable senior management in CLIL to select and foster the aspects of the three *savoirs* most required by their teachers, according to their type (language teacher, subject teacher) and their experience (as language/subject teachers, as CLIL teachers).

Aiming to acquire more of these components of CLIL teacher competences also facilitates a clearer career structure, as shown in Figure 10.2.

Levels of teacher
1 Starting (learning the principles)
2 Newly qualified teacher (putting principles into practice)
3 Core teacher (developing confidence and skills)
4 Post-threshold (upper pay scale)
5 Proficient (demonstrates confidence, experience and reflection)
6 Excellent/Advanced (exemplifying good practice)
7 Advanced skills/Specialist (leading and advising)

Figure 10.2 Career structure for development and progression

How can these savoirs be fostered?

The reality of any school system, in Europe and beyond, is probably such that anyone reading this chapter might dismiss the above *savoirs* as an impossible set of demands to satisfy. As we know, initial training should ideally help teachers acquire the personal attributes, professional knowledge, and skills necessary for their development in an evolving profession. However, training institutions, whether they are universities or training colleges, are often slow to respond to methodological changes and developments such as CLIL, adding it onto their standard courses at best. Germany, Sweden, the Netherlands, and the UK are slowly improving the general situation, but a further problem is that the trainers in these tertiary institutions might not have had much experience of these new developments themselves, and thus find it hard to give them the attention they merit.

As for in-service provision and ongoing professional development, the situation is equally questionable. Teachers are often left to their own devices, with very few schools having a transparent culture of teacher development. Apart from in the Netherlands, it is rare for teachers to be provided with a set of professional standards which might indicate those competences they should both implement and demonstrate. Despite the fact that CLIL may be prospering in a wide range of countries, staples such as peer observation are rare in countries such as Spain and Italy, and departmental heads are internally appointed or often do not exist. Directors of Study and government-appointed inspection teams tend to deal more with administrative than with pedagogical issues, and it is unusual to see a school principal in the classroom.

The outlook is not entirely gloomy, however. CLIL has enjoyed a boom period of growth unencumbered by such formal considerations, largely because the growth has been bottom-up, as we have already observed. But as we move into a more prescriptive top-down phase, stakeholders (see Chapter 9) will also need guidance in order to respond appropriately to the changes that will take place.

Materials

As we noted in Chapter 7, teacher-trainers are often influential but temporary figures. Good CLIL materials are, however, more permanent references. The success of a project depends on how successfully its principles are carried out by its practitioners—in this case, the teachers. One effective way of ensuring this is by providing teachers with materials which exemplify the very methodological principles that they should follow and implement in the classroom. Indeed, the development or purchase of exemplary materials can be a deliberate attempt, on the part of a CLIL management team, to encapsulate and articulate the CLIL approach through those didactic materials.

In the Basque Country's long-running *Eleanitz* project (Muñoa, 2012), and in Catalonia's XTEC project, the CLIL training process was predicated on the principles of creation, experimentation, feedback, reflection, and change, using a discrete set of context-led materials.

These didactic materials became the main tool with which to train teachers; and their experience with the materials provided the necessary feedback for continued revision and improvement, as can be seen in Figure 10.3.

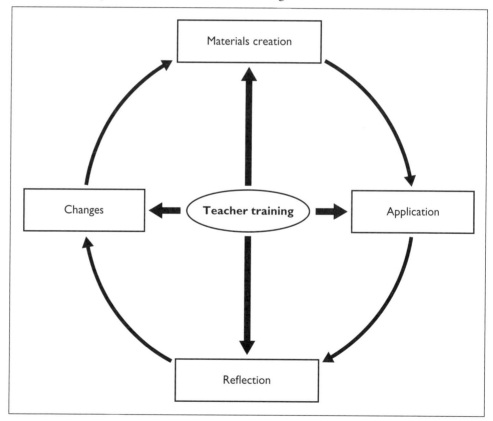

Figure 10.3 Interaction of materials and teacher training

This circular loop of 'create–apply–reflect–change' was crucial to the success of the Eleanitz project and has proved beneficial to both the materials writers/trainers and the teachers. The opportunity for writers to witness teachers piloting the materials first-hand, then feed back to them on the experience, was a privilege that could become more widespread practice. It enabled both parties to become more sensitive to the other's needs; and crucially, it gave the teachers a real stake in the creative process.

The experience of these projects suggests that in-service training is more effective when it stems from practice, which in turn permits a more coherent understanding of the theoretical underpinnings of the materials used. It is also crucial for the continuation and development of a project that good practice is identified and that teachers are eventually incorporated into the system as trainers, master practitioners, materials writers, and the curriculum designers of tomorrow. Ongoing training involving a judicious mix of teaching practice, presentation of new materials, observation, feedback, and discussion of principles seems a sound enough basis for successful practice.

Topics of interest

In the Basque project mentioned above, both primary and secondary teachers received in-service training, meeting four or five times a year at different schools. The host teacher for the session would invite the visiting teachers into class to observe a lesson in progress using the materials which they themselves were also using in their own classes. Afterwards, the teacher-trainer would chair reflection and discussion on the lesson. In order to provide some insight into the sort of issues CLIL teachers discuss, and the in-service input they can receive, Table 10.2 (overleaf) was provided as a tool by the trainer in the final meeting of the year to review the issues addressed during the four previous meetings. The names of the schools have been replaced by 'School A', etc. to preserve anonymity. The teachers were invited to recall the main issues that arose in the previous meetings and write them in the table in note form. They then discussed these issues in small groups and brought their thoughts to the plenary session.

The meeting at School A included the rather odd-sounding topics 'Braking and accelerating' and 'Lesson moves'. The former refers to task types: either a simple task or activity which is intended to be done quickly, as a way of transitioning into a deeper issue (thus the teacher 'accelerates'), or a more complex task or activity which involves all three dimensions of content (concepts, procedures, language) and plenty of planning and management (the teacher 'brakes', literally slowing the lesson(s) down in order to give students enough time to benefit from the content on offer). 'Lesson moves' refers to the three language features mentioned in Chapter 7, namely orientation, complication, and resolution. The teachers were encouraged to reflect on the structure of a lesson, and how these different stages involved different interaction and language demands. The other themes are more transparent, but provide insight into the sort of topics on which practising CLIL teachers need to focus.

Place	Topic	We talked about ...
School A (October)	Assessment and testing Braking and accelerating How to write good exams Lesson moves	
School B (December)	Reading strategies New vocabulary CALP Text–task relationship	
School C (February)	Student 'intervention' Teachers' question techniques Students talking in Basque or English	
School D (April)	Giving instructions Group work Group dynamics (theories)	

Table 10.2 Review of topics arising in training sessions

Teachers can also be helped by written guides which are not merely descriptive, but attempt to train as well. The technology unit from which we saw an activity in Chapter 7 (see page 187) is accompanied by a guide which not only walks teachers through every step of each activity, but also attempts to draw their attention to the content–language relationship. The entry for the activity is shown in full in Figure 10.4.

The full versions of the 'didactic objectives' to which the numbers refer are not included here, but the interesting thing to note is that in the 'Steps' section of the description, teachers are asked to work with language frames (evident in the actual activity) without involving themselves too deeply in explicit grammatical explanations. The objective remains directly conceptual, with the language frames the natural vehicles for the task.

The 'Key answers' section exemplifies possible sentences, so that teachers can see a wide range of possibilities and help students to produce them as accurately as possible. This is not a language lesson, as such, but it trains teachers to see and to facilitate the content–language relationship.

What provision exists?

The problem with answering a question about existing provision in a book is that provision (hopefully) develops and renders book-based information obsolete very quickly. However, a snapshot of certain types of provision, past and present, can still be useful.

MODULE 1	NEEDS Matching categories of need with actual inventions.		
Number	Activity type	Didactic objective	Interaction
09	Exploring	1, 2	Individual or pair work

STEPS

- Remind students of what you read in the text. Usually inventions are made because of a need—in response to a necessity. 'Necessity is the mother of invention.'
- Look at the speech bubbles and ask them what the men are saying. What do they think the operation consists of? (They're cutting off his leg.)
- Check that students know the meaning of the list of inventions. Ask for examples, maybe mime.
- Explain that they have to decide what was the need or necessity that led to their invention.
- Do an example together, eliciting responses from the students. E.g. *anaesthetic: to stop the person moving during an operation; to take away the pain.*
- Ask for another, using the scaffolds, and then let them continue, in pairs or individually, discussing the needs that led to the inventions and write a minimum of six. Encourage them to use either of the scaffolds, according to which comes most naturally. BUT they must use at least one 'stop from …' structure (the more difficult one).
- Ask them for their responses, again modelling the appropriate sentences.

KEY ANSWERS and COMMENTS

Some ideas:

Anaesthetic	to stop the person moving during an operation
	to take away the pain
The mobile phone	to contact anyone from any place
The air-bag	to protect passengers from being injured in car accidents
Gore-Tex	to make outdoor clothes and equipment waterproof
	to stop people from getting wet
The skyscraper	to use space in the air when space on the ground is limited
The tin can	to preserve food for longer
The tractor	to move heavy loads without having to use (and look after) animals
The flushing toilet	to dispose of human waste effectively in the towns
	to stop houses from smelling
The key	to keep property and objects safe
The X-ray machine	to see internal damage (e.g. broken bones)
	to treat more effectively
Heating	to keep people warm in the cold
	to stop people from feeling cold
Toothpaste	to keep teeth clean and healthy
	to stop teeth from rotting/falling out

* Notice that the gerund variation occurs after a negative sentence—*stop people from …-ing*. It won't always work.

Figure 10.4 Extract from CLIL technology guide (adapted from Ball et al., Subject projects 1: The world of inventions, Ikaselkar.)

We have already said that, due to contextual restraints, generic models are difficult to propose. But the internet and its accompanying online possibilities are an obvious way forward in the creation of some sort of cross-border provision. The British Council's 'CLIL Essentials' is one such example of a course that attempts to provide a basic grounding for less-experienced teachers (of CLIL), and the Cambridge TKT (Teacher Knowledge Test) also has a CLIL-based preparation module which offers a useful accompanying book (Bentley, 2010) to introduce teachers to the basics of the approach. This type of provision will inevitably undergo expansion as local contexts develop online courses for teachers. However, these courses do not qualify CLIL teachers, as yet.

Basic teaching qualifications still prevail, probably owing to the fact that if a country has a poorly developed system of CLIL, still in its infancy, it cannot demand high-level CLIL qualifications in its workforce. If the country has a well-developed system in place (for example, in the Netherlands), then in-service certification plus experience will usually suffice. So a CLIL qualification is rarely a mandatory requirement, but rather one of 'added value'. This may change.

In Britain, the Netherlands, and Austria, some universities now offer postgraduate degrees focused on bilingual education. In Germany, some of the federal states offer bilingual qualifications to teachers in curriculum subjects, obtained during or after their degree studies. In Spain, master's degrees focused exclusively on CLIL are offered in some universities, and state-subsidized language courses abroad are provided. Spain also has a system of regionally based training centres which offer in-service CLIL courses. In Finland, pre-service training is available for teachers who wish to pursue a CLIL path, and in both Poland and Austria, new teachers must specialize in a second subject during training. Since this can include further foreign language specialization, the system lends itself usefully to CLIL practice.

In Austria, Technical High Schools (HTLs) teach a wide range of technical subjects to students aged between 14 and 19, from construction engineering to design and marketing, depending on each school's specialist area. The schools are very prestigious educational institutions and places are coveted, with good job prospects on graduation. The Austrian government recently introduced legislation which has made it obligatory for HTLs to teach a proportion of their curriculum subjects through the medium of English (72 hours minimum per year) from September 2013. Each HTL has a designated colleague responsible for CLIL.

In anticipation of this, Universities of Education around Austria offer INSETT for HTL subject teachers. There are four modules of three days each, spread out over a period of 18 months. Each module has an assignment which involves participants preparing lessons based on what they have been taught. The participants then teach their lessons/assignments, collect feedback, and are supported at distance by a course tutor. Interestingly, the project now brings together subject and language teachers for co-operative training. Schools also have funding to organize their own local INSETT. It is an interesting model to consider.

Tertiary education

English-medium instruction (EMI) in tertiary education is a significant growth area, with over half of the world's international students being taught in English, and universities offering an increasing range of courses in this language (see Graddol, 2006).

In terms of teacher needs, there is a close interface with those of primary and secondary school teachers, although the universal prominence of lecture-type delivery creates certain differences. In basic terms, teachers at this level must possess the confidence to deliver a lecture in the target language, be accurate to the extent that they are understood, and be able to interact spontaneously with students in either a lecture or a smaller seminar context, as well as in more informal situations.

Where EMI practice is institutionally embedded, minimum requirements of language levels can be stipulated, and tested if necessary. In certain regions of Spain, for example, courses are now offered for university teachers who are either teaching or planning to teach parts of their courses through English—although in other contexts, it might be through another language. The content for a ten-week (30-hour) course offered at the University of the Basque Country includes the following, showing the clear overlap with CLIL practice:

- Lecturing to larger groups: staging and signposting
- Clarifying specialist terminology
- Questioning techniques and dealing with questions
- Checking understanding
- CALP (Cognitive Academic Language Proficiency)
- Working with smaller groups/tutorials
- Classroom management
- Activity/Task design and activity variety
- Helping students deal with texts
- Maintaining interest/attention
- Stimulating student participation
- Beginning and ending sessions
- Use of multimedia
- Continuous assessment and feedback (formal and informal)
- Testing: high versus low language risk (how to be fair)

(Ball & Lindsay, 2012)

Proposals and recommendations

What remains to be done in order to make CLIL a more homogeneous practice, with its parameters more clearly defined through a set of broadly agreed training initiatives? Our proposals would be as follows:

1 At an institutional level, there is a clear need for improved initial training. In a multilingual environment, there will be a move away from training teachers to become language specialists to developing their capacity to teach in two or more languages. This may also be reflected in less multilingual environments.

2 Training institutions should include courses and modules that make all teachers aware of the importance of language across the curriculum. They should also include a more widespread offer of CLIL modules on master's and other postgraduate courses. Language teacher-trainees should also be sensitized to the changes that are taking place with regard to their teaching area.

3 In certain countries, more hours of teaching practice are required on pre-service courses and during the initial year of teaching. There should be more opportunities to observe models outside teachers' own immediate environment, and more incentives to travel and observe other systems, either as a student or as a teacher.

4 A set of clearly stated professional standards for CLIL teachers is needed. These standards should provide a framework describing the *savoirs* necessary to develop as a teacher (see page 276). *The European framework for CLIL teacher education* (Marsh et al., 2010), for example, represents a good basis for establishing a set of ground rules (see page 276). With a general framework in place, specific competences can be more easily identified for CLIL teachers and CLIL teacher-trainers, but in context. Priorities, depending on experience, can also be identified.

These standards can be also broken down into stages so that each teacher has an officially recognized trajectory to follow in the school system. These standards would provide a clear benchmark, with transparent and consistent criteria for performance evaluation carried out in schools. They would also determine the subsequent INSETT needs of teachers, and what areas of their professional profile each CLIL teacher needs to further develop.

5 There is a need for more sharing of practice, and more investment in CLIL materials that can be applied across national borders. Teacher involvement in materials development can be a powerful training tool.

6 Teachers who are teaching through another language need regular opportunities to maintain and improve their language skills. Although we have emphasized methodological aspects over linguistic ones, teachers themselves report the need to feel confident and to develop. Language improvement as a separate phenomenon is often too slow and isolated from the subject-literacy awareness that CLIL teachers require. 'Looped' courses are good precisely because they involve practising the methodology of CLIL simultaneously with target-language input.

Summary

In this final chapter, we have tried to suggest that the profile of a CLIL teacher is of a more hybrid type. This reflects the greater concern in CLIL contexts with the impact of language on students' academic performance and the parallel need for increased awareness of subject-based discourse and literacy. We have also suggested that the increase in competence-based education is turning our attention towards the types of competences required by teachers, in order to respond to new developments in their profession—one of which is CLIL.

We have stated that methodological awareness for CLIL teachers should be of paramount importance, and that considerations regarding the affective well-being of students lead naturally to awareness of classroom management and language-related issues. These issues can be merged usefully with the concept of *savoir* and its various components. We also mentioned that good CLIL materials can be used as exemplars, and that they often underpin the theories of learning that gave rise to their creation. Finally, we suggested that although general training provision for CLIL is still at a nascent stage, a set of consensual guidelines would appear to be emerging.

Task

If you would like to look at a practical task to explore your own practice related to the content of this chapter, see Appendix 1 (page 296).

Further reading

Ball, P., & **Lindsay, D.** (2010). Teacher training for CLIL in the Basque Country: The case of the Ikastolas—an expediency model. In D. Lasagabaster & Y. Ruiz de Zarobe (Eds.), *CLIL in Spain: Implementation, results and teacher training* (pp. 162–188). Newcastle upon Tyne, UK: Cambridge Scholars Publishing.
The article proposes a model for in-service training for CLIL teachers, based on the long-term multilingual project in the Basque Country. The article suggests that appropriate didactic materials are crucial in the training process, and provides a set of principles for supporting a range of teachers, from those just starting out to the more experienced.

Burns, A., & **Richards, J. C.** (2009). *The Cambridge guide to second-language teacher education*. Cambridge: Cambridge University Press.
This substantial book contains contributions from a wide range of authors in the field of L2 education. The book is divided into seven different sections, each focusing on separate aspects of teacher knowledge and training. Both initial and in-service teacher-training issues are covered.

Coyle, D. (2008). CLIL—a pedagogical approach. In N. Van Deusen-Scholl & N. Hornberger (Eds.), *Encyclopedia of Language and Education, second edition* (pp. 97–111). US: Springer-Verlag.
An article which describes and explains Coyle's model of the '4Cs' (Content, Communication, Cognition, and Culture) as a basis for curricular planning in CLIL, but also as a training tool for teacher development and reflection.

Wolff, D. (2012). The European framework for CLIL teacher education. *Synergies, 8,* 105–116.
This short article presents an interesting framework for the professional development of CLIL teachers in Europe. The framework seeks to provide general guidelines for the education of CLIL teachers, and goes on to suggest that the CLIL model for teacher education should be used as the basis for a more general model within European education, be it subject or language training.

APPENDIX 1   TASKS

Suggested answers to these tasks (where applicable) can be found in Appendix 2 on pages 297–299.

Chapter 2

Write a single phrase against each key characteristic of CLIL in the table below, to remind yourself, in summary, of what you have understood about each of these ten defining parameters. One has been done as an example.

	Key characteristics of CLIL	Things to help me remember
1	Conceptual sequencing	*Different language occurs at different stages of a sequence.*
2	Conceptual fronting	
3	Task as priority, language as vehicle	
4	Making key language salient	
5	CLIL in three dimensions	
6	The text–task relationship	
7	Enhancing peer communication	
8	Guiding multimedia input	
9	Supporting student output	
10	Supporting thinking skills	

Chapter 3

1 CLIL in three dimensions
Find a lesson description from your teaching context and write out a three-dimensional objective to cover the sequence of activities. Use the model in Figure 3.1 on page 52 to help you.

2 Turning up the procedural volume
Look at Materials extract 4.D (on page 89) and try to devise a single activity, or a series of activities, that would serve to 'break down' this text procedurally for NNS students in a 'hard' CLIL class. Try to ensure that the students will not be required to read the text until they have understood the nature of the activity/activities that you propose.

3 Turning up the language volume
Using the text 'Diet and disease' in Materials extract 4.D again, which language structures would you make salient to the students? Write down a maximum of three. Base your decisions on the frequency of the structures and the key role that this language plays to illustrate the topic. (Of course, if you have done Task 2 above successfully, you may have already linked your procedural choices to the key language you encountered. If so, well done!)

Chapter 4

In Materials extract 4.E (see page 94), we identified the 'thinking processes' in the text as defining, explaining, and exemplifying.

- Take a textbook page from any content subject, or use the text in Materials extract 4.G, and identify the 'thinking processes' in the text.
- Find the non-subject-specific general academic terminology used in the text.

Chapter 5

- Take a textbook that you often use in class and locate a text where the shape and structure of the ideas will not be obvious to the learner.
- Try to identify a generic structure for the text with appropriate categories. You might think of using a table, a tree diagram, a flow diagram, a combination of these, or any other diagrammatical representation presented in this chapter.
- Think about how you might exploit the structure for guiding learners through their reading of the text and/or for the purpose of following teacher talk on the same topic.

Why did US agriculture not share in the boom of the 1920s?

The most striking example of an industry that was unable to share in the prosperity of the 1920s was agriculture, which employed more than a quarter of the working population. During World War I, American agriculture had boomed, as grain from the Midwestern and southern states had been exported to Europe. With the aid of new machinery, such as combine harvesters, production increased, prices rose, and American farmers were able to make substantial profits. But the good times came to an abrupt end following the armistice.

Why was this?

There were a number of reasons that agriculture missed out on the growth experienced elsewhere.

- Demobilization in Europe meant that former agricultural workers returned to their farms and began producing food again. American imports were no longer needed.

- American tariffs made selling to Europe even more difficult. European countries found it hard to sell in American markets, thereby earning the dollars with which to purchase American produce.

- American agriculture also began facing competition from Canada and Argentina, who began supplying grain to the world markets.

- American patterns of food consumption were changing. An increasingly prosperous population preferred more luxurious foods, such as fresh fruit and vegetables, to cereal products. Furthermore, the banning of alcohol under the Prohibition laws meant that the consumption of barley in making beer fell by 90 per cent.

All this meant that American agriculture was suffering from overproduction and prices fell. Profits were squeezed, and many small farmers could no longer afford their rents or mortgage payments. Evictions and forced sales followed. There were one million fewer farms in 1930 than in 1920. It was the small farmers and labourers who suffered the most. The larger operators, equipped with modern machinery, were still able to make profits. These included some of the fruit growers of California and Florida, together with the cereal farmers of the Midwest.

The plight of the farming sector was bad for the whole economy. This was partly because so many Americans, approaching half the total population, lived in rural areas, with their livelihoods dependent on the well-being of the farming community. As agricultural incomes dropped, so demand for manufactured goods dropped also, creating unemployment in the industrial areas.

Materials extract 4.G Linear text (Cantrell et al., 20th century history for Cambridge IGCSE, OUP, p. 251.)

Chapter 6

1 Create a scaffold (with sentence starters, substitution tables, or annotated visuals) for supporting an individual talk on a topic in your subject.

2 Create an information-sharing activity, using the template for creating an information-search activity on page 156, for speaking on a topic in your subject. Create cards with 'two things you know' and 'two things you want to find out' based on information from your subject.

3 Identify a text on a topic from your subject and create a writing frame for writing about it which includes headings, sentence starters, and a word list.

Chapter 7

Materials extract 7.V is taken from a Year 4 primary book on science. Despite being designed for native-speakers, the two tasks which begin the sequence are well designed and could easily be used by NNS learners.

Look carefully at the mini-sequence, then use this table to mark the presence or absence of each principle. There may be other principles or techniques that you notice. Two rows at the bottom of the table are provided for any additions you might wish to make.

Materials design principles	✓ / ✗
The primacy of task	
The three dimensions of content	
Guide input and support output	
Scaffolding and embedding	
Make key language salient	
The concept of difficulty	
Think in sequences	

Chapter 8

The sentences labelled 'Tails' below have been separated from the sentences that preceded them ('Heads') and jumbled up. As a quick summative test of this chapter on assessment, try to match the 'Heads' and the 'Tails' by writing the corresponding 'Tails' letters in the table provided on the following page.

'Heads'

1 Does the course use mainly listening/reading or speaking/writing? Do the assessment procedures reflect the predominant methodology employed during the course?

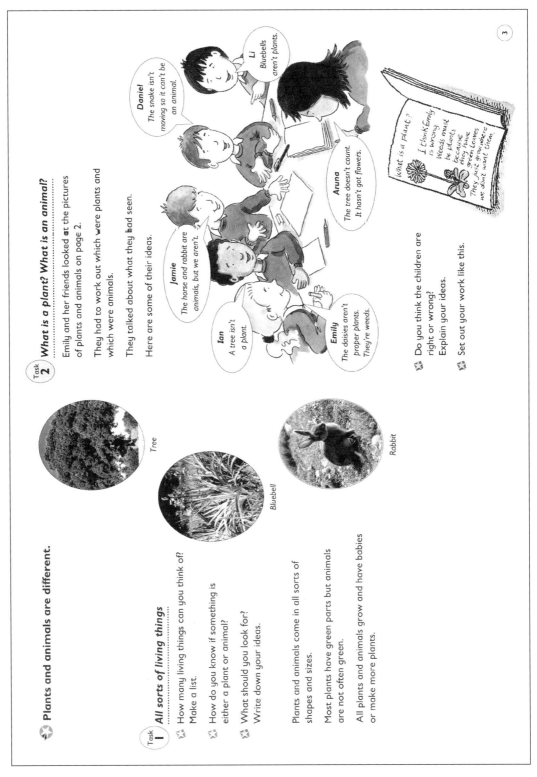

Materials extract 7.V Year 4 primary science book extracts (Feasey et al., Habitats, Ginn and Company, pp. 2–3.)

2 There is a risk of ambiguous subject-knowledge results, especially with learners with low L2 ability.

3 Assess several times during an academic term, for example using 'retrieval' or 'simple integration' tasks.

4 Assess over a period of time using a collection of varied responses.

5 Assess using the 'boxing weights' analogy and a rubric, for example.

6 Assess the topic content, but make it more procedural. So assess the ability to communicate and the ability to use the appropriate discourse type for the functions required.

'Tails'

a This is because we need to show degrees of subject/language knowledge and decide on the relative 'weight' of certain objectives.

b This is especially important for language teachers who incorporate more topic content into their classes, but also for subject teachers who need measures (formal or informal) to check on the stages of the learning of particular concepts.

c Does the exam content reflect and derive from the course objectives?

d The students must also display productive competences. What are the reasons for communicating? The target audience? Can they adjust the discourse to the particular target audience?

e The learner knows the subject, but cannot express it sufficiently in the L2.

f For example: test results, visuals, texts, oral responses, attitudes, self-assessments, etc.

1	2	3	4	5	6

Chapter 9

1 Evaluate your institution and its CLIL programme using the instrument in Table 9.1 (see pages 264–265). How does the institution score? Where are its strengths and weaknesses? You may have access to the data you need and to informed contacts in the school yourself. Otherwise, the advice in the box below, which relates to the 12 points in Table 9.1, may be useful.

2 In what aspects of performance do you think the institution can make improvements? If you were developing a CLIL policy on the basis of these scores, what would be the next key steps which the institution should take to improve its CLIL programme?

3 If the instrument does not quite apply to your institution, what changes would you make to it so that it becomes more appropriate?

1 Look at any data the school may have on subject achievement in CLIL subjects and compare it with data on subject achievement by comparable learners doing the same subjects in L1.

2 Check any test data which the school may have on the L2 ability of learners studying a CLIL subject and compare it with test data on the L2 levels of comparable learners studying L2 conventionally. Alternatively, talk informally to an L2 teacher.

3 Talk to a reliable source about the extent of school CLIL policy. This could be a member of senior management, a CLIL teacher, an L2 teacher, etc. Discuss all five issues in this category.

4 On the issue of the L2 ability of CLIL teachers, discuss this with either a CLIL teacher or an L2 teacher or both. On questions of school management awareness of—and support for—levels of language ability of CLIL staff, talk to a member of senior management. The school may or may not have a measure of L2 ability which is applied when making CLIL staff appointments.

5 Discuss this with CLIL staff or senior management. There may be formal qualifications which the school looks for when making CLIL staff appointments, but this is unlikely. Courses may or may not be available. It is more likely that staff will have informal views on whether CLIL teachers feel sufficiently pedagogically equipped.

6 Establish this by talking to CLIL staff or senior management.

7 Published materials may or may not be used. CLIL staff may make their own. Discuss with CLIL staff the degree to which the materials are suitable. Key issues will be whether the language level is appropriate to learners or whether the materials give enough support.

8 Discuss this with CLIL staff or senior management. Entry may be open, or there may be selection on the basis of language or subject ability. CLIL staff may have a view as to whether the arrangements are fit for purpose.

9 Establish this by talking to CLIL staff or senior management. CLIL staff may have achieved some consistency in the ways they assess, or there may be large differences.

10 Discuss this with L2 staff. If an L2 teacher is doing this, check the extent to which it happens: for example, does the L2 teacher attempt to find out the language demands of a subject?

11 Establish this by talking to CLIL staff, senior management, or parents.

12 Establish this by talking to CLIL staff or senior management.

Chapter 10

1 Choose a task or activity from the materials that you are using (either CLIL or otherwise) and try to write a guide using a similar template to that of Figure 10.4 (see page 283). Try to bring out the content–language relationship, as far as possible.

2 Put each of these three items in the correct column of the table below, according to their appropriate *savoir* (see page 276).

a Be open to, but constructively critical of, innovation.

b Develop awareness of subject-specific discourse features.

c Incorporate key CLIL features into lesson planning: scaffolding, modelling, fostering BICS and CALP.

savoir	*savoir-faire*	*savoir-être*

3 Which six of the 17 pedagogical attributes of 'Mrs Smith' (see page 274) would you prioritize for the introduction to a CLIL training course?

APPENDIX 2   SUGGESTED ANSWERS

Chapter 2

	Key characteristics of CLIL	Things to help me remember
1	Conceptual sequencing	Different language occurs at different stages of a sequence.
2	Conceptual fronting	Concepts, themes, and topics are prioritized in CLIL, even in 'soft' CLIL.
3	Task as priority, language as vehicle	The task should always be the first thing that the learner sees. The language is the means to fulfil the task.
4	Making key language salient	Subject teachers are not language teachers, but they must make their students aware of key language.
5	CLIL in three dimensions	An alternative way of viewing content (conceptual, procedural, and linguistic) and a way of balancing content demands in a lesson or unit
6	The text–task relationship	Make it clear to learners why they must read a given text. Make the text the vehicle.
7	Enhancing peer communication	Try to reduce IRF and think of ways to get learners talking in the L2 among themselves.
8	Guiding multimedia input	Always make sure learners have a task. Don't just 'show'.
9	Supporting student output	Learners must express themselves in speaking and writing in order to really consolidate learning.
10	Supporting thinking skills	Multilingualism seems to give learners a specific and wider set of skills. It also contributes to the development of competences.

Chapter 4

Describing change, and giving reasons and explanations

There were a number of reasons … missed out on …

… meant that … were no longer needed.

… made … even more difficult.

… found it hard to …

… also began facing competition from …

… were changing …

An … preferred more … such as …, to …

Furthermore, … meant that … consumption of … fell by …

All this meant that … was suffering from …

… were squeezed …

… many … could no longer afford …

It was the … and the … who suffered most.

The …, equipped with …, were still able to …

The plight of … was bad for the whole …

This was partly because …

As … dropped, so … dropped also, creating …

Chapter 7

Materials design principles	✓ / ✗
The primacy of task	✓
The three dimensions of content	✓
Guide input and support output	✓
Scaffolding and embedding	✓
Make key language salient	✗*
The concept of difficulty	✓
Think in sequences	✓

* The key language needed for truly distinguishing plants and animals has not been employed yet in the sequence. Some have, but at this early stage, the main language embedded allows the students some speculation and thinking. The key language (age-appropriate scientific vocabulary and related grammar, e.g. comparison) is not yet salient.

Chapter 8

'Assessment and the three dimensions' section

	Conceptual	Procedural	Language
Question 1	1	1	1
Question 2	4	4	5
Question 3	1	1	1
Question 4	3	1	3
Question 5	2	2	2

Task

1	2	3	4	5	6
c	e	b	f	a	d

Chapter 10

'Good practice' section

Repeated numbers in brackets represent 'secondary' effects/intentions.

Affective	Management	Language
5	1	(3)
9	2	4
10	3	6
(13)	(6)	7
15	11	8
17	13	12
	(14)	14
	16	(17)

Task 2

savoir	*savoir-faire*	*savoir-être*
b	c	a

GLOSSARY

***ab initio*:** Literally 'from the beginning'; used in this context to indicate pre-service teacher training.

activity: An educational process or procedure intended to stimulate learning.

additive bilingualism: A form of bilingualism in which the addition of a second language does not replace the first.

'backward' design: A method of designing a curriculum or a course by setting goals before choosing the instructional methods and the forms of assessment. In backward design, the educator starts by outlining the goals and the final task, then creates or plans assessment measures, and finally makes the lesson plans.

BICS (basic interpersonal communicative skills): A term originally coined by Jim Cummins which describes the social variety of language as opposed to the academic variety used in educational contexts (*CALP*).

Bologna Process: An attempt, initiated in 1999, to ensure comparability in the standards and quality of higher-education qualifications across Europe. One of its (several) purposes was to develop initiatives which would lead to better-quality teaching at the tertiary level of education.

CALP (cognitive academic language proficiency): A term originally coined by Jim Cummins which describes the academic variety of language used in educational contexts, as opposed to the social variety (*BICS*).

Cambridge ESOL (English for speakers of other languages): An agency of the University of Cambridge, England, providing a suite of qualifications in English.

Cambridge ESOL Advanced: A qualification in advanced academic and professional English language skills offered by ***Cambridge ESOL***.

catchment area: The surrounding area served by a school.

CEFR (Common European Framework of Reference): A guideline created by the Council of Europe to describe achievement levels of learners of foreign languages. It uses six 'reference levels', from the basic A1 to the highly advanced C2. These reference levels are now widely accepted as the European standard for grading an individual's language proficiency.

CLIL (content and language integrated learning): A way of teaching and learning subjects in a second language.

code-switching: A style of short-term alternation between languages in speech. Teachers or learners switch into an alternate language for a short stretch of talk and switch back.

competence-based education: Education which is based on students demonstrating that they have learned the knowledge and skills they are expected to acquire as they progress through their education. The goal of competence-based learning is to ensure that students are acquiring the knowledge and skills that are defined as essential to success in school, higher education, careers, and adult life.

complex integration task: A type of communicative task typical of a competence-based approach, where the learner is required to perform within the parameters of a given situation, displaying the competence (or degrees of it) by successfully using the topic content and skills which underpin that competence. The 'integration' is the combination of the content and the skills with the medium and the receptor (target audience), resulting in the specific competence. It is labelled as 'complex' because it occurs at the end of a sequence of work.

concept map: A diagram which helps learners organize information. Concept maps may include grids, flow-charts, spidergrams, etc.

conceptual fronting: A form of teaching which places initial emphasis on the conceptual content (subject knowledge), as opposed to the linguistic. In CLIL, the term serves to highlight the objective of a task or a class, and reinforces the notion that language is a tool at the service of concepts, not vice versa.

conceptual sequencing: The characteristic that distinguishes content-based syllabuses from language-based syllabuses. In content-based planning, the conceptual content that forms the basis of the syllabus is linear. In language-based planning, the language content is non-linear, and determined by categories of attainment level, such as beginner, intermediate, and advanced.

content-obligatory language: Language that is essential for understanding and talking about subject content.

continuous assessment: A form of assessment by which learners' knowledge is monitored continuously for the duration of a period of education.

CPD (continuous professional development): Training or advanced professional learning of a formal or informal nature, intended to help educators improve their professional knowledge, skill, and effectiveness.

cross-curricular language skills: Academic language skills which are used in many or all subjects, as opposed to subject-specific language and skills which tend to be limited to one subject or a restricted group of subjects.

DARTs (directed activities related to text): A group of learning activities which help the learner to read a school text, for example cloze, predication, sequencing, etc.

declarative knowledge: Knowledge about something or that something is the case, as opposed to procedural knowledge, which is knowing how to do something.

decoding: The reader's ability to apply knowledge of letter–sound relationships, including knowledge of letter patterns, to correctly pronounce written words. Also used in this book to refer to individual words representing code to which learners need to bring meaning.

dialogic talk: A form of educational talk associated with Robin Alexander, which he describes as having the following characteristics: collective (i.e. participants address learning tasks together), reciprocal (i.e. participants listen to each other and share ideas), supportive (i.e. pupils express their ideas freely and help each other to reach common understandings), cumulative (i.e. participants build on answers and other oral contributions), and purposeful (i.e. classroom talk is also structured with specific learning goals in view).

discourse marker: Normally, a word or phrase—such as a connector—which connects one sentence with another and describes the logical relationship between them, e.g. 'however', 'for this reason', 'by contrast'.

dual-language bilingual programme: A form of education through two languages, in which roughly equal numbers of language-minority and language-majority students are in the same classroom and the minority language is used for at least half of lesson time, with a separate language used in each period of instruction.

EAL (English as an additional language): 'An additional language' is the term given to a language which someone might acquire as a second, third, fourth, etc. language, in addition to their first language. Speakers of EAL speak English as a language which they have acquired in addition to their first.

ELL (English language learner): Learner of English as a second or additional language.

embedding: A technique which incorporates key vocabulary and topic-related grammar into educational materials. These key language features are placed strategically in the materials so that the learner encounters and uses them frequently.

EME (English-medium education): Education through the medium of English as a second language; also known as EMI (English-medium instruction).

evaluation: The collection, analysis, and interpretation of information about any aspect of a programme of learning as part of a recognized process of judging its effectiveness.

exploratory talk: A form of educational talk, associated with Douglas Barnes, which is hesitant, incomplete, and enquiring, and is used normally in pairs or small groups. It is informal and relaxed, and is used in the early stages of the development of a concept. It is opposed to ***presentational talk***, which is formal, audience-related, and offers a 'final draft' of talk for display and evaluation.

formative assessment: Assessment whose goal is to monitor student learning in order to provide ongoing feedback. This feedback can be used by teachers to improve their teaching, and by students to improve their learning.

general academic vocabulary: Vocabulary which is used in school discourse, as opposed to informal social discourse, for example 'consist of', 'provide'. It is not specific to subjects, but used across the curriculum.

graphic literacy: The ability to interpret and make meaning from information presented in the form of an image.

'hard' CLIL: CLIL programmes taught by subject teachers with a strong emphasis on the acquisition of subject knowledge, occupying all the available hours for the subject for a year or more and sometimes culminating in a public examination.

HOTS (higher-order thinking skills): Thinking skills which require more cognitive processing than others—such as analysis, evaluation, and synthesis—as opposed to the learning of facts and concepts.

HTL (Höhere Technische Lehranstalten): Upper-secondary technical and vocational colleges in Austria.

immersion education: A programme in which the L2 is the medium of instruction, where exposure to the L2 is normally confined to the classroom, which is taught by bilingual teachers, and which aims for *additive bilingualism*.

information gap: A type of task in which two learners aim to complete one set of information. One learner has part of the information and the other learner has the other part. By discussing or asking questions, each learner completes the whole set.

information transfer: A type of task in which learners transfer information from one medium to another, for example from a reading text to a graph.

input content: Subject content which is the focus of a lesson, especially relating to listening and reading activities.

INSETT (in-service education and teacher training): Teacher education and training which is carried on during the teacher's professional career, rather than before it, as in ITE. Also known as INSET (in-service education and training).

interactional language: The language used to build and maintain relationships.

IRF (initiation–response–feedback): A commonly occurring exchange characteristic of teacher–learner interaction, consisting of three moves: initiation (normally a teacher question), response (the learner answers the question), and feedback (provided by the teacher). Also known as a 'triadic pattern of questioning'.

ITE (initial teacher education): Teacher education and training which is carried on before the teacher's professional career, rather than during it, as in *INSETT*.

jigsaw task: A type of interactional reading or speaking activity in which groups of students read different parts of a text. After this, they regroup so that each group member has read a different part of the text and talks about it to the other group members, who listen and try to understand the contents of the text as a whole.

L1: A first, home, or community language.

L2: A second, additional, or foreign language.

L2-medium subject teaching: The teaching of subjects through the medium of a language which is a foreign, second, or additional language for the learner.

language-booster course: A language course provided in order to raise the level of language ability of learners so that they are better able to learn effectively within a CLIL programme.

language function: The communicative purpose of language, for example apologizing or asking for something in a shop. In school discourse, common communicative purposes tend to relate to thinking, such as defining, classifying, hypothesizing, etc.

language-majority student: A student who belongs to the majority group in society and speaks the language of that group.

language-minority student: A student who belongs to a minority group in society which uses a different language from the majority.

language-supportive strategy: Strategy which reduces the language demands of classroom tasks and makes it easier for learners to read, speak, and write about the subject, but also to listen to topic-related teacher talk. It can include listening, speaking, reading, and writing tasks; the use of visuals; an accessible teacher talking style; the use of questions; prompts designed to enable learners to talk; and opportunities for learners to use their L1.

language support: The provision of tasks and other teacher-interventions, whose aim is to reduce the language demands of classroom activities and make it easier for learners to read, speak, and write about the subject and to listen to the teacher talking about it.

language-sensitive activity: Activity which is assumed to reduce the language demands of classroom tasks and make it easier for learners to read, speak, and write about the subject and to listen to the teacher talking about it.

LoI (language of instruction): The language in which lessons are conducted; also referred to as *MoI* (medium of instruction).

looped course: A training course with dual overall objectives, only one of which is explicit. For example, CLIL teachers might attend a 'language improvement' course (entitled thus), but the methodology used by the tutor of the course may signal to the participants (implicitly) the methods that they themselves might apply when they return to class. In this case, the methodology is 'looped'. This is also referred to as 'looped input'.

LOTS (lower-order thinking skills): The foundation of skills required to move into higher-order thinking (*HOTS*); skills in which information only needs to be recalled and understood. LOTS include remembering information, and being able to understand and explain new ideas or concepts.

maintenance bilingual education: The education of minority-language learners in two languages—the majority and minority languages—which aims to maintain a language which might be lost in a community in which the majority language predominates. Half or more of curriculum time is taught in the minority students' home language.

MEC (Ministerio de Educación y Cultura): The Spanish Ministry of Education and Culture.

meta-disciplinary area: A competence or a procedure which does not belong to any specific subject discipline (for example, 'learning to learn') but which belongs to all curricular subjects. A meta-disciplinary competence is also applicable to any life situation: personal, social, academic, and work-related.

minority education: The education of language minorities.

minority language: A language spoken by a minority of the population of a given community.

MoI (medium of instruction): The language in which lessons are conducted; also referred to as *LoI* (language of instruction).

NNS (non-native speaker): Someone who speaks a language as a second, as opposed to a first, language.

output content: Subject content which is the focus of the lesson, especially relating to speaking and writing activities.

output hypothesis: A theory proposed by Merrill Swain, which claims that language input is insufficient for language acquisition to occur. Language output (speaking and writing) is also necessary and will best facilitate acquisition when learners are 'pushed', that is, when they are required by a language encounter to reshape their utterances.

partial immersion: A form of *immersion education* which provides roughly half of teaching in the L2, mainly in primary schooling.

peripheral language: Phrases and vocabulary which are neither specific to the subject nor part of general academic vocabulary, but of a more informal nature, necessary for the general discussion of a topic; the interactional language of classroom communication.

plenary: Learners seen as a whole classroom group, as opposed to small groups or pairs.

portfolio assessment: A purposeful collection of student work that exhibits a student's efforts, progress, and achievements in one or more areas of the curriculum.

presentational talk: A form of educational talk, associated with Douglas Barnes, which is formal, audience-related, and offers a 'final draft' of talk for display and evaluation. Compare ***exploratory talk***.

print-illiterate: Referring to people who cannot read, as distinct from other kinds of literacy, for example, visually or in terms of their use of social networks, etc.

procedural content: Content which relates to the 'how' of the curriculum; to the particular skills and demands of a given academic area; and to the classroom methods that support those skills and demands.

productive skills: Speaking and writing skills.

question loop: A type of task for asking and answering questions orally in the plenary classroom. Each student receives a strip of paper containing both a question and an answer to a separate question. One student begins by reading out their question to the rest of the class. Students look at their slips of paper to see if they have the answer. If they do, they shout it out, then read out their own question. The process continues until the questions loop back to the beginning.

realia: Real objects in or outside the classroom, in particular those which a teacher might bring into the classroom to illustrate a lesson.

rubric: An assessment tool which defines an ability to be tested in terms of a graded set of descriptors.

scaffolding: A teaching strategy used to move students progressively toward stronger understanding and greater independence in the learning process. Teachers provide successive levels of temporary support that help students reach higher levels of achievement than they would be able to achieve without assistance. The supportive strategies are gradually removed when they are no longer needed.

schema: Background or prior knowledge, relevant to a text, which allows the reader to make connections to the text they are reading and thus to increase comprehension.

scripted: A type of activity in which talk is provided in written form (or, in semi-scripted activities, partially provided) for the learner to read out.

SES (socio-economic status): The status of a person in society, as defined by their job, income, education, and social standing.

'soft' CLIL: CLIL programmes that take up only part of the curriculum time allocated to the subject (and therefore shorter), valued for their language benefits and often involving language teachers.

SSA (sub-Saharan Africa): The area of the African continent south of the Sahara Desert.

SSLIC (social science and language integrated curriculum): An acronym used by the multilingual school project in the Basque Country to refer to the direct links between the social-science programme (taught exclusively through English) and the content of the English syllabus, based on the procedural skills required for social science (analysis, comparison, data research and analysis, use of sources, etc.) and the discourse features that derive from those procedures.

subject-specific vocabulary: Vocabulary which is used in school discourse, as opposed to informal social discourse, and which is specific to subjects.

substitution table: A type of task which provides strong language support for speaking and writing, enabling learners to turn their attention away from the language being used and towards the subject matter. A sentence is provided which allows the learner to choose options in various columns, for example subject, verb, adjective, object, etc.: 'White/Red cells have a nucleus/have no nucleus/carry oxygen', etc.

summative assessment: Assessment whose goal is to evaluate student learning at the end of an instructional unit by comparing it against some standard or benchmark.

task: An educational process or procedure intended to stimulate learning, often comprising separate steps and requiring interaction among the learners in the form of activities.

three-dimensional CLIL: A way of viewing CLIL as having three dimensions: curricular concepts, procedures (the cognitive skills we use to work on the concepts), and language (the specific language items associated with the concepts).

total immersion: A form of *immersion education* which initially provides all of curriculum time taught in L2 and may later reduce gradually to half.

transversal: Used to refer to skills, competences, content, and even topics. Like *meta-disciplinary areas*, they are cross-curricular and can refer to cognitive skills or to 'lifelong' competences which are social, behavioural, and emotional.

two-way developmental bilingual education: See *dual-language bilingual programme*.

validity: The degree to which a test measures what it is intended to measure.

vehicular language: The language which is the medium of instruction for teaching and learning a subject.

WALT (We are learning to …): An acronym used in formative assessment, where the teacher makes the learning intentions (objectives) transparent to the students at the beginning of a sequence of learning. With younger children, WALT (short for the male name 'Walter') is often personified and displayed on a poster as a visual reminder of the learning objectives being pursued.

WILF (What I'm looking for …): An acronym (short for the male name 'Wilfred') which is often personified in the same way as *WALT*, and is WALT's friend. It is used for a similar purpose, but tends to focus the students on the criteria of assessment that the teacher will use to judge the learning at the end of any particular process. The criteria will derive from WALT's objectives.

ZPD (zone of proximal development): A concept defined by Vygotsky as 'the distance between the actual developmental level as determined by independent problem-solving and the level of potential development as determined through problem-solving under adult guidance, or in collaboration with more capable peers'.

REFERENCES

Aldasoro, M. (2013). *La unidad didáctica: materialización de un modelo educativo pedagógico basado en competencias* (The didactic unit: developing a pedagogic model based on competences). Conference Proceedings: Universidad del País Vasco, San Sebastián.

Alderson, J. C., & **Wall, D.** (1993). Does washback exist? *Applied Linguistics, 14,* 115–129.

Alexander, R. J. (2008). *Towards dialogic teaching: Rethinking classroom talk* (4th ed.). York: Dialogos.

Alidou, H., & **Brock-Utne, B.** (2006). Experience I—Teaching practices—Teaching in a familiar language. In H. Alidou, Boly, A., Brock-Utne, B., Diallo, Y.S., Heugh, K. & Wolff, H.E. (2006). *Optimizing learning and education in Africa—the language factor: A stock-taking research on mother tongue and bilingual education in sub-Saharan Africa* (pp. 85–100). Paris: ADEA.

Allan, D. (1997). The secrets of in-service training. *NovELTy, 4,* 43–55. British Council, Hungary, Pecs.

Association for Science Education. (2004). 'Diet and disease', *Science across the world.* www.scienceacross.org.

Asturias CLIL materials
http://web.educastur.princast.es/ies/sanchezl/archivos/materiales_dide1cticos.html

Austrian HTL portal
www.htl.at/htlat/schwerpunktportale/clil-content-and-language-integrated-learning/samples-of-good-practice.html

Baetens Beardsmore, H. (2008). Multilingualism, cognition and creativity. *International CLIL Research Journal, 1,* 4–19.

Baetens Beardsmore, H. (Ed.) (1993). *European models of bilingual education.* Clevedon, UK: Multilingual Matters.

Baker, C. (2001). *Foundations of bilingual education and bilingualism.* Clevedon, UK: Multilingual Matters.

Ball, P. (2014). British Council Regional Policy Dialogue 4: CLIL Policy and Practice: *Competence-based education for employability, mobility and growth.* Como: Italy.

Ball, P., & **Beobide, H.** (2010). *Geog 3.* EHI Elkar.

Ball, P., & **Lindsay, D.** (2010). Teacher training for CLIL in the Basque Country: The case of the Ikastolas—an expediency model. In D. Lasagabaster & Y. Ruiz de Zarobe, *CLIL in Spain: Implementation, results and teacher-training* (pp. 162–188). Newcastle upon Tyne: Cambridge Scholars Publishing.

Ball, P., & Lindsay, D. (2012). Language demands and support for English-medium instruction in tertiary education. Reflections on the Basque experience. In *English-medium instruction at universities: Global challenges* (pp. 44–61). Clevedon, UK: Multilingual Matters.

Ball, P., Elorza, I., García-Gurrutxaga, M. L, Garmendia, M., & Lindsay, D. (2007). *Subject projects 1*. San Sebastián: Ikastolen Elkartea.

Ball, P., Lindsay, D., Muñoa, I., & Viteri, L. (2013). *Subject projects 1*. San Sebastián: Ikaselkar.

Ball, P., Lindsay, D., Muñoa, I., & Viteri, L. (2014). *Subject projects 2*. San Sebastián: Ikaselkar.

Beckett, B., & Gallagher, R. (1996) *Coordinated science: Biology.* Oxford: OUP.

Beckett, B., & Gallagher, R. (2001). *New coordinated science: Biology, third edition.* Oxford: OUP.

Benson, C., & Kosonen, T. (Eds.). (2013). *Language issues in comparative education.* Rotterdam: Sense Publishers.

Bentley, K. (2010). *The TKT course CLIL module.* Cambridge: Cambridge University Press.

Beobide, H., & Ball, P. (2009). *Geography 3.* San Sebastián: Ikastolen Elkartea.

Beobide, H., & Ball, P. (2010). *History 4.* San Sebastián: Ikastolen Elkartea.

Bernstein, B. (1999). Vertical and horizontal discourse: An essay. *British Journal of Sociology of Education, 20,* 157–173.

Bertaux, P., Coonan, C. M., Frigols-Martín, M., & Mehisto, P. (2010). *CLIL teacher competences grid.* Retrieved from http://lendtrento.eu/convegno/files/mehisto.pdf

Biggs, J. B. (2003). *Teaching for quality learning at university, second edition.* Buckingham: Open University Press/Society for Research into Higher Education.

Bloom, B. S. (1956). *A taxonomy of educational objectives: The classification of educational goals; Handbook I: Cognitive domain.* New York: Longmans, Green.

Bourne, J., & McPake, J. (1991). *Partnership teaching: Co-operative teaching strategies for English language support in multilingual classrooms.* London: HMSO/DES.

Bousfield Wells, D. (n.d.). *Handbook for teachers of English as an additional language.* London: Hounslow Language Services.

Brice Heath, S. (1982). What no bedtime story means: Narrative skills at home and school. *Language in Society, 11,* 49–76). Cambridge, UK: Cambridge University Press.

British Council CLIL Essentials teacher training course. www.teachingenglish.org.uk/teacher-training/clil-essentials

Brock-Utne, B. (2010). English as the language of instruction or destruction—How do teachers and students in Tanzania cope? In B. Brock-Utne, Z. Desai, M. Qorro, & A. Pitman (Eds.), *Language of instruction in Tanzania and South Africa—Highlights from a project* (pp. 77–98). Rotterdam: Sense.

Brock-Utne, B., & **Skattum, I.** (2009). *Languages and education in Africa.* Oxford: Symposium.

Bruner, J. (1960). *The process of education.* Cambridge, MA: Harvard University Press.

Bullock, A. (1975). *The Bullock report: A language for life.* London: Department of Education and Science: Her Majesty's Stationery Office.

Burgess, J. (1994). Ideational frameworks in integrated language learning. *System, 22,* 309–318.

Buzan, T., & **Buzan, B.** (1996). *The mind map book.* New York: New American Library.

Cantrell, J., Smith, N., Smith, P., & **Ennion, R.** (2013). *20th century history for Cambridge IGCSE.* Oxford: Oxford University Press.

Catalonian CLIL materials http://srvcnpbs.xtec.cat/cirel/cirel/index.php?option=com_content&view=article&id=45&Itemid=73

Cedefop/Maastricht (2010). Retrieved from http://www.cedefop.europa.eu/en/publications-and-resources/key-documents

Chaudron, C. (1988). *Second language classrooms: Research on teaching and learning.* Cambridge: Cambridge University Press.

Clegg, J. (2002a). *Language across the curriculum. The British example: 'The national literacy strategy'.* San Sebastián: Jardunaldi Pedagogikoak.

Clegg, J. (2002b). The language of thinking. In *Ethical English: Teaching language through content and content through language* (pp. 97–99). Sofia, Bulgaria: Science Across the World and The British Council.

Clegg, J., & **Kelly, K.** (2009). *Geog.1 EAL Workbook.* Oxford: Oxford University Press.

Concept maps http://cmap.ihmc.us

Cortazzi, M., Rafik-Galea, S., & **Jin, L.** (1998). Seeing through texts: Developing discourse-based materials in teacher education. *The English Teacher, XXVIII,* 39–68.

Coxhead, A. (2000). A new academic word list. *TESOL Quarterly, 34,* 213–238.

Coyle, D. (2008). Retrieved from http://blocs.xtec.cat/clilpractiques1/files/2008/11/slrcoyle.pdf

Coyle, D. (2009). Foreword. In E. Dafouz & M. C. Guerini (Eds.), *CLIL across educational levels* (pp. 4–6). Madrid: Richmond/Santillana.

Coyle, D., Hood, P., & **Marsh, D.** (2010). *CLIL: Content and language integrated learning.* Cambridge: Cambridge University Press.

Creese, A. (2005). *Teacher collaboration and talk in multilingual classrooms.* Clevedon, UK: Multilingual Matters.

Cullingford, C. (1995). *The effective teacher.* London: Cassell.

Cummins, J. (1979). Cognitive/academic language proficiency, linguistic interdependence, the optimum age question and some other matters. *Working Papers on Bilingualism, 19,* 121–129.

Cummins, J. (1981). *Bilingualism and minority-language children.* Ontario: Ontario Institute for Studies in Education.

Cummins, J. (1984). *Bilingual education and special education: Issues in assessment and pedagogy.* Clevedon, UK: Multilingual Matters

Cummins, J. (1991). Language development and academic learning. In L. Malave & G. Duquette, *Language, culture and cognition* (pp. 161–175). Clevedon, UK: Multilingual Matters.

Cummins, J. (1994). The acquisition of English as a second language. In K. Spangenberg-Urbschat & R. Pritchard (Eds.), *Reading instruction for ESL students* (pp. 36–62). Delaware: International Reading Association.

Cummins, J. (2000). *Language, power and pedagogy: Bilingual children in the crossfire.* Clevedon, UK: Multilingual Matters.

Cummins, J., & **McNeely, S.** (1987). Language development, academic learning, and empowering minority students. In K. Tikunoff, *Bilingual education and bilingual special education: A guide for administrators* (pp. 75–94). Boston: College Hill.

Curriculum specifications for Science Year 6. (2006). Ministry of Education Malaysia. Retrieved from http://akses.skseriampang.net/HSP/04_Science/sc_yr6_eng.pdf

Dale, L., Van der Es, W., & **Tanner, R.** (2011). *CLIL skills.* Europees Platform.

Dalton-Puffer, C. (2007). *Discourse in content and language integrated learning (CLIL) classrooms.* Amsterdam: John Benjamins Publishing Company.

Davies, F., & **Greene, T.** (1984). *Reading for learning in the sciences.* London: Oliver & Boyd.

Djité, P. (2008). *The sociolinguistics of development in Africa.* Clevedon: Multilingual Matters.

Dobson, A., Perez Murillo, M., & **Johnstone, R.** (2010). *Bilingual education project: Spain: Evaluation report.* Madrid: British Council, Spanish Ministry of Education.

Elorza, I., & **Muñoa, I.** (2008). Promoting the minority language through integrated plurilingual language planning: The case of the Ikastolas. *Language, Culture and Curriculum, 21,* 85–101.

ESL Lounge www.esl-lounge.com

Europa: Summaries of EU legislation. (2006). Retrieved from http://europa.eu/legislation_summaries/education_training_youth/lifelong_learning/c11090_en.htm

European Platform (2013a). *Bilingual education in Dutch schools—a success story.* Haarlem: European Platform.

European Platform (2013b). *Internationalising education.* Haarlem: European Platform.

Feasey, R., Goldsworthy, A., Phipps, R., & **Stringer, J.** (2000). *Habitats.* Oxford: Ginn and Company.

Fink, L. D. (2003). *Creating significant learning experiences.* New York: Jossey-Bass.

Fleisch, B. (2008). *Primary education in crisis: Why South African children underachieve.* Cape Town: Juta.

Gallagher, R., & **Ingram, P.** (2001). *New coordinated science: Chemistry, third edition.* Oxford: Oxford University Press.

Gallagher, R., & **Parish, R.** (2005). *Geog 2, second edition.* Oxford: Oxford University Press.

Gallagher, R., Parish, R., & **Williamson, J.** (2014). *Geog.1, fourth edition.* Oxford: Oxford University Press.

Garagorri, X. (2010). *Euskal curriculuma.* Vitoria: Basque Government Publications.

Geddes, M., & **White, R.** (1978). The use of semi-scripted simulated authentic speech and listening comprehension. *Audio-Visual Language Journal, XVI,* 137–145.

Gibbons, P. (2002). *Scaffolding language scaffolding learning: Teaching second language learners in the mainstream classroom.* Portsmouth, NH: Heinemann.

Gibbons, P. (2009). *English learners, academic literacy and thinking.* Portsmouth, NH: Heinemann.

Graddol, D. (2006). *English next: Why global English may mean the end of 'English as a Foreign Language'.* London: British Council Publications.

Grandinetti, M., Langellotti, M., & **Ting, T. Y. L.** (2013). How CLIL can provide a pragmatic means to renovate science education—even in a sub-optimally bilingual context. *International Journal of Bilingual Education and Bilingualism, 16,* 354–374.

Harrison, P., & **Moorcroft, C.** (1996). *Science in action Book 3.* Dunstable: Folens.

Haslam, L., Wilkin, Y., & **Kellet, E.** (2005). *English as an additional language meeting the challenge in the classroom.* Abingdon, UK: David Fulton Publishers.

Hayes-Jacobs, H. (2006). *Active literacy across the curriculum: Strategies for reading, writing, speaking, and listening.* Larchmont, NY: Eye On Education.

Heugh, K. (2006). Theory and practice—Language education models in Africa: Research, design, decision-making, outcomes, and costs. In *Optimizing Learning and Education in Africa—the Language Factor* (pp. 56–84). ADEA/ GTZ/ Commonwealth Secretariat/UIE.

Hollingworth, S., & **Mansaray, A.** (2012). *Language diversity and attainment in English secondary schools: A scoping study.* London: London Metropolitan University.

Hudson, T. (2007). *Teaching second language reading.* Oxford: Oxford University Press.

Illich, I. (1971). *De-schooling society.* New York: Harper & Row.

Ioannou-Georgiou, S. (2012). Reviewing the puzzle of CLIL. *ELT Journal, 66,* 495–504.

Jaeppinen, A.-K. (2005). Thinking and content learning of mathematics and science as cognitional development in CLIL: Teaching through a foreign language in Finland. *Language and Education, 19,* 147–168.

Johnson, R. K., & **Swain, M.** (1997). *Immersion education: International perspectives.* Cambridge: Cambridge University Press.

Kauser, S., & **O'Donoghue, S.** (2010). *Oxford content and language support: Science.* Oxford: Oxford University Press.

Kelly, K. (2006). *Integruotas dalyko ir uzsienio kalbos mokymas* (Content and language integrated learning). Lithuania: Ministry of Education.

Kelly, K. (2009a). *Geography VPS.* Oxford: Macmillan.

Kelly, K. (2009b). *Science VPS.* Oxford: Macmillan.

Kelly, K. (2009c). *Your CLIL.* Macmillan. Retrieved from www.onestopenglish.com/clil/clil-teacher-magazine/your-clil

Kelly, K. (2010). Interview with Keith Kelly: British Council/BBC. Retrieved from www.teachingenglish.org.uk/article/interview-keith-kelly

Kelly, K. & **Kitanova, S.** (2002). Ethical English: Teaching language through content, and content through language. *Science Across The World.*

Krashen, S. D. (1988). *Second language acquisition and second language learning.* Jersey: Prentice-Hall International.

Lasagabaster, D. (2008). Foreign language competence in content and language integrated courses. *The Open Applied Linguistics Journal, 1,* 31–42.

Lee, C. (2006). *Language for learning mathematics: Assessment for learning in practice.* Maidenhead, UK and New York: Open University Press.

Lee, J. (2000). *Tasks and communicating in language classrooms.* New York: McGraw-Hill.

Lewis, M., & **Wray, D.** (1998). *Writing across the curriculum.* Reading, UK: University of Reading.

Lindholm-Leary, K. J. (2001). *Dual language education.* Clevedon, UK: Multilingual Matters.

Llinares, A., Morton, T., & **Whittaker, R.** (2012). *The roles of language in CLIL.* Cambridge: Cambridge University Press.

Lynch, T. (2009). *Teaching second language listening: A guide to evaluating, adapting, and creating tasks for listening in the language classroom.* Oxford: Oxford University Press.

Maastricht Communiqué (2004). Retrieved from http://ec.europa.eu/education/policy/vocational-policy/doc/maastricht_en.pdf

MacDonald, C. (1993). *Towards a new primary curriculum in South Africa.* Pretoria: Human Sciences Research Council.

Manoli, P., & **Papadopoulou, M.** (2012). Graphic organizers as a reading strategy: Research findings and issues. *Creative Education, 3,* 348–356.

Marland, M. (1977). *Language across the curriculum.* Oxford: Heinemann.

Marcus, N., Cooper, M., & **Sweller, J.** (1996). Understanding instructions. *Journal of Educational Psychology, 88,* 49–63.

Mariani, L. (1997). Teacher support and teacher challenge in promoting learner autonomy. *Perspectives, a Journal of TESOL-Italy,* XXIII.

Marsh, D., & **Langé, G.** (2000). *Using languages to learn and learning to use languages.* Finland: University of Jyväskylä.

Marsh, D. (2002). CLIL/EMILE—*The European dimension. Actions, trends and foresight potential.* UniCOM, Continuing Education Centre. Jyväskylä, Finland: University of Jyväskylä. Retrieved from http://clil-cd.ecml.at/LinkClick.aspx?fileticket=ekwp4udVLfQ%3D&tabid=947&language=en-GB

Marsh, D., Mehisto, P., Wolff, D., & **Frigols, M. J.** (2010). *The European framework for CLIL teacher education.* Graz: European Centre for Modern Languages, Council of Europe.

Mehisto, P. (2012a). Criteria for producing CLI learning material. *Encuentro, 21,* ISSN 1989-0796. Retrieved from www.unifg.it/sites/default/files/allegatiparagrafo/21-01-2014/mehisto_criteria_for_producing_clil_learning_material.pdf

Mehisto, P. (2012b). *Excellence in bilingual education: A guide for school principals.* Cambridge: Cambridge University Press.

Mehisto, P., Marsh D, & **Frigols M. J.** (2008). *Uncovering CLIL.* London: Macmillan Education.

Mercer, N. (2000). *Words and minds: How we use language to think together.* London: Routledge.

Mercer, N., & **Hodgkinson, S.** (Eds.) (2008). *Exploring talk in school: Inspired by the work of Douglas Barnes.* London: Sage.

Met, M. (1989). Learning language through content: Learning content through language. In K. E. Müller (Ed.), *Languages in elementary schools* (pp. 43–64). New York: American Forum.

Met, M. (1994). Teaching content through a second language. In F. Genesee (Ed.), *Educating second-language children: The whole child, the whole curriculum, the whole community* (pp. 159–182). New York: Cambridge University Press.

Ministry of Education Malaysia. (2006). Integrated curriculum for secondary schools. Curriculum Development Centre.

Mohan, B. (1986). *Language and content.* Reading, MA: Addison Wesley.

Muñoa, I. (2008). *Key factors to be considered by CLIL teachers.* Retrieved from www.eleanitz.org/sites/default/files/shared/Key%20factors%20to%20be%20considered%20by%20CLIL%20teachers.pdf

Muñoa, I. (2011). *CLIL as a catalyst for change: The case of the Ikastolas.* Retrieved from www.eleanitz.org/sites/default/files/shared/CLIL%20as%20a%20catalyst%20for%20change.pdf

Muñoa, I. (2012). *Key factors to be considered by CLIL teachers.* Retrieved from www.eleanitz.org/sites/default/files/Articles/Key%20factors%20to%20be%20considered%20by%20CLIL%20teachers.pdf

Muñoa, I., Ball, P., & **Garmendia, M.** (2008). *SSLIC English workbook 1.* Donostia: Ikastolen Elkartea.

Murphy, J. M. (1991). Oral communication in TESOL: Integrating speaking, listening and pronunciation. *TESOL Quarterly, 25,* 51–75.

O'Donnell, A. M, Dansereau, D. F., & **Hall, R. F.** (2002). Knowledge maps as scaffolds for cognitive processing. *Educational Psychology Review, 14,* 71–86.

Peacock, A. (1995). An agenda for research on text material in primary science for second language learners of English in developing countries. *Journal of Multilingual and Multicultural Development, 16,* 389–402. Clevedon: Multilingual Matters.

Pople, S. (2001). *New coordinated science: Physics, third edition.* Oxford: Oxford University Press.

Probyn, M. (2006). Language and learning science in South Africa. *Language and Education 20.*

Ribe, R., & **Vidal, N.** (1993). *Project work: step by step.* London: Macmillan.

Roberts, J. (1998). *Language teacher education.* London: Arnold.

Robson, W. (1991). *Medieval Britain.* Oxford: Oxford University Press.

Roegiers, X. (2000). *Une pédagogie de l'intégration.* Brussels: De Boeck.

Rogers, C. (1951). *Client-centered therapy: Its current practice, implications and theory.* London: Constable.

Roth, W.-M. (2005). *Talking science: Language and learning in science classrooms.* Lanham, MA: Rowman and Littlefield.

Science across the world: Acid rain over Europe. Retrieved from http://www.nationalstemcentre.org.uk/elibrary/file/5576/AR%20Complete%20Topic%20English.pdf.

Sierra, J. (2008). Assessment of bilingual education in the Basque Country. In J. Cenoz (Ed.), *Teaching through Basque: Achievements and challenges* (pp. 39–47). Clevedon, UK: Multilingual Matters.

Smyth, G. (2003). *Helping bilingual pupils to access the curriculum.* Abingdon, UK: David Fulton Publishers.

Snow, M., Met, M., & **Genesee, F.** (1989). A conceptual framework for the integration of language and content in second/foreign language instruction. *TESOL Quarterly, 23,* 201–217.

Swain, M. (1985). Communicative competence: Some roles of comprehensible input and comprehensible output in its development. In S. Gass & C. Madden (Eds.). *Input in second language acquisition* (pp. 235–252). Rowley, MA: Newbury House.

Thomas, W., & **Collier, V.** (1997). *School effectiveness for language minority students.* Washington, CD: National Clearinghouse for Bilingual Education.

Thomas, W., & **Collier, V.** (2002). *A national study of school effectiveness for language minority students' long-term academic achievement.* Santa Cruz, CA, and Washington, DC: Center for Research on Education, Diversity & Excellence.

Vygotsky, L. S. (1986). *Thought and language* (2nd Ed.). Cambridge, MA: MIT Press.

Wellington, J., & **Osborne, J.** (2001). *Language and literacy in science education.* Buckingham, UK: Open University Press.

Wells, G., & **Chang-Wells, G. L.** (1992). *Constructing knowledge together.* Portsmouth, NH: Heinemann.

Widdowson, H. (1979). *Explorations in applied linguistics I.* Oxford: Oxford University Press.

Wiggins, G., & **McTighe, J.** (1998). Put understanding first. *Educational Leadership, 65,* 36–41.

Wolff, D. (2012). The European framework for CLIL teacher education. *Synergies, 8,* 105–116.

XTEC site. http://srvcnpbs.xtec.cat/cirel/cirel/index.php?option=com_content&view=article&id=45&Itemid=73

Zwiers, J. (2008). *Building academic language: Essential practices for content classrooms.* San Francisco, CA: John Wiley & Sons.

Zydatiss, W. (2009). *Deutsch–Englische Züge in Berlin (DEZIBEL): Eine Evaluation des bilingualen Sachfachunterrichts an Gymnasien.* Frankfurt: Peter Lang.

INDEX

Page numbers annotated with 'g', 't' and 'f' refer to glossary entries, tables and figures respectively.